At the Limits of History

Keith Jenkins' work on historical theory is renowned; this collection presents the essential elements of his work over the last fifteen years.

Here we see Jenkins address the difficult and complex question of defining the limits of history. The collection draws together the key pieces of his work in one handy volume, encompassing the ever controversial issue of postmodernism and history, questions on the end of history and radical history into the future. Exchanges with Perez Zagorin and Michael Coleman further illuminate the level of debate that has surrounded postmodernism, and which continues to do so. An extended introduction and abstracts which contextualise each piece, together with a foreword by Hayden White and an afterword by Alun Munslow, make this collection essential reading for all those interested in the theory and practice of history and its development over the last few decades.

Keith Jenkins is Emeritus Professor, University of Chichester. He is the author of five books on historical theory and co-editor (with Alun Munslow) of *The Nature of History Reader* and (with Sue Morgan and Alun Munslow) *Manifestos for History*, all published by Routledge.

Hayden White is Emeritus Professor of the History of Consciousness, University of California, and teaches comparative literature at Stanford University. He is currently writing a book on *The Philosophy of the Preposition*.

Alun Munslow is UK Editor of *Rethinking History: The Journal of Theory and Practice*, and the author of several books on the nature of history; his most recent is *Narrative and History* (2007). He is Visiting Professor of History and Historical Theory at the University of Chichester.

At the Limits of History

Essays on Theory and Practice

Keith Jenkins

LONDON AND NEW YORK

First published 2009
by Routledge
2 Park Square, Milton Park, Abingdon, Oxon OX14 4RN

Simultaneously published in the USA and Canada
by Routledge
711 Third Ave, New York, NY 10017

Routledge is an imprint of the Taylor & Francis Group, an informa business

Typeset in Garamond by Taylor & Francis Books

British Library Cataloguing in Publication Data
A catalogue record for this book is available from the British Library

Library of Congress Cataloging in Publication Data
Jenkins, Keith, 1943-
At the limits of history : essays on theory and practice / Keith Jenkins.
p. cm.
1. History–Philosophy. 2. Historiography. 3. Postmodernism. 4. History–Methodology. I. Title.
D7.J46 2009
901–dc22

2008050132

ISBN10: 0-415-47235-0 (hbk)
ISBN10: 0-415-47236-9 (pbk)

ISBN13: 978-0-415-47235-7 (hbk)
ISBN13: 978-0-415-47236-4 (pbk)

For Sue, with love

Contents

Acknowledgements

I would like to thank Hayden White and Alun Munslow for kindly taking the time to write the Foreword and Afterword respectively for this volume; I feel exceptionally lucky to have had their support not just here but over the years. Beverley Southgate read the Introduction, as did Sande Cohen, Peter Icke, Stan Sliwinski and Mark Mason, and I thank them for their critical but always perceptive and helpful comments. Carole Farnfield will be much relieved to know that this is (probably) my last book, and that she will not have to turn my appalling handwriting into a clean typescript ever again; her help has always been immense. Above all, however, I want to express my gratitude to Sue Morgan who encouraged me to put together this collection of essays in the first place, who has read and commented on it at its various 'stages of production', and whose daily presence in my life reassures me that the best of all possible worlds can indeed actually arrive.

The essays that comprise this volume appeared in the following places and I am grateful to the publishers and authors for permission to reproduce them here.

Marxism and Historical Knowledge: Tony Bennett and the Discursive Turn, *Literature and History*, 3rd Series, 3/1, Spring, 1994, Manchester University Press, pp. 1–15;

Living in Time But Outside History, Living in Morality But Outside Ethics: Postmodernism and Elizabeth Deeds Ermarth, *Filozofski Vestnik,* XVIII, 2, 1997, Institute of Philosophy, SRC SASA, pp. 213–32;

Why Bother With History, *Rethinking History,* 1.1, Summer, 1997 (Taylor and Francis Ltd, http://www.informaworld.com, reprinted by permission of the publisher), pp. 56–66;

History, the Referent, and Narrative: Reflections on Postmodernism Now, *History and Theory,* 38, 1, 1999, Blackwell, pp. 1–24 (by, and with permission of, Perez Zagorin);

A Postmodern Reply to Perez Zagorin, *History and Theory,* 39, 2, 2000, Blackwell, pp. 181–200;

Rejoinder to a Postmodernist, *History and Theory*, 39, 2, 2000, Blackwell, pp. 201–9 (by Perez Zagorin);

Response to a Postmodernist: Or, A Historian's Critique of Postmodernist Critiques of History, *American Studies in Scandinavia,* 34, 1, 2002, University Press of Southern Denmark, pp. 47–64 (by, and with permission of, Michael C. Coleman);

Against the Historical 'Middle Ground': A Reply to Michael Coleman, *American Studies in Scandinavia,* 35, 1, 2003, University Press of Southern Denmark, pp. 1–22;

On Disobedient Histories, *Rethinking History,* 7, 3, 2003 (Taylor and Francis Ltd, http://www.informaworld.com, reprinted by permission of the publisher), pp. 367–85;

Modernist Disavowals and Postmodern Reminders of the Condition of History Today: On Jean François Lyotard, *Rethinking History,* 8, 3, 2004 (Taylor and Francis Ltd, http://www.informaworld.com, reprinted by permission of the publisher), pp. 365–85;

Ethical Responsibility and the Historian: On the Possible End of a History 'of a Certain Kind', *History and Theory,* 43, 4, 2004, Blackwell, pp. 43–60;

'Once Upon a Time': On History, November 2005, University of Chichester;

Postmodernity, the End of History, and Frank Ankersmit, in A. MacFie (ed.) *The Philosophy of History,* 2006, Palgrave Macmillan, Houndmills, pp. 138–54; reproduced with permission of Palgrave Macmillan;

The End of The Affair: On the Irretrievable Breakdown of History and Ethics, *Rethinking History,* 11, 2, 2007 (Taylor and Francis Ltd, http://www.informaworld.com, reprinted by permission of the publisher), pp. 275–85;

'Nobody Does it Better': Radical History and Hayden White, *Rethinking History,* 12, 1, 2008 (Taylor and Francis Ltd, http://www.informaworld.com, reprinted by permission of the publisher), pp. 59–74;

Sande Cohen: On the Verge of Newness, *Rethinking History,* 12, 4, 2008 (Taylor and Francis Ltd, http://www.informaworld.com, reprinted by permission of the publisher), pp. 437–62;

Cohen *contra* Ankersmit, *Rethinking History,* 12, 4, 2008 (Taylor and Francis Ltd, http://www.informaworld.com, reprinted by permission of the publisher), pp. 537–55.

Every effort has been made to obtain permission to reproduce copyright material. If any proper acknowledgement has not been made, copyright holders are invited to inform the publishers of the oversight.

Foreword

The postmodern messenger

Hayden White

> 'It is no surprise … that few academic historians liked the postmodern messenger.'
>
> Jenkins, '"Once Upon a Time": On History'

I have said it before and I now have a chance to say it again. Keith Jenkins follows a thought to the end of the line. I have watched him turn from a historian interested in philosophical issues into a philosopher interested in historiological issues. From there he seems to have morphed into a post-historian interested in post-philosophical issues. This, I take it, is the import of his celebration of the work of Sande Cohen, Elizabeth Ermarth, Alain Badiou, and Jean Baudrillard, all of whom tend to be simply dismissed by 'proper' humanists for having gone 'too far.' And of course, it goes without saying that going 'too far' is not only a mistake, it is a *moral* failing as well.

Such is the gist of Perez Zagorin's criticism of Jenkins' postmodernism, two specimens of which are included in this anthology. These essays are rife with adjectives such as 'absurd,' 'nonsense,' 'fantastic,' 'perverse,' 'reductive,' 'prejudiced,' 'problematic,' 'self-refuting,' 'amusing,' 'self-contradictory,' 'relativist,' 'sceptical,' 'tedious,' 'vain,' 'misleading,' 'laborious,' 'careless,' 'unsatisfactory,' 'leftist,' 'posturing,' and many more of this ilk. To which I feel compelled to reply, only half-jokingly, if Jenkins has got so much of the issue wrong or is so wrong on so much of the issue, he must be doing something right or at least relevant to current debates in the human sciences. For it is obvious – *pace* Zagorin – that Keith Jenkins is no wild-eyed monster bent on the destruction of Western Civilisation as Zagorin knows it. Indeed, as I read through these essays by Jenkins, I was once again reminded of how really quite commonsensical, rational, and measured are their tone and conceptual content.

To be sure, Jenkins envisions a utopian future more reminiscent of William Morris and the pre-Raphaelites – there is a lot of talk about dancing and mild pleasures – than that of Norman O. Brown ('polymorphous perversity') or the Baudrillard of *America* ('Where is the next orgy?'). In any event, what Jenkins calls 'new imaginaries' is a sufficiently capacious idea to permit inclusion of whatever might pass for a utopian dream by the most uptight historian. Critics of postmodernism who fear that it will lead to an attitude of 'anything goes' have got it precisely right, according to Jenkins. Who adds: and a good thing it is, too.

Of course, Jenkins' response to his critics or at least to critics like Zagorin *is* infuriating. For Zagorin, guardian of the ethics of propriety in matters intellectual, is really challenging Jenkins' right to discuss matters best left to the care of his betters. Why else would Zagorin ask for the kind of credentials he demands of Jenkins.? '[O]ne wonders,' Zagorin writes, 'what qualifications [Jenkins] has' for entering 'into questions relating to' historiography. We all recognise this 'one' who 'wonders' at the temerity of the outsider to blunder into a club which has its rules of membership and recognition. 'Has he ever written a work of history? Does he possess any substantial experience and knowledge of historical research and its problems?' Zagorin rhetorically asks.

Jenkins might have responded to Zagorin in kind, inquiring whether he, Zagorin, who works on political history, has any experience of politics that might qualify him to write on such a subject. Jenkins does not go this route because he knows that when it comes to assessing the cogency and force of a discourse like history or, for that matter, philosophy, there are no experts except those who designate themselves as such. It is quite otherwise with modern physical sciences, which stipulate the rules of the game, the language to be used in the description of their objects of study, and criteria to be used for the disconfirmation of discrete statements or propositions spun out of controlled observations. This is not the case with history. Nor with philosophy. Indeed, it appears that, in modern philosophy, the only problem of continuing concern is whether philosophy itself can ever be or become a scientific discipline.

But Zagorin's demand to see Jenkins' credentials, his license to comment on history and historiography, his insinuation that in order to consider a discipline like history critically, one must have been licensed in and have practiced it, portends the kinds of arguments that Zagorin will muster in his defence of the good old ways and the good old days, when people knew their place and stayed in it, giving proper respect to their betters and quietly enduring their status as patients rather than as agents of 'history.'

But Jenkins is questioning the legitimacy of professional historians' criteria for determining who has the right to study the past, in what manner, and to what end or purpose. The rules set up by professional historians for the licensing and vetting of historians – unlike those set up in chemistry or physics – are purely conventional and their authority purely customary. History is a practice utterly lacking in the theoretical foundations normally required for the establishment of a practice as a modern science.

But what's all the fuss? It is not as if one's views about history have any practical implications – by which I mean any 'moral and political' (Zagorin's terms) implications for most citizens. Historians study the past for itself alone and in its own terms, do they not? It is not as if one might decide to divorce one's spouse on the authority of some model divorcers offered up by 'history': Henry VIII, for example, or the late Duchess of Windsor. The historical past, studied in the manner promoted by contemporary professional historians, does not – and does not pretend to – offer anything in the way of moral or political instruction for the present. And, as Zagorin remarks, most professional historians just want to be left alone to do their thing, study their sources, and 'tell the truth' about the past, not so much to the general public as to their intellectual, social, and professional peers, in books and journals that they alone read.

Thus, we can ask quite legitimately why it is that Keith Jenkins himself thinks it so important to criticise, deconstruct, and otherwise attack professional historians and their histories. The essays that follow explain this more than adequately and have no need of explication by me. Jenkins knows what he knows and argues it forcefully, clearly, plainly, cogently, authoritatively. For him, if I understand him at all, historical studies today are only a variation of a whole cluster of pseudo-disciplines making up the humanities and so-called human sciences which have lost touch with the practical, which is to say, moral and political but also aesthetic and artistic, ideals which formerly gave them a utopian dimension that has since been utterly expunged from them in the interest of making them socially safe and servile.

Jenkins is a revolutionary, which means that he is also a visionary and a utopian, a kind of Blakean man of the Left who had, once upon a time, fallen among the custodians of the Proper and is now trying to awaken from the slumber of 'what goes without saying,' 'the heart of the matter,' the obvious, the Right Thing, what everyone knows, and all of the other commonplaces that substitute for thought in a historicised culture that mistakes its own past for its destiny. A sense of the authority of tradition appears to be utterly alien to Jenkins' way of thinking. In this he appears adamantly post-postmodern, for in postmodernism tradition and the past remain present even if in a parodied or ironic form. In Jenkins' work, even these are swept away.

Introduction

History limited

In this introduction I want to try and 'place in context' the essays which follow and which make up the bulk of the text. This 'context' has obviously got no pretentions to being the right or the only context (no such thing), but it is the one I read 'history today' in and through and which therefore enables me to render the said essays intelligible to myself and, hopefully, to you, the reader. And to achieve this 'contextualization' I want to outline, first, several of the features which I think characterise and mark contemporary history culture; second, I want to sketch-out my reactions to this phenomenon – reactions which inform and even govern the arguments the essays here contain – whilst, finally, in a section entitled 'Circumstances', I want to say a little bit about how the essays have been organised so that one can navigate one's way through them with relative ease.

History today: problematics

Once upon a time, here in the West, historians and philosophers of history tried to make the past bear the full weight of historical meaning(s). The various attempts to do this ended, pretty definitively, in the 1960s and 1970s, since when they have been emptying out all the meanings which had previously been put in until, today, the idea that the historical past has meanings – purposes, significance, teleologies – *in* it, meanings which can be found rather than manufactured, appears ridiculous: nobody really believes that any more. Consequently the past, conceived now as an absence, a nothingness, a blank canvas or screen onto which historians can paint or project any history to suit, means that all the meanings the past 'might be said to have' come from the *outside*. And, once intrinsic meanings (and values) have been evacuated from 'the past'; once everything is opened up to influences coming from *extrinsic* sources, then there is no stopping ... the outside simply goes on and on or, as Jacques Derrida has put it, 'The absence of a transcendental signifier extends the play of signification to infinity.' The past (all that has happened 'before now') thus becomes opened up to interminable readings and rereadings and so to an inexpungable *relativism* of accounts.

And of course there is a dependency here, an unequal exchange between the past and history whereby the past *depends* for its current (ontological) existence on its representers (say, historians) and their representations: no representation, no past. This is obviously not to say that the past didn't once exist and exist precisely in the way it did, but it is to say that for it to become transformed into history it is absolutely dependent on somebody making it so: all cultures have a past, not all of them have histories. Additionally, given that the past (as events, happenings, occurrences, etc.) is categorically (ontologically) of a different kind from history (as discourse, text, narrative, etc.) and with, incidentally, both the past and history being ontologically distinct from memory and its cognates, then the 'past itself' gives historians no help whatsoever in determining how it would, if only it could, historicise itself: if you wanted to write a history of the world it's not as if the world could suggest the shape it would prefer to be shaped as. Accordingly, loosed from each other, the past and its myriad historicisations float free such that, underdetermined, historians can make the past 'historical' any way they like, that is to say, in their *own* images.

Now, many historians baulk at this. For the past, although admittedly gone for good and so quite literally absent, nevertheless lives on – as they say – 'all around us', particularly through our acts of memory operating through social institutions and practices which both generate and embody them, and the fusion of which gives us our various (contingent) identities. But this argument – which is essentially about memory – is not much to the point if you are talking, as I am here, about the production of something very different, namely, histories as literary artefacts, as discursive representations produced (overwhelmingly) by historians. For most people certainly do *not* have these phenomena 'all around them'. Indeed, most people never have had, still don't and probably never will have what contemporary historians call a 'historical consciousness', that is to say, a consciousness of the historicised past like *theirs* ... a consciousness far removed from those unavoidable general processes of socialisation and enculturation which enable most people to get around in the world and get all the 'identities' they need to enable them to do so *sans histoire.* So if we want to bother to have the past-as-history, then it really does have to be brought back artificially (textually) through the various acts of the historian's imagination as generated by the application to that representational task of non-standardised (and non-standardisable) theories and methods: unlike memory, history is not of a natural kind.

To briefly expand these somewhat general and maybe abstract points – since I think they are crucially important given that they are already beginning to expose the problematicisation of the whole epistemic enterprise of doing history – let us imagine that, as a historian, you are asked to write a history of 'Yesterday in New York'. How could the (undoubted) existence of 'New York Yesterday' help you to do it? I mean, how would you *know* what you have to put in, or, put another way, *not* put in. Does the existence of 'New York Yesterday' yield its own criteria of significance which could inform/govern your selections? And then along come many more questions. For example, how would you *know* how to begin and end the organisation and the structuring into historical meaning of the traces 'New York Yesterday' left behind whilst also (somehow) taking into account all the things which happened but for which no traces remain yet which, 'yesterday', impacted constitutively on the things that are 'traceable'; how does inference (the problematics of which most historians massively underestimate)[1] work here exactly? Again, how would you determine and assess the power of those causal factors operating on/behind 'events' to bring them into existence such that they are explained and their meanings elicited when there is an irreducible *asymmetry* between cause(s) and effect? For whilst single effects (events – either simple or complex) are always available (we can 'see' that things happened) the problematic lies in the fact that no single 'historical' event (and this includes the problematic of intentionality as an 'event') has a single cause. Consequently – and logically given that one has a multiplicity of causes each with the inherent possibility of infinite regression – the problematic is that of calculating the necessary and sufficient causes of the event precisely in ways that do *not* commit the sin of regression to infinity. But then, short of that, how do you know how far back and how far afield you need to go to establish why and how the things that happened in 'New York Yesterday' happened in the way they did and not other? And millions of 'events' happened yesterday which you might have to explain, etc.; working on the assumption that agreement can be reached as to what constitutes a 'historical event' in the first place. So, how do you decide which cut-in and cut-out points are the correct ones in order to render up an account without all such decisions bearing all the signs of the 'undecidability of the decision' and its logical arbitrariness? A rhetorical question. For there is no non-arbitrary way. And this is not least because the typical way of 'fitting' events into some kind of meaning-making frame – by putting them 'into context' – only generates further undecidable decisions of its own. For, whilst 'contexts' may indeed be necessary (for meanings just are generated within whole-to-part or part-to-whole configurations), whilst 'contexts' are indeed required to frame events historians can then go on to (putatively) 'explain', such necessary enabling devices are also necessarily both arbitrary (you can always produce another context – and other people do), and unsaturable (you can always put more in, and other people do). Hence the jury is permanently out as to how you can *know* if you have constructed the 'right context' and filled it with the 'correct' substance required to yield, say, explanatory meanings of a historical kind with epistemic affects.

Now, to try and cope with these (and many, many other) problematics, could various theories and methods help you? Well, yes, indeed they could. In fact, they have to since history, not being of a 'natural kind', is absolutely dependent on theories and methods (or just 'theories' actually, since 'methods' are simply worked up, pragmatically useful theories to enable you to get whatever you want to get – are instrumental), for its very existence. For histories – as commodities circulating unevenly throughout cultures by no means spontaneously – have to be manufactured (theoretically) and driven (supply and demand) like everything else (so giving the lie, incidentally, to all those suggestions by so many historians to the effect that theory is irrelevant to historicisations ... no comment, I think, could be more irrelevant than that to any 'understanding' of history). But – another but – for theories to work (whatever their various ideological imbrications in this or that social formation), they have to have a definite object to work on, to which they can be 'applied'. Yet although we can certainly assume our object of enquiry – 'New York Yesterday' – once happened, given that it has now gone, then it can only be constituted as such an object of enquiry, thence to be 'interpreted' by theories and methods, if those very same theories and methods, working inferentially on the traces of 'Yesterday in New York', can 'bring it back' into some kind of imagined re-existence in the first place then to be worked upon ... by the same theories and methods! Chicken and egg or Catch-22; either way the once existence of New York *per se* (like that of the past *per se*) is unavailable to help in conjuring-up any way out of this paradox. And, of course, if the definite object of enquiry always eludes us (I mean, what is the referent for the word 'history'?) then theories/methods of a definitive kind do so as well. For, despite centuries of attempts to forge these into the 'practices' of historians which would then produce histories capable of satisfying knowledge claims and thus be put on an epistemologically sound foundation of a universalisable type, no such aspiration has ever been realised such that, lacking the 'real thing', historians have been left with a myriad of theories/methods which have transported them out of the realm of truth claims and into the realm of 'figural realism', a realm of an aesthetic and *not* an epistemic kind. And here history can at last be recognised for what it is: an act of the imagination (*illusio*) forever bereft of certainty and thus of a kind which, marked indelibly by enthymemic logic (the logic of contingent probabilities through inference), can only figure-forth proposals (try looking at things this way or that way ...) which, being premised on probabilistic argumentation consigns it to where Aristotle consigned it over two-thousand years ago: within *rhetoric.* For since, to recap, history has no definitive *object* of enquiry nor any definitive *mode* of enquiry, then such a discourse belongs quite properly to the realm of rhetoric since this is of a kind that, not dealing with any definite class of objects is 'merely a faculty for the furnishing of arguments'. And, since arguments can never be true or false but only valid or invalid, no history, based as it is on such argumentation, can ever be, as a historical account, of a truthful kind. Moreover, since histories are never 'in and for themselves' but only always for 'someone', then, as I have already noted in passing, histories have a determinate suasive (political/ideological) impetus. No matter how much historians protest their innocence (their putative objectivity and dis-interest) historical texts are always positioned sausively. Accordingly, marked from end to end by enthymemic logic (from the undecidability of the decision *via* problematic contexts to probabilistic (abductive) inference), histories will remain as things inferential always remain: conjectures and proposals inviting refutation and as such always logically *open.* Here historical epistemology and 'truth' is trumped by history's inescapable aesthetic, figurative, rhetorical 'nature'. It was, of course, ever thus: histories always have been and always will be of an 'aesthetic kind'.

After which general 'conclusion' with regard to theories and methods, the details of any relatively systematic body of these phenomena are exactly that: details. But it might be important – since they are bandied around so cavalierly by most academic (empirical) historians – to briefly mention the capricious/arbitrary 'nature' of that multitude of concepts and categories that historians use within theories and methods to metamorphose the traces of the past – 'New York Yesterday' – into historical intelligibility. So, for instance, given that phenomena as such are of no intrinsic type, then it's not obvious how you determine which phenomena go where. What exactly 'belongs to' the concepts of, say, class, gender, progress, regress, decline and fall? What 'falls into' the organising categories of the economic, the social, the political, cultural, ideological? How is it decided, and who decides, where to draw the limits, to consign and distribute phenomena so that they might conceivably allow (but how would we know) 'Yesterday in New York' to shine through?

All of which raises to the level of consciousness (and thus to the level of the problematic – which all the above are leading to) the fact that there are no *translation rules* to carry us from the traces of past phenomena (stuff, data, facts, etc.) to the correct meaning-making expressions of them; no logical passage from syntax to semantics; no entailment from fact to value and from is to ought; no high-road to the truth between epistemic elements 'unearthed' empirically in the so-called 'research phase' of the historians' work (where epistemology with regard to singular or clusters of singular statements of a corroborative kind vis-à-vis some type of trace can 'operate'), and their combination through colligatory procedures generating *narrative substances* which, individuated by the contingently placed historians' 'point of view' can, at best, usher-forth part–whole and/or whole–part relationships as proposals about the historicity of the phenomena now brought into discursive frames. And, of course, this reference to narrative substances – and hence to narratives – makes it clear that, given that there are no 'stories' in past phenomena (that events just don't have in them the shapes of stories), then historians are not only able to impose any narrative (substance) they like on 'the past' but they *have* to do so given that the past, however construed, has no narrative substance of its own. Consequently, such narratives can only give an impression or image or icon of some previous phenomena (like 'Yesterday in New York') which, always depicted from an individuating point of view, cannot be submitted to definitive true/false criteria at the level of the synthetic account. An impression/reading/point of view, articulated through narrative substances where the point of view determines the significance of its parts (and not vice versa) cannot be of an epistemic kind. And not only that, for of course historical texts as complex narratives have to have, simply to be the narratives they are, all the elements common to narratives *per se.* That is, they have to be troped and emplotted and sustained by various modes of argumentation, their articulation depends upon textual poetics, rhetorical figures and devices, compositional strategies, intertextual understandings, variable/contingent theories and methods, governing positions, personal-to-holder theses and so on and so forth which, though not totally ignoring empirical/epistemological elements are, as already indicated, massively underdetermined by them. The resultant texts are *about*, let us say, 'New York Yesterday', but they're a long way from somehow *corresponding* to it. Moreover, New York's traces, the only New York available to us, do not include any of these theoretical/methodological things, yet these things are the *only* way historians have of producing the literary artefact that is, historically speaking, New York *today.*

Now, faced with only these few problematicisations of the knowledge status and intellectual incoherence of contemporary historicisations – for one could go on raising such problematics for ever (for when would you know that the returns are all in …) – well, you do wonder how historians manage to get away with it; how, and with such confidence, they blithely write book after book and article after article *as if* the sorts of things mentioned above are of little or no concern to them. Certainly few historians mention any of them in their books and how they have addressed them. Of course, part of the coping strategy is to bracket-off these kinds of problematics as 'theory' and therefore as being undeserving of attention (which, given their own histories are theoretical all the way down suggests their own productions are unworthy of attention too). But – and this is a point all too often unregistered – even amongst theorists of history I have never actually read anyone who has attempted to tackle all these (and other) questions in a joined-up and relatively comprehensive way (as opposed to discrete discussions of facts, or events, or inference, or causality, or narration, etc.), that might convince me that the discourses historians traffic in have the right to consider their practices as constituting a *discipline* … history as a science being out of the question since at least Aristotle. So I can only conclude (infer) that most mainstream academic historians can only carry on intellectually undisturbed because such disturbing questions never get raised – and/or stay raised – at the level of consciousness. But how can this disinterest – or maybe disavowal – conceivably happen? Well, the theorist Michel de Certeau probably gets it right – the operation in question is rather *sly.* For how is it possible, he queries in amazement, for a discursive practice and its institutional home to constitute a specific kind of work and writing – history – that makes this highly problematic and *fictive* phenomenon appear to be untroubled by its own inadequacies and soldier on as if nothing was amiss? How is it possible asks de Certeau,

> that a narrative form claims to produce not a fiction but a (past) real? … What peculiar kind of sustained, permanent ambiguity is it that historians practice, one by which a 'real' past is taken for granted, another 'real' past is represented in texts, and a 'real' present is effaced from their production?[2]

Well, these are good questions indeed, and de Certeau's answer ought to give historians more than a brief pause for thought:

> The operation in question is rather *sly* ... [for] the 'real' as represented by historiography does not correspond to the 'real' that determines its production. A *mise en scene* of a (past) actuality, that is, the historical discourse itself, occults the social and technical apparatus of the professional institution that produces it ... the discourse gives itself credibility in the name of the reality which it is supposed to represent, but this authorised appearance of the 'real' serves precisely to camouflage the practice which in fact determines it. Representation thus disguises the praxis that organises it.[3]

Thus it is that we conveniently overlook the fact that history is always coded, that it is language- and value-based and, as such, can have no objective or natural basis – 'the past'. Consequently, as Sande Cohen has put it, confirming de Certeau, the way that history legitimates itself is not by returning it to 'the past' for its authentication, its 'checking' and its 'accuracy' – to 'how it essentially was' – 'but to "training", "discipline" and norms ... cultural operations before they are "historical" ... in their formation and outcomes, it being historiography that turns every social coding of time (and decoding) into retrospective "truths" found in "The study of history".'[4]

Now – and moving on – insofar as it is the politico-institutional locations and practices of historical cultures that infuse histories of every kind with life (with regard to metanarrative histories, say, The Party, The Reich, certain ontotheologies; with regard to academic histories certain discursive practices and professional/peer-approved standards which determine and regulate what passes for proper civilising and identity providing histories – 'roots', 'traditions', 'contexts', 'identities' of a predominantly liberal, bourgeois kind ...), then it would follow that if these collapsed or were weakened, then the histories (inter)dependent on them would collapse or be weakened too. And clearly the notion of collapse encapsulates exactly what has *already* happened in the case of metanarratives (the collapse of the Marxist/proletarian project and Third Reich racial millennialism; the irrelevance of redemptive eschatologies in what are, despite certain throwbacks, our secular 'God is dead' days); whilst a weakening, to say the least, is now arguably happening to the academic history *genre.* Here, its practices intellectually incoherent and its practitioners pretty much reduced to talking to themselves (in the United States as Robert Rosenstone has commented, an academic history which sells 1,000 copies is regarded as a hit – this in a population of around 300 million ... whilst history's more public 'heritage wing' fulfils an *overt* leisure and entertainment agenda embracing commercial commodification such that for most academics it isn't really 'history' at all – and they're right), then academic history's availability and relevance for the contemporary 'social' has now slipped out of our main cultural/ideological conversations as the whole of capitalist culture reaches its logical conclusion in the short-term everyday everydayness of market exchange value and that all-pervasive relativism (and nihilism) which, as was noted at the beginning of this introduction, has now emptied out all traces of intrinsic value from everything.

Accordingly, this relativism (know it or like it or not) now acts as the total (ising) axiom, the unquestioned quasi-foundation for our personal and social living. The basic reasons as to why this is the case seem obvious. Thus, today we live in a bourgeois, liberal, capitalist market economy based on exchange value. And exchange value is, by definition, relative value; the value of X has a value relative to Y depending upon supply and demand contingencies that are related to the specificities of the mechanisms of market forces, etc. Consequently, here in the West – and globally wherever the market cash-nexus runs as the determinant of value – then exchange/relative value runs too. Accordingly, it is just inconceivable to imagine that in social formations so saturated with relative value as ours that cultural expressions of value – for example the value/values of histories of every type – should escape contamination. And they don't. As a result – to recap a little so to round this argument off – the days of (modernist) metanarrative histories, histories where everyday happenings were collected together to form some kind of immanent unity thence to be yoked to some teleological trajectory taking 'us' from the past through the present to an assured future whence things contingent were now seen as expressions of historical necessity, well, as I've said, those fantasies have gone. And the fragmentation of such alleged unities has impacted upon academic *petite-narratives* too which, by no means escaping the desire for unity (for objectivity, epistemic surety, truth), now lack the intellectual resources to resist their own fragmentation, splintering and breaking apart despite all those vain attempts by 'revisionists' to reform things into secure, hegemonic discourses.

Now, there is a sense in which (as critics of the most influential current of critical thinking in the last four or five decades – postmodernism – have pointed out) such 'splintering' postmodernism (for it's postmodernity/postmodernism I am talking about here) is the archetypal expression of contemporary capitalism. Postmodernism is just what the capitalist doctor ordered as its relativism opens up the remaining restrictive practices of social formations to endless flexibilities and fluidities and thus to myriad forms of exploitation both nationally and internationally. Of course. *But* – and hopefully it's a big but – the critical elements of postmodernism as *critical theory* indicates that, although sired and born by capital and ideologically necessary to it, it is *not the property of capital* and is therefore capable of being turned *against* its origins and its current home. As such, postmodern critique – based on a positive reading of the *aporia,* of the undecidability of the decision – can be used to undercut all those attempts to still galvanise unjust and undemocratic socio-economic and political systems by reference back to some kind of privileging foundations (generally of a natural kind) *as if* they had escaped from, or could temper or neutralise relativism, when it had opened things up too far. And academic history is essentially one of those tempering phenomena ...

hence the attempt – too late in the day obviously – to resist critical postmodern relativism (often pejoratively) referred to as *extreme* or *absolute* or *vicious* or *rabid* relativism ... a sort of 'relativism plus' I suppose, in the name of academic standards or, in some cases, even on behalf of civilization itself ('barbarians at the gate' and all that). Thus we are currently witnessing all manner of 'history makeovers' as the attempt is made to upgrade and update those old staples of historical anti-relativism through various 'neo's' (neo-realism, neo-empiricism, neo-epistemology), and that whole trend toward finding and pinning down hard varieties of *real* experiences (sublime or not it makes no difference) *via* the directness of testimony, witnessing, and various forms of personal and collective memory. But to no avail. For postmodern relativism is *not,* to the chagrin of those historians who just don't seem to get it (for if they did then they couldn't possibly write the anti-relativistic polemics which is what their anti-postmodernism effectively boils down to ... historians whose number includes, say, the Spiegels, the Bentleys, the Ginzburgs, the McCullaghs, the Zagorins, the Colemans, the Roths *et al.*, i.e. pretty much the whole of the history profession), some kind of 'blip' against which a sensible dose of some or other 'neo' and still more effort in the archives will see off since, imbricated within capital, relativism is here for the duration. The saturation of capitalist social formations by relativism *means* saturation. There are no dry areas. We're all relativists now. And from a radical postmodern perspective – the perspective of this book – that's fine. 'We' can live happily enough with relativism in order to help bring about changes of an emancipatory and democratic kind both within and beyond capitalism – for surely (global) capitalism cannot be as good as it gets – cannot be 'the end of history'.

Now, talking of *perspectives,* if this historicization of contemporary history culture doesn't convince epistemologically committed defenders of the faith who still hope for some kind of certainty beyond the reach of time and chance, there is a logical, quasi-foundation to support singular relativism that (probably) cannot be refuted. To explain very briefly.

Academic historians are, typically, only too happy to embrace a sort of 'non-extreme relativism' on the basis of a liberal–pluralistic, domesticated *perspectivalism* of phenomena on the basis that, while we all read things from 'our own perspectives', nevertheless this potential multiplicity of perspectives doesn't lead to subjectivism because we can all agree what we have different perspectives *on*. Consequently, this common object constrains 'outrageous' perspectives so leading towards a consensus: thus relativism (subjectivism) contained. But, as modern and postmodern theorists – from Nietzsche to Lyotard to Lacan to Derrida have explained – and as Žižek has recently argued, a perspective remains 'absolutely singular' because the subject's gaze is always constitutively *in* the object gazed at – say a historical event – in the form of an ineradicable blind spot or stain. Thus, I am always in the painting I paint, the history I write; my own 'material presence' guarantees my singularity. Here my materialism is not, as Žižek says,

> the direct assertion of my inclusion into the objective reality (such an assertion presupposes that my position of enunciation is that of an external advisor who can grasp the whole of reality). It rather resides in the reflexive twist by means of which I myself am included in the picture constituted by me – it is this reflexive short-circuit, this necessary redoubling of myself as standing [both] outside and inside my picture [text, etc.] that bears witness to my material existence. Materialism means that the reality I see is [therefore] never 'whole', not because a large part of it eludes me, but because it contains a stain, a blind spot, which signals my inclusion in it.[5]

Singular relativism thus subverts all attempts to tame perspectival relativism. Accordingly, academic historians can never achieve what they would most like to achieve, namely, to be able to cling on to epistemic life at all costs.

So we can perhaps conclude by saying that relativism now trips unchallenged right across our social formation. Accordingly, today, at the very time when historians are desperately insisting (as a kind of 'after-burn') on the relevance of history as a precondition of informed practice (which is 'why history matters'), history cannot provide – that is, historians cannot provide – any objective/universal idea of direction, aim, purpose, meaning, truth, etc. At the very moment when the chips are down, at the very moment when historians think we desperately need history of a reliable and usable kind, such histories are not available – or even relevant. Sande Cohen has seen this clearly:

> Consider then the idea that history has become metaphysical again, in the precise sense that things have happened (e.g. a *chronicity* of disasters in Africa) that are so disruptive to representation that one must doubt every sense of telos, direction, aim, end, finality, truth. Doubt here is kin to a form of scepticism that has been called 'classical' and for good reason: by what judgement can one *measure* 'history' and through which comparisons does the telos of, say, the technological series (extensions of lifespan in selected areas) subsume or not the series called the '*telos* of literacy' (falling off in the West)? Representational synthesis has become a question of metaphysics: it discloses passive and active elements. And might not one also say that it is incumbent to account for experiences that are situational to the degree that it is not possible to invoke history as a mediation of differences, that there is a new subjectification that unevenly accompanies metaphysics? In short, history has been *shifted*: from context-providing, the concept of history has become a trap of representation; from serving as the platform of truth, a condition of judgement's possibility, the concept of history is a *stake* in conflicts, the outcome … of which might be unknown … there is no such thing as history that is 'not for'.[6]

History again slips out of ostensibly disinterested knowledge here to become ideology, mythology, bereft of unproblematic purpose. It's a hard lesson for historians to learn, schooled as they are to think in terms of the past as providing a fund of wisdom essential for contemporary understanding. But just as, one might say, the fact that birds use twigs to build their nests does not mean that the meaning (purpose) of twigs lies in the fact that birds make use of them – that twigs are made for birds – then it doesn't follow that just because historians use 'the past' then 'the past' was made for historians. Historians – not least those safely ensconced in History Departments – all too often seem to think that they and the past were just made for each other. That illusion – for illusion it is – surely has little future now. Accordingly, all this, and much, much more, comes to constitute, for me, the problematical condition of 'our' history culture today, a condition wherein academic history (my main focus in the essays in this book and elsewhere) is marked by intellectual incoherence of its *own* making – it cannot hit the epistemological goals it has set itself – and by an increasing irrelevance to the compelling problems that await us in the future and of which *none* are inherently historical (nothing is). Historians, in cultures like ours, are thus becoming redundant, are beginning to themselves dissolve into a *trace.*

Reactions

Over the past thirty years or so I have toyed with *three* general reactions to the lightly sketched impressions of the parlous state of history culture sketched out above.

First, as soon as I became aware and began to take on board – in the early 1970s – postmodern type arguments, I increasingly divorced myself from those academic historians who, knowing or intuiting that something was unconvincing about the knowledge claims made for their historical representations, chose either to ignore or pit themselves against postmodern influences (postmodernism understood here – as throughout my writings – as a general term under which lived (and live) varieties of post-structuralism, post-Marxism, post-feminism, post-colonialism and deconstructive currents, etc.), influences which unfailingly pointed to where history's weaknesses lay. Looking back, I don't think I have ever really understood historians' general antipathy to theory as such, but I did and I do understand their antipathy (and in some cases pathological hostility) towards postmodernism. For what 'postmodern' theorizing was to do in the last three or four decades of the twentieth century was to deconstruct the foundationalist and essentialist presuppositions of the Western Tradition – and especially that tradition in its 'modernist' phase – until it had emptied out every trace of intrinsic meaning/value including, as we have seen, any residual traces within historical metanarratives and, for those paying attention, from the (alleged) epistemic productions of academic historians. Consequently, for such attention-payers, their overwhelming reaction was, if not outright rejection, a reluctant taking on board of certain 'useful' postmodern elements – its linguistic and aesthetic turns, its refinement of knowledge claims, etc. – in order to strengthen their historicizations, whilst at the same time outlawing its unpalatable 'extremes' ... and extremists. But for radical postmodernists that kind of revisionist domestication just misunderstood the postmodern intention. For (at least as I read them) postmodern critiques were not designed to help modernist histories of whatever *genre* to survive by helping them to get *smarter*; postmodern critics wanted to see modernist, empirical/epistemologically striving histories *replaced* not least because, if their analyses of histories being of an aesthetic–rhetorical kind were correct (which they are) then there had never actually been histories of any other kind. Whether empirical/epistemologically striving historians knew it or not all histories – just to be histories – had to be the kind postmodernists had raised to the level of consciousness whilst, politically, modernist histories, imbricated in the exigencies of the Western nation state, had overwhelmingly played (and still play) a crucial conserving role of helping to ensure, by stitching together a 'knowable' past to an 'understandable' present to a 'controlled future', what Sande Cohen has correctly seen as its main function, namely, to bring about *the exclusion of new rival claimants to the future.* For where, asks Cohen, are those works of history 'that positively alienate the beliefs and judgements of their readers' in ways that 'do not allow for the standard equipment of improvement, enlightenment', not least when it isn't hard to recall 'how many well-known historical writings from the past [and contemporaneously] have supported political regimes that were murderous'?[7] Historians all too rarely *damage* the present *status quo.* Consequently, accepting these types of 'postist' arguments, it never really occurred to me that I should ever want to profess histories of a modernist kind.

My *second* reaction – having thrown in my lot with postmodernism – was to argue the case for postmodern history as *replacement.* The postmodern histories I envisaged would ideally have been overtly politically positioned on the left and highly reflexive theoretically and methodologically. Here the talk was all about alternative experimental histories characterized by explicit authorial interventions; about multi-faceted and multi-levelled, paratactical and thus non-linear, endlessly open narratives which, although ironic, were not ironic enough to disable commitment. This history was intent not just to derail the train of thought and imagination characterized as modernist, but to shunt it into the sidings where it could peacefully pass away unmourned and soon unremembered, an interesting experiment of timing and politicizing 'time' through a peculiar type of historicization (geographically specific and about two hundred years old at best) which, because of its epistemic fetishism delayed our understanding of history as the aesthetic being it always was as it sent generations of truth-seekers down the wrong network. It would have been better if histories had never been modern. Thus, postmodern histories linked to radical politics now seemed to be the only real option around. And I think I held to this sort of position until the mid 1990s when I underwent something of a change of mind.

My *third* reaction and, for what it's worth, my current position, is that we can now live without histories of either a modernist or a postmodernist kind.

Of course, insofar as this happy day has not yet arrived, insofar as a culture like ours still thinks it needs to think today and tomorrow *via* a 'contextualising' backward glance, then I still think histories should be of a postmodern kind and therefore will continue to support them in the interim. But, in the best of all possible worlds, I think that we can and we ought to live our finite lives in time but 'outside of histories'.

Now I had been moving towards this position for several years before articulating it at length for the first time in the late 1990s. During the mid 1990s it had begun to occur to me that the end of *viable* 'modern' histories may well make us consider the usefulness or not of histories as such, including viable postmodern ones vis-à-vis that unfinished project of emancipation that Derrida had urged us never to forget. So, whilst in earlier books and papers I had argued for the end of modernist histories in the name of postmodern replacements which might help sustain the Derridean project, I now began to wonder if that project needed history at all – viable or not. Accordingly, it was this position that I developed at length for the first time in *Why History? Ethics and Postmodernity,* published in 1999.

The arguments within *Why History?* are too complicated to outline in the two paragraphs I've allowed myself here; besides, I return to them in several of the essays in this volume. But, for now, let me say that when, in preparing and writing *Why History?*, I ran my eye over what could be claimed as being perhaps the greatest clutch of cultural theorists the world has ever seen, an incomparable generation of theorists running from the mid 1960s to the late 1990s – theorists who, as I've already said, deconstructed in the space of but thirty years or so the Western Tradition running back to at least Plato – something immediately struck me. Here is a list of just some of them: Roland Barthes, Louis Althusser, Michel Foucault, Gilles Deleuze, Felix Guattari, Jacques Lacan, Jacques Derrida, J. F. Lyotard, Jean Baudrillard, Gayatri Spivak, Luce Iragary, Judith Butler, Jacques Rancièrre, Ernesto Laclau, Richard Rorty, Alain Badiou. And what struck me, when I looked at this list of (heterogeneous) critical theorists, was simply this: not one of them was a historian in ways 'proper' historians would recognise. And when I extended the list to twenty then thirty theorists, there still wasn't a historian amongst them. And when, incidentally, a little later Hans Bertens and Joseph Natoli ran up their own list for their book *Postmodernism: The Key Figures,* out of the fifty-three theorists included, only one was a historian: Hayden White. Consequently, I began to think – to cut a long story very short – that if Derrida and Rorty could provide just about all the emancipatory analyses, ethics and rhetoric needed without being historians, if Baudrillard *et al.* could do without history, then we all could.

And so in *Why History?* I developed certain arguments allowing me to conclude that we now have no need – in the sense of really *need* – to have histories around at all – including postmodern ones. That, to put it bluntly, when it comes down to radical/revolutionary politics of emancipation and empowering democracies, whether we have a historical (historian's) consciousness or not is, at best, an *option.* Of course, to repeat, postmodern histories, if they exist, could continue to work relative to their own lights. But in terms of urgent emancipatory *praxis* – the only light I was using in *Why History?* (and since) – such works may not be much to the point in a culture arguably so post-historical in its postmodernity. And by now it is too late, surely, still to be modern.

This position is not, let me insist, a pessimistic one; quite the reverse. Given the 'state of the situation' of our short-term, throw away, forgetful 'three minutes culture', the case for history (always remembering that, because there is no definitive history *per se*, then what kind of history may be required is an undecidable political decision) is difficult to sustain. Histories, as sometime providers of theoretical and practical 'bases' for emancipation have had their chance, have had their day in the sun, histories which, I'm afraid to say, on the reckoning of the balance sheet of forces for good versus evil, by no means balance out evenly. And so without regrets or nostalgia I think we can now wave history goodbye and look forward to a future – which is where we all have to live after all – unburdened and unspoilt by the historicised/historical past.

A short *PS.* In his essay *The Burden of History* (1966), Hayden White argues *against* Nietzsche's claim that history 'is a costly and superfluous luxury of the understanding', going on, after the paragraph I am going to quote, to answer the question posed in the last sentence of it with a *yes.* But it seems to me that, on this occasion at least, White has given the devil the best tune, such that I think that the answer which now *ought* to be given can only be *no.* But I can't speak for you.

Thus, in thinking that, *pace* Nietzsche, history is indeed worthwhile, White asks:

> But to what purpose ultimately? Merely to exploit the human capacity for play or mind's ability to frolic in images. There are worse activities for a morally responsible man, of course, but merely to demand the exercise of our image-making abilities does not necessarily lead to the conclusion that we should exercise them on the historical past. Here it would be well to bear in mind the line of argument which descends from Schopenhauer to Sartre and which suggests that the historical record can never become the occasion of either significant aesthetic or scientific experience. The documentary record, this tradition maintains, first invites the exercise of the speculative imagination by its incompleteness, and then discourages it by requiring that the historian remain bound to the consideration of those few facts which it does provide. To both Schopenhauer and Sartre, therefore, the artist [historian] is well advised to ignore the historical record and limit himself to the consideration of the phenomenal world as presented to him in his everyday experience. It is worth asking, then, why the past ought to be studied at all and what function can be served by a contemplation of things under the aspect of history. Put another

way: is there any reason why we ought to study things under the aspect of their past-ness rather than under the aspect of their present-ness, which is the aspect under which everything offers itself for our contemplation immediately?[8]

Circumstances

The above considerations have provided the background thinking for my putting together, in 2008/9, the essays in this volume. Since 1990 I have written and/or edited seven books on historical theory and before and alongside them various articles, chapters and papers. What I have done here is to pick out just over a dozen or so of the latter, all published over the last fifteen years, wherein I have tried to work out some of the *limits* of history and, I suppose on occasion, its possibilities or lack of them. I hope that, collected together, they might be useful to students of history – not least those coming to its study for the first time – and I just want to say a little bit about how the essays reproduced here have been organised.

The essays appear in chronological order since they reflect some of the changes in my thinking which is, in this respect, inevitably unidirectional. In their original form some had abstracts and some did not; where they did these have not been retained, where they didn't I haven't written new ones. But what I have done for all the papers is to write some short, prefacing remarks about the more immediate circumstances of their production. These prefacing remarks are not meant to close down (through direction, etc.) the reader's own reading of them, but to offer some brief remarks as to what I see as the *raison d'etre* for the papers: that's all.

There are also three papers in this volume that I didn't write, two by Perez Zagorin and one by Michael Coleman, and I ought to explain this. In 1999 Perez Zagorin wrote an article for the journal *History and Theory* in which he took issue with postmodernism in general and my *The Postmodern History Reader* (1997) in particular. I wrote a reply to Zagorin and, although *History and Theory* rarely carry 'exchanges', they agreed to this one if Zagorin would agree to write a reply to my reply. In the event he did. Thus I include here Zagorin's two papers as well as my own, single paper.

In 2002, Michael Coleman published a paper, again attacking postmodern history theorists in general and myself in particular, and the journal where Coleman's paper appeared, *American Studies in Scandinavia*, agreed, not least through the encouragement of Coleman, to carry a reply if I wished to write one. Which I did. Accordingly, Coleman's paper as well as my reply appear here.

In the essays which follow there are a few repetitions. That is to say that over the years I have sometimes put into a later publication a few sentences and, on occasion, a few paragraphs, pretty much verbatim. Thus, for example, let us say, at random, that essay 'nine' has a paragraph or two taken from essay 'four'. Now, it occurred to me that for this volume I should delete the paragraphs in the later essay – essay nine. But this assumed that readers would read essay four before essay nine (instead of nine before four), or that they would actually read both essays, which some readers won't necessarily do. So, at the risk of some occasional repetition I have left all the papers intact and thus autonomous. I apologise for my self-plagiarism and I don't want to exaggerate its extent; besides, although the odd sentence/paragraph may reappear, the essays in which they do so by no means use them in the same way: same words, different meanings.

Finally, a brief word about the register and vocabulary the papers are written in. The vast bulk of what I have written over the years has been written for 'students of history' and *not* for my 'history peers' or 'history colleagues'. I have never wanted to write scholarly, probably esoteric, footnote-clogged texts for those already 'in the know' and already 'on the inside', and I hope I never have. Most professional, academic historians are too-long-in-the-tooth to think too much outside of the box anyway (or inside it if their anti-theoretical attitudes are anything to go by), and so I have always had younger, fresher, and thus hopefully more open-minded audiences in mind. This doesn't necessarily mean to say that some of the things I have written may not appear 'difficult' – quite a few students have told me that they are – but I prefer to think of any such difficulty as being a challenge and encouragement to thinking rather than being technically over-complicated. Moreover – and despite the common accusation by many historians that theory, and especially postmodern theory, is 'a load of jargon', in fact the precision with which most of the theorists I am familiar with write – including Lyotard, Derrida, Baudrillard – is very far from that. So, the essays appearing here are hopefully accessible enough to be both 'popular' and challenging. And I suppose, in this regard, I ought to end by saying that, because I have always wanted to try and influence or change young historians' (young at heart historians') minds vis-à-vis the shibboleths of the profession, then most of the things I've written have been *polemical.* Again I don't want to exaggerate this; compared with many writers the things I have written may well not have enough of what I think all theoretical writings about history *ought* to have: a positive, left, political, *cutting edge.*[9]

Notes

1 I said in the text that most (empirical) historians underestimate the problematics of inference. This really needs a paper of its own, but I can put a few, indicative points here.

The *normal* way in which historians see the problematic of inference is as follows. Historians in the *archive* 'find' various *traces* from the past. Some of these, if pragmatically useful become *sources* and some of those become *evidence* for the argument/thesis the historian is running. Though sometimes 'vague', historians don't normally go to the archive without purposes in mind ... otherwise why go to *that* archive, *that* deposit, *that* shelf, *that* box ... after which the 'problem' – that of *inference* – is all about the accuracy of the extrapolations from traces/sources/evidence to the argument and its eventual status as 'history' as expressed in the finished text. In the 'training' of the historian the problematic of inference is often addressed, but these discussions rarely produce a method of how *exactly* to select, how *exactly* to test inferences, of how *exactly* you make so many undecidable decisions and judgements, such that in the end various 'mystifications' come to the rescue: one gets 'a feel for the archive'; 'experience suggests that' ... any lingering concerns often papered over by normalising any scepticism over accuracy as 'scholarly caution', counter extrapolations of alternative interpretations as 'tolerant (liberal) pluralism', and by lowering expectations: one shouldn't expect more than provisional findings from historians anyway. All of which sits awkwardly against a practice wedded to notions of accuracy, facticity, reliability, objectivity and 'truth at the end of enquiry'.

Seen in the above light, the problematic of inference becomes ultimately resolved by experience, but the point I want to make is that experience cannot make inferential judgements/decisions *sound.* The further problematicisation of inference thus includes the following:

(a) Historians always access the past (its traces) not as it *was* but as it *is*, i.e. the state/condition of the archive is itself subject to the contingencies of time and space; i.e. wear and tear is itself historicised.

(b) Historians cannot be – if they want to be historians – anything but anachronistic, hindsightful, and present-centred. The idea of sloughing-off the present so as to access the past in and for itself as it essentially was *without* benefit of hindsight is not only impossible but *anti-historical.* 'History', to be 'history', necessarily involves 'looking back'. The problematics of doing so are rarely systematically explored.

(c) 'History' always involves at least two processes of production: the first whereby one produces (via the archive, through all the things that have made you the historian you are) the material which can be constituted as an object of study which is, then, a second-order activity, worked on to produce (via inference, etc.) a historical text. In other words, histories are always *prefigured.* The problematic here is that how this process works is not exactly known, not least because few historical texts suggest any doubt as to their own authority on their surface. Yet they should, as Hayden White has pointed out, 'when it is a matter of trying to *mark out* what appears to be a new area of human experience for preliminary analysis, *define* its contours, *identify* the elements in its field, and *discern* the kinds of relationships that obtain among them. It is here that [historical] discourse must establish the adequacy of the language used in analyzing the field to the objects that appear to occupy it. And discourse effects this adequation by a *pre*-figurative move that is more tropical than logical' (*Tropics of Discourse,* Baltimore: Johns Hopkins University Press, 1978, p. 1). I am unaware of how courses on 'method' in universities grapple with this tropological aspect of inference, if at all.

(d) Finally, to inference more directly. Two points:

  (i) the past was made up of everything that happened but also everything that didn't but could have happened if other decisions, events, occurrences had occurred. But the traces that remain, the only past we *now* have, are traces of what happened. Yet, these are traces of a past constituted by things that both did and didn't happen, *all* of which ought to be taken into account. The first problem: how do you factor in constitutive absence?

  (ii) The second problem is the *size* of this absence. For the vast majority of things that *did* happen, like the vast majority of the things that happened last year or 'Yesterday in New York', left no direct traces. In fact – and overall this must be a conservative estimate – I would say that 99 per cent of the things that happened in the past (just like 99 per cent of the things that happened 'Yesterday in New York') never get recorded. So the problem of inference becomes that of how you infer a 100 per cent past, either simple or complex, if only 1 per cent of its actuality left traces. Of course, 1 per cent of all possible traces is a lot of 'stuff', and hence the problem of inference as most historians 'experience it', that is, the problematic of selection. But this pales into insignificance when the 'real' problematic is of somehow inferring from 1 per cent of traces (whose typicality isn't obvious) to some kind of putative whole (for historians always have to make sense of things in terms of part-whole or whole-part relationships) when the other 99 per cent has 'gone without trace'. No wonder that in the end 'experience' is the final arbiter between 'decisions', but experience of what exactly? Of ever being successful (but how would you know?), or the experience of little-dwelt-upon failures? Well, whichever way things fall, it is problematics like these which undercut all appeal to epistemic claims for the discourse of history as the inferential acts of the imagination they ultimately are.

Apropos 'inference' and 'New York Yesterday', Beverley Southgate commented that my use of 'New York Yesterday' reminded him of Thomas Pynchon's reference 'to each of us having our "own rat-house of history". In which state of ... relativism, with everyone having "their private versions of history", there must, Pynchon calculates, be about "five million different rat-houses" in the city of New York alone ... '.

2 de Certeau, M., quoted in Jenkins, K., *Why History? Ethics and Postmodernity,* London: Routledge, 1999, p. 91.

3 Ibid., p. 93.

4 Cohen, S., *Passive Nihilism: Cultural Historiography and the Rhetorics of Scholarship,* London: Macmillan, 1998, pp. 127–8.

5 Žižek, S., in Douzinas, C. (ed.) *Adieu Derrida,* Houndmills: Palgrave, 2007, p. 128. Incidentally, and *apropos* relativism and political commitment, it is sometimes wondered how one can (how I can) espouse relativism with such certainty and not commit a performative contradiction, i.e. that to say that all judgements are relative is to make an absolute statement which is obviously disallowed if 'everything is relative'. Two things can be said about this. First, I take relativism not as 'the truth' but as an *axiom*; it's the premise from which I work. I'm open to the possibility that relativism can be refuted, but until such a refutation (of a foundational/universal type) comes along, I'll assume it doesn't exist. Second, the idea that, if relativism invades politics/ethics, then how can I strongly forward a position given its non-foundational status, the point is this: I take it that there are no absolute grounds for my decisions. That my decisions – like yours and everyone else's – are undecidable. But note that once I have made my (*aporetic*) decision, then I can push it/run with it as hard as I can. Indeed, the whole point of making a decision is that, once made, you stick with it: otherwise why bother making a decision in the first place? So there is nothing contradictory or paradoxical or inconsistent about deciding on undecidable (singular–relativistic) 'grounds' and then acting as if that decision was justified and pursuable. Indeed there is, as they say, 'no alternative'.

6 Cohen, S., in Brueggemann, A. and Schulman, P. (eds) *Rhine Crossings,* New York: State University of New York Press, 2005, p. 274. At the very end of his latest book, *History Out of Joint* (Baltimore: Johns Hopkins University Press, 2006), Cohen, in estimating the value, if any, history may have in a culture like ours writes: 'To close with another beginning: what would it require in our "advanced" society – that has been historicised – to openly say that historical representation is just material for discussion – we wish to test ourselves with it instead of stepping inside its comfort zones. What would one make of a society where history was actually taken seriously for its disjunctions instead of seeking identifications within it?' (p. 261).

7 Cohen, S., 'On the Body and Passion of History and Historiography', *Rethinking History,* 12, 4, 2008, pp. 515–536.

8 White, H., 'The Burden of History', in idem, *Tropics of Discourse: Essays in Cultural Criticism,* Baltimore: Johns Hopkins University Press, 1978, pp. 27–50, 46.

9 With regard to politics, ethics and history, I have long been influenced by the works of Ernesto Laclau. For a succinct summary of his position on radical politics and history see his 'The Time is Out of Joint', *Diacritics*, 25, 2, 1995, pp. 86–96.

1 Marxism and historical knowledge

Tony Bennett and the discursive turn

In the 1980s I was becoming an adherent of the radical politics and political theory of Ernesto Laclau, out of which came a form of 'discursive Marxism' or 'post-Marxism', a Marxism influenced not least by Jacques Derrida and which had jettisoned the notion of historical inevitability whilst retaining key elements of Marxist method and political commitment. My reading of various texts by Paul Hirst and Barry Hindess (not least their *Pre-Capitalist Modes of Production* (1975)), wherein Marxist history had also been rejected, also influenced my move towards post-Marxism, whilst I had also become familiar with the 'cultural studies' and literary theory of Tony Bennett. In 1990 Bennett published his book, *Outside Literature,* in which, in chapters 2 and 3, he rejected Marxist history as teleology but kept a form of historical knowledge which I didn't think he needed to. And so I wrote this paper which was both respectful of Bennett yet critical of him insofar as I didn't think he took the rejection of history to its logical conclusions. Hindess and Hirst did do that, however, and I found their argument both logical – they indeed took their reasoning to its logical conclusion – and convincing. So in this paper I worked Bennett, Laclau, Hindess and Hirst together vis-à-vis my then embryonic notion that we were coming to a certain 'end of history' ... and that this was (probably) a good thing.

The question of what is history, the question of how the events and situations of the past can be represented in words and the status of such resultant knowledge, the question of whether it is possible to find some 'real' basis beyond contingency for the verbal propositions and interpretations which historians construct about the past, and the question inextricably bound up with these concerns – of how historians and histories are made or allowed to function within different social formations – these are things that do, or should, concern historians constantly.

Today, under the intellectual pressures produced by varieties of deconstructionist, post-structuralist and postmodern analyses, historians from across the political–intellectual spectrum are addressing such questions more urgently than for some time, seeking at the level of theory for some 'real' foundations for historical knowledge not undercut by a rhetorical scepticism and relativism. This reassessment is being articulated within current 'bourgeois' terms as the need for objectivity, unbiasedness, balance, disinterestedness, non-present-centredness and a study of history 'for its own sake' (as opposed to, say, history 'for the proletariat's sake') and, on the political left, by the somewhat reluctant reorientation and reconstitution of Marxism into its own 'postist' phase as post-Marxism.

Accordingly it is this rethinking of history into a post-Marxist variant which I want to look at in this paper through an examination of some of the arguments put forward by Tony Bennett in his recent book, *Outside Literature*.[1] This is not, it has to be said, the only thing that Bennett is concerned with in *Outside Literature*. At least since the publication of *Formalism and Marxism*, Bennett has been addressing, in various articles and papers, the interconnected areas of literary theory, literary value, literary genres, the historicity of texts and more general questions related to ways of reading popular culture from a critical Marxist perspective.[2] And in *Outside Literature* he revisits these areas in extremely perceptive and thought-provoking ways. But, as I have indicated, in addition to these old preoccupations, Bennett also examines for the first time, in any substantial or systematic way, the problems that have accumulated around the possibility of gaining, in these 'postist' days, some secure grounds on which the claims we make about the past can be grounded in viable and usable Marxist forms so as to be able to work the practices of capitalist 'new-times' in the direction of continuing socialist political desires.

Bennett cannot be accused of making his task for a procedural and substantive post-Marxist history an easy one, on four counts. First, accepting broadly Saussurean and post-Saussurean arguments that language is a system of differences with no positive terms, Bennett takes it that, rather than 'reflecting' the social world of which it is a part, language precedes and appropriates that world, carving it up according to its own (ultimately arbitrary) rules of signification and severing it from any necessary or intrinsic connection to external referents. As a result, historical modes of explanation and interpretation that depend upon the idea of there being an 'objective' reality existing independent of language and which assume a one-to-one fit between evidence and inference (as Samuel points out, the usual basis of functional analysis and the normal procedure in historical empirical research)[3] are undermined. Instead we are invited to 'read the signs': to read the past as a text in ways that always encourage a rewriting and to consider past social formations as a series of spectacles in which 'appearances are double-coded, meanings occult and images opaque'.[4]

Second, Bennett effectively accepts related, Derridean-type arguments as to the unavoidable surpluses of signification produced by signs, surpluses that make it impossible to establish intended meanings in acts of speaking and writing in consistent and stable ways so that the (themselves discursively constructed) readers are confronted, ultimately, by an indeterminacy of meaning, the *aporia*, in the face of which a definitive 'once and for all' closure is endlessly deferred.[5] Accordingly, this dissolution of the materiality of the sign arguably ruptures any necessary relationship to a knowable pre-discursive reality, this again suggesting the impossibility of achieving a definitive history since, as Spiegel puts it, it denies the ability of language to ultimately relate to or account for any reality other than itself, history thereby becoming a sub-system of linguistic signs constituting its object according to the contingent rules of the linguistic universe inhabited by the historian.[6] In this construction 'the past' becomes not so much a real presence in 'history' but an effect of presence created by textuality, as notional a term as the 'real world' alluded to in realist fiction, only ever existing in those present discourses that articulate it and thus as vulnerable to the waywardness of deconstructionism as any other discourse: there is no *hors-texte.* Accordingly, the upshot seems to be a past that can be infinitely re-described; that can be played and re-played as an (endless) arrangement of styles, tropes, genres and signifying practices, destabilising it as a discrete area of knowledge: as Hebdige puts it, 'the only history that exists here is the history of the signifier and that is no history at all'.[7]

Third, cognisance of these kinds of argument leads Bennett to broadly agree with Lyotard's formulation of post-modernism as characterised by 'incredulity towards metanarratives', metanarratives that obviously include Marxism.[8] For, unfortunately, says Bennett, it is now rather obvious that the idea of history with a capital 'H' (of history as construed as an object capable of being deciphered and which when deciphered could be known as the embodiment of a process that was from its very origins being propelled irresistibly towards its world-communist *telos* by class-struggle) was never more than a desirable story, a useful fiction that had and has no more truth 'in it' than any other of the historical fictions around (liberalism, conservatism, whiggism, ... in fact all the 'isms'), the reason why this one has been so stubbornly maintained being because Marxists have traditionally thought that, for their story to really gain a hold on the consciousness of the working classes, then it had to actually be 'truer' than all those other creations. That Marxism really had to correspond to the true processes of 'History' ... that the advance towards communism was dependent upon it being the 'real' culmination of the objective direction of historical development and being known (scientifically known) as such. For if, says Bennett, the historical process was not 'really' such an objective journey towards communism, then there could be no 'real' foundation for its representation as such and therefore no 'real' possibility of it being believed in or acted upon. Marxism to be capable of mobilising the workers had to be quite literally true:

> History, so to speak, cannot [in this theory] be duped into progress by tricking its subjects into believing that it has an objective progressive tendency. Its course must *be* one of progress in order to *be known* as such, and it must *be known* as such in order to realise itself.[9]

But none of this is the case of course. The past 'itself' never did and never will 'lead' anybody anywhere. The past is expressive of no purposeful essence that can be known 'historically'. Rather, history has to be recognised for what it is: an organising concept, a metaphor ... the past as if it was history; the past as if it was what the Marxist reading said it was.

Fourth and finally, these Saussurean, Derridean and Lyotardian-type arguments lead Bennett towards a general acceptance of aspects of post-Marxism as construed particularly by Chantel Mouffe and Ernesto Laclau, theorists who have already effectively incorporated these points into Marxist discourse, Bennett agreeing very much with their 'development' of three areas of 'traditional' Marxist thought: society, epistemology and class.[10]

With regard to society, Bennett agrees with Mouffe and Laclau that the basic concept so fundamental to traditional Marxism – that society can be constituted as an intelligible object of knowledge – is now flawed. For if, it is argued, social relations are partly discursive, and since discursive relations are partly relations of meaning and thus liable to fluidity and indeterminacy, then it becomes hard to see how the idea of society can be regarded as supplying a conceptually fixed or stable object of which there might be systematic and accumulating/lasting knowledge. Consequently, Laclau and Mouffe reject any real distinction between discursive and non-discursive practices, arguing that it is necessary to abandon as an area of analysis the premise of society as a sutured, self-defined totality. For the discursivity inherent in social relations, they argue, means that one cannot find a unifying principle (such as that traditionally supplied by the 'economic base' or the 'mode of production') capable of serving as the organising centre for the concept of society as a rationally ordered whole. They thus reject the view that society be seen as an integrated totality within which each part is fixed in its position in relation to every other part by virtue of its relationship to a central underlying principle (or contradiction) which underpins (acts as the base for) all social relationships. Instead Laclau and Mouffe see society as a vast network of dispersed differences caught up in an incessantly mobile set of discursive (and thus contingent) relationships, such a flexible condition being too unstable for analysis in the form required by Marxist theoretical study, as well as being unable to constitute the grounds for some political transformation whereby as a consequence of a change in the relations of production society as such will be totally restructured.

Epistemologically, the argument accepted by Bennett is that an insistence on the discursivity of social relations dismantles the thought–reality opposition which he sees as supplying the conditions for the old central question of epistemology as such, namely, how can a relationship of correspondence between thought and reality be established in order that the truth claims of the former might be vindicated by the latter? For, as Bennett notes, the desire for a normative epistemology by means of which Marxist truth claims – and thus its political correctness – might be privileged above those of rival theories has generally been accompanied by a concept of materialism according to which reality is seen as supplying a fixed reference point (an unproblematic referent) in relation to which competing truth claims can be adjudicated. However, as discourse is everywhere and constitutes the meanings for everything, no such pre-discursive reality exists on which to ground such an epistemology, the result being that the forms of closure promised by Marxists just do not work, just do not provide any adequate means of deciding between the contradictory truth claims of different discourses. Laclau and Mouffe have summarised this succinctly: 'Just as the era of ... universal discourses ... has come to an end ... so too ... has the era of normative epistemologies.'[11]

Finally, with regard to class, Bennett argues that the anti-unifying thrust of post-Marxism has been accompanied by a retreat from – or recognition of the relative decomposition of – the working classes as the vehicle for the transformation of capitalist society into a socialist one via a moment of revolution. What is now in crisis, says Bennett, is thus the very idea of a socialism which rests on the centrality of a homogenous working class and on revolution as the inevitable way forward. For as Laclau and Mouffe put it,

> The plural and multifarious character of contemporary social struggles has finally dissolved the last foundation for that political imaginary. Peopled with 'universal' subjects and conceptually built around History in the singular, it has postulated 'society' as an intelligible structure that could be intellectually mastered on the basis of certain class positions and reconstituted ... through a founding act of a political order. Today, the Left is witnessing the final act of the dissolution of that Jacobin imaginary.[12]

So, having accepted these four positions, Bennett's task – to try and show that some kind of definitive and usable knowledge of the past is historically possible – really does seem to be a formidable one. For, as Bennett is very well aware, there is no chance at all of trying to return to the 'pre-postist' view – by now intellectually archaic – of seeing history as a discourse committed to the recovery of the past in some unmediated and transparent pre-discursive state, in some naive realist way. For, as an effect of discourse, history is clearly unable to function as an extra-discursive source of anything else: 'Historical explanation thus turns out to be a way of telling stories without any particularly convincing means, where such stories differ, of deciding between them', all these sorts of arguments as to the limits of certainty appearing to Bennett to be 'unassailable', a product of the discursive turn of the twentieth century.[13]

And yet, formidable or not, unassailable or not, Bennett will try to rescue Marxism from precisely this discursive turn. For in his view a firm 'footing' in a 'known' reality is both a necessity for any credible Marxist reading and, in fact, still a possibility:

> Textualising the past in such a way that it can be rendered permanently undecidable serves little purpose. Keeping the past open ... serves every politics in principle but none in practice. For the latter requires, however provisionally, that the past be fixed, that what can be said of it ... be subject to definite limitations, substantive and procedural, if those truths ... are to count for much. This is not a matter of closing down the past but

> simply of recognising that its openness cannot be infinite if the truths produced there are to prove actionable.[14]

'That the past be fixed'; 'That what can be said of it ... be subject to definite limitations'; that the past to be 'actionable' must not be capable of 'infinite' readings; these are the imperatives that will thus push Bennett towards trying to show how the 'truth' of the past can be known. So, how does he try to do it, and how successful can he possibly be, after accepting, as he has, so many postist positions? Well, in effect, Bennett will run three arguments, the first of which might be called a damage limitation exercise; here the attempt is made to argue that not anything can be said about the 'facts of the past'. Second, Bennett then abandons the by now hopelessly wrecked notion of an upper-case History in favour of a lower-case version that can arguably access the past by craft-like methods and 'skills' modelled on legal procedures. And, third, Bennett then argues that if the first two strategies fail then it still doesn't matter; that a Marxist analysis will be true (true enough) if it can re-organise the past for present purposes in ways that mobilise the remaining working classes politically. In the end Bennett will use as the criterion of historical truth the old Marxist test of the unity of theory and practice.

Bennett's first argument, then, runs as follows. So alright, historians can never recover the past as it actually was. Nevertheless, what is at issue in historical scholarship – and what is all that there can ever be at issue says Bennett – is what can be derived from the historical record or archive. Of course such records and archives are highly volatile and changeable (thus apart from the effects of various forms of institutional labour by archivists, librarians, etc., which goes into their organisation/production, the composition of such 'deposits' may vary considerably over time, as witnessed for example by the influence of feminist historians in expanding what now counts as the historical record). Nevertheless, these traces of the past still occupy a distinct position in relation to the works produced and then distributed in what Bennett calls the 'public historical sphere' (i.e. in books, articles, lectures, in various expressions of the past in public and published histories). For such records act as the bottom line which underwrites the public limits that historians have to obey, functioning not as the real referent in the sense of an extra-discursive real 'but *as if it were* such a referent in the sense that it constitutes the last court of appeal for historical disputes, the point at which, so to speak, they hit base – but a base within discourse'.[15]

From this position Bennett is then able to suggest that once what is called 'the past' is recognised as an already 'worked up' record/archive, as a social product, then it is also necessary to recognise it as a highly differentiated one. For this allows that the issues involved in historical scholarship can be re-thought in ways that do not insist that they be posed as part of a general epistemological problem concerning the nature of the historian's access to the past *as such*. For historians have never and will never access the past *as such*; what is accessed are the various mutable arrangements of the record or archive – the traces of the past. On this account history is thus the *discipline* through which historians working at the level of the *public historical sphere* (as, say, salaried workers in universities) come into contact with the historic record or archive in order to be either corrected by it or allowed to change with it. Either way they cannot ignore it. As such, history – while being the 'product' of historians – cannot just be what historians want, rather they have to follow those specific rules governing –

> the discursive moves which may be made in relation to this record, including those regulating the re-organisation of that record itself in periods of marked historiographical controversy. It is these rules, which historians are right to insist on as constitutive of their discipline, which limit the arbitrariness of 'the past' ... in the sense that either its maintenance ... or its transformation, depend on certain conditions being met – even though, of course, these may themselves be bones for contention.[16]

Bennett's suggestion is therefore that history is best seen as a specific discursive regime governed by distinct procedures through which the maintenance and transformation of the past as a set of currently existing realities is regulated. It constitutes a disciplined means for the production of a 'historical past' which exercises a regulatory function in relation to the public past (i.e. history). And for Bennett the existence of this fixing and limiting 'historic past' is what is crucial, the mere fact that such a referent (the record/trace that the historian refers to as the source of his derived interpretation) turns out to be intra-discursive and mutable, not being held to disable the 'historical enterprise'.

This comprises Bennett's first argument, that the past as traces already in discourse (the historic past) acts as the referent for the historian *as if it* was pre-discursive and is respected accordingly. Consequently history's productivity (the texts historians produce) consists precisely in its

> capacity to reorganise its referent and thus transform 'the past' – not as it was but as it is. Understood in this way, the cogency and productivity of historical inquiry may be admitted without the question of its relations to 'the real past' ever arising. This is not to doubt that such a past existed but is merely to say that, from the point of view of what is at issue in historical debates ... it may be allowed to go its own way – as it surely has.[17]

Now, it may have been noticed that, whilst in Bennett's first attempt the discipline of history is governed and limited by distinct procedures, these do not even pretend to reach some pre-discursive reality, and that the past that is reached is extremely mutable. For, as Bennett has noted, here there are 'marked areas of historiographical controversy'. The record/archive is treated only 'as if' it were a real referent. This is a 'historic past' which is subject to the sorts of 'rearrangement' and 'extension' that feminists carry out, the result of all these sorts of *loopholes* being that, for Bennett, the spectre of disabling relativism has not yet been banished. For, as Bennett says, if from such already textualised 'sources' –

> narratives are all that we can have and if all narratives are, in principle, of equal value – as it seems they must be if there is no touchstone of 'reality' to which they can be referred for the adjudication of their truth claims – then rational debate would seem to be pointless. If the non-accessibility of a referent means that the theorist is 'drawn into labyrinths of textual "undecidability" where any kind of systematic truth-claim could only tell the story of its own undoing' – then why bother? ... The upshot ... would be ... the free circulation of communal myths and values.[18]

And here one might be tempted to reply, 'Yes, that does seem to be the upshot.' But that is not Bennett's response. For in Bennett's view the relativism of the kind suggested here can be resisted successfully without resurrecting the idea of accessing some pre-discursive referent/reality. It by no means follows, he argues, that if certain propositions cannot be shown to be absolutely true then we cannot establish their provisional truth. Nor does it follow that just because we cannot escape the narrative–textual nature of history then anything goes, that all narratives are to be regarded as equal vis-à-vis their propositional content. Such a violent all-or-nothing logic can be put aside for that desired 'rational debate' which will in practice allow for the 'empirical regulation of propositional statements' without the question of access to a pre-discursive past ever arising. Drawing on the work of Mark Cousins and addressing himself not to upper-case History but to lower-case history as a 'craft' with particular 'skills', rules and procedures similar to those embodied in the law, Bennett will thus develop his second argument in the attempt to square the relativist circle.

For both history and the law address two primary questions: did a specific event occur or not and, if so, into what class of event does it fall? These questions, when answered, occasion further probings: who was responsible for the event, what links of causality can be established in relation to the event and other pertinent events, etc. In a court of law such questions are pursued by means of tight rules that govern the admissibility of, and the relevant credence to be given to, different types of evidence which for an event to be legally recognised must be assembled in such a way that it is accepted as a representation of the event which is 'beyond all reasonable doubt'. As Cousins himself writes:

> It might appear that the legal process attempts to establish what really happened in the past, but 'really' is used in a specialised sense. 'Really' is what is relevant to the law, what is definable by law, what may be argued in terms of law and evidence, what may be judged and what may be

> subject to appeal. 'Reality' as far as the law is concerned is a set of representations of the past, ordered in accordance with legal categories and rules of evidence into a decision which claims to rest upon the truth. But this truth of the past, the representations of events, is a strictly legal truth.[19]

Similarly, says Bennett, the past for the historian is never the past as such but only the past as a product of the protocols of investigation which characterise the discipline of history as it establishes, classifies and orders the relationships between events relevant to the research being undertaken. In this way the procedures of historians may be said to produce (uncover) events whose representations are called historical facts. In this formulation the reality of those events consists of nothing but the status of historical facts that is accorded to those representations whose 'evidential' status has passed procedural scrutiny. As Bennett admits, this 'knowledge' cannot claim to rest on any *foundation* other than its own procedures, or to know anything other than the facts which such procedures produce and validate; nevertheless, this does not open the door for some kind of sceptical relativism. As Cousins argues:

> to reject any general foundation to historical truth or any general truth of History does itself not undermine a notion of historical truth as such. There is no need to enter a form of scepticism about statements about the past. It is enough to recognise that the justification for truth claims about the past are [sic] part of the particular practice of historical investigation. Historical facts are not illusions; we may as well say they are true.[20]

Of course, says Bennett, such truths/facts which serve as the only possible check on the forms in which the past is re-presented are not absolute. Obviously there remains a degree of indeterminacy between the historic past and historians accounts but, Bennett argues,

> only a degree, for this indeterminacy is located against a bedrock of what are taken to be determinate historical truths. It is true that this bedrock may be shifted in the sense that some truths may be added to it while others are subtracted as specific historiographical disputes are worked out. Yet such disputes never throw the totality of the 'historical past' into question.[21]

Yet, this reassurance given, Bennett is very much aware of the obvious weakness in all this, namely, that whilst all these kinds of procedures can prevent any sort of 'facts' from being deemed 'reasonable' and whilst they may indeed help us to see *what* happened, historians are above all concerned (and Marxists especially so) not only with the establishment of factual *propositional statements* which, as propositional statements, can indeed be subject to truth/falsity logical analysis, but with the *evaluative* arrangements of 'facts' in causal processes and the establishment of what past 'events' meant and mean vis-à-vis a (logically) infinite range of preferences/criteria precisely *not* given by the events of the past as facts. In other words, there may well be procedures to establish much of the *syntax* of the past (and these are crucially important of course) but there is no procedure whatsoever that can absolutely guarantee its *semantics*. For no method, no procedure, no discipline, no set of so-called 'historian's skills' – precisely because they are only *formal* mechanisms for going about doing things – can demonstrate 'beyond all reasonable doubt' any *substantive* theory for, as form and substance (as fact and value), they are ontologically separate and (arguably) not-entailable. And despite his optimism Bennett recognises this, recognises that after all this work he is still not far away from his relativistic starting point, a recognition he explicitly confronts. For sadly there is, says Bennett,

> nothing within the protocols of historical enquiry that can prevent historical representations which violently traduce the 'historical past' from gaining an effective currency [in historians' accounts and the public historical sphere] and so becoming a major social force ... the ascendancy of fascist myth, for example.[22]

Bennett cannot thus do other at this juncture than reformulate the question of historical knowledge in more directly political and thus substantive (as opposed to formal or procedural) terms:

> If there neither is nor can be an absolute warrant for Marxist accounts of history then how does Marxist historical interpretation [or liberal or Whig or Tory or idealist or feminist ...] differ from fascist myth?[23]

Accordingly, Bennett runs (as his third and last general argument) two particular approaches to try and solve this problem, the first of which is extremely slight and which actually still carries with it the baggage of the procedural. For if, he argues, fascist myths were to gain ascendancy, then this would be because of the failure of the specific form of reasoning embodied in the procedures of history to establish their pertinence or carry much weight in the general political arena. But this is really no 'argument' at all, suggesting only that historical procedures as such, were they to have carried their *proper* weight, would have inevitably led to a non-fascist interpretation, a conclusion which unfortunately only resurrects yet again the false idea that *formal* methods somehow entail a substantive theory (in this case anti-fascism). What then, is Bennett's second approach?

Here, Bennett's starting point is again 'fascist mythology'. For if, he argues, 'fictional histories' (like fascist mythologies) can actually mobilise sections of the population, and if they can do so in *desirable* ways (i.e. if they are running in a socialist/Marxist leftward direction and not in, say, a fascist/rightist direction), then such histories are actually alright. Of course in the best of all possible worlds it would be wonderful if the 'findings' of lower-case history as a formal discipline should actually coincide and support the larger substantive Marxist metanarrative (as in a sense Marx's own 'empirical' work on nineteenth-century British capital was held to support the larger historical trajectory of which it was but an exemplary *moment*, the particular and the general thus corresponding). But given, says Bennett, that we live not so much in the best of all possible worlds but arguably in a postmodern one that has driven a coach and horses through all kinds of correspondences including that one, then the 'correctness' of Marxism will have to stand or fall before the traditional unity of theory and practice, that the correctness of Marxist analysis can still be shown if, despite its failure to be absolutely true, it is *true enough* to mobilise desirable social forces behind it.

Bennett thus concedes that one can admit the force of postmodernist type critiques of all *certaintist* discourses. One can even admit the loss of organisational centres and bases (the centricity of the bourgeois/proletarian class-struggle; the *realist* economic base) around which conflicts were held to have their roots. One can also concede the passing of those grand metanarratives – that shortening of the time perspectives of those long pasts and long futures constructed by nineteenth-century teleologies as they have collapsed into abbreviated forms. And one can recognise that the expression of Marx's own analysis in the form of a historical narrative as opposed to some other form was just his peculiar way of putting things rather than somehow being 'necessary'. But does all this really matter? If Marxism, says Bennett, cannot secure its own relation to reality as a knowledge relation and if it must accept its own discursivity and acknowledge that it is submitted to the effects of language and textuality, then so be it ... for how could it be otherwise? So Marxism is in the end constructed out of a whole battery of rhetorical and figurative devices! For that is fine as well; I mean, says Bennett, show me a political position which has not got all of these features?[24]

No, in the end none of these critiques really matter – any more than they seem to matter to all those other discourses. What would matter, would be if it could be somehow shown that the existing stock of metaphorical, rhetorical and figurative devices used in Marxism had *disabling* theoretical and political consequences that could be remedied only by the use of another completely different set of devices. What should be a concern for Marxism, says Bennett, is not that it should be able to secure its own discursive construction of the real absolutely – for no discourse can do that – but rather that it can secure its constructions and framings politically in ways which make them count above rival contending ones in terms of their ability to organise the consciousness and practices of historical agents.

And if, concludes Bennett, the question is then still raised as to where the 'real' foundations and justifications for such practices can be demonstrated beyond all reasonable doubt, then the unfortunate but inescapable answer now arrived at is *nowhere* if it is a case of looking for an absolute justification in terms of epistemology, methodology, ethics or 'history'. For in the end the only justification in these areas seems to be a self-referencing political one:

> it seems to me [claims Bennett] that socialism can extricate itself from the mire of an epistemological and ethical relativism only by means of a political desire which functions as cause and justification of itself ... and which supplies the criteria – always contested – for the determination of the ends to which political and theoretical practice are directed. If that's not felt to be enough, I would ask: what other foundation could there be which is not a demand for transcendence [a demand which given the impossibility of it being met] ... denies the possibility that such a demand might ever be realised?[25]

This, then, is Bennett's argument, and in conclusion it might be asked just how far he is successful in doing what he principally set out to do, namely, to 'fix' the past such that what can be said of it would be subject to 'definite limitations' so as to effect a real political influence on the present in Marxist ways through the development of an approach to historical knowledge via a disciplined set of lower-case procedures. And it would seem that the answer – to what is after all a political desire – is, politically, not very successful.

For what is Bennett's political argument? It is this. If one wants to have a political effect on contemporary politics, if one wants 'history' to count, then historians *qua* historians can only make a difference to the political present by organising and reorganising the past in politically pertinent ways that will have some plausibility by virtue of the adopted procedures. Bennett appreciates that nowadays any upper-case version of this organisation/reorganisation of the past will be laughed out of court and so argues that, if Marxism as post-Marxism is to have any effects, then it will have to do so by more modest interventions via lower-case methods. And this Bennett is happy to do; hence his first and second arguments where he attempts to establish a set of disciplined procedures to set him a course between a now hopelessly inadequate empiricism on the one hand and a sceptical, rhetorical, self-referencing textuality on the other. Consequently it is then possible for Bennett to conclude his methodological analysis by arguing that, if one sees history as he has suggested – not as a discipline aiming at a knowledge of the past in the sense of the hitherto existing but as a way of '*producing knowledges which surface and have their effects within the past*, where the past is conceived as a complexly laminated, social zone of representation' – then, viewed in this way,

> historical inquiry may be allowed both a cogency and a political pertinence in the sense of having a direct and compelling influence on the present ... In subjecting representations of the past to a disciplined regulation, in its elaboration of rules and procedures for the disciplined interrogation of evidence which allow new knowledges to emerge and transform the face of the past, history does indeed make a material difference to and within the present.[26]

But does it? Or rather, to be more precise, *does it and will it do so in desirable Marxist ways* (for otherwise as a Marxist why bother)? For let us say that we do acknowledge the logic and cogency of Bennett's first and second arguments, and that we do admit them to be informed by his third. Then the question becomes: how would that make Marxism have a compelling political pertinence in the future that is any more pervasive than its pertinence now? For in a society like ours it would still be possible – precisely because of Bennett's essential third argument – to 'pick off' such a reflexive sophisticated methodological approach in simple *ad hominem* ways; that is, irrespective of method, who 'trusts' a Marxist reorganisation of the past? In that sense, although Bennett argues (because his reconceptualisation of how historical knowledges are produced go beyond empirical formulations) against the conclusion put forward by Hindess and Hirst in their 'maverick' *Pre-Capitalist Modes of Production*,[27] it is not so clear that they don't still have a point. For Hindess and Hirst's argument – that because the past has gone and because it cannot be known as it 'truly' was, and since the mediation of the past into history is self-referencing, and since Marxist interpretations are not necessarily superior to any other by dint of method, then one may as well stop trying to bolster politics by what can only ever be a *relative historical interpretation* and just concentrate on politics as such – these points still seem to be too stubbornly plausible to be easily sidestepped. In which case one may at least consider concurring with Hindess and Hirst that a Marxist position is neither necessarily strengthened nor weakened 'within the present' by the possession of such a 'relative interpretation', however constructed, which is to say that, in effect, Marxist history *doesn't* really have (and certainly doesn't *necessarily* have) a compelling cogency and pertinence by virtue of its disciplined knowledge claims *après* Bennett after all.

In terms of political efficacy, then, Bennett's position seems rather more problematic than he allows for. But where Bennett's arguments are arguably a considerable advance over less reflexive views as to how historical knowledge is constructed is not within the political but (if one might 'pretend' for a moment that historical study might be considered as history *per se*) within history so construed. For here Bennett's arguments with regard to the question of how historical knowledge seems to be constructed are, if I might use one of his terms, unassailable. For Bennett's methodological clarifications (which have a richness merely hinted at here) of how the past as textualised traces (the historic past) is mediated into historian's discourse in the public sphere, constitutes one of the most convincing, lucid and economical accounts available. This is a rather less ambitious and more unfortunate conclusion to reach than Bennett's own methodological *and* political desires, but it is perhaps inevitable given that these two areas are not really 'connected'. For it remains difficult to see how one can turn a formal disciplinary mechanism (which is by definition an *empty* mechanism) into a way of producing a substantive position which would, in its Marxist version, be politically pertinent and compelling by virtue of its method, no matter how reflexively acute.

Notes

1 Tony Bennett, *Outside Literature* (London, 1990).
2 Tony Bennett, *Formalism and Marxism* (London, 1979). For some recent attempts to undercut the threats coming from post-structuralist and postmodern directions by a reassertion of a 'proper' (bourgeois) history around the study of the past for its own sake (own-sakism) see, for example, Lawrence Stone's articles in *Past and Present* No. 133, 1991, pp. 217–18 and No. 135, 1992, pp. 189–94; along with those of G. Spiegel, *History and Post-Modernism*, No. 135, pp 194–208. See also Arthur Marwick's '"A Fetishism of Documents"? The Salience of Source-based History', in H. Kozicki (ed.) *Developments in Modern Historiography*, (NewYork, 1993), and G. R. Elton, *Return to Essentials* (Cambridge, 1991).
3 Raphael Samuel, 'Reading the Signs', *History Workshop Journal*, 32, 1991, pp. 88–109, p. 89.
4 Ibid., p. 89.
5 Gabrielle M. Spiegel, 'History, Historicism and the Social Logic of the Text in the Middle Ages', *Speculum*, Vol. LXV, 1990, p. 62.
6 Ibid., p. 63.
7 Dick Hebdige, *Hiding In The Light* (London, 1988), p. 171.
8 J. F. Lyotard, *The Post-modern Condition*, (Manchester, 1984).
9 Bennett, *Outside Literature*, op. cit., p. 60.
10 Ernesto Laclau and Chantel Mouffe, *Hegemony and Socialist Strategy* (London, 1985). See also Ernesto Laclau, *New Reflections on the Revolution of Our Time* (London, 1990).
11 Bennett, op. cit., p. 23.
12 Ibid., p. 24.
13 Ibid., p. 52.
14 Ibid., p. 281.
15 Ibid., p. 50. In order that Bennett's arguments are distorted as little as possible by my 'interpretation', I have given a close reading of his text *via* long and short quotes. To cut down on the footnoting I have referenced only the longer extracts; the bulk of the arguments I have used appear throughout Chapters 2 and 3.
16 Ibid., p. 50.
17 Ibid., p. 51.
18 Ibid., p. 54.
19 M. Cousins, 'The Practice of Historical Investigation', cited in Bennett, ibid., p. 56.
20 Ibid., p. 56.
21 Ibid., p. 57.
22 Ibid., p. 57.
23 Ibid., p. 62.
24 Ibid., pp. 58–62 passim. See also Tony Bennett, 'Texts in History', in Derek Attridge *et al.* (eds.) *Post-structuralism and the Question of History* (Cambridge, 1987), pp. 63–81, p. 65.
25 Bennett, in Attridge, op. cit., pp. 66–7.
26 Bennett, *Outside Literature*, op. cit., pp. 76–7.
27 Barry Hindess and Paul Hirst, *Pre-Capitalist Modes of Production* (London, 1975).

2 Living in time but outside history, living in morality but outside ethics

Postmodernism and Elizabeth Deeds Ermarth

In the mid-1990s I was asked by Oto Luthar if I would write an article for the Slovenian-based journal *Filozofski Vestnik.* At the time I had just completed my *The Postmodern History Reader* (1997) and was working on a new book *Why History? Ethics and Postmodernity,* which came out in 1999. My penultimate chapter was on Elizabeth Ermarth whose works – and especially her *Sequel to History* (1992) – I thought were quite brilliant. And yet, amongst professional/academic historians, her explicit commitment to postmodernism – which still continues – meant her book was written off as some sort of extreme tract that could hold little interest for students of history. They couldn't be more wrong. So, since I was working on Ermarth, the paper I sent to Oto Luthar was precisely on *Sequel to History.* After that, I used most of this article as the basis for my chapter on Ermarth in *Why History?* Though towards the end of my reading of Ermarth I make some criticisms, overall I was and remain a great admirer of her work, and I hope that readers unfamiliar with her writing may find this article a good reason for going to her direct.

In those sophist days before the 'start' of the Western Tradition, the suspicion that the finite and the contingent was all that there was, the idea that the phenomenal world was the only actual world, the understanding that the basis for living finite lives was the aleatory and the ludic, led to attitudes and theorisations expressed in varieties of ontological, epistemological and ethical relativisms vis-à-vis the significances and meanings conferred on the 'metaphysics of existence'. And why not? If from the 'facts' of the 'evidence' no non-contingent, absolute 'ought' unequivocally emerged, if individual and political life – past, present and future – seemed interpretable interminably (you can talk about politics forever …), if there seemed no rhyme nor reason to anything or anybody in themselves (indeed, if it was realised that the 'secret' of the essence of the 'thing in itself' was that there was no such essence), then no other viable conclusion seemed available other than a relativistic 'anything goes' coupled with the ultimate acceptance of the idea that 'might is right'. Consequently it is here, against these conclusions, that the Western Tradition begins, in the refusal, by Plato, to see sophist scepticism and relativism not as *solutions* to the problem of the finite, the contingent and the aleatory (a way to live with these actualities, to put your feet up and be relaxed about them) but rather as continuing *problems* (seen now precisely as 'the problems of scepticism and relativism') still to be solved. Accordingly, because sophists and, later and differently, pyrrhonists and other sceptical solutions for living life 'here and now' were not deemed to be solutions at all, so the finite world – whose anti-logic articulations Plato well recognised as providing no basis for anything other than various relativisms – had to be supplemented/supplanted by something 'beyond the reach of time and chance', an 'infinitive fix' to bring temporary/temporal chaos into permanent and absolute order. Living in the shadows of Plato, the history of the Western Tradition has thus overwhelmingly been the history of various articulations of this apparently necessary, stabilising fantasy – this infinite fix – in the guise of eternal verities expressed either in the anglicised upper case (Forms, God, Essence, Nature, Human Nature, The Categorical Imperative, Spirit, Class Struggle, Dialectic, Market Forces, Reason, History ...) and/or in older linguistic expressions all suggesting immanence and centrings that had an invariable presence (*eidos*, *arche*, *telos*, *energeia*, *ousia*, etc.), imaginaries all bearing down upon us wearing the insignia of Truth.[1]

It is a curious fact, but a fact nevertheless, that such a variety of infinite fixes was not immediately regarded with widespread incredulity (as opposed to local, marginalised and shadowy scepticisms and relativisms – critiques overwhelmingly recuperated by the dominant tradition to be construed as its ever-threatening 'other'). One might have thought that the very fact that, 'historically speaking', there have been so many expressions of such upper-case demands, would have made people immediately consider such eternal imperatives as mere reified projections of their own interpretive (relative) desires and that to obey such chimeras was to chase themselves back into their own logically tautological and solipsistic lairs. But again, historically speaking, this fact – of one thing to be expressed but so many narrative/metanarrative expressions – seems only to have convinced adherents of them that, strange though it may seem, their own preferred interpretations were not really interpretations at all but *the* Truth. Thus we have witnessed – restricting ourselves now to fairly recent historical articulations of this 'existential metaphysic' though one very obviously based on much 'older frames of mind' – various foundational progressivisms, positivisms, Marxisms, Whiggisms, Fascisms, etc., metanarrative fixes ultimately of the 'ends justify the means' type. To banish the finite and contingent and to turn such phenomena into some kind of demanding necessity, these formulations we have died for.

Contemporary postmodernism is a phase – however hesitatingly and qualifyingly specified as non-teleological, non-stagist, and as merely a 'different' moment/condition from and/or after modernity – postmodernism has finally, I think, ended the plausibility of such metanarratives. Today there seems to be everywhere that incredulity towards them which Lyotard famously essayed: few if any of us believe in such fantasies any more. Through the efforts of various linguistic, narrative, deconstructive and discursive turns, we now realise that there never has been, and there never will be, any 'knowable' forms, essences, natural natures, histories, etc., beyond contingency. That we will never have access to a founding originary, and hence to no inevitable destinations, teleological trajectories or dialectics of closure; that we have no conduit to any kind of extra-discursive transcendental signifier, full-presence or omniscient narrator/narrative. In fact, we postmodernists have now just about unpacked the imaginaries of the non-relativist Western Tradition so that we are effectively 'back at the beginning': rhetorical neo-sophists. For we *post*-modernists are, in an interesting reversal, also *pre*-Western Traditionalists, *pre*-modernists. In a very precise way we are now *pre*-platonic, *pre*-Christian, *pre*-Kantian, *pre*-Hegelian, *pre*-Marxist, *pre*-market, *pre*-fascist, in the sense that these attempts to put us in touch with various foundations having failed, then we now have to face – at the end of the Western Tradition – the same existential/metaphysical problems the sophists faced before it began. Accordingly, we now have the chance to consider contemporary takes on sophist-type sceptical and relativistic *solutions* to the metaphysics of existence precisely as solutions and not at all as problems 'still to be solved' Such solutions to finiteness and the endless equivalences of anti-logic may not be the same type of solutions as Plato's or Kant's or Marx's or contemporary 'certaintists', but they are solutions nevertheless – and ones which the actuality of living in postmodernity is forcing upon us whether we like it or not.[2] These solutions suggest – at least to me – that we can now live pre/postmodern lives in ways which have no need for any infinite fix to stabilise contingency and chance, no need for any upper-case, metanarrative history (or lower-case professional/academic histories – but that is another story)[3] to stabilise time in a particular temporality, and no need for a capitalised Ethics – an Ethical System – to stabilise 'disinterestedly' the 'interested' tastes and styles of our own personal and public morality: that we can forget these sorts of history and ethics altogether.

To any remaining non-sophists, this may seem to be a rash move to make, but my thinking on the non-rashness of it might seem less reckless if I briefly reformulate some of what I have just said and so further prepare the ground for what all these preliminary remarks are actually leading up to, namely, an examination (expository much more than critical) of a text by Elizabeth Deeds Ermarth – *Sequel to History: Postmodernism and the Crisis of Representational Time*[4] – wherein she essays, in what I will argue is one of the most important considerations of postmodernism, history and ethics/morality available, what I construe as ways of living *in* time but *outside* history, *in* morality but *outside* ethics. My reformulation of our current condition – my further stage setting for Ermarth – can be put as follows.

It still seems rather obvious and commonsensical to say that perhaps the main reason why historians study the past is because they think that what this work may produce – a historical consciousness – is a good thing. Yet beyond this minimalist intention common endeavour and agreement tend to collapse. For given that it is the idea of the good which defines the desired type of consciousness, that is to say, if a good historical consciousness is anything the definer so stipulates – which it is – then because 'we' live amongst so many competing notions of the good with no universally acceptable/neutral criteria for adjudication between them, so not only does any ultimate closure become endlessly deferred, but the very idea of a good historical consciousness is similarly affected: we now have no clear sense of what a good history/historical consciousness is. There are various contemporary reactions to this 'relativist' conclusion, but perhaps the most popular is not to try – and keep on trying – to find a 'real' history/historical consciousness beyond constitutive interests, but to admit one's position (one's interests) so to be as reflexive, ironic (*après*, say, Richard Rorty) and as 'open about one's closures' as one can be. Thus we witness increasingly historians quite openly flagging their positions – feminists and post-feminists, post-Marxists, post-colonialists, neo-phenomenologists, neo-pragmatists, etc. – and, at the level of the lower case, umpteen 'revisionists'. But my argument is that this positional explicitness is still 'too historical'. For I think that we are now at a moment when we might forget history altogether and live our lives without reference back to a past tense articulated in ways which we are historically familiar with. Maybe we can forget the historicised past and – because we do still have to (temporarily) live together – just talk about that: ethics talk. And yet, this alternative may also be, in turn, too ethical. Why can't we forget ethics too?

Here, in distinguishing ethics from morality, a little bit of arbitrary defining (there is no other) may be useful. For the problem with ethics is that normally we link up that notion with the idea of a system: an ethical system. Such an idea of an ethical system – say Kant's – has, at its centre, the further notion of universalism, that is, an ethical system is one which, if universalised, would allow ethical judgements to be made about all and every contingent situation when one has to make a choice – when one has to decide what one *ought* to do. But such a total, transcendental system is an impossibility and, in the event that this should be held not to be so, actually not ethical anyway. For if there was such a thing as a total ethic so that in every situation one only had to apply it, then one would not be making a choice at all but merely applying a rule – in which case the implementation of such a rule absolves the subject from actually making a decision. Consequently, there is no morality (choice) involved here, but just the application of a necessity. But if, as I am assuming, morality involves choice in such a way that a system of 'ethical necessities' would not be moral at all, then free choice, untrammelled by reference back to any 'system', would just have to be subjective, contingent, situationist, pragmatic, aleatory, and thus always ultimately unsystematisable and ungroundable, i.e. sophist-like. It is this situation, the situation where every moral choice is ultimately undecidable (the *aporia*) but where decisions always have to be made, which makes Derrida talk about the 'madness of the decision', Baudrillard the 'radical illusion of morality', Levinas the ontological violence inflicted on the other to make it the same, and Laclau talk about the 'philosophy of the undecidability of the decision'.[5] The upshot of all this – to cut a long story very short – is that we are now all left within an unbounded space–time, with nothing certaintist to fall back on to underwrite our public/private self-styling, and with no fixed horizons (common skies) to guide us ... with no ultimate ethical stabilisers ... least of all any stabilisers we may have thought issued from a past constructed historiographically by us but in such a way so to render forth the illusion that that past/history was self-constituting so as to help us live better lives, the (historicised) past as the great pedagogue, always teaching us 'its' lessons *as if* they were not always only our own projections. Consequently, that illusion now transparently obvious, so the suggestion that we 'forget history and ethics' for 'temporality and morality', postist/sophist-style, now forces itself upon us – or rather – we now force it upon ourselves.

As already suggested, Ermarth addresses both facets of the postmodern condition I have been discussing; to recall, the question of what would it be like to live *out* of history but *in* time, *out* of ethics but *in* morality. As I read her, I think that she is much more successful arguing for the former rather than the latter, where she seems to perhaps not fully recognise the problems or, if she does, to be insufficiently relativist about them, needlessly drawing back from where I take the logic of her argument to be driving her. But I return to this criticism after my reading of Ermarth's text which, it must be reiterated, has a richness and suggestiveness which defies easy summary and which I urge readers to go to and appropriate for their own purposes, as I have done here. Relative to the above stage setting, then, my own take own on (just aspects of) Ermarth runs as follows.

Let us stipulate, as *metaphysics*, the givenness of existence (the *gift* of the world, being) as something which just existentially *is* (I mean, we don't have a choice about unconditionally accepting these gifts). And let us say that this given, this thing-in-itself, is actually eternally unfathomable. Then let us stipulate *ontology* as the effort to bring this given within the closure of meaning, to very precisely try to make it fathomable and known (epistemological). Let us go on to say that this restriction, once on-going, then performs that constant (violent) appropriation by which we seek to enlarge our meanings until the metaphysical is exhausted and 'its' meaning reduced to 'ours', its 'otherness' now 'corresponding' to the 'same': to us. Then let us say that, of course, this attempted closure can never fully occur, that what Bataille calls the 'general economy' of existence resists our most persistent cultural drives towards the production of meaning and the grounding of such meaning (the attempt to eliminate the *excess*) within our 'restrictive' productionist economy. And then let us recognise this struggle between the metaphysical and the ontological/ epistemological – between the unrestricted (infinite) general economy and the restrictivist productive one – constitutes at one and the same time both the possibility of meaning and the guarantee that a full meaning (total presence, self-identity, etc.) is unachievable, that the gap between the thing-in-itself (the other, radical alterity, etc.) and our theoretical appropriations of it remain, no matter how apparently close(d), infinitely and eternally apart, but that 'the rhetorical beat must go on, endlessly repeating the sequence by which the lure of solid ground is succeeded by the ensuing demystification.'[6]

Now, all this can be read as simply saying that, in a culture, 'nothing is of a natural kind.' Everything to be meaningful and productive has to be within the 'productivist economy', its excess cordoned off and kept on the outside (from there to haunt it – haunt it with the thought of its always imperfect closures), an economy which, to be communicable, is necessarily coded. Accordingly, to be in a culture is to live in and through a code, a language, to be within the (theoretical) imaginaries (metaphysical, ontological, epistemological) which constitute reality (the 'effects of the real') so that 'residence in a language' *is* residence in reality (the real *is* imaginary, the imaginary *is* real), this including, of course, that metaphysical imagining of what, theoretically outside of the productivist economy, the excess may be like (i.e. the excess isn't any more 'really real' than the cultural inside, it's just a regulative idea, a potentially productive silence, another simulacrum).

The imaginary which Ermarth is most interested in is the discursive production of Western time. We don't know what the stuff we call time actually is; time, to be 'time', always has to be timed (given temporality). And it is the peculiar way in which Western time has been timed in what Ermarth calls its modern, linear, historical form (which she traces back to at least as far as the Renaissance), the capsizal of that (arbitrary) form in 'postmodern times', and its replacement by a timing of time that is precisely not 'historical' but is rather conceived in feminist-friendly, chaos-friendly, hopscotch, figural, *rhythmic* timings, that is the concern of her text.

Ermarth is of the opinion that postmodernism has just about got all the imaginary formulations needed to end modern linear history and begin rhythmic time, and she's glad. For whereas modernist discourse has got used to its imagining of time so to regard it as 'real time' – has forgotten its inventedness (its temporal fix) so regarding it as a neutral, objective phenomenon – postmodernism urges us to recall that such a reality is always the 'mediated construct of a founding subject', that time is a function of position (p. 18). For Ermarth, 'objects', including phenomenal timings, are best seen not as 'objectively' there but rather as the 'subject objectified' or, better still, as the 'subject performatively objectifying' from specific enunciative locations (the '*locutions* of culture'), this latter construal giving impetus to the move away from a fixed Cartesian ego/subject in favour of a subject-in-process, performatively and playfully constituting then living within such constitutiveness whilst interminably unsettling such temporary shelters/residences seen now as old metaphors congealed into the appearances of literal truths and awaiting dissolution by new, more pragmatically useful ones ('the beat goes on … '), ones opening up – as Ermarth construes postmodern potentiality – erotic possibilities. These possibilities, not being within the restricted economy of linear history, thus effectively draw on the (metaphorical) resources of the general economy, the metaphysical excess, it being the (counter)penetration of that excess, imagined by Ermarth as feminist-friendly, rhythmic time, into the male (phallologocentric) productivist historical economy, that potentially destabilises it, this explaining, not least, the opposition, fear and indeed intense hatred postmodernism often engenders amongst modernists/'historians'. For Ermarth, postmodern rhythmic critiques of modernist linear histories involve a critique of everything within the moribund productivist, modernist economy:

> What postmodernism supplants, then, is the discourse of representation characteristic of the long and productive era that produced historical thinking ... Across a broad range of cultural manifestations a massive re-examination of Western discourse is underway: its obsession with power and knowledge, its constraint of language to primarily symbolic function, its ethic of winning, its categorical and dualistic modes of definition; its belief in the quantitative and objective, its linear time and individual subject, and above all its common media of exchange (time, space, money) which guarantee certain political and social systems ... There are some who fear that postmodernism, by depreciating traditional causalities, portends an end to morality itself [Ethics] and the fear is not unfounded so far as traditional morality [Ethics] is concerned (pp. 5–9).

Unlike so many postmodern historians, then, who, as I have noted already, see postmodernism as the beginning of new kinds of history (post-feminist, post-colonial, etc.), Ermarth isn't interested in interpreting the past 'rhythmically'; rather she sees it as offering a present and a future without history 'as we know it' but with a new type of existential temporality. At times she is guarded about this; 'my intention', she writes, 'is not to lobby for post-modernism at the expense of history', but to locate 'a major discursive shift in our understanding of temporality and to explore some of its implications' (p. 10). Again she writes:

> Whether or not it is meaningful to speak of a 'new' history remains an open question, although the term 'history' has become so saturated with dialectical value that it may no longer be very buoyant ... I attend mainly to how postmodern narrative time works, what it offers, and what its implicit requirements, gains, and losses may be. The work that undermines history also opens new questions and provides new opportunities in practice. (pp. 14–15).

But these (unnecessary) qualifications noted – these bits of modernist nostalgia which will resurface in her hesitation over accepting the relativising logic of her position – on the whole Ermarth is up-beat:

> My thesis in brief is this: postmodern narrative language undermines historical time and substitutes for it a new construction of temporality that I call rhythmic time. This rhythmic time either radically modifies or abandons altogether the dialectics, the teleology, the transcendence [the infinite fix] and the putative neutrality of historical time; and it replaces

> the Cartesian *cogito* with a different subjectivity whose manifesto might be Cortazar's 'I swing, therefore I am.' (p. 14).

Against this general thesis, then, Ermarth's text is composed of a series of densely elaborated arguments which, ironically, have the overall form of an old binary opposition. Ermarth's text is basically structured around the attempt to show (a) what is wrong with modern(ist) linear, phallologocentric *history* and (b) what is right with *rhythmic time* and what are its possibilities.

Ermarth's accusations against 'history' add up to a catalogue of faults that is heavy indeed. Modernist historical sequencing, patterning, rationalising and 'accounting for', converts chance into causality and, often, into demanding necessities that justify sometime ends–mean scenarios of a totalising, totalitarian kind. Tamers of the contingent and the ludic, their (generally) narrative-encased accounts function to make us feel at home in the existential givenness in the way that 'legends always have, as collective myths that confirm various primary "truths" about "the way things are"'. Belief in a temporal medium that is 'disinterestedly natural' and homogeneous consequently makes possible those mutually informative measurements between one historical moment and another that support most forms of knowledge so that 'History has become a commanding metanarrative, perhaps *the* metanarrative in Western discourse' (p. 20). It is here, in narrative/metanarrative that the mythical figures of 'historical objectivity' and 'true meaning' appear, articulated typically through the disinterested narrator/omniscient narrator, 'the Narrator as Nobody', issuing forth the illusion of 'History Speaking'. This achievement – of naturalising the imaginaries of realistic time and space and of a commonly recognised set of continuities and of neutrality – enables 'us' to 'arrive at' our hypotheses, formulate our laws, produce our experiments, 'our capital and our knowledge', so producing 'an invariant world'. Here, any dissenting voices, any excessive interpretive play, are marginalised as pathological: it is only the 'accidents' of language, nationality, gender and ideology, that obscure 'objective truth' and a potentially 'cosmic vision'. These conditions notwithstanding, 'if each individual could see all the world ... all would see the *same* world ... in this, perhaps, temporal realism or history betrays its religious origin' (p. 30). And this tendency to go cosmic, to universalise, is political:

> Considered historically the present requires a future to complete or at least improve it, and consequently a dialectical method for getting there just as this same present has been produced dialectically by the past. By emphasising what is linear, developmental, and mediate, historical thinking by definition involves transcendence of a kind that trivialises the specific detail and finite moment. In the mobile culture of historicism every moment *has* to be partial so that we can pursue development, so we can seek a completion that, by definition and paradoxically, we can never actually find but that has emblems along the way: more information,

> more clarity, more money, more prestige, more of the constituents of heaven (p. 31).

And, of course, such destinations, heavily Western and heavily male orientated, have just about excluded nine-tenths of the world, a fraction which includes most women. Consequently it is this 'fact', the exclusion of this fraction from history, that makes Ermarth's discarding of history not only one to be at ease with but a necessary one: 'Is it possible to exist *outside* history? [Yes] Women know; they have existed there' (p. 17).

For those precisely excluded by the Western myth of history, postmodernism thus ushers in, in its potentially new timings, potentially new emancipations. Unlike historical emancipations – always then not now, always there not here – postmodern emancipatory imaginaries are 'presentist'. Thus, postmodernism,

> calls our attention *not* to fictions of origins and ends but to the process of consciousness itself as it constructs and deconstructs such fictions and, most importantly, as it enables readers to perform those new acts of attention required by a writing [and a practice – for to be in language is to be in 'reality'] that is going nowhere because it has already arrived (p. 86).

As opposed to the heavy seriousness of history, then, postmodern timings are altogether lighter and more bearable by comparison. Accordingly the bulk of Ermarth's text is taken up with the general possibilities of residing in a postmodern language/practice and, more particularly, of the possibilities for women: the benefits seem enormous.

As I read her, Ermarth's positive arguments start from the same sort of assumptions that I briefly alluded to in my preparatory remarks, namely, that the world (and the world gone by) is neither significant or absurd: it just *is*. We kid ourselves if we think that through our 'scripture, literature, picture, sculpture, agriculture, pisciculture, all the tures in this world', we've ever really got it taped (p. 98). The world, the past, existence, remain utterly problematic, and exhilaratingly so: 'All our literature has not succeeded in eroding their smallest corner, in flattening their slightest curve' (p. 97). For it is this sublime otherness which 'springs up before us' in those 'exciting moments of danger' when the covers are blown. The point here is not simply that this destroys habitual practices, the point is now to make 'a deliberate action of what has heretofore been automatic, a political agenda' (p. 99). Such an agenda will retain its metaphorical status upfront; if we can never know literally what the world is 'in itself', then our appropriations of it are always metaphorical, rhetorical: the past *as if* it was history. Yet – and I return to Ermarth's failure to happily accept any metaphors – not any old imaginary will do for her. After clearing the decks, a specific agenda which on occasion *seems* to suggest that it is itself a necessity (given the way the world actually is) is outlined. Here is a bit more of the deck clearing:

> The most subversive theory is the one that resists the habit of Western knowledge to totalise, to go for first and final cause. In Western epistemology, for example, the structure of induction and deduction … implies that theory must somehow be adequate to practice, or that practice must conform to theory. The postmodern idea of theory as a guerrilla tactic – if you haven't got one make one up – flies in the face of this … centuries-old discursive habit. The practice of postmodern theory … requires a fine sense of play and a total willingness to live without discursive sleep … (p. 99).

So, what does playing guerrilla with Ermarth theoretically entail? How does she carve out of an indifferent time a feminist-friendly temporality? Put skeletally, I would portray Ermarth's near-two-hundred page celebration in the following two or three page way.

Rhythmic time is her favourite trope. As opposed to modernist history/ 'tellable' time, rhythmic time has no time for transcendence: it has no essences, no universals, no immanence, no point. Rather rhythmic time – parataxis on the move – depends on local arrangements whose 'amplifications' are unpredictable. Rhythmic sequences fork and re-fork, exfoliating, proliferating thematic threads which come to arbitrary ends, a chaotic coming together of 'details patterned paratactically, which is to say asyntactically, which is to say meaninglessly'; details are unexpectedly complex and rich without becoming 'information'. This way of reading the world is essential equipment for a postmodern at ease with herself. Ermarth elaborates:

> The … paratactic moves forward by moving sideways. Emphasising what is parallel and synchronically patterned rather than what is linear and progressive … Paratactic narrative [and lives] move … in several directions at once (p. 85).

Such stylistic self-fashioning (to reside in a language is to reside in 'reality') offers new discursive practices, multi-level thinking which makes available multiple beginnings and endings, which pluralises perspectives, mixes and remixes, dubs and redubs those interpretive frames that subjects-in-process live through so as to make the past – including those causal powers which have blindly impressed thus far her behavings, bear her impress: to be free of the 'burden of history' is the aim; to be in control of her own discourse, to be a happy *cronopios* (p. 35) (Ermarth's text is dedicated 'to cronopios everywhere' who, refusing histories of infinity and dialectics, face with joy finite lives). Postmodern time is thus cronopios time: it's performative, it's improvisation, it's individual and collective, it's bricolage, it's jazz. Forget the 'conditionings' of history; make the event.

Drawing on the semiotic dispositions of language (after Kristeva) and coupling it with Derrida's notion of the endlessly ludic character of language (and thus life), Ermarth extols the possibilities of that play which, in its endless deferments, prevents systems ever becoming closed. It is this sort of play that ruptures modernist history, dependent as it was/is on ontological axioms to keep the system secure and safe from the (feminine) excess:

> Derrida's argument has the implications that *structure itself is referential* in the sense that it always depends for its stability on reference elsewhere to some justifying absolute that exists 'beyond' the structure and exceeds it. It is *this referentiality* to an Elsewhere – to a 'full presence' … that validates the structure and justifies its effort to achieve maximum rigidity or … completeness. By reference to something outside it … 'truth' or 'natural law' or 'reality' or … 'history' – structure depends on something … that limits absolutely its play of differentiation. However, to the extent that a structure limits play … it becomes 'ruined' … no new formulations, no new experiments or adventures are possible. By contrast, the incompleteness of living systems guarantees … play remains open … systems that seek to exclude play are also seeking death (p. 148).

Ermarth is seeking life. Utilising the concept of the figure (*figura*) Ermarth hints at a future of play where meanings remain open. Events may be congruent but they don't necessarily connect, may be adjacent but not related, may be sequenced but are not synthesisable. Things just don't add up, they are not aggregatable; no dialectical closure is possible. Postmodern figures – temporary meanings in a chaos that makes such meanings self-referentially meaningful, makes unequivocal truths, meanings and purposes, non-permanent:

> This disorientation for its own sake is very unlike the effect of medieval *figura*, which makes truth only temporarily inaccessible … Postmodern *figure* makes univocal truth permanently inaccessible. On the 'other side' of a medieval figure is a clarifiable structure and a stable, cosmic meaning. On the 'other side' of postmodern figures is the marvellous mystery consisting of the fact that these figures *are* the tangible world, and that the tangible world is discourse, is language, is figure … There are no messages … only messengers (p. 184).

It is this endless play of a 'meaningful meaninglessness' – being on the edge of the abyss but not regarding this as abysmal – that arouses eroticism. Not, Ermarth hastens to add, eroticism in the 'narrow, shabby sense', but in the sense of having the capacity to surprise – forever. This is subversive. In a productive culture which lives in the linear, the purposeful, then play conjures up notions of waste: of wasting time, squandering, of time misspent. Digressive, paratactic play defying dialectics, however, confers for Ermarth 'an exquisite pleasure by relieving the mind of its already recognisable … meanings … To restore to language its electricity … its power to shock, to derail it from the track of conventional formulas', is to be postmodern. This isn't easy. It involves a capability for the kinds of play 'not currently primary values of the cultural formation in which we presently operate our universities, watch our markets, and pursue our careers'. But it can be done: 'Once we have given up antidotes to finitude – Kantian categories and vodka – we face finitude and its opportunities' (p. 193).

This challenge to history, to the closure of systems, to live a life that is alive rather than a living death, this is what makes rhythmic, ludic time, the future Ermarth wants: for this you can forget history and (I think) systems *per se* – including Ethical ones:

> This manoeuvre of imagination in play in language [in a life] is one that does without history, without a millenary kingdom, without Kantian categories or vodka, without Marx, Freud, or 'all the religions dreamt up by man' ... In their place this postmodern writing [living] offers its precision, its erotic (chance) conjunctions, its rhythmic series: the coloured bits or elements of kaleidoscopic arrangements, and whatever patterns emerge. These are the materials for the anthematic figure, a mandala, a polychromous rose design, a rhythmic, momentary, fleeting, life-affirming arrangement. Trying to give these arrangements fixity, or to control this rhythm in advance, would be like trying to redirect the arrow after it has left the bow (p. 210).

This essaying of existential-type, postmodern possibilities *after the end of history* seems exhilarating; if nothing else Ermarth's optimism displaces those more common, mournful musings on the loss of one of the West's most potent, organising mythologisations – history – articulated not least by those who have most to lose. It may therefore appear churlish to now level against Ermarth's 'visions' some concluding criticisms, thereby remaining trapped within the ritualistic (modernist) convention of the expositor turning critic as he or she – having lived parasitically off the text – has the 'correcting' last word. But I 'intend' my criticisms to be constructive. It seems to me that Ermarth succeeds in her critique of modernity's way of organising temporality – linear history – such that it is indeed possible to conceive of a life without it; to live *outside* that history and *within* a new rhythmic temporality where 'history as we have known it' has no more relevance; is passé. This signals the end of history as modernists have conceptualised the past and thought they had 'known it'. But – and this is my 'but' – I think that it is also possible to live *outside* of Ethics (Ethical systems) and *in* the type of morality suggested by Derrida, Lyotard, Baudrillard, Rorty, Fish *et al.*, namely, that of the 'undecidibility of the decision', the force of which suggests the acceptance of a pragmatic, sophist-type relativism. For I think that Ermarth, despite the drift of her argument, draws back from this; in the end her notion of rhythmic time has the ring of truth about it.

At various points throughout her text, then, Ermarth draws back from embracing the relativism which I think her arguments propel her towards. Thus, for example, whilst insisting that there is nothing outside of language (the text, simulacra) such that 'nothing exceeds its practices or its play, nothing escapes its limitations, nothing acts as a cosmic or natural "ground" and justification', including, obviously, the linguistically constructed concept of time (including, obviously, rhythmic temporality), this fact, she adds, this recognition, 'is quite far removed from any relativist catastrophe' (p. 140). Again, in relation to the historicised past, whilst the idea that the past is invented 'threatens the moral universe with total solipsism', the reader/writer of the past, no more than the reader/writer of any text, cannot do what he/she likes with it; in fact, its existence demands a 'disciplined' reading/writing because it – texts and the past as a text – 'requires new acts of attention' (pp. 71–2). Postmodernism, whatever else it is, she warns, is not some sort of cultural and moral bonfire.

Now, one of the reasons why Ermarth seems to be saying these things is something which suggests that she is still within the grip of the Western Tradition where relativism is seen – and this goes back to my comments at the start of this paper – not as the sophist-like solution to the problems of living in an indifferent world, but as a problem still to be solved (hence her comment, above, wherein relativism is seen not as a happy solution but rather as a 'catastrophe'). What Ermarth seems to be seeking is a nice consensus around the erotic possibilities of postmodernism (basically one where everyone imagines reality as she does) for without 'consensus available as a basis for conducting affairs, what is there but force?' (p. 61). This is a fear which has standing behind it that typical 'modernist' objection to postmodern relativism, namely, that such a relativism leaves us helpless before another holocaust:

> Practically speaking, the debates about postmodernism come down to discussion about what, if anything, provides a reality principle for any construct. Postmodern writers and theorists do not deny the existence of the material world ... nor, so far as I know, does anyone familiar with the issue seriously deny the exclusiveness of discursive languages to which we necessarily resort in order to say anything 'about' either the material or the discursive worlds – statements that inevitably are interpretations and, consequently, a pre-interpretation of an apriori formulation. But if discursive rules provide untranscendable constraints, what constrains the discursive rules? The question is haunted by the spectres of holocausts which, in various national forms, have already demonstrated what appears to be no restraint. If anything can be justified in some Name, is there no way to choose between justifications? If every interpretation, every system, every set of laws is a closed, inertial system and if there is no longer validity for any privileged position ... how can a person or polis choose between ... this or that course except by chance? (p. 59).

Well, chance may, Ermarth allows, have much to do with it, and she will go on to consider surrealist pronouncements in favour of 'objective chance' (basically choosing between things once such things have been put 'under a description'), but, leaving that aside in this paper (as Ermarth herself does at this point in her text), I want to concentrate, as she does, on whether there are any general grounds for constraint. Here, Ermarth reviews and rejects 'answers' given by, variously, Jameson, Lyotard, Katherine Hayes and Barbara Herrnstein Smith, the reason for their failure seeming to lie in the fact that they don't comprehend the way postmodernism has changed our understanding of 'reality'; like the concept of history, 'reality' doesn't mean what it used to. Classically, explains Ermarth, reality implied something stable and self-identical, but 'physical reality' (which non-idealist postmodernists do not doubt) has been redescribed in postmodern idioms by people like Ilya Prigogine and Isabelle Stengers, whose treatment of reality as 'chaos as a phase of order' means 'reality' is in a 'constant process of fundamental redefinition, so that the term "fundamental" does not even really apply' (p. 62). Consequently, to give up on 'classical' reality does not mean we give up on postmodern 'chaotic' notions of reality as things which *actually* constrain us:

> The fears of moral catastrophe that postmodernism raises in some are usually posited on classical assumptions ... [But] nobody denies the presence of conditions external to our descriptive and linguistic systems, nobody hopes for complete solipsism of the kind that some ascribe, completely wrongheadedly, to postmodernism and that would in any case only be possible in a classical system ... To give up the 'reality' or 'realities' that constrain behaviour and inscribe value does not mean anarchic relativism in which 'everything is permitted' and brute power rules ... The failure of a totalising absolute like historical time may raise the fear that 'everything is permitted' but ... there is no such thing [as that] (p. 62).

Rather, the chaos theory and the 'dissipative structures' described by Prigogine and Stengers introduce us to a 'new concept of matter' that suggests a 'new conception of order that is independent of the closures and finalities of classical dynamics and that permit us to see how "*nonequilibrium brings order out of chaos*"' (p. 63). Thus, for example, the element of chance in a stochastic (probabilistic) process – where an 'end' becomes the possibility of a new 'beginning' which is not controlled in the classical sense by that 'end' – opens up new sources of life, new rhythms of continuance in ever-new states and modes: 'The more determinist laws appear limited, the more open the universe is to fluctuation and innovation' (p. 63). Without wanting, as Ermarth puts it, to draw 'facile political analogies' from Prigogine and Stenger, this is what she does indeed go on to draw. In a probabilistic process, she argues, things must be considered in the context of the moment when individual behaviour can be decisive or ineffectual but not predictable:

> Even small fluctuations may grow and change the overall structure. As a result individual activity is not doomed to insignificance. On the other

> hand, this is also a threat since in our universe the security of stable, permanent rules seems gone forever. What social (that is, moral) implications this may have remains to be seen, but it is not clear that there is any greater threat of moral catastrophe in probabalistic social descriptions than has already been shown in logocentric ones (p. 65).

Postmodernism thus acknowledges not single but multiple constraints; postmodern time and space are warped and made finite by

> the play of chance and necessity in the processes of life themselves … 'Reality' … never stays 'the same'; it is not inert but interactive … This awareness of finitude, of limit, is the basis of an entirely new aesthetic and provides the main restraint on construction that postmodernism respects (pp. 65–6).

Now, this seems to me to be a most peculiar argument. One can see why Ermarth is running it, of course, probabilistic/chaos theory seems to be another way of talking about rhythmic time. But whilst this certainly undercuts 'classical' moral foundations (i.e. the 'chance' to draw a stable *ought* from a stable *is*) we Rorties and Lyotards have given up on trying to draw any entailed *ought* from any *is*, stable or unstable. I mean, let us say the 'actual' physical world is like Ermarth's (moral) rhythmic description of it après Prigogine and Stenger. And say everyone accepts this: liberals, Marxists, feminists, neo-Nazis; everyone. What difference would it make? Is a political, constrained consensus between Ermarth and neo-Nazis going to be arrived at because the way an (indifferent) world is in terms of physics? This seems unlikely, not least because, irrespective of physics, their moral differences remain incommensurable simply because they're 'moral' all the way down. Whilst views on the physical world may by chance affect politics it is difficult to see how they can determine them in any sort of is–ought way that involves entailment: Prigogine and Stengers are red herrings in this respect.

There is another point here too with regard to closure. For it looks as if Ermarth, in following Prigogine and Stengers, is saying that chaos theory/rhythmic time are somehow closer to the way 'reality' actually is than other metaphoric 'correspondences' are. But surely she can't be saying that. Because, if she is, her notion of rhythmic time as being nearer to actuality and therefore the best (true) basis for a life, better than old modernist, historical life, is just as much a closure, albeit of a different substantive 'content', as the historical was. I mean, what if we don't want to embrace rhythmic time even if it can be shown to be nearer to actuality, to 'nature'? What if we don't want to embrace a 'naturalistic fallacy' but want to retain our freedom to choose, to choose, say, a newly constructed, emancipatory linearity? If Ermarth is being faithful to her own creative theorising, then presumably she ought not to *care* if anybody chooses to live non-rhythmically in non-feminist-friendly ways. Or is she saying that we ought to be rhythmic because linear time is somehow *intrinsically* repressive, *intrinsically* masculine, that rhythmic time is *intrinsically* feminist friendly, and that these connections cannot be reversed, that rhythmic time just cannot be repressive in its experimentations, as if from the activity of postmodern 'play' we couldn't all end up temporarily playing neo-Nazi? But what could stop this? Something *intrinsic* to 'play'? It would seem that here Ermarth is simply substituting one closure (linear history) with another (rhythmic time) which we ought to follow because it is nearer actuality and thus, presumably, nearer to actualising emancipation.

To be sure, Ermarth says she isn't doing this. As she writes at the end of her text (repeating earlier, similar disclaimers), the 'multilevel play described in this book belongs to an effort to renew social codes by restoring powers that have been repressed ... not ... to enforce another repression' (p. 212). But I think that she can only say this because she *knows* what is best for us and knows we won't necessarily feel it as repression. Thus, for instance, seeing human beings as subjects-in-process just is a better way of seeing them as opposed to seeing them in terms of the Cartesian *cogito*; thus, postmodernism and feminism have an affinity because of their joint insistence that the chief political problems (of language – to have residence in a language is to have residence in 'reality') can 'only be solved by writing a new language, one uncontaminated by the old, radioactive terms, so that one thing seems *certain*: no effort to come to terms with social agendas will succeed without the recognition that history itself is a representational construction of the first order, and that new social construction cannot take place until history is denaturalised' (p. 56). These seem fairly certaintist, non-relativistic remarks to me, thus raising the question of how reflexive Ermarth has been about the status of the closures she is suggesting for others; I mean, for a linearist to be trapped in rhythmic time could be a nightmare. But maybe Ermarth has thought of that; she admits a revision of existing hegemonic arrangements of the type she is suggesting may hurt. So alright. But arguably what isn't alright is where she seems to forget that such new arrangements are nothing more than her own personal preferences, ungroundable in either chaos theory or ethics in any way whatsoever.

The reason for me saying this is that I think this sort of personal relativism is the only position postmodernism makes available. This way of putting things may make it look as if I'm committing a 'performative contradiction' (of saying that you must absolutely believe me when I say that the only truth is relativism which then appears to be an absolute truth, etc.) but I think this old 'contradiction' is not a contradiction at all but a paradox, and paradoxes, unlike contradictions, can be resolved. This particular one as follows.

In the restricted, modernist economy, it seemed that symbolic value was based on use value, that there really were real intrinsic needs, capacities, meanings and so on, and these stabilised symbolic exchange mechanisms. In the postmodern (restricted) economy, however, having shed every last notion of intrinsic value (*use* value) exchange takes place at the symbolic level only – at the level of the simulacra. Thus, unrestricted by use/intrinsic value, any symbolic value can be exchanged with any other, in effect, 'anything goes'. Any-thing can be exchanged with any-thing else because things themselves (and certainly 'things – in – themselves') quite 'literally' don't enter into it; any equivalence will do. So, for example, you can, if you like, exchange love and justice for Ermarthian feminism (make them equivalent) or, staying with her allusion to the holocaust, exchange love and justice for it (make them equivalent). Again, rhythmic time is equivalent to a type of liberation for Ermarth which for a non-Ermarthian might be equivalent to, as she puts it, a catastrophe. So which is it? Well, 'it' isn't either; 'it' isn't anything until it is given a value, and any value can be given to anything. We may wish that this was not the case, but it seems to me that it is.

From my point of view, then, I think it could be said that the transcendent has taken its revenge on Ermarth. On the one hand it has allowed her to have her way with history – who knows or cares what it means any more – letting her concentrate on organising the future in desirable, rhythmic forms. But, on the other hand, Ermarth seems to have been seduced into thinking that there could be something in rhythmic time that isn't just convenient for her own political desires but is actually closer to the way the world actually is, thus heading off relativism. But the idea 'behind' the notion of simulacra that we can know the gift of the world, etc., beyond endlessly interpretable mediations, is a radical illusion. A simulacrum is not something which conceals the truth; it is the most plausible truth we have. Indeed, it is this 'truth' which hides the fact that there is no truth, so that in that sense we can say, paradoxically, that the simulacrum is 'true'. In *The Perfect Crime*,[7] Baudrillard argues that, whereas the old philosophical question used to be, 'Why is there something rather that nothing?', the postmodern question is, 'Why is there nothing rather than something?' The acceptance of the latter formulation suggests to Baudrillard (and to me) that if we are bound only to the interminably unstable equivalencies of signs and appearances self-reverentially spinning around themselves (Baudrillard's 'orbital culture') then relative value runs – forever. Yet, this is not a problem. For maybe we can relax about this and agree, with Wittgenstein, that the fact that there have never been the sorts of foundations we once thought there were (but that we humans have still created moral discourses) means that we never needed such foundations in the first place, nor will we, so that the very idea of foundationalism is 'one well lost'. Besides, that absolutist conceit has caused too many problems – not least those of the certaintist holocaust, that supreme *modernist* event.[8] For as Richard Rorty has pointed out:

> Anti-pragmatists [and anti-postmodernists and anti-relativists] fool themselves when they think that by insisting ... that moral truths are 'objective' – are true independent of human needs, interests, history – they have provided us with weapons against the bad guys. For the fascists can, and often do, reply that they entirely agree that moral truth is objective, eternal and universal ... and fascist ... Dewey made much of

> the fact that traditional notions of 'objectivity' and 'universality' were useful to the bad guys, and he had a point.[9]

This is not to say, Rorty adds, that this inability to answer 'the bad guys' is the result of pragmatism or relativism being wicked or inadequate theories, but that philosophy is just not the right weapon to reach for when trying to resolve, when all discursive attempts have failed, such moral and political differences. Thus, the inevitability of moral 'philosophy of the decision' relativism needn't be any more of a problem for us than it was for the sophists, and it shouldn't be one for Ermarth. But I think it is. Yet, though arguably 'still in the grip of the tradition', Ermarth's text is nevertheless one which enables us to imagine the possibility of living our lives not only *outside* history and *in* time, but *outside* ethics and *in* morality in quite self-conscious ways. *For in fact, if only we had known it, this is the way we have always had to live our lives.* In this respect – and it is in this respect that postmodern reflexivity is so useful – we might just as well relax and say, with Baudrillard: '"Nothing" hasn't changed.'

Notes

1 J. Derrida, *Writing and Difference*, Routledge, London, 1978, p. 289.
2 I am indebted to Philip Jenkins whose various arguments on Baudrillard I have drawn on in passing.
3 See the Introduction to my *The Postmodernism History Reader*, Routledge, London, 1997.
4 E. D. Ermarth, *Sequel to History: Postmodernism and the Crisis of Representational Time*, Princeton University Press, Princeton, 1992. Rather than footnoting my references to Ermarth, I have inserted them parenthetically in the paper.
5 See the various arguments of Rorty, Derrida, Lyotard, Laclau, *et al.*, in C. Mouffe (ed.), *Deconstruction and Pragmatism*, Routledge, London, 1996.
6 S. Fish, *Doing What Comes Naturally*, Oxford University Press, Oxford, 1989, p. 493.
7 J. Baudrillard, *The Perfect Crime*, Verso, London, 1996, p. 2.
8 On the holocaust as a modernist event, and the problem of its representation, see, for example, Hayden White's, 'The Modernist Event', in V. Sobchack (ed.), *The Persistence of History*, Routledge, London, 1996, pp. 17–38.
9 R. Rorty, 'Just One More Species Doing Its Best', *London Review of Books*, vol. 13, no. 14, 25, July, 1991, pp. 3–7, p. 6.

3 Why bother with history?

In 1996 I had been involved in discussions with the then History Editor at Routledge, Heather McCallum, about the possibility of setting up a new journal in historical theory, and I was more than happy to support the appointment of Alun Munslow as the founding (UK) Editor. Once in post, Alun invited Robert Rosenstone (California Institute of Technology) to be the US Editor, and then got together prestigious Editorial and Advisory Boards. The first issue of the journal – entitled *Rethinking History: The Journal of Theory and Practice* – was published in the summer of 1997 and I was asked by Alun – or maybe I volunteered – to write an article for it. In the event it may not have been the most appropriate paper because in it I discussed some of my developing thoughts on the possible 'end of history', but it appeared and has since been republished in various collections of essays. Happily, the journal has gone from strength to strength, publishing some of the most thoughtful and experimental pieces on historical theory and practice available and always (well, nearly always) in accessible ways.

I start with some comments by Geoffrey Bennington which I hope will help me to make the two points that I want to consider in this paper. My first point is that postmodern ways of thinking probably signal the end of history/historiography as 'we' have known it in its modernist upper-case (metanarrative) and in its lower-case (professional/academic) forms. And that as a consequence, this capsizal of History/history not only carries with it a reconsideration of the nature(s) of the discursive phenomena which have lived under these signs, but also raises the ethical question of whether or not we still need, in these postmodern times, to reconsider them at all. Maybe we can just 'forget history'; maybe we can now lead lives within grammatical formulations which have no reference to a past tense articulated in ways which are, as it were, 'historically' familiar to us.

My second, subordinate point, refers to lower-case professional/academic historiography more particularly and the ways its peculiar methods of appropriating/consuming the past are also fatally problematicised by postmodernism. I think most people would agree that in the bulk of the literature it is the capsizal of metanarrative constructions which has received most attention: it would seem that few people believe in such teleological fantasies any more. And yet, for many people (for many proper/professional historians), that metanarrative collapse seems to have left lower-case historiography intact; indeed, the collapse of its 'rival' seems to have served only to bolster its claims to be 'proper' history. But my point is that I think this evaluation is a mistaken one. For as I read it, the specificities of the fall-out occasioned by the capsizal of the upper case have caused fatal collateral damage to the lower, the result being the effective end of the whole (modernist) History/history ensemble. And at this juncture I refer back to my first, major point, that under the impact of postmodernism, modernist constructions as we have gotten used to them are not only no longer viable, but that the need to bother with the past at all – not least for ethical purposes – is questionable: that perhaps we don't need what we might call a 'historical consciousness' any more. In effect, I suppose that what I'm going to be running here is a sort of 'end of history' argument. Let me begin doing so then, taking as my 'way in' the comments by Bennington I've already mentioned I'll be using.

In his article, 'Demanding History', which appeared in the volume *Post-structuralism and the Question of History* (1987) (edited by D. Attridge, R. Young and Bennington himself), Bennington argued that traditional (modernist) historiography is characterised by two demands. First of all, *history itself demands*. That is to say, 'it' demands that 'we' do certain things: that we do its bidding, that we come to know it so as to become 'familiar' with it, that we obey its laws, lie down before its evidence, and so on. Secondly, *history is demanded*. It's demanded by us. We want it. We demand that it performs, say, the role of the great pedagogue, delivering up its secrets, its meanings, its reality and its ethics, so that we can 'learn lessons from it', orientate ourselves within it, find and legitimate our identities, and thus benefit from its study: either way, consciousness of the demanding/demanded past – a historical consciousness – is considered to be 'a good thing'.

Now, these two ways of positioning history (history demands – history is demanded) are part of an interesting opening move in Bennington's own essay. But, rather than follow him further here, I merely want to dwell for a little while on the observations I've just mentioned and extend them in ways which – though I'm sure Bennington is aware of them – he hasn't bothered to do himself. I have three points to make that are germane to my own double-faceted argument.

First, vis-à-vis the statement *history demands*, I think we need to make the (expected) qualifying distinction between upper- and lower-case historiography/historians, that is, between metanarrative type upper-case and professional/academic lower-case demands. Thus, upper-case historiography has suggested and occasionally still suggests that 'we' (we objects of the historical process, 'we' who are *subjected* to it) do the bidding of a history which has its own *raison d'être* … its own immanent meaning(s), its own trajectory and teleology … this is a history which is going somewhere irrespective of whether we know it or not, so that the best we can do is to try and 'discover' its 'objective' journey/destination not, normally, to resist it, but to become its (increasingly 'historically conscious') bearers, its fellow-travellers. Typically this capitalised History has got, of course, its own capitalised Ontology, its own preferred way of making itself known (Epistemology), its own Method, and (and this is crucial) its own substantive Ethic ... for it is this ethical dimension which makes this history's demands not only necessary to comply with but necessarily good; in this construal to be at one with the march of history is to be with the angels – as it were.

Obviously, I could go on describing the characteristics of such a metanarrative history for some time, but I'm sure this type of construction and its various expressions are familiar. Of course, the very fact that, historically, there have been so many expressions of upper-case History's demands, might make us immediately consider the idea that these demands are actually just our own interpretive desires. But, 'historically' speaking, this fact – of one past but many metanarratives – has overwhelmingly served to convince adherents of them that, strange though it may seem, their preferred interpretation is not really an interpretation at all but 'the truth'. Thus we have witnessed various foundational Marxisms, Whiggisms, Fascisms, etc.: metanarratives ultimately of the essentialist 'ends justify the means' type; metanarratives which demand that we recognise that we *all* belong to a history that is bigger, better, more prioritising, more compelling and, indeed, more demanding, than our own, personal histories; that it is to 'it' that our first loyalties lie.

Now, the demands issuing out of such upper-case histories are, in some ways at least, very different from the demands made on us by history in the professional/academic lower case. But that's not to say that the lower case is any more permissive, any less 'normative'. Lower-case professional/academic historiography insists with as much conviction as any upper-case history ever did that it (and it alone) really is 'proper' history, and that a 'proper' understanding of the past can only be achieved if its strictures are jealously followed. Though the demands made by history in the lower case may be less overtly (and less theoretically) formulated, they are no less certaintist (and in fact no less theoretical) for that. Lower-case professional/academic historiography – a historiography every bit as local, as temporally located and as ideologically positioned as any other demanding construct – really does think that its own peculiar *species* of historiography is identical to its *genus*, that it 'truly' is history *per se*. Accordingly, and as indicated, this type of historiography has its own (arbitrary) demands. For example, 'It' demands that we study it for its own sake (own-sakism) as opposed to studying it (explicitly) for the sake of, say, the proletariat, the bourgeoisie, or women. 'It' insists that only disinterested, objectivist study will make it reveal the way it really was (as distinct from how we would like it to have been) – the past 'in and for itself' – the 'only past worth having'. 'It' insists on, at least, epistemological if not ontological realism. 'It' insists that its 'facts' can be best discovered and authenticated empirically (and not 'theoretically' – as if empiricism wasn't just another theory). 'It' valorises its original sources and especially its documents (documentarism). 'It' refuses to go along with the idea, common to poststructuralism/postmodernism, that language is not some sort of (modernist) reflection of the world it somehow captures in words, but is constitutive of that world. 'It' just won't let us recognise that language is anterior to the world it shapes, that what we experience as reality is a linguistic construct, the effect (the 'reality effect') of the specific language system we inhabit, structuring it 'like a language' according to its own rules of signification. 'It' refuses to let us admit that there is no world that is not ordered as a language, as textuality. 'It' refuses to let us happily bask in the knowledge that there is nothing meaningfull 'outside of the text'. 'It' demands that historians accept that whilst its truth(s) may never be absolutely/transparently known, to find those truth(s) – 'its' truths – is the only legitimate function of the 'proper' historian.

Moreover, the fact that this last aim cannot ever be achieved – the fact that lower-case historiography is obviously 'interpretive' – indeed, the fact that a 'true interpretation' is very obviously an oxymoron (I mean, you can have a 'true truth' and an 'interpretive interpretation' but not the two together) is, Job-like, transformed from a weakness into a strength. For, whilst in lower-case historiography, various interpretations are held, in principle, to be capable of a synthesis (one past so in principle one account ...), unsynthesisable interpretations just are a fact of 'professional' life. Out of necessity, then, such interpretive 'openness' has to be re-articulated back into, and normalised as a welcome feature of professional historiography, its 'open nature' and its 'tolerance' of the 'different' (of difference) being embraced; here, lower-case historiography gains credit for its liberal pluralism and for its championing of academic freedom as opposed to the suffocating closures of the (ideologically fixated) upper case. The historicised past studied under these (its) demands, then, constitutes proper, normative, professional history: this is what must be done. This is the only sort of 'real' history there is – as the various Introductions and Primers to professional/academic history absolutely insist, this is the only way to proceed: this is how history ought to be; this is how history *per se* must be 'practised' (Elton, 1969; Tosh, 1991; Marwick, 1989; Stanford, 1994).

I turn now to the second point I want to make, which is, to recall, to develop Bennington's idea that not only does History/history make demands on us (of the type I've mentioned) but that we make demands on it: that *we demand history*. That we demand that it gives us – again to recall – trajectories, meanings, legitimisations, 'practices' and ethics which we can learn from and so 'place ourselves' in a past-backed-up-present (and future). But, after having put the matter that way, I don't think it should take us too long to realise the rather obvious point that it is these sorts of demands (the demands we make of history) which have actually constructed and thus constituted the (reciprocal) demands we have pretty much taken thus far as issuing *independently* from history (from the past) itself. My second point is simply this then: that those upper- and lower-case histories which demanded/demand that we did or do their bidding *do not independently exist and never have done*. Their demands are always only ours. Those 'demanding' histories are mere figments of, projections of (at this point in our 'actuality'), the Modernist imagination. Insofar as we have thought that there really is a history (a past) that has its own demands, then we have forgotten that we've merely been throwing our voice. As soon as you think about it, the idea of a historicised past existing independently of our variously present-day constitutive concerns is an absurd one. At which point Bennington's dualism – Bennington's interesting binary opposition – can be 'deconstructed'. *All* the characteristics alleged to belong to 'the past' belong to us. *All* the demands allegedly from the past are demands we make of the past. Accordingly, we now recognise – and more importantly (and threateningly) some of us now act in the 'knowledge' – that there never has been, and there never will be, any such thing as an upper-case past that is expressive of some kind of demanding/commanding essence, whilst the ridiculous idea (demand) that the only legitimate/proper study of the past is lower-case own-sakism is recognised for what it is, as simply the mystifying way in which a modernist bourgeoisie conveniently articulated and still articulates its own professional code, its own guild practices, *as if* these issued not from 'it' at all, but from out of the past itself. Accordingly, the whole modernist upper-/lower-case ensemble now appears as an ultimately self-referencing, problematic expression of our various interests, an ideological discourse *per se* without any real access to the past as such, unable to engage in a dialogue with anything other than an 'always already' historiographically constituted historicised past. In summary form we might thus say that the past as constituted by its existing traces is always apprehended and appropriated textually through the sedimented layers of our previous interpretations and through the reading habits and categories developed by our previous/current methodological practices. And whilst we suspect that there may well be a 'real past' (an actual past) metaphorically underlying all our disparate versions of it, we 'know' that that past, that 'real referent', is ultimately inaccessible, and that all we have are our versions ... but that that hardly matters, since versions are all we've ever had. Accordingly, the notion of a putative 'history-before-all-historiography' (like the putative 'world-before-all-versions-of-the-world') is, as Richard Rorty has put it, 'one well lost' (Rorty in McHale, 1992, p. 5). Or, put another way, historiography *per se* now appears to be just one more foundationless positioned expression in a world of foundationless positioned expressions as we collapse the 'referent into representation'.

Staying with the demise of lower-case professional/academic historiography for just a moment longer and then going on from it, the idea of a past 'in itself' to be studied for its 'own sake' really is a hopeless ambition. For postmodernists 'know' (and in saying this they are not susceptible to the favourite modernist charge of committing a performative contradiction) ... postmodernists know that the past has neither rhyme nor reason in it, that it is unfathomable, sublime, shapeless, formless. Consequently, postmodernists recognise that to give to something formless a form, to give to something shapeless a shape, to give to the non-storied the form of a narrative structure as if such a narrative corresponded to the structures of real stories lived in the past (narrativity after Hayden White) (White, 1973, 1987, pp. 1–25) to do all these things is to realise that historiography – despite its sometime empirical features – is, in the forming of its 'narrative substances' (Ankersmit, 1983, 1994) an aestheticising practice. Accordingly, because aesthetics are not subject to true/false interrogation – I mean, what is the truth of a shape – such a discourse cannot logically support true/false 'significations' beyond the level of the statement or the chronicle, nor, and *I want to concentrate from now on this*, can it provide any grounds for ethical judgements. Thus, post-modernism ushers in the spectre of the severing of any necessary connection between any kind of historiography and any kind of ethical system. Consequently, one of the main reasons why traditional historians of both cases have said they study the past – to learn 'its' lessons, to learn from 'its' mistakes, and to morally legitimate current desires and identities – is something that the past/history/historiography just cannot do. Yet, despite this, I think it is pretty much taken for granted that a historical consciousness is, ethically speaking, still a 'good thing' to have. But how can it be? For if it is a notion of goodness which defines the desired type of consciousness, that is, if a 'good historical consciousness' is anything the definer defines as good (which it is), then, because today there are so many explicit, competing notions of good with no neutral (foundational) criteria for adjudication between them, so not only does the ultimate closure of 'the good' become endlessly deferred, but the idea of what constitutes a 'good historical consciousness', or indeed a 'good history', is similarly affected: we now have no clear sense of what a 'good historical consciousness' is. Nothing can be gained ethically from a study of the past if that past is unavailable to us 'in itself' (i.e. as a self-constituting thing with its own ethics and not those we have ourselves put into it). For if we only get from the past the ethics (the lessons, the 'guides to action') which we put into it (which we do) then why bother with this circumvolution? Why not just have 'ethics talk' and leave the temporal dimension out of it? Why not just 'forget history' and historians?

But then, why not forget ethics too? Here a little bit of arbitrary defining (there is no other) may be useful. For the problem of ethics is that normally we link up that notion with the idea of a system: an ethical system. Such an idea of an ethical system (say Kant's) has, at its 'centre', the further notion of universalism; that is to say, an ethical system is one which, if universalised, would allow ethical judgements to be made about all and every contingent situation when one has to make a choice – when one has to decide what one ought to do. But such a total (transcendental) system is impossible and, in the event that this should be held should not be the case, not ethical. For if there was such a thing as a total ethic so that in every situation one only had to apply it, then one would not be making a choice at all but merely applying a rule – in which case the implementation of such a rule absolves the subject from actually making a decision. Consequently, there is no ethics (choice) involved here, merely the application of a necessity. But if – as I am assuming – 'morality' involves choice in such a way that a system of 'ethical necessities' would not be 'moral' at all, then free choice, untrammelled by reference back to any 'system', would just have to be subjective, contingent, situationist, pragmatic, aleatory and thus always ultimately unsystematisable, ungroundable. It is this situation, the situation where every moral choice is ultimately 'undecidable' but where such choices still have to be made (the situation we are in today) which makes Derrida talk about the 'madness of the decision', Baudrillard talk about the 'radical illusion of morality' and Laclau talk about the 'philosophy of the decision' (Mouffe, 1996). The upshot being – to cut a long story very short – that we are now left within an unbounded space, with nothing certaintist to fall back upon and no fixed horizons to guide us, with no ultimate ethical stabilisers – least of all any stabilisers which we may have thought issued from the past constructed historiographically by us but in such a way so to render forth the illusion that the past was constituting itself for us – to help us. Consequently, that radical illusion now made transparent, so the suggestion that we forget 'history and ethics' now forces itself upon us – or rather, we now force it upon ourselves.

There are, I think, many additional reasons to those I have just mentioned, to make me think that 'ethically speaking' forgetting history and ethics might be an interesting move to make (I'm thinking here of the sorts of argument which would jack up the linguistic register and the arguments I'm using several notches: say, arguments such as Derrida's play on the notion of the gift and the consequent idea of full presence and absence/lack which runs as a leitmotif throughout Western metaphysics (Bennington and Derrida, 1996); of Levinas' critique of that same metaphysics as the history of our committing 'ontological violence' on the object (Levinas, 1985); of Baudrillard's critique (1996) of our pathetic susceptibility to being seduced by the object/'reality' which runs, again, throughout Western metaphysics until our postmodern escape into a happy, carefree acceptance of a non-essentialising simulacrum as the beginning and end of Truth, Reality, Meaning, and so on and so forth (Mouffe, 1996)). But I want to remain, for now, in the rather mundane register I have chosen to use and to come to my third and final set of comments – comments to strengthen my argument that, *the demands of history* being collapsed into *our demands for history*, so we might forget history and sort out our present problems in the present. I have two comments to make vis-à-vis this third point.

The first comment to underline the futility of going to the past for ethical/moral lessons as variously used and deployed within historiography – and which I've already hinted at – is because that past is utterly promiscuous: it will go with anybody – Marxists, Whigs, racists, feminists, phenomenologists, structuralists, empiricists, Eltonists, Foucauldians, 'postists' – anybody. And this is because, as we have seen, the past has no resistance of its own; the past as such doesn't exist *historically* outside of historians' textual constitutive appropriations, consequently, being constructed by them it has no independence to resist them at the aesthetic 'level of signification'.[1] The historicised past *itself* thus contains nothing independent of us that we *have* to be loyal to, nothing we *have* to feel guilty about, no facts we *have* to respect, no truth we *have* to find, no problems we *have* to solve – for the past doesn't have any problems – only historians have those as they *displace* current ideological problematics from the present into the past as if, once removed, they become amenable to resolution; that if we 'understand' the 'historical conditions' of 'this and that' then the problems of 'this and that' can be some way to being solved. But obviously this displacement is illusory. Given that it is the historians who have the problems, not the past, the solutions to their problems lie in them and their present, not in history. In that sense the past doesn't 'actually enter into it' – except rhetorically.

This conclusion – that 'historical' problems and 'historical' solutions are always *historians'* problems and conclusions – leads to my second and final point in this third and final comment. Which is this. Given that history is constituted by the work of historians (historiography) the idea that we can 'learn lessons from the past/history', actually translates out as simply, 'we can learn lessons from historians'. At which point the fairly obvious question arises as to how many of us would trust historians as 'moral guides', as 'lesson givers', and as providers of and legitimators of our identities, any further than we could, how can I put it, throw them? The reification[2] of historians' work as the work of 'history', the designation of historians' problems as 'historical' problems, the habit of thinking in terms of 'historical' ontologies, 'historical' epistemologies and 'historical' methodologies rather than 'historians', all these ideas, to re-use Rorty's phrase, are ones 'well lost'. The collapse of Bennington's dualism, the absorption of *history's demands* into *our demands*, should firmly lay these particular sleights of hand to rest.

To sum up. I began by saying that a working of Bennington's couplet *history demands/we demand history* may lead us to the point where we not only rethink the 'nature' of history, but also whether we still need a history at all: what is the point of going to the historicised past? And I said that, in saying this, maybe I was talking about a version of the 'end of history'. And I suppose I've now given some reasons why this is possibly the case. The idea that there really is a past-as-history that makes upper- and/or lower-case (normative) demands on us, as distinct from 'the fact' that we simply project on to the past our own (normative) desires as if they were not ours at all, is an interesting modernist trick which postmodernists feel under no obligation to continue with. Postmodernism therefore does, I think, signal the end of history as modernists have construed it – and maybe the way in which we need to bother construing it at all. By which I don't mean, it almost goes without saying, that actual life is ending, that there won't (probably) be a tomorrow and a next year. Nor do I mean, again it almost goes without saying, that ethical/moral problems and discussions about ethically/morally positioned representations of the past may not continue, the point being, however, that postmodern implications have so transformed the concepts of History/history and ethics/morality that they are now no longer the same, that traditional ways of posing (and therefore of allegedly answering) the questions no longer make much sense. What I want to say, then, is that today we seem to be living through the last years of the peculiar ways in which modernist historians *conceptualised* the past, the (illusory) way that they tried to make ethical and moral sense of it in upper- and lower-case forms – the idea that, separate from us, the past 'itself' (as if the past had a 'self') could make normative demands on us and that, separate from it, we could make normative demands on it which it would understand, and respond to, if only we got its 'number' – a dualism now happily collapsed, and which collapse maybe signals the end of 'history demands'/'we demand history' altogether. To end with a few words from Freud suitably jumbled up: for those particular illusions there may well have been a past; it is problematic, however, if there is now much of a future.

Notes

1 Although I don't think for a moment that F. R. Ankersmit would agree with much that I have said in this paper, his views on the aesthetic nature of historiography, his rejection of the 'historists' historical object as a reified past in favour of a 'nostalgic' historical sensation, and his qualified postmodernism as a movement beyond the 'Kantian paradigm of knowledge and meaning' into the possibilities of a new, disaggregated world that lies ahead of us, stand behind some of the ideas expressed here. See especially Ankersmit's recent collection of older papers and new essays, *History and Tropology: The Rise and Fall of Metaphor* (1994).

2 Particularly interesting in the context of postmodern ways of expressing older notions of reification is Jean Baudrillard's notion of 'the idea of reversibility' (Baudrillard, 1996). Thus, for example, Baudrillard points out that whilst much has been made of the way in which the 'subject constitutes the object' few have raised the question of the way in which the 'object constitutes the subject'. That is to say, while we post-Cartesians can now admit that we subjects constitute objects (e.g. we historians constitute history/historiography) we have not been too aware of how such an object (history/historiography) once in place then constitutes us, tells us how to behave towards it, tells us how to treat it as if it was self-constitutive. That history would only give up its secrets if it was looked at in, say, Marxist fashion, or empirically, or if we approached it 'properly', i.e. objectively, open mindedly, in ways which were balanced, etc. In this way the reified object really does look as if it has a life of its own as we forget that we gave this discourse all the life it has as we meekly obey 'its' strictures; in this way Baudrillard talks of the 'revenge of the object'. But a further interesting point about reversibility is not only the insight it offers into the way our demands of history are reified such that the histories we demand in turn demand us, control us, but that we can never get out of this subject–object/object–subject reversal into a higher resolution or synthesis whereby we can ever really sort out and thus know what we had made of the past/history and what the past/history (us) had made of us …

References

Ankersmit, F. R., *Narrative Logic* (The Hague, 1983).

——, *History and Tropology* (Berkeley, CA, 1994).

Attridge, D., Young, R. and Bennington, G. (eds), *Post-structuralism and the Question of History* (Cambridge, 1987).

Baudrillard, J., *The Perfect Crime* (London, 1996).
Bennington, G. and Derrida, J., *Jacques Derrida* (Chicago, 1996).
Elton, G., *The Practice of History*, (London, 1969).
Laclau, E., *Emancipation(s)* (London, 1996).
Levinas, E., *Ethics and Infinity* (Pittsburgh, 1985).
Lyotard, J. F., *The Differend* (Minnesota, 1988).
McHale, B., *Constructing Postmodernism* (London, 1992).
Marwick, A., *The Nature of History* (London, 1989).
Mouffe, C. (ed.), *Deconstruction and Pragmatism* (London, 1996).
Stanford, M., *A Companion to the Study of History* (Oxford, 1994).
Tosh, J., *The Pursuit of History* (London, 1991).
White, H., *Metahistory: The Historical Consciousness in the Nineteenth Century* (Baltimore, MD, 1973).
——, *The Content of the Form* (Baltimore, MD, 1987).

4 History, the referent and narrative

Reflections on postmodernism now

Perez Zagorin

In 1999 Perez Zagorin wrote an article in the journal *History and Theory* attacking postmodern histories and historians, including my *The Postmodern History Reader* (1997). I contacted the journal to see if it would accept a response – not a usual practice for *History and Theory* – but it agreed to do so on this occasion if Zagorin would write a 'reply' to my 'reply' – which he reluctantly did. Both Zagorin's and my article appeared in the same issue of the journal in 2000. At the time I thought that my reply was centred pretty much on what Zagorin had said but, as his reply makes clear, he clearly thinks I had missed the point. Maybe he was right; the papers do in a sense speak past each other. But I think that's not to dismiss them. So far as I can see the papers raised a series of 'positions' – of arguments and counter arguments – that were 'in the air at the time' and which are still being recycled today in various ways.

Sixty-odd years ago the historical profession in the United States was confronted for the first time with the troubling specter of relativism in the form of a questioning of the possibility of objectivity in the investigation of the human past. The authors of this challenge to objectivity were two distinguished members of the profession, Charles A. Beard and Carl L. Becker, who promulgated their position in various essays and books during the 1930s and later. Both men took some of their arguments from philosophy and showed traces of the influence of European thinkers such as the Italian idealist philosopher Benedetto Croce. Basically pragmatists in their outlook, they did not despair of historical knowledge or recommend any changes in historical practice. They simply maintained that no student of the past could escape the dominance of the practical problems of the present in determining his or her interests, values, and presuppositions, and that this relationship to the present made historians unable to achieve an objective approach to the past or to know it as it actually was. The extended debate provoked by their relativistic perspective persisted down through the 1950s and beyond before it finally faded away. In 1988 the entire controversy was retrospectively surveyed in Peter Novick's excellent study, *That Noble Dream*. Novick himself held, as he stated in his introduction, that objectivity was not only a delusion but an essentially confused concept. It was thus quite paradoxical that some reviewers of his book praised it for its objectivity, thereby implying its self-refuting character in the manifest contradiction between its author's practice as a historian and his professed disbelief in objectivity.[1] Moreover, if we ask what effect the objectivity debate had upon historians, we see no sign that it shook their commitment to objectivity as an ideal. At the most it may have persuaded some of them that objectivity was not an easy goal and perhaps also induced them to become more conscious of their values and biases as inquirers. As Novick acknowledged, however, the historical profession as a whole continued to give allegiance to objectivity as a regulatory principle and to believe that some approximation to it was attainable.[2] In taking this view, it seems to me that its members were implicitly recognizing a fundamental truth, namely, that objectivity, rightly understood and its limits grasped, was not a chimera, but an intrinsic aspect of historical reason which could not be abandoned as an aim or standard without also abandoning history itself as one of the foremost of the human and social sciences.

In the aftermath of the objectivity debate has come postmodernism, whose skeptical questioning and redefinition of history involves a much more radical form of relativism than was ever envisaged by Beard, Becker, and others of their persuasion. By now postmodernism has been with us for well over two decades and generated an extensive literature of exposition and controversy. Today anyone with a theoretical or philosophical interest in historiography, literary studies, or language knows all the cards in the postmodernist deck and how its theories have been applied to history. Possibly this leaves out the majority of professional historians who, as usual, appear to ignore theoretical issues and would prefer to be left undisturbed to get on with their work while no doubt hoping the postmodernist challenge will eventually go away.[3] But among the historians who have taken part in the postmodernist debate or attach some importance to the philosophical and methodological foundations of their discipline, a variety of responses can be distinguished. There are some who evince great alarm at the incursions of postmodernism, considering the latter as a new kind of nihilism threatening the very existence of history as an intellectual discipline, and who tend to regard themselves as a beleaguered minority defending the citadel of reason against its hordes of enemies. This, one might not unfairly say, is the impression created by the treatment of postmodernism in writings like Keith Windschuttle's recent polemic, *The Killing of History*, Geoffrey Elton's *Return to Essentials*, and several of the essays on the subject by Gertrude Himmelfarb.[4] Opposite to these are a small number of historians favorable to postmodernism, who embrace it as providing new and profoundly original insights into the nature of history which must decidedly affect historical practice. Among the exemplars of this point of view are the editors and most of the contributors to F. R. Ankersmit and Hans Kellner's volume of essays bearing the revealing title *A New Philosophy of History*, and the recent books on postmodernism and historiography by David D. Roberts and Robert F. Berkhofer, Jr.[5] Still other historians, while giving respectful and sympathetic consideration to postmodernist ideas or perhaps acknowledging certain contributions postmodernism has made to historiography, draw back or dissent from some of its extreme theoretical claims. Such is more or less the attitude expressed in essays by John Toews and Gabrielle Spiegel, in the collaborative work on the present condition of history by Joyce Appleby, Lynn Hunt, and Margaret Jacob, and in the dispassionate comments contained in Georg Iggers's recent survey of twentieth-century historiography. *In Defence of History*, by the British scholar Richard J. Evans, is another instance of a work that, while generally very critical of postmodernism, nevertheless holds that it has benefited historiography in certain ways.[6]

There thus appears to be a wide spectrum of opinions among historians with respect to postmodernism, ranging from substantial agreement and broad endorsement, to noncommittal examination, qualified criticism, and specific reservations, to complete rejection and uncompromising hostility.[7]

When looking at the current scene, it's also impossible not to notice that one of the odd effects of postmodernism has been to turn some historians, and a much larger number of literary scholars, into philosophers, which means, in most cases, into bad philosophers, judging by the poor arguments and weak reasons often encountered in the postmodernist debate. And in this connection it's hard to overlook the fact that of all the various areas of the humanities, philosophy is the discipline in which postmodernism has made the fewest inroads and gained the fewest converts. Most philosophers in the United States, as in Britain also, remain attached to the analytical tradition which has shaped the general approach to philosophy since the 1940s and the demise of logical positivism. It is a tradition that, in giving centrality to logic and the analysis of language and concepts, assumes standards of clarity and care in reasoning, as well as a respect for facts, of which postmodernist advocates often fall short. In consequence, philosophers in the United States are usually disinclined to take postmodernism seriously.[8] The writings of influential postmodernist thinkers like Derrida and Foucault are rarely studied in university philosophy courses. As Hilary Putnam, a leading contemporary philosopher, has lately remarked in a survey of the past half-century of philosophy, there has been no reception by American philosophers of continental philosophy,[9] and it is from the latter that postmodernism entirely derives. Similarly, nearly all the well-known philosophers in this country and Britain who have shown the greatest interest in the philosophy or theory of history during the past forty years—I refer to thinkers like Maurice Mandelbaum, William Dray, W. H. Walsh, Patrick Gardiner, and Morton White—have been almost entirely unresponsive or opposed to postmodernist approaches to historiography that have appeared since the 1970s.[10] Of course, it is arguable that the interest of analytical philosophers in the philosophy of history has been unduly narrow, that in focusing as they have done to a considerable extent on the problem of historical explanation, they largely ignored other questions of great significance such as hermeneutics or the theory of interpretation and the role of language itself in the production of historical knowledge. Even if this charge should be accepted, however, analytical philosophy's resistance to verbal obfuscation and its insistence on the necessity of clarity and logical correctness seem to me to posit standards of intellectual discourse that are as valid for historians as for philosophers.

These and the reflections that follow have been prompted by a reading of the essays by diverse authors collected in the *The Postmodern History Reader* under the editorship of Keith Jenkins, and of many of the other articles and books published in recent years in the postmodernist debate.[11] As these writings show, postmodernism is an amorphous concept and a syncretism of different but related theories, theses, and claims that have tended to be included under this one heading.[12] They all have their origin in modern German philosophy, especially in Nietzsche and extending to Heidegger, in the adaptation of this philosophy by various French intellectuals since the 1960s, and in poststructuralist theories of language likewise originating in France in the 1960s. In the most general sense, postmodernism stands for the proposition that Western society in recent decades has undergone an epochal shift from the modern to a postmodern era said to be characterized by the final repudiation of the Enlightenment's legacy of belief in reason and progress and by a pervasive incredulity toward all metanarratives imputing a direction and meaning to history, in particular the notion that human history is process of universal emancipation. In place of grand narratives of this kind, so it is held, have come a multiplicity of discourses and language games, a questioning of the nature of knowledge together with a dissolution of the idea of truth, and problems of legitimacy in many fields. Such is the understanding of the postmodern era outlined in one of the most influential statements on the subject, Jean-François Lyotard's *The Postmodern Condition*.[13] Both Lyotard and numerous other writers have likewise connected the appearance of postmodernity with a number of technological and social transformations in the later twentieth century that have given rise to a new global economy and to an electronic, computer-regulated, media-saturated, and mass consumer society.

Needless to say, the argument claiming to discern a new postmodern epoch in Western society is a highly debatable one. The changes offered in evidence might also be plausibly interpreted as further unforeseen developments of modernity itself with all its many paradoxes and possibilities. In any case, it should be borne in mind that the concept of the postmodern, sometimes also thought of as synonymous with that of a posthistorical age, is by no means novel and can be found as far back as the nineteenth century in philosophers like Cournot and Nietzsche. In the past, moreover, it has been very largely identified with a strand of historical pessimism and cultural conservatism regarding the nature and prospects of modern society that includes among others not only Nietzsche, but Max Weber, Spengler, the German sociologist Arnold Gehlen, Aldous Huxley, and the critical theorists of the Frankfurt school, all of whom held in one way or another that the modern age was rapidly leading to an era of cultural sterility, bureaucratic and technological domination, and the disappearance of personal autonomy and nobility in human life.[14]

In addition, it must be pointed out that, well before it became what some now consider to be a hallmark of the postmodern, incredulity concerning metanarratives was a familiar theme in Western thought. There have always been those since the eighteenth century who denied the credibility of such narratives. Adversaries of the French Revolution, like Edmund Burke and a varied line of nineteenth-century thinkers, historians, and social philosophers such as Tocqueville, Carlyle, Burckhardt, Herzen, and Taine, all rejected the grand narrative of emancipation in which the revolution figured as an emancipatory turning point. Much of the philosophical, historical, and political criticism directed against Marxism and communism over the years has included a rejection of the validity of their metanarrative of history as a redemptive process leading through class struggle and revolutions to socialism and a communist world order, a belief which Raymond Aron, one of its critics, called "the opium of the intellectuals."[15] When in his early career the historian Ranke criticized speculative philosophies of history like Hegel's or Fichte's as fabrications, and affirmed that the office of history was only to show what had actually happened, he was seeking to ban the metanarrative from historiography.[16] A century later, near the close of World War II, the philosopher Karl Popper argued in his famous work, *The Open Society and Its Enemies*, that history has no meaning and thereby strove to demonstrate the impossibility of all metanarratives.[17] And in 1949, Karl Löwith, another philosopher, concluded his valuable study, *Meaning in History*, with the judgment that "the problem of history as a whole is unanswerable within its own perspective. Historical processes as such do not bear the least evidence of a comprehensive and ultimate meaning. History as such has no outcome."[18]

Finally, and not least important, the advent of the postmodern announced by Lyotard and others seems itself to be based upon a metanarrative or totalizing account purporting to explain the entire course of modern history and its outcome in the present and future. At the outset, therefore, the theory of postmodernism presents a striking inconsistency, since it is obliged to proffer a metanarrative to sustain its thesis of the demise of the metanarrative.

Leaving aside, however, the broad meaning of postmodernism discussed above, and viewing it in a more specific philosophical sense and in its bearing upon historical knowledge, its two principal features may be said to be its conception of language and its rejection of realism. It is a philosophy of linguistic idealism or panlingualism claiming that language constitutes and defines reality for human minds, or rather that there is no extralinguistic reality independent of our representations of it in language or discourse. It regards language itself as a system of signs that refer only to one another internally in an endless process of signification that never arrives at stable meaning. The infiltration and spread of this conception of language during recent years is a major aspect of what is usually described as "the linguistic turn" in history and some of the other human sciences. Postmodernism thus denies both the ability of language or discourse to refer to an independent world of facts and things and the determinacy or decidability of textual meaning. By the same token, it also dismisses the possibility of objective knowledge and truth as goals of inquiry. In maintaining these views, it claims to be both antimetaphysical and postmetaphysical. The critical reader, however, will have no difficulty in perceiving that this idealist philosophy is itself a species of metaphysics founded on unproved and unprovable assumptions concerning the nature of language and what there is.[19]

The postmodernist theory of language is largely the product of poststructuralist misinterpretations of the work of the Swiss linguist Ferdinand de Saussure, whose lectures before the First World War were posthumously published in 1916 as the *Course in General Linguistics*. Saussure considered himself a scientist of language, not a philosopher or metaphysician. In teaching that the proper object of the science of linguistics should be *langue* or the synchronic, ahistorical study of language as a total system, rather than *parole* or the diachronic, historical study of language as spoken and temporally evolved, he became the founder of structural linguistics. His explanation of language as a system of signs distinguished solely by their opposition and difference from one another (a principle he formulated in the well-known dictum that "in language there are only differences without positive terms"), and his definition of the sign as a signifier arbitrarily linked to a signified, did not cause him, however, to renounce realism or deny that words could refer to objects in the world. Although formed by an arbitrary connection between a particular sound and a particular meaning, the sign as he defined it was itself a concept with a referential relation to things. Saussure therefore never supposed that the world is constructed in language and does not exist independently of our linguistic descriptions. As a number of scholars have shown, these idealist opinions were not his, but conclusions drawn from and imposed upon his work by subsequent poststructuralists and literary theorists who are responsible for the postmodernist philosophy of language.[20] Yet, in spite of this fact, we continue to see discussions of postmodernism by historians who still go on repeating that language can't refer to anything beyond itself as though it were a true proposition owing to Saussure. In an essay reprinted in *The Postmodern History Reader*, Gabrielle Spiegel attributes to Saussure the belief that "reality does not exist 'beyond' the reach of language" and that language and texts cannot reflect the world, which "is only a linguistic construct" and "merely another articulation of language or discourse."[21] Joyce Appleby similarly imagines that for Saussure "words always refer to other words rather than to objects outside the text."[22] Jane Caplan also, in undertaking to explain postmodernism to historians, reiterates the mistaken view that a "central tenet" of Saussurean linguistics detaches signification "from any external reference, whether to the past or the real."[23] These statements, however, are simply misrepresentations of Saussure, who never endorsed the fantastic notion that the world is the creation of language and has no existence outside it.

A number of other themes commonly associated with postmodernism stem from the very wide influence of Michel Foucault, whose writings indicted

Enlightenment reason for introducing new, unperceived modes of oppression and sought to show how in every society, power shapes and unites with knowledge in the form of "regimes of truth" and dominant discourses that prescribe the limits of the knowable and sayable in particular cultures.[24] In historiography and other fields these postmodernist themes, often tinged with an admixture of Marxism, have been widely incorporated in radical versions of feminism, multiculturalism, and affirmations of ethnic or sexual identity. Among them are opposition to humanism and to the idea of mankind and a common human nature as pernicious myths; the assurance that what passes for reason or truth is invariably the product of the ideological and political interests of hegemonic groups whose domination shapes discourse; and the pervasive suspicion of an insidious cultural imperialism, ethnocentrism, or sexism implicit in all statements of general moral principles.

Although the postmodernist theory of language as expounded in the writings of its foremost spokesman, Jacques Derrida, has been damagingly criticized by both philosophers and linguists, this fact has not prevented it from making headway in certain disciplines.[25] In the form of deconstructionism and literary theory, and in association with the approach to literature known as the New Historicism, postmodernism and its manner of dealing with texts has become the predominant influence in the study and teaching of literature in American universities.[26]

History, by contrast, has shown itself to be considerably more resistant to postmodernist trends. This, at any rate, is the strong impression I have derived from the postmodernist debate among historians as well as from my reading of historical books and articles in diverse fields and from the statements of well-known academic historians. It is no doubt true that in several areas such as women's studies, social history, and cultural and intellectual history, a number of scholars have been receptive to postmodernist conceptions of language and discourse. Yet, on the other hand, the vast expansion of the historical horizon during the past generation to encompass the histories of women, racial and ethnic minorities, and all kinds of marginalized or forgotten groups and communities owes none of its original inspiration to postmodernism and has developed mostly in independence of it. The like is true of the enormous growth of social history and the concentration upon the lives of ordinary people in the past, which has been another of the major changes in historiography during the same period. By now it seems fair to conclude that postmodernism is a distinctly minority phenomenon among professional historians, most of whom are unwilling to accept its view of history because they find it so contrary to their own personal understanding and experience of historical inquiry. To all appearances, the prevailing attitude of historians in the United States might be typified in the statement made in 1994 by Bernard Bailyn, a leading senior scholar of early American history, that "the accuracy and adequacy of representations of past actualities, the verisimilitude or closeness to fact of what is written about them, remain the measure, in the end, of good history … "[27] In a younger generation of historians, Thomas L.

Haskell persists in the defense of objectivity, and, while describing his response to postmodernism as "ambivalent," nevertheless contends that its emphasis on language cannot relieve history of the need for words like "rationality," "logicality," or "truth."[28] Similarly, Alan B. Spitzer, by profession a historian of modern France, in a book that examines some major historical controversies, including the notorious case of the concealment of his pro-Nazi, anti-Semitic wartime writings by the prominent Yale literary scholar and decontructionist Paul de Man, has used these examples to oppose the postmodernist dismissal of the ideas of truth and objectivity and to demonstrate that the latter are indispensable in the practice of history.[29]

Even among historians who in response to the linguistic turn have focused their attention on the role of discourse in culture and politics, most continue to be realists in believing that history's object is the knowledge of the past as a vanished reality which is capable of being reconstructed. Thus the French scholar Roger Chartier, a leading member of this school, does not fail to remind us that history is a "confirmable, verifiable knowledge" of a "past reality" and that only on the basis of a "critical realism" and a striving for truth can historians resist "the perversion of their discipline" and "mythical reconstructions of the past governed by the needs of communities, imagined or real, national or not, that create or accept historical narratives to suit their desires and expectations."[30] Such comments, which point out the dangers in the extreme relativism that postmodernist philosophy represents, help explain why most historians, even those who are sympathetic to it in certain respects, are reluctant to embrace its theory of history. If any considerable number of them were to adopt its principles, it is difficult to see how the larger society could continue to place any trust in the veracity and sincerity of history as a genuine discipline of knowledge directed to the human past. By the same token the latter would also be rendered incapable of performing its vital and ever more necessary intellectual function in the schools, universities, and wider culture of today's world.

Those who are familiar with the present state of historiography can easily note various things they find wrong with it. The massive over-production of academic historical writing and the inferior quality of a considerable portion of what gets published is one. The overt ideological and political biases that tend to direct or influence work in certain fields of history is another. The fragmentation of the historical discipline into an ever-increasing number of highly specialized areas whose detailed results remain unintegrated into a more comprehensive vision and understanding of the past is yet a third and very serious problem. With regard to this last point, I believe that we are in desperate need of large-scale works of history that can assist the present generation to orient itself amid the complexities of the historical process by providing some wide and relatively integrated perspectives on the modern development of Western and other societies and cultures and their interrelations.

Postmodernist theorists, on the other hand, are critical of what they term normal historical practice for quite different reasons. What bothers them are such things as its continuing faith in the possibility of objective history, its stubborn conviction that history isn't just concerned with texts and discourses but aspires to provide in some non-absolute yet valid sense a true representation and understanding of the past, and its alleged complicity with and ideological support of the political and economic status quo.

Consider Keith Jenkins's introduction to *The Postmodern History Reader*, a reductive and prejudiced critique of normal historical practice as the product of bourgeois ideology and interests. Jenkins is confident that we are living in the condition of postmodernity and have no choice about it. He maintains that "histories are just theories about the past and how it should be appropriated" and that "only theory can constitute what counts as a fact ... " For this last point he offers the misplaced argument that facts cannot exist except under some description. It is a poor argument in this context, though, because a description isn't a theory, and the fact, for example, that Hitler became chancellor of Germany in 1933 is not known or established as the consequence of any theory.[31] For postmodernist Jenkins, the idea that it might be possible to study the past for its own sake (which is usually taken to mean the attempt to understand an earlier human culture or society first and foremost in terms of its own self-conceptions and values rather than in order to serve an immediate practical or political interest of the present) is ridiculous and merely "the mystifying way in which a bourgeoisie articulates its own interests as if they belonged to the past itself."[32] He is simply unable to conceive the viability or value of the historical effort to restore to comprehension a vanished past with its distinctive ways of life and modes of thought, although it's the kind of project many historians undertake. He also asserts that, if historians reject a futuristic orientation in doing history, it's because they don't desire a future different from the present in which capitalism dominates the world. What this proposition completely ignores, of course, is the well-founded conviction held by most historians that the business of history is with the past as a possible object of knowledge, not the future.[33]

A critical comment in a similar vein appears in Robert F. Berkhofer Jr.'s essay in the same volume. One of his theoretical objections against normal historical practice is that it tries to create the illusion of an omniscient, neutral narrator in works of history, and that "by assuming a third-person voice and an omniscient viewpoint," historians aim to gain power over their readers in the name of reality. This view, which he also frequently repeats in his book, *Beyond the Great Story*, attributes to historiography what theorists of narrative identify as one of the conventions of realist fiction, which usually involves an external, invisible, impersonal, and all-knowing teller of the story who fosters the illusion that the literary text is a direct record of reality. It's extremely doubtful, though, that any educated reader of a history has ever credited its author with the degree of omniscience ascribed to the creator of a realistic fiction. A reader of this kind would consider it impermissible if the authors of histories repeatedly obtruded their personal voices, opinions, and experiences into their writings, instead of subordinating themselves completely to the subject at hand. Such a reader understands very well that a historical work differs in essential ways from an invented fiction like the novel, that it doesn't pretend to know or tell everything, and that it is always a selective reconstruction of the past from a great manifold of facts, a selection dictated by the subjects, problems, and questions the author proposes to deal with. This same reader is also aware that a history is written from a point of view, that its statements are susceptible of disproof, that it embodies comments and judgments relative to controverted questions, and that it doesn't profess to be a mindless and mechanical transcript of reality but an attempt at understanding. An informed reader observes too that a history, unlike a novel in the realist genre, consists not only of specimens of narrative but of arguments, footnotes of documentation and justification, acknowledgments of what isn't known, discussions and evaluations of sources and evidence, and critiques of the views of other scholars. This kind of reader, which is the one we seek to educate in university courses in history, will always find differing accounts and interpretations of the same subject to make him or her aware of historical disagreements. Berkhofer's claim that normal historical practice permits historians to assert their power over readers by creating the illusion of their omniscience of the real is thus without substance. It makes sense only as a part of the postmodernist attack on historical realism and on the presupposition accepted by most historians that historiography is concerned with the actuality of the past and with facts attested by evidence.[34]

The belief that traditional historiography invariably supports the status quo is also held by David D. Roberts, whose book *Nothing But History* endorses the postmodernist conception of history as the only one suited to our post-metaphysical culture. "History is always written by the victors," he supposes, and historical thinking always tends to justify "the present power configuration by affording privilege to the course of the actual … "[35] While it's certainly the case that history is mainly concerned with the actual rather than with the might-have-been, one nevertheless wonders how on earth Roberts could have arrived at the conclusion that only the victors write the histories, since it's far from being generally true. Not only has historiography in both the past and the present nearly always involved differences and contestation, but there are classic histories written by losers, not winners. One thinks, for instance, of Thucydides, himself an exile, the author of a history relating the defeat of Athens, his city; or of Tacitus, the greatest of Roman historians, whose *Annals* and *Histories* were not the work of a victor but of a man who lamented the irrecoverable loss of Roman republican liberty; or of the Earl of Clarendon, a Royalist who wrote a considerable part of his *History of the Rebellion* in the circumstances of a revolution that overthrew King Charles I, the sovereign whose cause he strove to justify. A significant part of contemporary German historiography is the work of scholars of a defeated nation seeking to explain how the German people submitted to the Nazi regime and the crimes it committed. Many histories have exposed the discreditable methods by which power has been acquired and exercised, and many others have been written to vindicate lost causes, religious minorities, and oppressed peoples. And especially in recent times and in those societies where freedom of thought and expression is the rule, historical controversy has been so common that it has been rare for any single historical viewpoint or account to achieve an exclusive ascendancy.

The postmodernist theory of history comprises two principal theses that entail a much more sweeping type of skepticism than anything to be seen in the earlier relativistic doubts concerning objectivity. The first thesis is that of anti-realism, which maintains that the past cannot be the object of historical knowledge or, more specifically, that the past is not and cannot be the referent of historical statements and representations. Such representations are therefore construed as referring not to the past but solely to other and always present historical statements, discourses, and texts. By thus depriving historical knowledge-claims of any relationship to the actual past, postmodernism dissolves history into a species of literature and makes the past itself into nothing more than a text. The second thesis is that of narrativism, which assigns priority in the creation of historical narratives to the imperatives of language and the tropes or figures of speech inherent in linguistic usage. According to this thesis, the fictional stories invented by writers and the narrations fashioned by historians do not differ from one another in any essential respect because both are made out of language and equally subject to the latter's rules in the practice of rhetoric and the construction of narratives. The manner in which historical narratives are emplotted, the connections they posit among events, and the interpretations and explanations they present are thus seen as constructions imposed upon the past rather than being founded on, constrained by, or answerable to facts as disclosed by the evidence. From the narrativist standpoint, the tropes and literary genres employed by historians prefigure and determine the vision, interpretation, and meaning of the facts. By the same token they also place historical narratives in the same category as the fictional discourses of novelists and artists, so that it is impossible to make a distinction between histories and fiction or to adjudicate between differing historical interpretations on the basis of facts or evidence.

A peculiar paradox inherent in the first or anti-realist thesis calls for notice before I attempt to address it more directly. Like historians, postmodernist authors tell stories about the past that they seem to hope and believe are true and consistent with the facts. Elizabeth Ermarth, a contributor to *The Postmodern History Reader* who wishes to regard everything as a text and who aims to subvert the conception of time she associates with modernism and traditional historiography, makes many factual statements ostensibly about the past: for example, that modernity began with the Renaissance and Reformation, that the ancient Greeks had no conception of the subject, that the period of Einstein's papers on relativity was also that of Kafka's stories and of the cubism of Picasso and Braque, that the German Higher Criticism of the Bible historicized Christianity, and so on. She also frankly confesses that her own text about postmodernism is "written in the language of representation [that is, realism], assumes a consensus community, and engages in historical generalization and footnotes," a position she justifies with the ingenuous argument that "one need not give up history to challenge its hegemony … "[36] David Roberts's book is likewise a work of intellectual history tracing the development of certain ideas about history from Vico through Nietzsche, Croce, Heidegger, and others down to Derrida, Foucault, and the contemporary postmodern, postmetaphysical era to which he considers historiography must adapt. Berkhofer too includes numerous historical summaries of the views of various writers on history, and in order "to demystify normal historical authority" he calls upon historians to investigate the premises and politics of historical interpretations and methods, a task that is itself historical in character.[37] What then is the status of these historical descriptions, analyses, and interpretations by postmodernist theorists of history? They read like conventional accounts and appear to be intended as true and objective representations referring to individuals, books, thoughts, and events in a real past, and it's hard to see how their readers could understand them in any other way. Yet their authors evince no awareness of the problematic and self-refuting character of their historical pronouncements in light of their postmodernist opposition to historical realism. Berkhofer is likewise proposing an infinite regress, because the historians who investigate the premises and politics of historical interpretations will need, if his recommendation is to be followed, to have their own politics of interpretation investigated by other historians, and so on ad infinitum.

The rejection of historical realism has been an essential theme in the philosophy of poststructuralism and postmodernism. It was given canonical formulation in Derrida's *Of Grammatology* in which, denying that reading could "legitimately transgress the text … toward a referent" or a "reality," whether "metaphysical, historical, psychobiographical," or other, he laid it down that "there is nothing outside of the text." Roland Barthes, one of the most prominent of French literary theorists, advanced a similar opinion in a discussion dealing with historical discourse, of which a selection is printed in *The Postmodern History Reader*. Analyzing this discourse from a semiotic angle, Barthes contended that the reference it presumes or makes to a past reality is spurious, a deceptive effect of language, and that the signified in such discourse is devoid of referent other than the discourse itself.[38] Berkhofer is likewise opposed to historical realism and emphasizes the profound challenge that "dereferentialism" presents to traditional historical understanding.[39] His reason for rejecting realism in history consists of first putting the question, "what is the referent for the word, 'history,'" which is then followed by the answer that "it cannot be the past as such, because that is absent by definition." In spite of the historian's presumption of a past actuality, he explains, "no one can point to the past in the same way that one can point to a horse or a tree (or even a picture of them), as the objects to which the words 'horse' and 'tree' refer." He then goes on to approve the opinion of literary theorists that reference in history can only relate to other histories or texts.[40]

Such reasoning should remind us of the continuing relevance of Bertrand Russell's observation that "it is the essential function of words to have a connection of one sort or another with facts, which are in general non-linguistic. Some modern philosophers ... tell us that the attempt to confront language with fact is 'metaphysics' and is on this ground to be condemned. This is one of those views which are so absurd that only very learned men could possibly adopt them."[41] Certainly, it is difficult not to feel some discomfort in reporting Berkhofer's rejoinder to realism as though it were a serious argument, based as it is on the narrowest, most stultifying sort of an acquaintance or empiricist theory of knowledge according to which we can know only what we can presently see or point to. It's also a most unreasonable argument, because it implies the incoherent conception that for past events to be the referent of statements in works of history, they must first stand before us as present objects of perception. That is, of course, an absurd notion, since the past and past events can survive as objects of knowledge only through the evidence of their existence that is found in the present, and such evidence acquires its definition and status as evidence only if and insofar as it is taken to refer to actual events, persons, institutions, ideas, and so on, which occurred in the past.

At the present time there are quite a few analytical philosophers around, like William Alston, Rom Harré, Roy Bhaskar, Hilary Putnam (in a modified way), Thomas Nagel, Nicholas Rescher, Israel Scheffler, John Searle, Roderick Chisholm, and others, who defend some version of realism either in regard to knowledge and truth or in an ontic sense as the affirmation that the world, material objects, natural phenomena, and so on, exist independently of mind or language.[42] In general, though, these philosophers don't address the question of realism from the standpoint of historiography or seem to perceive any special problem in talking about the reality and existence of events and things that are past. We need not, however, consider the subject of realism in its several different meanings or aspects in order to respond to the postmodernist skepticism concerning the past as the referent of historical statements. Perhaps the best reply that can be made to this skepticism is that the idea of the past as independently real or actual does not depend on any theory and is not a philosophical conclusion. It is, rather, a requirement of historical reason and a conceptual necessity, vouchsafed by memory as well as implicated in human language that includes past-tense statements, and is entailed by the very idea of history as a distinctive form of knowledge which has the human past as its object. To deny the existence of the past as something actual to which historians can refer is therefore futile, because it is an essential condition of the possibility of history as an inquiry.

The narrativist or what might also be termed the tropological thesis belongs to the postmodernist constellation of ideas because it eliminates the distinction between historical and fictional narratives and hence denies to historiography the kind of truth-value it claims in its accounts and representations of the past. While analytical philosophers of history prior to the advent of postmodernism expressed considerable interest in the role of narratives in history, their reflections did not lead in a skeptical direction. The aim of these philosophers was chiefly to clarify the function of narratives and to show how they contributed to the task of historical explanation.[43] The later and by now widely familiar narrativist thesis that has become part of the postmodernist syndrome has been largely inspired by Hayden White's book *Metahistory* (1973) and the subsequent essays in which he elaborated his position.[44] One of its testimonials is the recent collection of articles, *A New Philosophy of History*, whose introduction by Hans Kellner presents an exposition of this position. The latter has had little appeal to historians, however, who are unable to recognize themselves in it, and it has found its main reception among the literary specialists who lean toward the postmodernist conception of language.

Initially the narrativist view does not deny the reality of the past or the possibility of giving a true description of individual historical events such as might be noted in a simple record of discrete successive occurrences in the form of annals. White argues, however, that when events or facts come to be incorporated into coherent historical narratives, they must then be emplotted in a story that has a beginning, middle, and end. Such plots, he maintains, do not correspond to or represent the reality of the events themselves, which are merely a continuous and meaningless flux. They are accordingly stories the historian invents by means of language and rhetoric in order to endow the endless succession of events or facts with some order and meaning. He also contends that, in devising the story line of such narratives, historians will be obliged, in the same way as are authors of fictional narratives, to emplot the facts according to one or another of the principal literary genres—comedy, romance, tragedy, irony, or satire. (Epic does not seem to figure here.) Likewise, in constructing their narratives, historians will also have a choice among the several principal rhetorical devices or tropes such as metaphor, metonymy, synecdoche, or irony, one of which will predominate in generating the stories and interpretations they present. "Any given set of real events," White claims, can be emplotted in a number of different ways, because events themselves are devoid of meaning and are neither "intrinsically tragic, comic, farcical and so on." Hence they "can be constructed as such only by the imposition of the structure of a given story type on the events" and "it is the choice of the story type and its imposition upon the events that endow them with meaning."[45] "To emplot real events as a story of a specific kind," he summarizes his position, " … is to trope these events. This is because … there is no such thing as a 'real' story. Stories are told or written, not found. And as for the notion of a 'true' *story*, this is virtually a contradiction in terms. *All* stories are fictions, which means, of course, that they can be 'true' in a metaphorical sense and in the sense in which a figure of speech can be true."[46]

The initial concession which the narrativist thesis makes to historical realism is thus soon cancelled by its extreme constructionist theory of what historians do. Erasing the demarcation between works of fiction and historical narratives, it regards the latter as formalized verbal objects to be estimated in literary terms, and it discards the concept of a real and knowable past for one in which the past and its possible meanings are seen as purely literary and tropological constructions. White accordingly emphasizes "the inexpungeable relativity" of all histories "as a function of the language used to describe and thereby constitute past events as possible objects of explanation and understanding."[47] He similarly holds that "when it comes to the historical record, there are no grounds to be found in the record itself for preferring one way of construing its meaning rather than another."[48] While the narrativist thesis is willing to grant to historiography a kind of truth, it is exactly the same sort as that conveyed in fictional writings, which depict imaginary and invented worlds, but not the truth that historians suppose themselves to pursue, which depends upon the factuality of historical representations and their fidelity in comprehending the reality of the historical past.

In an essay entitled "'Figuring the Nature of the Times Deceased': Literary Theory and Historical Writing," White has endeavored to respond to some of the numerous criticisms directed against his narrativist thesis, among them that it rules out the referentiality of historical discourse and collapses the difference between fact and fiction. In reply, he points out that tropology stresses the metalinguistic over the referential function of discourse and also redefines the relations between fact and fiction by showing how linguistic protocols constitute the facts.[49] These answers do not appear to me to meet the objections and misgivings White's views have aroused among both historians and philosophers. The defects of his narrativist thesis are evident. Few readers or persons with any genuine experience of doing history will ever be persuaded that there is no fundamental difference between historical and fictional narratives because both are creations of language. Nor has White succeeded in giving sense to, much less justifying, the proposition that historical facts are constituted by and derive their existence from the protocols of language. Equally implausible is the claim that historians are under no constraints of fact and meaning in producing their narratives and are free to emplot and interpret past events in whatever way they prefer. As William Dray has inquired, "does the historian really have *carte blanche* with regard to how a set of events like Stalin's decimation of the kulaks or the demise of the North American Indian should be emplotted? If he 'chooses' to represent it as comic, should those who find this unacceptable regard it as simply a poetic *gaucherie* or should they resist it as morally obtuse?"[50] It is highly questionable, moreover, that historical narratives do and must conform to one of several different genres. Not only are there many works of history which cannot be classified in this way (to what particular genre does Herbert Butterfield's *The Origins of Modern Science* belong, or Richard Southern's *The Making of the Middle Ages*, or G. R. Elton's *The Tudor Revolution in Government*, or LeRoy Ladurie's *Les Paysans de Languedoc*, or Leo Strauss's *The Political Philosophy of Hobbes*?), but such genre categories as tragedy and irony are much too abstract and broad to serve as very enlightening descriptions of particular histories. In general, it remains unexplained how the extreme constructionism White espouses can possibly be consistent with an acknowledgment of the existence of singular past events as independent objects of knowledge.

These and other failings of White's narrativist thesis have been pointed out by philosophical critics like William H. Dray and Noël Carroll.[51] Historians have expressed a similar dissatisfaction. In questioning White's debilitating relativism, Roger Chartier observes that the complex, demanding operations historians use to investigate the past would be totally pointless if historical and fictional discourses were identical and if "the reality of the events emplotted" were of no importance for the kind of knowledge history can give.[52] One may guess that nearly all historians, whatever differences there might be among them, would endorse the conviction voiced by Bernard Bailyn that "the distinction between history and fiction is profound"; and they would surely also agree with him that "history is an imaginative construction ... but [it] must be ... closely bounded by the documentation—limited by the evidence that has survived, and ... by the obligation to be consistent with what has previously been established. It must somehow fit together with what is already known."[53] Historians of the Holocaust in particular have been disquieted by the assertion that historical facts are products of discourse, not true evidence of an antecedent reality, and that past events may be emplotted in any way a historian might choose.[54] As Chartier has noted, there seems to be no basis under White's view for invoking the facts of the historical record to refute the rewriting of history in revisionist narratives which allege that the Holocaust is a myth invented by Zionist propaganda and that the death camps and gas chambers never existed.[55]

White's narrativist thesis insists that no meaning or interconnection is to be found in the historical facts themselves, and that any meaning or relationships attributed to them is a construction imposed by the historian. This sweeping proposition is doubtful for at least two reasons. The first is that even ordinary individual human perceptions are not a chaotic experiencing, but consist naturally of structured and meaningful configurations. Similarly, a human being's experience of living in time is not a mere temporal chaos or an unmarked succession of minutes, days, and years. On the contrary, human experience and activity are narratively structured, so that people can and do find sequences and stories in their life histories that help them make sense of their own existence in the past and present. Such narratives are likewise implicit in the collective experiences and actions that have had the effect of uniting individuals into larger groups and communities whose members are conscious of possessing a common identity through the narratives they share.[56] The second reason is that historical facts are not mere isolated entities but can be seen to exist in an immanent relationship to other facts and to exhibit an intelligible structure and order which allows the historian to treat them as distinctive subjects. The development of the atomic theory of matter, or Roman law, or Gothic architecture, or republican institutions, or the doctrine of the divine right of kings, or Renaissance humanism forms in each case an intelligible order of interrelated facts which, as histories, imply their own criteria of relevancy. Each of these developments presents internal relationships of temporal succession, causal linkage, and other kinds of connection or reciprocities that enable the facts to constitute parts of the same history. While I do not suppose that there are any absolute origins, beginnings, and endings, narrative sequence or structure may be regarded as in some measure an attribute of the events themselves. The impeachment and resignation from office of President Richard M. Nixon, for instance, is a story whose facts largely determine its beginning and end. Likewise, the history of the battle of Stalingrad designates an event whose beginning, middle, and end are to some degree immanent and not simply freely invented and imposed upon a featureless temporal flow by the historian. There may of course be several alternative choices of where to begin, but these won't be arbitrary and are definitely limited by the facts themselves. You wouldn't, for example, begin a history of the battle of Stalingrad with the Crusades or the accession of the Romanov dynasty in Russia in 1613 or even with the death of Lenin in 1924. In the same way, the end of the battle is also to a great extent a property of the facts which constrain the narrative. It didn't come in 1944 or 1945 but in February 1943 at or shortly following the time the remnants of the German 6th army surrounded by Soviet forces at Stalingrad at last surrendered and were taken prisoner.[57]

It is evident that the narrativist thesis not only greatly underestimates the variety of histories, which is in fact far too numerous to be categorized, but also overestimates the role of narrative by identifying historiography entirely with the narrative mode. To be sure, many histories, especially political ones, consist of a relation or story of events; but even these may not be purely narrative, since they are also apt to contain numerous explicit analytical and explanatory comments, observations on disputed facts and issues, and other features generally absent from literary narratives such as the novel. Many histories, on the other hand, are not reconstructions and recountings of a succession of events in the obvious form of a story. Instead, they may be broad surveys of various aspects of a period, or accounts of the evolution of an idea, or descriptions of the development and functioning of institutions, or analyses, interpretations, and critical treatments of particular historical problems. Although works of this kind are likely to include pieces of narrative and to pay attention to some aspect of change over time, they are not fundamentally cast in a narrative mold. As examples one may cite such histories as Jacob Burckhardt's *Civilization of the Renaissance in Italy*, Moses Finley's *Politics in the Ancient World*, L. B. Namier's *The Structure of Politics at the Accession of George III*, Alfred Cobban's *The Social Interpretation of the French Revolution*, Lucien Febvre's *The Problem of Unbelief in the Sixteenth Century*, A. O. Lovejoy's *The Great Chain of Being*, H. C. Lea's *A History of the Inquisition of Spain*, or Roland Mousnier's *The Institutions of France under the Absolute Monarchy*, none of which really fits the category of narrative history.

Generally speaking, it cannot be too strongly emphasized that whatever form historiography may take, whether predominantly narrative or something else, it is not and cannot be purely a mimesis, description, or picture in words. History is above all and in its essential character a work of thought and of analysis and synthesis. Historical inquiry always operates through reflective processes of selection based on relevance to the problems and questions that the historian poses with respect to his or her subject. Its purpose has never been to produce a verbal copy, simulacrum, or literal recapitulation of the past, a task which would be otiose and stupid if it were not an impossibility. Its primary aim—which description, narrative, and all the other means available to historiography serve—is *understanding*: to understand past human actions, thoughts, beliefs, values, institutions, polities, cultures, social relationships, environments, and so on and the changes that have occurred in them and in human societies as a whole with the passage of time.

Historians who are not unqualifiedly critical of postmodernist philosophy have occasionally noted some of its positive contributions. In his *In Defence of History*, Richard J. Evans, a distinguished scholar of German history, observes that

> postmodernism in its more constructive modes has encouraged historians to look more closely at documents, to take their surface patina more seriously, and to think about texts and narratives in new ways. It has helped open up many new subjects and areas for research, while putting back on the agenda many topics which had previously seemed to be exhausted. It has forced historians to interrogate their own methods and procedures as never before, and in the process has made them more self-critical … It has led to a greater emphasis on open acknowledgment of the historians' own subjectivity, which can only help the reader engaged in a critical assessment of historical work.[58]

In a similar spirit Thomas Haskell, a scholar of United States history, declares his admiration for the "multifaceted explosion of interest in theoretical and epistemological issues in the human sciences" postmodernism has provoked and welcomes the "postmodern revival" of concern "with problems of explanation, interpretation, and epistemology … "[59]

These comments may have their point, but I wonder whether the price paid for the benefits mentioned has not been excessive. Postmodernism has sown a great deal of intellectual confusion in some of the humanistic disciplines, and it has also been a major factor in promoting the very considerable politicization that has occurred in them in recent years. In importing its theories of history and literature into the classroom, and in the concentration of its followers on questions of race, class, and gender, it has pretty certainly been one of the contributory causes of the drastic and disturbing decline of the position of the humanities in the universities that has been going on since the 1970s.[60] The appeal of postmodernism is to be explained not only by the radical questioning it has broached in history and other disciplines, but by its position in the politics of the academy. Most postmodernists situate themselves on the political left and have tended to be supporters of the movement in the universities for women's and gender studies, Afro-American studies, ethnic studies, and gay studies. They have been among the defenders of multiculturalism and the promoters of cultural and postcolonial studies. In a United States that has become increasingly conservative in its politics and economic direction since the presidency of Ronald Reagan, postmodernism, which often manages to incorporate elements of Marxism and evokes the allegiance of a miscellany of scholars in different areas, exists as one of the last relics of the political mood of the 1960s and as an academic outpost of radical dislike of the conservative trends in American society. Others, of course, who are not postmodernists, may share this dislike to some extent. What is commonly not understood or is overlooked, however, is that the skepticism and relativism endemic to postmodernist philosophy cuts the ground from any moral or political stand its adherents might take; for if historical facts are pure constructions and objectivity and truth have no place in history, the humanities, or the social sciences, then there is no particular reason to give any credence to the intellectual claims and moral or political arguments that postmodernists themselves may advance.

Among the greatest of privileges that biological evolution bestowed on human beings and the genes and brains they carry is the power of language and verbal communication in speech and writing. Language has endowed humans with a unique ability to cope with their environment and to understand the universe in which they live. Only the possession of language has made it possible for human beings to create and transmit culture and to possess a history rather than being doomed to the static condition of colonies of bees or termites that have persisted unchangingly for countless thousands of years. Although numerous philosophers in past centuries well understood that language is not only our supreme means of making sense of the world but can also be a cause of systematic error, misunderstanding, deception, and falsehood, not until quite recently did some thinkers come to regard it as separating us from the reality of things by confining us to a world that is constituted entirely by language. This last conclusion is one of the outcomes of the linguistic idealism of postmodernist theory. In the domain of history, the same theory asserts that the past is inaccessible to us as an object of knowledge and cannot be the referent of historical writings, which must refer solely to other writings, texts, and discourses. Arguing that historians have ignored the vital importance of language in their discipline, proponents of the narrativist thesis claim credit for demonstrating that language is not a transparent medium through which historians perceive the reality of the past, and that rhetorical tropes and literary genres prefigure and determine the character of any historiographical representation.[61] Contemporary narrativists, however, might be described as lost in the tropics of discourse, and their views give rhetoric a bad name; for this ancient discipline, honored in classical antiquity and the subject of famous works by Aristotle, Cicero, Tacitus, and Quintilian, was always understood to be dedicated to the art of persuasion and the cultivation of eloquence.[62] It was supposed to be a means of contributing to the dignity and power of history; classical and later authorities on rhetoric, not being constructionists, never entertained the thought that language and rhetoric made history indistinguishable from fictional tales, deprived historians of the actuality of the past, and engendered the explanations and interpretations they set forth.[63]

Whatever contributions may be attributed to postmodernism, it is not a tenable set of theories. Founded on a mistaken conception of the nature and function of language, it fails to accord with some of the strongest intuitions and convictions that historians bring to their work, and does not illuminate the nature of history as a discipline dedicated in principle to a true depiction and understanding of the human past. It is probable that its influence will increasingly fade, as seems to be already apparent. Any useful purposes it has served in compelling historians to think afresh about the nature of their inquiry, or in showing them new ways to read texts, or in helping to broaden the horizons of historiography through the inclusion of subjects and forms of life either neglected or ignored by earlier generations of scholars, are to its credit; but such purposes have no dependence on any particular postmodernist doctrines and may be pursued from other and quite different philosophical standpoints. As Kant once said of skepticism, it is not a dwelling place for the human mind; I believe that the same is equally true of postmodernism.

Notes

1 Peter Novick, *That Noble Dream: The "Objectivity Question" and the American Historical Profession* (Cambridge, Eng., 1988), contains full references to the writings of Beard and Becker and other works in the objectivity controversy. Thomas L. Haskell, in an interesting review-essay on Novick's book, "Objectivity Is Not Neutrality: Rhetoric vs. Practice in Peter Novick's *That Noble Dream*," *History and Theory* 29 (1990), 129–57, was one of the commentators who praised it for its objectivity and also defended the concept of objectivity against its critics.

2 Novick, *That Noble Dream*, 2. Robert F. Berkhofer, Jr., a historian favorable to postmodernism, confirms my view that the objectivity controversy did not cause the American historical profession to renounce objectivity as a goal; *Beyond the Great Story: History as Text and Discourse* (Cambridge, Mass., 1995), 205–7. Patrick Joyce has made a similar observation about the endurance of the ideal of objectivity among British historians in "The Return of History: Postmodernism and the Politics of Academic History in Britain," *Past and Present* (1998), 207–35.

3 One version of this attitude is perhaps exemplified in the following remark by the distinguished medievalist Brian Tierney: "Metahistory is a fascinating subject in its own right, considered as a branch of epistemology or linguistics, but it has little to do with the activity of the simple working historian."; *Religion, Law, and the Growth of Constitutional Thought 1150–1650* (Cambridge, Eng., 1982), vii–viii.

4 Keith Windschuttle, *The Killing of History: How Literary Critics and Social Theorists Are Murdering Our Past* (New York, 1997); Geoffrey Elton, *Return to Essentials: Some Reflections on the Present State of Historical Study* (Cambridge, Eng., 1991); Gertrude Himmelfarb, "Telling It As You Like It: Postmodernist History and the Flight from Fact," in *The Postmodern History Reader*, ed. Keith Jenkins (London, 1997); "Some Reflections on the New History," *American Historical Review* 94 (1989), 661–70; and see also some of her essays in *On Looking into the Abyss: Untimely Thoughts on Culture and Society* (New York, 1994). Among historians

who take a negative view of postmodernism are also a number of Marxist scholars who oppose it because of its incompatibility with historical materialism; for examples, see the essays by Bryan Palmer, "Critical Theory, Historical Materialism, and the Ostensible End of Marxism: The Poverty of Theory Revisited," and Neville Kirk, "History, Language, Ideas and Postmodernism: A Materialist View," in *The Postmodern History Reader*.

5 *A New Philosophy of History*, ed. Frank Ankersmit and Hans Kellner (Chicago, 1995); David D. Roberts, *Nothing But History* (Berkeley, 1995); Berkhofer, *Beyond the Great Story*.

6 John Toews, "Intellectual History after the Linguistic Turn: The Autonomy of Meaning and the Irreducibility of Experience," *American Historical Review* 92 (1987), 879–907; Gabrielle Spiegel, "History, Historicism, and the Social Logic of the Text in the Middle Ages," and "History and Postmodernism," in *The Postmodern History Reader*; Joyce Appleby, Lynn Hunt, and Margaret Jacob, *Telling the Truth about History* (New York, 1995), chapters 6–7; Georg Iggers, *Historiography in the Twentieth Century* (Hanover, N. H., 1997), chapters 8–10; Richard J. Evans, *In Defence of History* (London, 1997), 248. Evans's book is to be commended not only for its balance and a number of its discussions but for its helpful bibliography pertaining to historiography and postmodernism (284–301). For further comment on his view of the positive side of postmodernism, see below, 22.

7 See also the varying attitudes expressed in a forum devoted to the theory of history in the *American Historical Review* 94 (1989), which touched upon issues connected with postmodernism and included comments by David Harlan, David Hollinger, Allan Megill, and others. Similar evidence of the spectrum of opinion is also found in the forum on the book by Joyce Appleby *et al.*, *Telling the Truth about History*, in *History and Theory* 34 (1995), 321–39, with statements by Raymond Martin, Joan Wallach Scott, and Cushing Strout.

8 The only present-day American philosopher of note trained in the analytical tradition who shares some common ground with postmodernism appears to be Richard Rorty, although he describes himself as a neopragmatist.

9 Hilary Putnam, "A Half Century of Philosophy Viewed from Within," *Daedalus* 126 (1997), 201.

10 These philosophers all belong to the analytical tradition, and the problems they chiefly addressed in the philosophy of history, such as the nature of historical explanation, have since receded in favor of others that have been given prominence by "the linguistic turn"; for an interesting account of this development, see the essays by Richard T. Vann, "Turning Linguistic," and Arthur Danto, "The Decline and Fall of the Analytical Philosophy of History," in *A New Philosophy of History*. Both Danto and Louis Mink, another of the analytical philosophers who gave his attention to the philosophy of history, are perhaps partial exceptions to my comment in the text in that neither has rejected the stress on narrative which, as I shall point out later in this essay, has been a feature of postmodernist conceptions of history. Nevertheless, in his essay cited above, on pages 71, 74, and 78–9, Danto dismisses deconstructionism as a philosophical position and appears to accept the famous "covering-law" theory of historical explanation advanced by Carl Hempel, an eminent analytical philosopher.

11 The present writer has himself been a participant in this debate and has criticized postmodernism in an essay reprinted in *The Postmodern History Reader*; Perez Zagorin, "Historiography and Postmodernism: Reconsiderations," which originally appeared in *History and Theory* 29 (1990), 317–35.

12 Writings dealing with the nature of postmodernism are legion by now. For some useful guides to the concept, see the discussion by Steven Best and Douglas Kellner, *Postmodern Theory* (New York, 1991), chapter 1, and Allan Megill, "What Does the Term 'Postmodern' Mean?," *Annals of Scholarship* 6 (1989), 129–51.

13 Jean-François Lyotard, *The Postmodern Condition* [1979] (Manchester, Eng., 1984). Lyotard has elaborated his conception of the postmodern in a number of works discussed in Best and Kellner, *Postmodern Theory*, chapter 5.

14 See Lutz Niethammer, *Posthistoire: Has History Come to An End?* (London, 1992), who presents an account of this line of thinkers preoccupied with the thought that Western

civilization was giving way to a posthistorical or postmodern age of decline, mediocrity, and loss of creativity. In an interesting essay dealing with postmodernism and the end of history, Perry Anderson discusses the relevance of Cournot and Gehlen, as well as of Hegel; see Anderson, "The Ends of History," in *A Zone of Engagement* (London, 1992).

15 Raymond Aron, *The Opium of the Intellectuals* (New York, 1957).

16 See the remarks of Maurice Mandelbaum, *History, Man, and Reason* (Baltimore, 1971), 61, and Ranke's statements in the preface to his *Histories of the Latin and Germanic Nations 1494–1514* (1824) and from one of his fragments of the 1830s critical of philosophers of history who postulate a steady movement of the human race toward perfection, printed in Fritz Stern, *The Varieties of History* (Cleveland, 1956), 57, 58.

17 Karl R. Popper, *The Open Society and Its Enemies* [1943], 2 vols. (London, 1947), II, chapter 25.

18 Karl Löwith, *Meaning in History* (Chicago, 1949), 191.

19 This fact is acknowledged by Lyotard, who said of the postmodernist theory of language that "one does not at all break with metaphysics by putting language everywhere"; quoted from his *Discours, Figur* (Paris, 1971), 14, by Best and Kellner, *Postmodern Theory*, 149.

20 Ferdinand de Saussure, *Course in General Linguistics* (New York, 1959), 120. For the misreadings of Saussure by poststructuralists and literary theorists, and in particular by Derrida in developing his deconstructionist approach to language, see especially the careful analyses by Raymond Tallis, *Not Saussure* (London, 1988), chapter 6, and the same author's letter to the *Times Literary Supplement* (7 November 1997), 19; John Ellis, *Against Deconstruction* (Princeton, 1989), chapter 2; Leonard Jackson, *The Poverty of Structuralism* (London, 1991), chapters 1, 3, 5–6.

21 Spiegel, "History, Historicism, and the Social Logic of the Text in the Middle Ages," in *The Postmodern History Reader*, 181.

22 Review in the *Times Literary Supplement* (31 October 1997), 10; and see also the hopelessly muddled account of Saussure by Appleby and her co-authors in *Telling the Truth about History*, 214–15, which concludes that the Swiss linguist made it possible to argue that "reality is always shrouded by language."

23 Jane Caplan, "Postmodernism, Poststructuralism, and Deconstruction: Notes for Historians," *Central European History* 22 (1989), 265.

24 See Michel Foucault, *Power/Knowledge: Selected Interviews and Other Writings 1972–1977*, ed. Colin Gordon (Brighton, Eng., 1980).

25 For examples of such criticism, see John Searle, "Reiterating the Differences: A Reply to Derrida," *Glyph* (1977), 198–208; "The Word Turned Upside Down," *New York Review of Books* (27 October 1983), 74–79; "Literary Theory and Its Discontents," *New Literary History*. 25 (1994), 637–67; Tallis, *Not Saussure*; Jackson, *Poverty of Structuralism*; Ellis, *Against Deconstruction*; Jenny Teichman, "Deconstruction and Aerodynamics," *Philosophy* 68 (1993), 53–62; E. R. Davey, " 'The Words Which We Are Using Do Not Satisfy Me ... ' Interpreting Derrida: A Dissenting View," *Journal of European Studies* 27 (1997), 1–32.

26 See the essay by M. H. Abrams, "The Transformation of English Studies: 1930–95," *Daedalus* 126 (1997), 105–31.

27 Bernard Bailyn, *On the Teaching and Writing of History* (Hanover, N. H., 1994), 8. As a view similar to Bailyn's and still, I think, pretty largely representative of the historical profession, it is worth adding the avowal of A. Brunt, a sophisticated scholar and one of the foremost British historians of ancient Greece and Rome, that "It seems to me beyond question that the aim of the historian is to discover 'how things really were', even if he recognizes that he can never achieve complete success."; *The Fall of the Roman Republic and Related Essays* (Oxford, 1988), endnote on historical facts and evidence, 508.

28 Thomas L. Haskell, *Objectivity Is Not Neutrality* (Baltimore, 1998), 8, 9.

29 Alan Spitzer, *Historical Truth and Lies about the Past* (Chapel Hill, 1996), chapter 3. In discussing the de Man case, Spitzer shows, as other writers have also done, the way in which postmodernist defenders of de Man like Derrida and others contradicted their own theoretical principles by using arguments appealing to historical evidence, textual meaning, factuality, and truth.

30 Roger Chartier, "History between Narrative and Knowledge," in *On the Edge of the Cliff: History, Language, and Practices* (Baltimore, 1997), 26, 27; there are numerous other passages in this and some of the other essays in this collection to the same effect. Chartier also takes care to note (19–20) that "experience is not reducible to discourse," and to caution against treating everything as a text, because there are many practices that bear no resemblance to discursive strategies.

31 Jenkins takes this argument from Arthur Danto's *Analytical Philosophy of History* (Cambridge, Eng., 1965), 218–19, but misunderstands it. What Danto says there is not that a theory alone can decide what is to be taken as a fact, but that a phenomenon must first be placed under some description before it can be explained, a very different matter.

32 In an essay critical of John Dewey's pragmatist and presentist approach to historical inquiry, the philosopher and historian of ideas A. O. Lovejoy gave a convincing account of the notion of the study of the past for its own sake or in its own terms, and of the educative function of such a study; see his "Present Standpoints and Past History," reprinted in *The Philosophy of History in Our Time*, ed. Hans Meyerhoff (New York, 1950).

33 Keith Jenkins, "Introduction: On Being Open about Our Closures," in *The Postmodern History Reader*, 3, 6, 14, 15, 16, 17.

34 Robert F. Berkhofer, Jr., "The Challenge of Poetics to (Normal) Historical Practice," in *The Postmodern History Reader*, 152; some of the material in the essay is taken from Berkhofer's *Beyond the Great Story*, which makes the same argument against the supposed mystification perpetrated by the historian's text in its pretense of godlike omniscience and its aspiration to power over readers (see 38, 64, 68, 229).

35 Roberts, *Nothing But History*, 6, and see also 209.

36 Elizabeth Ermarth, "Sequel to History," in *The Postmodern History Reader*, 57 and passim.

37 Berkhofer, *Beyond the Great Story*, 247.

38 Roland Barthes, "The Discourse of History," in *The Postmodern History Reader*, 121–22.

39 Berkhofer, *Beyond the Great Story*, 9.

40 Berkhofer, "The Challenge of Poetics to (Normal) Historical Practice," in *The Postmodern History Reader*, 149–50. This same argument is repeated in the author's *Beyond the Great Story* in chapter 3, "Historical Representation and Truthfulness," 63–4.

41 Bertrand Russell, *My Philosophical Development* (New York, 1959), 148. See Russell's similar remark on the relation of language to "something which is not verbal, for the sake of which … words … were invented. The purpose of words, though philosophers seem to forget this simple fact, is to deal with matters other than words. … "; *An Inquiry into Meaning and Truth* (London, 1940), 140–41, quoted by Israel Scheffler, "Epistemology of Objectivity," in *Starmaking: Realism, Anti-Realism, and Irrealism*, ed. Peter J. McCormick (Cambridge, Mass., 1996) 55. This last comment, although cited as a criticism of the logical positivist philosopher Otto Neurath, applies equally to the postmodernist theory of language.

42 I take the underlying thesis of realism to consist in the claim that the universe, the world, objects, events, and so on exist independently of our representations of them in thought and language. Searle, for example, defends this position as "external realism"; John Searle, "Does the Real World Exist," in *Realism, Antirealism and Epistemology*, ed. Christopher B. Kulp (Lanham, Md., 1997). Alston, on the other hand, defends a realist conception of truth according to which a statement (proposition, belief, etc.) is true if and only if what the statement says is actually the case; William B. Alston, *A Realist Conception of Truth* (Ithaca, N.Y., 1996). Both of these positions are of course consistent with each other and each would seem to imply a correspondence theory of truth.

43 William H. Dray's essay, "On the Nature and Role of Narrative in History," in his book, *On History and Philosophers of History* (Leiden, 1989), contains a helpful review of the discussion of historical narrative by analytical philosophers of history, including W. B. Gallie, Morton White, Arthur Danto, and Louis Mink.

44 Hayden White, *Metahistory: The Historical Imagination in Nineteenth-Century Europe* (Baltimore, 1973); *Tropics of Discourse: Essays in Cultural Criticism* (Baltimore, 1978); *The Content of the Form: Narrative Discourse and Historical Representation* (Baltimore, 1987).

45 Hayden White, "Narrative in Contemporary Historical Theory," in *The Content of the Form*, 44.
46 Hayden White, " 'Figuring the Nature of the Times Deceased': Literary Theory and Historical Writing," in *The Future of Literary Theory*, ed. Ralph Cohen (London, 1989), 27.
47 Hayden White, "Historical Emplotment and the Problem of Truth," in *The Postmodern History Reader*, 392.
48 Hayden White, "The Politics of Historical Interpretation: Discipline and De-sublimation," in *The Politics of Interpretation*, ed. W. J. T. Mitchell (Chicago, 1983), 136.
49 White, " 'Figuring the Nature of the Times Deceased'," 34–5.
50 William Dray, "Narrative and Historical Realism," in *On History and Philosophers of History* (Leiden, 1989), 161.
51 See the careful discussion of White's views in Noël Carroll, "Interpretation, History, and Narrative," *Monist* 73 (1990), 134–66, and Dray, "Narrative and Historical Realism," and Dray's review of White's *The Content of the Form* in *History and Theory* 27 (1988), 282–7. Among his comments in this review is that White's central position is "frustratingly underargued," and that when his constructionist thesis is put in question, he lets "rhetoric rather than logical argument assume too much of the burden of its defense" (283). Carroll's conclusion, following his exposure of the fallacies and gaps of reasoning in White's narrativism, should also be noted: "his reduction of all narrative to the status of fiction seems a desperate and inevitably self-defeating way in which to grant the literary dimension of historiography its due" (161–2).
52 Roger Chartier, "Four Questions for Hayden White," in *On the Edge of the Cliff*, 35.
53 Bailyn, *On the Teaching and Writing of History*, 72.
54 See Saul Friedländer, "Probing the Limits of Representation" and Berel Lang, "Is It Possible To Misrepresent the Holocaust?" in *The Postmodern History Reader*. (The Lang article was originally published in *History and Theory* 34 [1995], 84–9.)
55 Roger Chartier, "Four Questions for Hayden White," in *On the Edge of the Cliff*, 36–7.
56 David Carr, *Time, Narrative, and History* (Bloomington, Ind., 1986), has sought to show that narrative structure is a genuine feature of all human experience rather than a construction retrospectively imposed; see the interesting discussion of his work in Dray, "Narrative and Historical Realism," in *On History and Philosophers of History*, 134–56.
57 Dray's essay "Narrative and Historical Realism" presents an acute critique of the constructionist conception of narrative and argues for the view that narrative structures in works of history have their basis in the events themselves.
58 Evans, *In Defence of History*, 248.
59 Haskell, *Objectivity Is Not Neutrality*, 8, 9.
60 An article by James Engell and Anthony Dangerfield, who are both academics in the fields of English and comparative literature, documents on the basis of extensive data the very serious decline of the humanities in the universities since 1970 as measured by the drop in degrees awarded, disparity in faculty salaries, lower quality of students, diminished funding, and other criteria; see their "The Market-model University: Humanities in the Age of Money," *Harvard Magazine* 100, no. 5 (1998), 48–55, 111.
61 See Hans Kellner's introduction to *A New Philosophy of History*.
62 Although I say that rhetoric was a discipline honored in antiquity, it is also true that since Plato's day there has been an intermittent quarrel between philosophy and rhetoric. In dialogues such as his *Phaedrus* and *Gorgias*, Plato condemned rhetoric as a corrupt art that cared nothing for truth, and the same indictment has been echoed by many later philosophers; see Brian Vickers, *In Defence of Rhetoric* (Oxford, 1988), chapter 2 and passim, and Perez Zagorin, *Francis Bacon* (Princeton, 1998), 177–8.
63 Vickers, chapter 9, notes some of the misunderstandings and misuse of classical rhetoric in contemporary literary theory, deconstructionism, and narrativism. On the relationship between rhetoric and the practice of history among ancient historians such as Tacitus and theorists of history such as Cicero, see the studies by T. Wiseman, *Clio's Cosmetics* (Leicester, Eng., 1979), and A. J. Woodman, *Rhetoric in Classical Historiography* (London, 1978). Both

scholars argue that because Greco-Roman writers regarded historiography primarily as a literary genre in which rhetoric played a great part, they held a different view of historical truth than have the moderns; accordingly, they attached less importance to truth and did not ban the use of fictional invention. A. Brunt takes an opposite position in "Cicero and Historiography," *Studies in Greek History and Thought* (Oxford, 1993), which maintains that the role of rhetoric in ancient historiography did not deflect either historians or Cicero in his observations on history from considering truth as the supreme requirement of historiography; see also Brunt's essay, "Introduction to Thucydides," in the same volume.

5 A postmodern reply to Perez Zagorin

I

The understanding Perez Zagorin has of postmodernism and history – which he correctly thinks is typical of that held by most of his professional colleagues – is actually a misreading which deserves to be closely examined. I shall show that actually reading postmodernism and history "correctly" affords Zagorin and those who might agree with him even less comfort than reading it "wrong." Reading things "right" (and in the context of helping insure that despite the failure of the first experiment of the emancipatory project of modernity, the "discourse of emancipation" is not forgotten) suggests that the end of history would be "a good thing." Of course, trying to reach this upbeat conclusion in favor *not* of postmodern history but of a postmodernism *sans histoire* when starting from a critique of this whole phenomenon involves risks. Initially, at least, it allows Zagorin to set the agenda, thus, for example, possibly pushing me into too defensive a stance. But as my arguments develop I hope to break free from too myopic an encounter with Zagorin's obsessions as I move towards that positive reading of postmodernism for which I shall be striving.

II

According to Zagorin, then, postmodernism (and postmodern history) is, in its (allegedly) antirealist, antireferential, linguistic idealism, committed to a view that reality – and the past as once-reality – is a self-referencing text, a linguistic artefact scarcely distinguishable from fiction. Unable or not bothering to establish an ontologically independent reality "out there," it leads to a dangerous, unstoppable hyper-relativism and/or nihilism, with such severe ontological, epistemological, methodological, and ethical consequences ("anything goes") that a strong critique of it is urgently required. For Zagorin this involves not just a defense of historical knowledge and the integrity and practices of the professionals who produce it (for this could be construed as too narrowly self-serving) but also, casting the net of legitimation wider, of Reason, of Ethics, of Culture and, in the final analysis, even of Civilization itself. Zagorin rehearses this general position throughout his article, leaving little doubt as to what he "intends" to say.

Thus, on page seven, Zagorin announces that, leaving aside the broader meanings and significance of the postmodernism he has been discussing until that point (and to which I shall attend later), and viewing more narrowly its "specific philosophical sense and in its bearing upon historical knowledge," its two principal features "may be said to be its conception of language and its rejection of realism." For Zagorin, postmodernism is "a philosophy of linguistic idealism," a metaphysics which claims there is "no extra-linguistic reality independent of our representations of it in language or discourse." Such language/discourse is thus constituted by self-referencing sign-systems caught in an incestuous "process of signification that never arrives at stable meaning."[1] Consequently, postmodernism denies the ability of language/discourse to refer to an independent world of "facts and things and the determinacy or decidability of textual meaning." Additionally, it categorically "dismisses the possibility of objective knowledge and truth as goals of inquiry," a dismissal pointing to "the dangers in the extreme relativism that postmodernist philosophy represents."[2] Its relativism entails an attitude towards narrative according to which, bereft of "a real referent," the fictional stories "invented by writers and the narratives fashioned by historians" do not differ in any "essential respect." Accordingly, opposing this, Zagorin aligns himself with such "realist" and "proper" philosophers as Harré, Bhaskar, Putnam, Searle, and Nagel, all of whom defend "some version of realism either in regard to knowledge and truth or in an ontic sense as the affirmation that the world, material objects, natural phenomena, and so on, exist independently of mind or language."[3] He also finds allies in such "proper" historians as Himmelfarb, Evans, and Chartier. Chartier, despite sometimes toying with the "linguistic turn," still insists history must be retained as a discipline believing in the "confirmable, verifiable knowledge" of a "past reality" because "only on the basis of a 'critical realism' and a striving for truth" can it hold out against those postmodern perversions which would replace objective knowledge with "mythical reconstructions of the past governed by the needs of communities, imagined or real, national or not, that create or accept historical narratives to suit their desires and expectations."[4] Here Zagorin espies perhaps the greatest threat his notion of postmodern skepticism and relativism pose, namely, that they render history "incapable of performing its vital and ever more necessary intellectual function in the schools, universities, and the wider culture of today's world," in that it cuts "the ground from any moral or political stand" both its opponents and – ironically observes Zagorin – its adherents might take. For if "historical facts are pure constructions and objectivity and truth have no place in history … then there is no particular reason to give any credence to the intellectual claims and moral or political arguments that postmodernists themselves may advance."[5] Here postmodernists are apparently hoist on their own petard, stupidly committing – a routine "modernist" accusation this – a performative contradiction.

Now, can these heavy charges of antirealism, antireferentiality, linguistic idealism and hapless relativism, and so on, be made to stick in the way Zagorin puts them? Or can they be redescribed, nuanced, and thus understood in ways which, while straightening out a few matters, do not allow such rearticulations to be recuperated by a then reinforced modernist historiography but instead render the situation much more critical than Zagorin supposes? Obviously my answer – as already announced in my opening remarks – is "yes," and it is this answer that I now begin to develop in the following sections.

III

Despite Zagorin's repeated assertions to the contrary, so far as I know, not a single "postmodernist" – not Foucault nor Derrida nor Baudrillard nor Lyotard nor Rorty nor Ankersmit nor Butler nor Ermarth nor White, most of whom figure in Zagorin's account – is actually an antirealist. Indeed, this is a ridiculous accusation. For no postmodernist disagrees with the crucial distinction Richard Rorty so representatively draws between "the world" as being "out there" and our human appropriations of it which are not, between the claim that the actual/social world is out there in all its stubborn, brute actuality, and the claim that all the meanings and significances and truths it "can be said to have" are "in here," in our languages. As Rorty puts it:

> We need to make a distinction between the claim that the world is out there and the claim that truth is out there. To say that the world is out there, that it is not our creation, is to say, with common sense, that most things in space and time are the effects of causes which do not include human mental states. To say that truth is not out there is simply to say that where there are no sentences there is no truth … truth cannot be out there – cannot exist independently of the human mind – because sentences cannot so exist – or be out there. The world is out there, but descriptions of the world are not. Only descriptions of the world can be true or false … the world can, once we have programmed ourselves with a language, cause us to hold beliefs. But it cannot propose a language [or beliefs] for us to speak.[6]

Not a hint of antirealism as Zagorin has construed it is present here nor, we might note in passing, any trace of a linguistic idealism which might be defined in ways denying the (ontic) actuality of the world – or world's past. Rorty's "commonsense" assumption – one postmodernists pragmatically share – is that the world exists independent of, and is irreducible to, human mental states. Of course it is a trivial truth (and note in passing that Rorty sees no problem in using the term "truth" to refer to the actuality of things once put under and made "real" relative to descriptions which embody their own and sometimes comparable modes of verification, and so forth) that, if no "human mental states" existed then we would not be able to say that the world exists independent of them. But the assumption Rorty and postmodernists make is that we do exist and do so as the sorts of beings we think we are (complete with what we choose to call our central nervous system), happily agreeing that the world in all its actuality – including in that actuality previous and current human institutions – is out there, and that it is to *that* to which we *refer* through the mediations of our various linguistic/discursive *practices*. Thus, with regard to *referentiality* it can be confidently said that postmodernists willingly accept that discourses refer to an ontic actuality. They go on to hold, "commonsensically," that for this actuality to be meaningful – to be made real by and for us – then it becomes so through the only medium we have to make this happen, namely, by the creation of "reality-effects" performatively constituted through various symbolic codes.

For it is another "trivial" (and tautological) truth – but one with massive ramifications – that in a culture nothing cultural "is of a natural kind." Obviously anything to be made meaningful and productive for us – to have the aura of reality and thus value conferred on it – has to be brought within our varying (and thus "historically relative") productivist economies/logics, economies which, to be communicable, are necessarily coded, necessarily "signed." Consequently, to live *knowingly* in a culture just is to have residence within discursive practices; to be "literally" fabricated and performatively constituted and reconstituted within imaginaries which then produce what passes for "reality" without our knowing if our realisms (our simulacra) ever *correspond* to the way that that "actuality" would, if only it could, discourse about itself. For we can never know that. We can never compare our beliefs with things that are not beliefs to see if they are somehow "identical." This is not to say – and again note that no postmodernist ever says it – that there is nothing out there to hold beliefs about, but to say, again with Rorty, that the *causal* independence of some bit of "stuff" – say gold or a text – from the inquiring chemist or critic does not mean that they can perform the (impossible) feat of stripping their object bare of human concerns, see it as it is "in itself," and then compare the extent to which beliefs measure up to it. No; postmodernists accept the *causal* stubbornness of the gold or text. But they think this should not be confused with an *intentional* stubbornness, an insistence on being described in a certain way, its own way. For, as Rorty concludes, "the only way to get a non-institutional fact [or description] would be to find a language for describing an object which was as little ours, and as much the object's own, as the object's causal powers," and this (the ultimate objectivity) eludes us.[7]

Yet, if postmodernists cannot be categorized along Zagorin's lines as antirealists, antireferentialists, and naive linguistic idealists, then what are they? That is to say, if postmodernists hold the general line I have been describing, then why on earth do Zagorin and so many other historians still routinely assume (it has become a sort of *doxa*) that they are precisely antirealists and all the rest? Over the last paragraph or so I have already been starting to answer this question, which is that what makes postmodernists seem to be what they clearly are not is that, while none of them are antirealists, they are *all* antirepresentationalists.

What exactly does "antirepresentationalist" mean here? Again, so succinct is Rorty's articulation of it that it is economical to stay with him for a few more paragraphs.

As a card-carrying antirepresentationalist, Rorty sees it as his task to make a lot of the distinction between representationalism and antirepresentationalism because he thinks the old dichotomy between realism and antirealism only makes sense (and then as nonsense) *within* representationalism, a paradigm he thinks we should have abandoned years ago.[8] He believes we should have developed beyond the position held by most realists – including Zagorin – who still consider it useful to think of mind or language as representing "reality" and who then get upset when it becomes ultimately impossible to determine precisely where and when, within this construal, "representations of reality end and reality begins – and vice-versa." For this belief gives rise to unproductive disagreements between realists and antirealists, skeptics and antiskeptics ("Representationalists typically think that controversies between sceptics and antisceptics are fruitful and interesting. Antirepresentationalists typically think both sets of controversies pointless."[9]) Accordingly, Rorty thinks we should escape from these useless passions by all becoming antirepresentationalists; by viewing knowledge not as a matter of getting reality right but of acquiring pragmatic habits allowing us to *cope* with the contingencies of "our worded world." Rorty again:

> The antirepresentationalist is quite willing to grant that our language, like our bodies, has been shaped by the environment we live in. Indeed, he or she insists on this point – the point that our minds or our language could not (as the representationalist sceptic fears) be "out of touch with reality" any more than our bodies could. What he or she denies is that it is explanatorily useful to pick and choose among the contents of our minds or our language and say that this or that item "corresponds to" or "represents" the environment in the way some other item does not. On an antirepresentationalist view, it is one thing to say … an ability to use the word "atom" as physicists do, is useful for coping with the environment. It is another thing to explain this utility by reference to representationalist notions such as the notion that the reality referred to by "quark" was "determinate" before the word "quark" came along [or that] the reason why physicists have come to use "atom" … is that there really are atoms out there which have caused themselves to be represented … caused us to have words which refer to them. Antirepresentationalists think that attempt hopeless. They see no way to explain what "determinate" [or "cause"] means in such a context except by chanting one of a number of equally baffling words … so antirepresentationalists think [the idea] that we use "atom" as we do and that atomic physics works because atoms are

as they are is no more enlightening than "opium puts people to sleep because of its dormative power."[10]

Agreeing with Wittgenstein, Rorty thus suggests we recognize that questions that we should have to "climb out of our own minds to answer" should not be asked. Wittgenstein was suggesting that both realism *and* idealism share representationalist presuppositions "we would be better off dropping" – which is precisely what postmodernists have done and Zagorin hasn't.

Postmodernists, then, are happy to acknowledge both an "actuality" out there and that there is no way to appropriate it without the use of some self-referencing word like "actuality" to do it, happy to acknowledge that there is no way to get out of our readings and writings, out of our discourses, out of our textuality. Consequently, at this point I think we can begin to accept, quite matter-of-factly, that there is nothing *meaningful* "outside of our texts."

Now, this reference to there being "nothing outside of the text" announces the arrival of Derrida, a Derrida who, while mentioned only fleetingly by Zagorin, stands behind so many of his worst fears. I therefore want to look at Derrida in some (albeit very basic) "detail" because Zagorin's hostile misunderstanding of him is so typical, and because a "properly" understood Derrida is even less comfort to him than the straw man he imagines. But before doing this it might be useful briefly to underline and thus stress how the antirepresentationalism of postmodernists is far more disturbing for Zagorin than the "antirealist" position he thinks they hold and which "is bad enough."

The point is simply this. Within the representationalist paradigm Zagorin inhabits (his "reality") there at least seems a chance that "realism" could just somehow be right, that an objective correspondence between word and world could be somehow achieved at increasingly synoptic levels, skepticism and relativism refuted, and truth – "right side up and gotten plain" – *found.* Within Zagorin's representationalism the hope still remains that, while the meanings of the world and world's past have, admittedly, to be expressed symbolically, this communicative necessity need not imply that such symbols cannot "objectively reflect" reality. The extra-discursive, it hopes, can somehow prevent those endless linguistic mediations which always threaten to rhetorically substitute – as rhetoric does – its "own forms for the forms of reality." This holds out the possibility of "factual facts," "objective objects," "true truths" and – for this is the ultimate desire of realists of all stripes – the establishment of some sort of logical entailment from fact to value so as to banish the dreaded moral relativism.

Antirepresentationalism, however, holds out no such hopes; it is playing no such game. Antirepresentationalism insists that, for example, while our words refer, insofar as they generate meaning, they can only ever refer *indirectly* – via innumerable mediations – to an actuality that always remains unavailable in its sublimity, its otherness, its radical alterity, its excess. In short, as Hayden White has cogently put it: "There is no such thing as one correct way of speaking and representing the world because language is arbitrary in its relation to the world it speaks about"; everything can be redescribed.[11] In this antirepresentationalist paradigm the interesting question is thus no longer the modernist one – "why is there something rather than nothing?" but the postmodern version, "why is there nothing rather than something?" a question making it clear that we humans will have to continue to do what we have always had to do – to make up, as Baudrillard has put it, "something out of nothing" – it's the story of our lives![12]

Now, it seems to me that there is such an element of obviousness about the antirepresentationalist position just described that its "commonsense" portrayal here maybe makes it appear inconsequential and non-radical: is that what all the fuss is about? And in a way it is non-radical, save for the fact that what, at the moment, makes it seem so dangerously subversive for the likes of Zagorin (and for the sort of "representative" practice that operates on his sort of preferences) is their continued commitment to representationalism. Consequently, insofar as representationalism remains the dominant ontological and epistemological paradigm, postmodern antirepresentationalism will be read as an enormously critical threat and not, as postmodernists read it, as having an enormous liberating potential – a liberation precisely from representationalism.

For postmodernists accept a postmodern future without any signs of the angstridden, doom-laden, panicky consciousness Zagorin *et al.* perhaps understandably display, given that we have come to the end of *their* "representationalist" modernity and the end of the elements constituting it – like *their* history. Postmodernists, as the much and undeservedly maligned Elizabeth Ermarth puts it,

> no longer require an "objective" world to guarantee – like some sort of bank for intersubjective transactions – the relations between one consciousness and another, or to guarantee an identity between illusions. There is only subjectivity. There are only illusions. And every illusion, because it has no permanently objectifying frame, constitutes reality and hence is totally "objective" for its duration. The postmodern event [thus] comes in negotiating the transitions from one moment to another.[13]

Again this is not to say – and no postmodernist says it – that individuals are so "contingent" that there is a total lack of structure allowing anybody to do anything with impunity. Rather, what is meant by the contingency of the performative "person" and the moral/political "undecidable decisions" they make, is that opportunities for self-ness and otherness occur at the limits of an always partially deconstructed "context" wherein that "self" can ultimately appeal only to *its* self as the sole semantic source. And again this is not seen as a problem. For why, asks Ermarth's Robbe-Grillet, should this

> be grounds for pessimism? Is it so distressing to learn that one's own view is only one's own view, or that every project is an invention? Obviously I

> am concerned, in any case, only with the world as my point of view orientates it: I shall never know any other. The relative subjectivity of my sense of sight serves me precisely to define my situation in the world. I simply keep myself from helping to make this situation a servitude.[14]

"I simply keep myself from helping to make this situation a servitude." Here, I think we have an encapsulation of not only Robbe-Grillet's and Ermarth's position, but Derrida's too. Despite Zagorin's attempt to personify Derrida as a confused charlatan, so as to be able, not least, to similarly paint postmodern fellow-travelers, neither he nor they are that. So what, basically, is Derrida saying about Zagorin's concerns that so annoys him and how do they actually once again add up to a position worse than he thinks? This basic Derrida might be put as follows.

IV

If a word was meaningful "in and for itself" it would be a transcendental signifier, a signifier embodying full presence/self identity. But we have no access to a signifier like that. Consequently, a signifier necessarily gets its meaning *relative* to other signifiers; it always needs *supplementing* by another signifier (or set of signifiers) to become a concept – a signified. But because the second signifier(s) which supplements the first and on which the first relies (so that its meaning is derived from what it is not – it is thus dependent on "the other") is not entailed, then the meaning that is always potentially realizable when signifiers are joined is a contingent and thus ultimately an arbitrary and logically unstable one. For there is no "logical" guarantee that, "next time," the supplement "which comes" will be the same as that which arrived "last time" (things are always getting lost in the post ...) so that future meanings are always logically open. Moreover, given that meanings (signifieds) are always embedded in more or less extensive chains of signification (genres of discourse/discursive practices) themselves similarly constituted, so the meanings of words via chains of signification cannot be relied upon to be arranged in the same way in what are always different (and non-suturable) contexts: history never repeats itself.[15] All meanings are constituted not by self-sufficient signs, then, but always through the phenomenon of *différance*, the term *différance* signaling that, in Derrida's usage, the second, qualifying signifier differs both *spatially* from the first (it doesn't occupy the same syntagmatic location) and *temporally* (in that it – and meaning – always come late, is never simultaneous) and so *deferred*. It is this space–time structure that is, for Derrida, irreducible: you can never get meaning "into the world" without *différance* operating.

Yet if *différance* is the "condition of possibility" for meaning-making, this condition is also – *simultaneously* – the condition that ensures permanent/absolute meanings are impossible. Accordingly, *différance* being at once both the "logical" condition of the possibility of meaning and the "logical" impossibility of fixity, this construction and deconstruction of meaning obeys (for Derrida is no enemy of "logic") the same "logic." Consequently, for Derrida this interminable play of differences that is both constitutive and destructive of meaning simply is *différance*. This is why, for him, *différance* is neither a word nor a concept but rather the necessary condition, the playing movement constitutive of words and conceptuality themselves: there is no meaning outside of, or before, semiological *différance*. Derrida thus calls the resultant sign a *trace*, in that, for a meaning to be "present" in it, it must be related to something absent, a trace of "the other's" meaning, so that meanings are (signs are) the result of a "differential network of traces." It is (to introduce the further crucial element of Derrida's lexicon) this time–space structure of *différance* through traces that he terms *archi-writing* or *writing in general*, a structure within which full presence is only ever an effect. There are thus no origins (and thus no teleologies) here, only traces of traces ("The supplement is always the supplement of a supplement. 'One wishes to go back from the supplement to the source ... [but] one must recognise that there is a supplement always already at the source.' Language, text and writing are [thus] constituted by ... a network of traces and referents, references to other references, a general referability without single origin or destination."[16]) Here all teleologies, immanencies, essences, substantive metanarratives and dialectical closures – all the onto-theologies – drop out of the frame.

Now it is this extended concept of *archi-writing* which (as the conditions of possibility for meaning entering the world) thus constitutes for Derrida a new science of writing (grammatology) and within which his statement *Il n'y a pas de hors texte* (or, better still, *Il n'y a pas de hors contexte*) has to be understood as a "logical" outcome. For when Derrida uses the phrase "there is nothing outside of the text," the text he is referring to is *this* text – *le texte en général*.[17]

Accordingly, it is very clearly *this* notion of the "general text" which allows Derrida to arrive without fuss at his already noted, infamous conclusion that, given that all meaning is necessarily within this extended notion of the general text, then there is, by virtue of logic and definition, nothing meaningful outside it.

Now, I have already noted that Zagorin says that Derrida and postmodernists think that it is language that constitutes meaning and thus what passes for us humans as "reality." We can now see how this is – but now in the above context – "true." Zagorin also says that meaning is made, for postmodernists, out of a self-referential sign system (in this context the *general text*) and this is also – in the above context – true. But then Zagorin goes on to add that postmodernists must therefore deny any extra-discursive reality (that is, actuality) independent of such discourses ("linguistic idealism") to which language refers – which is false. In fact, what Derrida is arguing for is not any sort of linguistic idealism at all, but rather and very precisely a form of *linguistic materialism*, in that it is this "grounding" of meaning in actual contexts that ensures that any repetition of meaning is always different because "history doesn't repeat itself" – and hence Derrida's term for this: *iterability*.

Derrida's "grammatology" is thus materialist through and through. But so typical is Zagorin's fallacious inference – and so widespread is the taking of the term "text" literally and empirically (as if it was equivalent to a book, say, instead of *le texte en général*) that a further underlining of what Derrida means vis-à-vis his statement "there is nothing outside of the text" with regard to referentiality as Zagorin conceives it is in order to squash any remaining mistakes once and for all.

To say it as categorically as possible: Derrida *never* denies that signs/words refer to "things" outside of language. When he says there is nothing outside of the text he obviously does not mean that the extra-discursive does not exist nor is he asserting – as Richard Evans (praised by Zagorin) has accused Derrida of asserting – that concentration camps are literally texts ("the insistence that all history is discourse diverts attention from the real lives and sufferings of people in the past. Auschwitz is not a text. The gas chambers were not a discourse. It trivializes mass murder to see it as a text."[18]) This is not only an incredibly offensive remark to a Jew who has little reason to forget the death camps, but also mind-blowingly "wrong." As we have seen, Derrida's notion of the general text in no way implies that the world is some sort of vast library; deconstruction is not bibliophilia. Rather – as Critchley has noted – text *qua* text/context is *always* glossed by Derrida to consist of the entire "real-history-of-the-world." It does not deny or suspend reference to history, to the world, to actuality, but simply insists that these things appear in meaning *not* as an immediate experience of presence but as "a network of differentially … signifying traces", of experience as a "ceaseless movement of interpretation within a limitless context."[19] As Derrida himself calmly says:

> It is totally false to suggest that deconstruction is a suspension of reference … I never cease to be surprised by critics who see my work as a declaration that there is nothing beyond language … [yet] every week I receive critical commentaries which operate on the assumption that what they call "post-structuralism" … amounts to saying that there is nothing beyond language … and other stupidities of that sort.[20]

What Derrida means by there being "nothing outside of the text/context" is glossed by him thus:

> What I call "text" implies all the structures called "real," "economic," "historical," "socio-institutional," in short all possible referents … "there is nothing outside of the text" … does not mean that all referents are suspended, denied, or enclosed in a book, as people have claimed, or have been naive enough to believe and to have accused me of believing. But it does mean that every referent and all reality has the structure of a *différantial* trace … and that one cannot refer to this "real" except in an interpretive experience. The latter neither yields meaning nor assumes it except in a movement of *différantial* referring. That's all.[21]

Let's hope this "that's all" is enough for Zagorin. And let me add immediately that, *contra* another of Zagorin's misunderstandings, Derrida never says that words and discourses are not *stabilized* in material practices. For Derrida insists that there is a crucial distinction – unnoticed by Zagorin – between the *logic* of *différance* (which indeed ensures no meaning can be permanently stabilized) and the *relative* stabilizations of discourse by power relations. These relative stabilizations (by virtue of the operation of "binary oppositions," and so forth) make his deconstruction of such "verticals of authority" necessary in the name of emancipations and democracies "to come," for they legitimate the hierarchical power relationships which infuse them with life. As Derrida says:

> [What] a deconstructive point of view tries to show, is that since conventions, institutions and consensus are stabilizations (sometimes stabilizations of great duration, sometimes micro-stabilizations) ... this means that they are stabilizations of something essentially unstable and chaotic. Thus, it becomes necessary to stabilize precisely because stability is not natural; it is because there is instability that stabilization becomes necessary. Now, this chaos and instability ... is at once naturally the worst against which we struggle with laws, rules, conventions, politics and provisional hegemony, but at the same time it is a chance, a chance to change, to destabilize. If there were continual stability, there would be no need for politics, and it is to the extent that stability is not natural, essential or substantial, that politics exists and ethics is possible. Chaos is at once a risk and a chance, and it is here that the possible and the impossible cross each other.[22]

Stabilizations – even those of such duration that they give the illusion of being permanent and absolute ("beyond the reach of time and chance") – are thus always contingent and relative to context. The cause of the opposite "illusion" is their more or less "permanent" articulation of the interests of various "regimes of truth," regimes of power – regimes, as the above passage suggests, Derrida hopes deconstruction will subvert in the interests of the left. For while Derrida and postmodernists know, *pace* Zagorin, that deconstruction is logically deconstructive of all and every position based as they all are on the indestructible logic of *différance*, as a self-proclaimed "man of the left" he nevertheless hopes that deconstruction will

> serve to politicize or repoliticize the left with regard to positions which are not simply academic. I hope – and if I can continue to contribute a little to this I will be very content – that the political left in universities in the United States, France and elsewhere, will gain politically by employing deconstruction ... Deconstruction is hyper-politicising in following paths and codes which are clearly not traditional ... that is, it permits us to think the political and think the democratic by granting us the space [to do so].[23]

Derrida's political task – his ungroundable choice – is thus to wed the logic of *différance*/deconstruction to his emancipatory desires, to be openly political not least in the portals of the oft-denied but the in fact equally political academia of contemporary social formations. How does Derrida arrange this in ways that are again worse for Zagorin's position than he thinks? Let me briefly outline a way of using Derrida to position Zagorin pretty precisely as an unreflexive occupier of the *second* of *three orders of violence.*

To make (to realize) a meaning, to bring a meaning into the world is ultimately an act of violence – a violence of "writing" that can be called *first-level violence.* Since there is no one-to-one natural correspondence between word and world, no literal entailment of signifier to signifier and thence to the signified and thence to the putative referent, to get the actuality of the world into a language it never asked to be put in is always to establish both a power and a metaphorical relationship (a tree *as if* it was a tree, the past *as if* it was history ...). Yet, accurate as this is, Derrida thinks the notion of a metaphorical relationship still runs the risk of carrying realist overtones, in that it may suggest that there is a meaningful reality to which the text refers, albeit figuratively. For, as David Roberts points out in his *Nothing but History* (a work to which Zagorin refers but whose thesis eludes him), because when we "work back from the 'text' seeking a reassuring connection to some prevailing real world, we find no stopping point, no solid ground,"[24] then the founding concepts of meaning are instances not of metaphor generally but the (metaphorical) trope of *catachresis*: a violent production of meaning, an imposition, an abuse. As Derrida puts it:

> I have always tried to expose the way in which philosophy is literary, not so much because it is *metaphor* but because it is *catachresis.* The term metaphor implies a relation to an original "property" of meaning, a "proper" sense to which it indirectly or equivocally refers, whereas *catachresis* is a violent production of meaning, an abuse which refers to no exterior or proper norm.[25]

Yet this call to meaning is, of course, a necessary one if any meanings are to be conferred at all, since this violent imposition is – as already noted – both the condition of the possibility of meaning and, simultaneously, the failure of this naming gesture ever to be what it would like to be: literal, full-presence. For it is precisely *différance* – as the irreducible tension (*aporia*) between the idealized transcendent gesture and the necessity of empirical inscription, that is the site of its unavoidable, potential undoing.

How can this undoing be developed in what is termed the *level of secondary violence*, Zagorin's intellectual hideout? Well, the logic of *différance* again says it all.

For Derrida *et al.*, every sign wants to say what it "really" means. This is the sign's motivation; the idealized gesture of the quasi-transcendental (to achieve full-presence, and so forth). Yet, for the sign to operate as a sign it must be irreducible to one context; it must be repeatable (albeit differently) in other contexts (iterable), otherwise it just would not be a sign. Consequently, the necessity of *material* inscription/reinscription guarantees the logical impossibility of the purity of the transcendental gesture. Nevertheless, the "myth" of the transcendental (universals, absolutes ...) remains the animating force behind the signs of, say, Justice, Law, Ethics, or History, such that it is here that the aporetic tension inevitably resides. For while the originary violence of the sign enables us to *think* the *idea* of the transcendental gesture, that gesture is never realizable at the empirical level. Consequently, Justice or Law or Ethics or History are actually only accessible at the level of the empirical/iterable (as laws, justices, ethics, histories) and yet are irreducible to them. Historical discourse, then, just cannot escape indeterminacy, cannot escape *différance*, of being always both the idealized gesture *and* iterable – that is, always open to new inscriptions (to retextualizations/recontextualizations). The fulfillment of the idealized gesture is thus permanently delayed, will always be "to come," will always be belated. We shall never know what History/history "really is" (for that will remain secret and undepictable – like the name/face of God). Its putative aim – the truth-full reconstruction of the past – is both an impossible myth, yet the one which figures as the motivation behind historians' productions. We shall (courtesy of *différance*) never know what the nature of history is any more than we shall know The Law, or Justice, or Ethics, or God: we shall never know the past "in and for itself," for its "own sake."

Now, it is precisely this fact (and if there is a fact this is it) that Derrida thinks we have tried to forget, to disavow. And it is this refusal to remember the violent, arbitrary, contingent, all-too-human illusory relationships of words to things – this call to make "something out of nothing" – in favor of literal truths, permanent categories, ontological certainties, invariable essences, and absolutist ethics, that goes under the name of *secondary violence*: the abuse of *forgetting* (that is, *catachresis*).

This "mind-world" of secondary violence – of realism, of representationalism, of non-relativistic ethical imperatives – is, as I say, the one Zagorin inhabits. And it is these suppressed/repressed actualities which Derrida and others (Baudrillard, Lyotard, White ...) wish us to recall precisely by deconstructing via *différance* those protective, fictive shelters of secondary violence which, if I can put it this way, the overwhelming thrust of the Western Tradition (of which modernity was its swan song) erected as barriers against "the other(s)." I mean all those "infinite fixes," those rigid designators, those binary oppositions, those various/sometime white, ethnic, gendered, onto-theological fantasies which, embodied in phallo-logocentric articulations, have included among their vehicles numerous histories, not least those sometimes finding expression in upper-case (metanarrative) and lower-case (certaintist/academic/professional) forms. And Derrida, as I read him (along with other radical postmodernists) is motivated to remove all and every remaining, privileging carapace insofar as they have (and do) help legitimate reasons excusing acts of *third-level violence*, that is, the everyday empirical violence of rape, exclusion, murder, genocide, and war. And why not? For today, says Derrida, such violence has reached new heights. For never before

> have violence, inequality, famine and thus economic oppression affected as many human beings in the history of the Earth and of humanity. Instead of singing the advent of the ideal of liberal democracy and the capitalist market in the euphoria of [Fukuyama's] end of history, instead of the "end of ideologies" and the end of the great emancipatory discourses, let us never neglect this obvious, macroscopic fact, made up of innumerable singular sites of suffering: no degree of progress allows one to ignore that never before, in absolute figures, have so many men, women, and children, been subjugated, starved, or exterminated on the earth.[26]

I have no need to give further detail here about the complex relationship of "Derrida" and "deconstructionism" to politics, characterized as it is among various Derrideans who disagree whether deconstruction *qua* deconstruction can be held to have any substantive politics or is able to engage in old-style "critiques."[27] But I hope I have now said enough to correct various misunderstandings Zagorin holds about textuality, realism/antirealism, and the like. I also hope I have made the point, in passing, that, *pace* Zagorin, Derrida is no nihilist, no irrationalist, and no simple antihumanist. Nor is he even a straightforward skeptic or relativist; nor is another way of spelling deconstruction "destruction." Rather, Derrida is correct to place himself in the "classical discourse of emancipation":

> I am very sentimental and I believe in happiness; and I believe that this has an altogether determinant place in my work ... I believe there is an enormous amount to do today ... in all domains and all the areas of the world and society. Even if I would not wish to inscribe the discourse of emancipation into a teleology, a metaphysics, an eschatology, or even a classical messianism, I none the less believe that there is no ethico-political decision or gesture without what I would call a "Yes" to emancipation ... Emancipation is ... a vast question today and I have to say I have no tolerance for those who – deconstructionist or not – are ironical with regard to the grand discourse of emancipation. This attitude has always distressed and irritated me. I do not want to renounce this discourse.[28]

This Derrida, *this* politics, is, I think, more than enough to disturb Zagorin (there is no need for hyperbole and demonizing) whose dislike of – often Derridean-inspired – postmodernist politicizations of "the humanist disciplines" (sowing intellectual confusion with their relativism; encouraging women, gender, Afro-American, ethnic, postcolonial and gay studies, and promoting multiculturalism)[29] is etched into his own (political) position. There is no need to spin postmodernism in absurd antirealist modes. For read as what I have argued it is – above all a critique of Western phallo-logocentrism – it has more than enough power to turn our attitudes to Western metanarratives – including those historical articulations partly constitutive of modernity – to unabashed incredulity. And of course it does not take too much imagination then to work out that the sort of critiques of metaphysical, ontological, epistemological, methodological, and ethical foundations that have brought about the capsizing of historical metanarratives can be equally applied to all those categories when they are held in "lower-case" professional/academic forms, so that that type of history, too, now appears to be just one more foundationless expression of interests (history is *not* an epistemology) in a world of foundationless, positioned interests. Which of course is what it is. And it is this point – that we are all antifoundationalists now – that Zagorin just cannot get. This is illustrated when he plays what I have already referred to as an apparent trump card: that the "skepticism" and relativism postmodernists champion undercuts – if only they knew it – their own positions. But of course they do know it. And they don't care. Because it doesn't matter. For what worries Zagorin – that without foundations you are too weak to rebuff or refute foundational opponents – misses the point that there aren't any credible foundational opponents around any more. Postmodernists are not weak because they have no foundations because nobody has foundations; we are all relativists now, all postmodern now. Accordingly, it is at this point that we arguably reach not only the end of history but the end of ethics too (in the sense that philosophy could ostensibly ground *the* ethical code) and emerge foundationally naked into the world of the politics of hegemony. Ernesto Laclau has seen this more clearly than most:

> The metaphysical [logocentric] discourse of the West is coming to an end, and philosophy in its twilight has performed a last service for us in the deconstruction of its own terrain. Let us think, for instance, of Derrida's undecidables. Once undecidability has reached the ground itself – once the organisation of a certain camp is governed by a hegemonic decision – hegemonic because it is not objectively determined, because different decisions were also possible – the realm of philosophy comes to an end and the realm of politics begins. This realm will be inhabited by a different type of discourse … which … constructs the world on the "grounds" of a radical undecidability.[30]

V

At the beginning of this Reply I said that I wanted to move, by its end, to an argument which suggests that postmodernism possibly signals the end of history as we have known it, not only in its modernist metanarrative and professional, academic forms, but history *per se*. So far I have not broached this thesis directly, concentrating on refuting what I take to be Zagorin's more general misunderstandings of antirepresentationalism, textuality, Derrida, and so on, so as to give at least some plausibility to postmodern-type historical approaches. I have done so on the grounds that, *if* we are now to have a history at all, then something like a highly reflexive, overtly positioned type of approach offers some of the best intellectual resources for developing historicizations of the past in ways "which have not yet been" – ways that are post-Zagorin.

But I now think that this position fails to face up to the further challenges issuing from postmodernism (construed as a mongrel mixture of deconstructionist, poststructuralist, postfeminist, postcolonial, post-Marxist approaches), challenges which I think should not be resisted but exploited. The reasons I say this are developed at length in a book I have recently published: *Why History? Ethics and Postmodernity*.[31] I give a brief résumé of my argument here in ways directly connecting it to Zagorin's argument that postmodernism is not only founded on a "mistaken conception of the nature and function of language" – which I hope I have refuted – but also that it is "probable that its influence will increasingly fade, as seems to be already apparent," not least because, despite postmodern claims, the world is not undergoing "an epochal transition from the modern to a postmodern age."[32] For I think that Zagorin is as wrong on this latter point as he is on his view of language, antirealism, Derrida, and so on. His failure to recognize this "reflects" his failure to comprehend that we are living in a culture wherein it is now too late still to be modern, and where the future is no more containable within the discourses of modernity than the "modern epoch" was containable within the discourses of "the medieval." This is the argument I now wish to state baldly.

When I came to thinking about writing *Why History?* I started off with the question in mind as to what we might now need in terms of new *imaginaries* such that the possibility of emancipation could be rethought after the Enlightenment projects of modernity (projects to try to create in bourgeois and proletarian forms "human rights communities") could be held to have failed on their own terms, and if historical imaginaries might still be among them. I took it initially as a plausible hypothesis, and then axiomatically, that the phenomena of postmodernity and postmodernism (our postmodern condition raised to the level of theoretical consciousness) could best be read as coming *after* modernity. So-called "postist" thought could thus be profitably construed as offering a kind of *retrospective* on it in such a way as at least to raise the question of what, vis-à-vis emancipation, we are to do now and what, if anything, might we need from the past appropriated in even its most developed "postist" forms to help us to do it. In posing these questions I originally came up with a positive response, not least because I had long had in mind – to the extent that it seemed commonsense – George Steiner's observation that it is not the literal past that determines our present or future (save, possibly, in a genetic sense), but "images of the past," images which, as selective as any other "myth," gives each new era its sense of identity, of regress and of new achievements such that "the echoes by which a society seeks to determine the reach, the logic and the authority of its own voice, come from the rear."[33] But I am no longer so sure about this. For postmodern theorizing may well have made us realize that the "myths" that may take us from the present into the future may best be *of* the present and *of* the future. Perhaps we do not need – and maybe never have needed – to measure "changes" against what are always highly selective appropriations of the past, not least because such practices are enormously damaging in their restrictive cloyingness and "reality." As Sande Cohen argues, "the dissemination of models of 'history' promotes cultural subjects who are encouraged to think about non-narrative relations – capitalism, justice, and contradictions – in a narrative manner"; narration therefore "screens the mind from the non-narrative forces of power in the present, insofar as 'historical' narration reduces present semantic thought (connotation) to forms of story, repetition, and model, all of which service cultural redundancy ... what actually occurs by means of 'historical thought' is the destruction of a ... semanticized present."[34] Consequently, I see no reason why we cannot now gather the strength to rid ourselves of "the burden of history," and construct measures of radical emancipation from *current* imaginaries *sans histoire* and especially postmodern ones which, articulated critically in the future anterior verb tense means that we recognize (and act on the recognition) that the seemingly best "will never have been good enough."

This appreciation, that thanks to the nonhistorical imaginaries which can be gleaned from postmodernism we can wave goodbye to history without any nostalgia, first occurred to me most vividly when I began to think seriously about the insistent demand – made particularly by "traditional" historians of all stripes across the left–right spectrum – for postmodernists to come clean and explain "what exactly does a postmodern history look like?" You can see the anxious thinking behind such a request. So strong have (modernist) histories been in the formation of our culture, so central their place in the bourgeois and proletarian imagination, that it appears as if history *per se* is a natural phenomenon; I mean, there is always a past so what could be more natural than that there should always be historicizations of it? Accordingly, it is this (in fact naturalist fallacy) which, I would argue, explains both why it is still very much an expectation (an expectation many postmodernist historians share) that, after the end of modernity (and modernity-styled histories) we might expect to see, as a constituent of postmodernism, postmodern histories; and why the perceived threat of such constructions superseding modernist ones makes defenders of them (Zagorin, Richard Evans, Gertrude Himmelfarb, Roger Chartier, Elizabeth Fox-Genovese, Christopher Norris *et al.*) rush to the barricades as such "new histories" begin to situate themselves in the spaces created by the now withering hegemonic bulk of the old, modernist genres.

But of course history is not a natural phenomenon and there is nothing permanent about it. Because, as has been already noted, by definition in a culture nothing is of "a natural kind"; so no discourse can be anything but a contingent artifice. There is no reason to think that time need necessarily be timed historically. Although we apparently live in time (and time in us), timings of time have been (and are) articulated historically only in very specific kinds of social formation. It is tautological to say so, but it needs stressing, that we have obviously never seen anything like nineteenth- and twentieth-century, Western, upper- and lower-case genres ("histories as we have known them") at any other time or place. There have never been, on any other part of the Earth, at any other time, ways of historicizing the past *like that*. For histories such as these are both unique (historians like telling people that history is made up of unique phenomena) and ephemeral (they are equally good at telling them that everything is temporary/temporal), and there is no reason to exclude modernist historical discourse from these broad – but true – commonplaces. Consequently, there is no reason why, in "postist" social formations beyond modernity, postmodernism need drag modernity's particular and peculiar habits of historicization with it, or – for example – the ways such habits have been used by the European nation-state. For despite the current postmodern meltdown, so radioactive with old modernist connotations is history, that to think radically new ("to make up rules in the absence of rules" *après* Lyotard) it is arguably a distinct handicap to think through contaminating, passé categories. Accordingly, if a postmodern politics is to begin to set agendas, it is unnecessary to cast any part of them in familiar historical genres whose time has now literally passed as the "necessity" which once infused them with life (the organization of the bourgeois and proletarian "public spheres") disappears. From this perspective what are "historically" curious (and an aberration) are modernist historicizations of the past – the way the past, present, and future were/are made sense of in metanarrative and lower-case discursive practices: those crazy, fabular ways that came to be seen as normal and, miraculously for "a time," as universal types and even true – a time now passing. Consequently, although future-gazing is a hostage to fortune, it is not too fanciful to imagine that, in a hundred or two hundred years' time, in social formations that have developed new imaginaries which are deemed appropriate, modernist upper- and lower-case histories which once played such a vital role for us will not much – or even at all – feature for them and that ways of encoding the past which (curiously and sadly, it may come to seem if anyone bothers to recall it) some people – Zagorin among them – thought might last forever, were themselves just local, temporary phenomena that postmodernists started taking apart in the late twentieth century.

In summary form, then, as I read it, there are now two main sorts of recognizable and "still together" historical types in (albeit moribund) existence – the old upper and lower cases. But the old upper-case metanarratives of yesteryear are now too decrepit and discredited to be wheeled out again even as farce, while the lower case – which once had limited emancipatory ambitions as expressed in Whig and progressivist forms – has long been politically conservative, has long withdrawn from this world to become studiously "own-sakist," studiously "academic." Consequently, broadly speaking, nothing much in the way of a politically up-front emancipatory discourse can be expected from it. And so it is for this reason that, as I have said, it has looked (and looks) to some as if postmodernism will have to invent its own type of history for its own projects, given the uselessness of the other two. This explains the anxious queries as to what it will be like: better the enemy you know! But why need it look like anything? Why need it exist? If postmodern critiques have shown that the past will go with anybody, if it will obey any reader, if it will thus support everything in general and nothing in particular, if, moreover, the status of historical knowledge beyond the statement and the chronicle has been fatally undercut and made problematical by postmodern "skepticisms," relativisms, and neo-pragmatisms anyway, then not only is the question raised as to what would a *viable* postmodern history look like, but what a viable historicization of the past *per se* might look like raises its head. From the point of view of emancipatory discourse, why would you want to hitch your future-oriented wagon to a knackered old horse that answers to the name of history?

Thus my current argument is that we might now begin to forget historical discourses of the past and begin to live amid the ample and agreeable imaginaries provided by postmodern-type theorists (say Roland Barthes, Michel Foucault, Gilles Deleuze, Jacques Derrida, Jean-François Lyotard, Jean Baudrillard, Luce Irigaray, Julia Kristéva, Gayatri Spivak, Judith Butler, Ernesto Laclau, Chantal Mouffe, Richard Rorty, Elizabeth Ermarth – these are a few of the better-known names) who can generate enough emancipatory rhetorics to eliminate any further kind of foundational or non-foundational past. To be sure, such theorizing may need to refer on occasion to what one might call "philosophies of time," but such theorizing need not be derived from, be parasitical on, nor be predicated upon (any more than it is now) the kind of historical accounts provided by traditional/empirical historians. Besides, it is counterintuitive to argue that, "despite everything," we will always need a history to place ourselves in the present, to think the future and (and this is the sometime position of some postmodernists) for articulating, say, notions of identity essential for solidarity. For such arguments are counterintuitive not least in the simple sense that postmodern-type theorists just do very well indeed without either modernist or postmodern histories. Some of the most brilliant thinkers of our current condition – for example most of those listed above – just are able to write book after book without being historians in any sense the likes of Zagorin would recognize as "acceptable." Accordingly, my argument is that if Derrida and Rorty *et al.* can do without history then we all can. Of course, traditional historians working in either case – and postmodernists working in a differently conceived history genre which suits them – can obviously continue doing so relative to their own lights. But in terms of emancipatory *praxis – the light I am using* – such work is not, I suspect, much to the point in a culture that is so radically posthistorical in its postmodernity. Here a *post histoire* future that is not a replication or further installments of the old looks exciting and inviting.

All this is not to say – and I am definitely *not* saying – that such mongrel-mixed theorizing should be taken uncritically, least of all by those who can see much virtue in it. But I hope that there might be, in a world much lacking in virtue, a potential that may be realized in ways that point to better things to come; and that we do not give up or renounce, as Derrida urges us not to give up or renounce, "the discourse of emancipation." Engaged with or not by historians, recognized or not by historians, to me postmodernism seems to be a vehicle through which, at the end of the experiment of the modern, *a little bit of newness may be entering our world.* And I think it likely that such new imaginaries – of surprising things to come – may well not include in their number "histories as we have known them" or, even, histories at all.

Notes

1 Perez Zagorin, "History, the Referent, and Narrative: Reflections on Postmodernism Now," *History and Theory* 38 (1999), 7.
2 Ibid., 10.
3 Ibid., 16.
4 Ibid., 10.
5 Ibid., 23.
6 Richard Rorty, *Contingency, Irony and Solidarity* (Cambridge, Eng., 1989), 4–6.
7 Richard Rorty, *Objectivity, Relativism, and Truth* (Cambridge, Eng., 1991), 84.
8 Ibid., 2.
9 Ibid.
10 Ibid., 5–7.
11 Ewa Domanska, "Interview: Hayden White," *Diacritics* (Spring, 1994), 96.
12 For a succinct introduction to the theories of Jean Baudrillard, see Rex Butler, *Jean Baudrillard: The Defence of the Real* (London, 1999).
13 Elizabeth Deeds Ermarth, *Sequel to History* (Princeton, 1992), 111.
14 Ibid., 110.
15 Derek Attridge makes and extends the same point: "For Derrida the literary text is not, therefore, a verbal outcome or a hermetically sealed space; it is not the site of a rich plenitude of meaning but rather an emptying-out of meaning that remains potently meaningful; it does not possess a core of uniqueness that survives iterability, but rather a repeatable singularity that depends on an openness to new contexts and therefore on its difference each time it is repeated." *Jacques Derrida: Acts of Literature* (London, 1992), 16.
16 Jacques Derrida quoted in Nicholas Royle, *After Derrida* (Manchester, 1995), 22.
17 Simon Critchley, *The Ethics of Deconstruction* (Oxford, 1992), 38.
18 Richard Evans, "Truth Lost in Vain Views," *Times Higher Education Supplement* (12 September 1997).
19 Critchley, *The Ethics of Deconstruction*, 39.
20 Jacques Derrida, "Deconstruction and the Other," in Richard Kearney, *States of Mind* (Manchester, Eng., 1995), 172–3. Derrida discusses "history" throughout his work but especially in *Of Grammatology* (Baltimore, 1976); *Writing and Difference* (London, 1978); *Positions* (London, 1981); *Spectres of Marx* (London, 1994); and *Politics of Friendship* (London, 1997). A particularly good introduction to "Derrida" is in the work, jointly authored by Derrida and Geoffrey Bennington, *Jacques Derrida* (Chicago, 1993).
21 Jacques Derrida, *Limited Inc.* (Evanston, 1988), 148.
22 Jacques Derrida, "Remarks on Deconstruction and Pragmatism," in *Deconstruction and Pragmatism*, ed. Chantal Mouffe (London, 1996), 83–4.

23 Ibid., 85–6.
24 David Roberts, *Nothing But History* (Berkeley, 1995), 200.
25 Derrida in Kearney, *States of Mind*, 172.
26 Jacques Derrida, "Spectres Of Marx," *New Left Review* 205 (1994), 50. For similar sentiments see Derrida, "The Deconstruction of Actuality," *Radical Philosophy* 68 (1994), 28–41.
27 For "engaged discussions" of Derrida and politics by what might be broadly called "Derrideans" see, for example: Richard Beardsworth, *Derrida and the Political* (London, 1996); Geoffrey Bennington, *Legislations* (London, 1994); Simon Critchley, *Ethics–Politics–Subjectivity* (London, 1999); Ernesto Laclau, "Deconstruction, Pragmatism, Hegemony," in Mouffe (ed.), *Deconstruction and Pragmatism*, 54–60; Christopher Norris, *Derrida* (Baltimore, 1987).
28 Derrida, in Mouffe (ed.), *Deconstruction and Pragmatism*, 77–82.
29 Zagorin, "History, the Referent, and Narrative," 22.
30 Ernesto Laclau, *Emancipations* (London, 1996), 123.
31 Keith Jenkins, *Why History? Ethics and Postmodernity* (London, 1999).
32 Zagorin, "History, the Referent, and Narrative," 24.
33 Jenkins, *Why History?*, 4.
34 Sande Cohen, *Historical Culture* (Berkeley, 1988), 1.

6 Rejoinder to a postmodernist

Perez Zagorin

I take little pleasure in writing this rejoinder to Keith Jenkins's defense of postmodernism against the strictures in my earlier article. Most of his reply is merely a retread of other people's views, while the issues he deals with are chiefly related to questions of epistemology, language, and meaning, which have been discussed repeatedly by many philosophers. To go over them again is like being forced to eat a diet of hay and stubble.

Much of what Jenkins has to say represents an attempted imposition and usurpation of philosophy upon history. History, or historiography, is an independent empirical discipline of great sophistication with a long tradition behind it, which has given rise to many masterpieces. It is in no need of instruction or reform by philosophers or philosophical neophytes. If philosophy is to have a fruitful relationship with history, it must accept the historian's methods and ways of thinking as it finds them. The main contribution it can make to historiography (and I do not underestimate its importance and value) is to help it to clarify its own understanding of its discipline and the presuppositions on which the latter depends. An outstanding instance of a philosophic contribution of this kind is William Dray's recent book on R. G. Collingwood's idea of history, a deeply informed, sympathetic, and penetrating critical examination of Collingwood's conception of historical inquiry. Not the least of the reasons that make this volume so illuminating is Dray's broad knowledge of how historians carry on their work.[1]

Jenkins's essay deals directly with historiography only in its final pages, and, insofar as he enters into questions relating to this subject, one wonders what qualifications he has for doing so. Has he ever written a work of history? Does he possess any substantial experience and knowledge of historical research and its problems? Has he ever spent any length of time in an archive striving to understand and reconstruct the daily life, the institutions, structures, beliefs, values, or any of the events of a long past society through the study of the records and documents it has left behind as evidence? Does he know what it is to read a manuscript written in an ancient hand and determine its contextual background and its provenance, meaning, and significance as part of an evidential synthesis to which it is related?

Since classical antiquity, some of the most interesting and valuable observations about the nature of history as an inquiry have come from the pens of practicing historians and of a small number of philosophers like Francis Bacon, Vico, Marx, Croce, and Collingwood who were likewise competent students and investigators of the human past. Jenkins's remarks, however, contain no indication that he knows what doing history is all about or even remotely comprehends its indispensable importance and contribution to our own and future civilization. Instead, writing as an epigone of deconstructionism, what he mainly brings to his discussion are a few thoughts repeated and elaborated from the writings of Derrida and Rorty, themselves philosophers with little knowledge of historical inquiry, who are among the present-day stars of the postmodernist comic opera in which Jenkins himself plays only a walk-on role.[2] He justifies his presentation with the oft-heard but dubious claim that these philosophers are continually misunderstood and misread by their critics. Hence he is chiefly concerned to set them and me right on our alleged misconceptions. It is amusing, though, that in some of his comments he adopts a frequent postmodernist and deconstructionist device of framing certain epistemic terms in warning quotation marks. Thus, he talks of reading postmodernism "'correctly,'" reading it "'wrong,'" and reading it "'right'" (181), and he complains that a certain remark about Derrida is mind-blowingly "'wrong'" (190). Are these terms supposed to have a different meaning when enclosed in quotation marks? Can we read something "correctly" but not correctly? And is being "wrong" or "right" not the same as being wrong or right? This manner of argument is typical of the self-contradictions of postmodernist theory in purporting to assert that it knows something while simultaneously aiming to undermine claims to objective knowledge.

Jenkins is not a careful reader. He charges me, for instance, with attempting to personify Derrida as a "confused charlatan" (188), an expression that does not appear in my earlier article and which I would not think of using in controversy, despite the confusions Derrida's deconstructionism has sown among many literary scholars and some historians. Jenkins also wrongly terms me an ally of Gertrude Himmelfarb (182), a social and political conservative from whom I take care to distance myself in my article. Moreover, in a grossly erroneous statement, he attributes to me an "angst-ridden, doom-laden, panicky consciousness" that we have come to the end of modernity (187), when, of course, the entire tenor of my article, which foresees the decline of postmodernist theories, belies this description.

For all his desire to get free of history, Jenkins appears to be a fervent believer in historical inevitability. Convinced that the postmodern epoch is inescapably upon us, he criticizes my failure to comprehend "that we are living in a culture wherein it is now too late still to be modern … " (196). I am always surprised at the certainty with which postmodernists, as if they were prophets, confidently proclaim the arrival of a postmodern age. One of the principal hallmarks they attribute to the latter is the discrediting of all metanarratives and totalizing accounts of the course of history as directed toward a goal, which are considered to be illusions of the preceding modern age. Their own historicist conception of the emergence of a postmodernity which we resist in vain is itself, however, merely another metanarrative to which they in turn have fallen captive. It obviously pretends to a knowledge of the present and future that is beyond its power.

Anyone reflecting on the history of the twentieth century is of course aware of the multitude of radical changes that have affected every area of life at an increasing rate and with worldwide impact. In spite of the persistence of old enmities and the emergence of new ones in the wake of the collapse of communism in Europe, a great tide of technological innovations and far-reaching economic developments is bringing the parts of our planet ever more closely together, drastically reducing the effects of both time and distance. The future, nevertheless, remains invisible, while the diagnosis and assessment of the dominant trends of the present and their possible outcomes is an intellectual problem of enormous complexity. No one knows for sure whether the present is best understood as an epochal transition to a new era which represents a major breach with the past, or whether, as I said in my previous essay, the world is experiencing the continuing and unforeseen consequences of modernity with its many paradoxes and possibilities.

This is not an issue I want or need to debate further. It is nevertheless worth pointing out to postmodern prophets like Jenkins that some of the foremost contemporary sociologists who have studied the subject most closely do not accept the idea of a postmodern epoch. I refer in particular to Anthony Giddens in Britain and the late Niklas Luhmann in Germany. In wide-ranging discussions of the transformations Western society has undergone since the nineteenth century, both reject the distinction between the modern and postmodern. Giddens regards the sociocultural features of the present as indications of the emergence of a "post-traditional" society and the "radicalization of modernity." Luhmann, retaining the idea of the modern as the meaning of our time, observes that "the characteristics of today's modernity are not those of yesterday and not those of tomorrow, and in this lies modernity."[3] At present it probably makes very little difference whether we think of ourselves as modern or postmodern. Perhaps Jenkins would be more modest and reserved in his judgment on the question if he did not imagine that postmodernity licenses his talk of what he calls emancipation and his wish to get rid of history.

In my article I characterized postmodernist philosophy as a species of linguistic idealism which is opposed to realism and the ideas of truth and objective knowledge. Jenkins calls this description incorrect and wants it known that postmodernists are not anti-realists but anti-representationalists. As an example he cites Richard Rorty, who he says sees no problem in using the term "truth," and whom he quotes as conceding that there is actually a "world … out there." What Rorty would have us do, he says, is give up as futile and unnecessary the idea that our thought or language can provide us with a representation of reality (184–6).

Rorty is a brilliant, versatile, and controversial philosopher whose attacks on epistemology and proposals to redefine philosophy as a part of literature have aroused considerable interest in the academic world. He is held in much higher regard by literature professors and postmodernists like Jenkins, however, than he is by philosophers, many of whom have been very critical of his ideas. Both his widely discussed book of 1979, *Philosophy and the Mirror of Nature*, and a number of his subsequent writings include a repudiation of realism, so that Jenkins must be the only person around who imagines that Rorty isn't an anti-realist. It would therefore seem that Jenkins is confused about philosophical realism and what it connotes. To help clarify the issue, let us formulate it as the proposition that the external world, material objects, and in general the way things are don't depend for their existence or nature on our sensory experience or our ideas of or references to them in language or discourse. More broadly, it entails that truth consists of theories and statements that accurately represent or correspond to the facts of how things are or were in the world. In relation to historiography, realism means that the events of the past are unalterable and independent of the historian's cognition of them and attempts to reconstruct them, and that the vanished human past is capable of being an object of reference and truthful representation through the evidence it has left.

Neither Rorty, who calls himself a neo-pragmatist, nor other postmodernists are realists in this sense. Charles Taylor puts it exactly right when he says that "Rorty offers a great leap into non-realism; where there have hitherto been thought to be facts-or-truths-of-the matter, there turn out to be only rival languages, between which we end up plumping … because in some way one works better for us than the others."[4] In short, as Taylor and other critics such as Hilary Putnam and Susan Haack have shown, Rorty is not a realist but a relativist of a certain type.[5] He is someone who considers it pointless to suppose that there is a way things really are independent of how we talk about them, who would therefore rid philosophy of the notion of truth as correspondence to fact, and who thinks that "is true" is just a compliment we give to sentences we agree with.[6] Truth for him is relativized to signify no more than whatever particular beliefs work best for us or are most in accord with the standards and beliefs of our culture, our community, or our cultural peers. It is odd that he seems to have forgotten that agreement has nothing to do with truth. Paradoxically, since Rorty surely knows that large parts of his culture and many of his peers reject relativism as false, he ought by his own criterion to abandon it; but since he seems to think that it is in some sense nevertheless true or "true," he is evidently caught in a self-refuting bind,[7] although this is a problem that escapes Jenkins's notice.

Lest the question of realism be thought remote or unimportant, I will quote a passage from John Searle's recent book, *The Construction of Social Reality* (1995), which includes an exposition and defense of what he terms external realism and of the correspondence theory of truth:

> I actually think that philosophical theories make a tremendous difference to every aspect of our lives. In my observation, the rejection of realism, the denial of ontological objectivity, is an essential component of the attacks on epistemic objectivity, rationality, truth, and intelligence in contemporary intellectual life. It is no accident that various theories of language, literature, and even education that try to undermine the traditional conceptions of truth, epistemic objectivity, and rationality rely heavily on arguments against external realism.[8]

Jenkins quotes with approval the following observation by Hayden White, which he imagines is a refutation of representationalism: "There is no such thing as one correct way of speaking and representing the world because language is arbitrary in its relation to the world it speaks about" and "everything can be redescribed" (187). This comment about representationalism, which must be considered as a corollary of realism, is clearly mistaken on several counts. First, while language is arbitrary with respect to the association of a particular phoneme with a particular signifier and the concept it designates, it is not arbitrary with respect to reference or meaning. Once a language such as English is in existence, there is nothing arbitrary in the fact that the sound and letters "dog" always mean or refer to a dog, or that the two syllables "promise" always refer to the act of promising. Second, although it is very true that anything can be redescribed, it can't be redescribed in any way whatever. If the Amazon River is the longest river in the world, it can be redescribed as located in South America, as flowing through several different countries, and in many other ways as well, but it can't be redescribed as the shortest or the next longest river in the world; and if 22 June 1941 is described as the day Germany invaded the USSR, it can be redescribed as a day after the summer solstice or a day of fine weather or somebody's birthday, but not as the day the USSR invaded Germany. Facts and meaning exert their own constraints on redescription. Third, it is anyhow not the case that representationalism entails the view that there is only one correct way of speaking about or describing the world. On the contrary, since the world and everything in it manifestly has very many aspects, representationalism finds no difficulty in recognizing that, for example, any entity, event, object, or work of imagination can be described in different ways, depending on one's interests, the questions one asks, one's criteria of relevance, and so on. If all of these different descriptions are non-contradictory, they may also be true; if they correspond to the facts, they are true.

When he comes to Derrida, Jenkins tediously expounds his theory of language and *différance* as though its mistaken notions and leaps in logic had never been the subject of extensive criticism by linguists and philosophers.[9] Much of what he has to say is irrelevant to my article, which touched on Derrida only slightly and in passing. I will merely take note here of his vain effort to explain Derrida's well-known dictum that there is nothing outside the text.

On the face of it this is a very implausible proposition. It does not appear to be metaphorical and seems to say that everything that is is part of a text. Derrida puts this another way when he also denies that reading can get beyond the text to any sort of referent or reality either historical, biographical, metaphysical, or other. One wonders what could motivate or justify his statement. Jenkins quotes Derrida's own gloss on it that "What I call 'text' implies all the structures called 'real,' 'economic,' 'historical,' 'socio-institutional,' in short all possible referents ... 'there is nothing outside the text' ... does not mean that all referents are suspended, denied, or enclosed in a book ... " Jenkins goes on to stress that "text" means "text in general" and does not imply that the world is some sort of vast library (190). Nevertheless, there is still great difficulty in making sense of Derrida's position. Texts are intentional acts of human beings and linguistic representations of things and facts which are very largely non-linguistic; they consist of words and sentences; they are produced by authors who choose their words in order to express an intended meaning; they are made to be read, deciphered, or interpreted; they require for their physical realization such things as paper, ink, print, pens, parchment, stone, clay tablets, and so on, none of which is a text; they differ from non-linguistic entities like mountains, electrons, the Empire State building, space ships, and so on, as well as from social structures, institutions, families, economies, events like the assassination of Julius Caesar, and human history in general, which includes texts but is not a text itself.

When we read, for instance, a letter written by Oliver Cromwell, we do not think of Cromwell as someone who is part of a text, but as a real person of the seventeenth century whose letter provides evidence about himself, his thoughts and actions, as well as perhaps about other facts pertaining to the past. In what way, then, can it be the case that there is nothing outside the text, and how are referents preserved if they are simply texts themselves? Jenkins's defense of Derrida's statement therefore fails, and he gives away the game when he speaks of "the illusory relationships of words to things" (193). To say that there is nothing outside the text is synonymous with the anti-realist claim that things exist for us only in language, and that no referential relationship is possible between words and world. It denies that the world and of course the past too have an independent existence external to language to which mind and language give us access. This conception of text, a fallacious consequence of Derrida's philosophy of language, is a category mistake and deeply misleading. It is one that few historians or philosophers would ever be likely to accept.

Jenkins's attempt to rehabilitate the congeries of ideas that he musters under the name of postmodernism is careless and unsatisfactory in many ways, but it would be too laborious and tiresome to discuss them all. One feels that it is useless, for instance, to offer any response to his endorsement of the conclusion that we do not require an objective world and that "there are only illusions" and "only subjectivity" (187), a position that refutes and makes nonsense of his own arguments. The evolution of language is the complex result of many factors and among the phenomena least subject to human will and control; yet Jenkins, true to the spirit of Foucault, implausibly maintains that meanings are determined by "power relations" and that to bring a meaning into the world is "ultimately an act of violence" (191, 192). In an abuse of both good sense and language he describes realism and representationalism as a type of violence and associates the former with being in favor of literal truths, permanent categories, ontological certainties, invariable essences, and absolutist ethics (193). Rejoicing in the fact that "we are all anti-foundationalists" and "relativists now," he rejects as irrelevant the critique that postmodernism's denial of truth and objective knowledge cuts the ground from under its own political and moral pronouncements (195). He has apparently not yet heard the news that the demise of foundationalism in epistemology, which is one of the major achievements of twentieth-century philosophy, does not leave us with relativism as the sole alternative or compel us to abandon the notions of knowledge and truth. Even without an incorrigible and absolute foundation for knowledge such as Descartes and later Bertrand Russell sought, most philosophers would still probably consider truth to mean correspondence with the facts and regard true knowledge as the principal goal of any inquiry; and it still remains the case that we continue to appraise all knowledge-claims for their degree of truth, and to require good arguments, conformity to logic, sound evidence, objectivity, reasons that can withstand criticism, and, in general, rational support and justification for beliefs and propositions about the world and the human past, as well as for statements of moral and political values concerning what is the good, right, or just thing to do.

Throughout his essay Jenkins adopts the leftist rhetoric and posturing we have come to associate with postmodernist and deconstructionist discourse and which in recent decades has been *de rigueur* in some university departments and disciplines. He prejudicially condemns the Western tradition for its complicity in the everyday violence of rape, exclusion, murder, genocide, and war (194), ignoring that none of these sins is limited to the West and that from the Western tradition mainly have sprung the ideals, theories, and values that today inspire the struggle for peace, freedom, tolerance, human rights, economic security, and racial and gender equality throughout the world. He identifies himself with Derrida's embrace of "the grand discourse of emancipation" (194), in the name of which he wants to see the end of history as now practiced. Jenkins's rhapsody to an undefined and seemingly unlimited emancipation presents a caricature of the non-political mind when it wants to revolutionize the world. His own postmodernist philosophy gives us no reason to attach any value to his political judgments, which are no less arbitrary than they would be if he were an advocate of racism and sexism. He leaves in obscurity what the emancipation he seeks will consist of and how it will come about. Rather than anything genuine or credible, it resembles a vague, apocalyptic apparition hovering spectrally in the future. Will it establish the reign of political correctness of which we have had a foretaste in our universities and elsewhere in recent years? Or is it to be a new version of a utopia of complete socioeconomic equality and freedom in succession to the socialist utopia once envisaged by Marx, Lenin, and Mao, whose bankruptcy was demonstrated by the terror, despotism, and injustice accompanying the attempts to put it into practice in countries like Soviet Russia, China, and Cambodia?

Jenkins argues that it is time to abandon history as currently practiced because it is moribund, conservative, withdrawn from the world, and academic, so that no emancipatory discourse can be expected of it. He wants to construct his "radical emancipation" out of "imaginaries ... gleaned from postmodernism" and in this way liberate the world from "the burden of history" (197). Possibly there will no longer be any historiography in his emancipated world, but something other in its place; or else a new type of historiography will appear, altogether different from that of the present, embodying an emancipatory discourse which will leave the past behind once and for all (197–200). Described in plain and prosaic terms, a historiography of the kind Jenkins hopes to see, though extremely misty, would probably forsake its critical senses and respect for evidence, be thoroughly serviceable to a repressive political orthodoxy, and breed lies and myths without restraint. But Jenkins's notion of historiography is fortunately a fantasy rather than something to be taken seriously.

If Jenkins were much more of a historian than he is a postmodernist, a relativist, and a disciple of deconstruction, it would probably be unnecessary to argue over most of the issues I have touched. Like nearly all physical and biological scientists, historians also are naturally and intuitively realists and adherents of the correspondence theory of truth. These convictions are ones their experience and reflections on the study of the past lead them to form. Almost all scientists are inclined to believe that the way things are in nature is independent of mind and language; and while they doubtless consider it pretentious to say they are searching for Truth, they do think that scientific research and theories, if successful, enable them to learn how nature works. Most historians similarly take it for granted that the past is independent of their thinking about it and that they are studying, analyzing, relating, and explaining actions, events, thoughts, structures, and processes that were part of the actual past human beings lived. This is not an arbitrary assumption or an illusion of language; it is a truth that is conceptually linked to the possibility of history as a discipline whose foremost collective purpose is to achieve an understanding of the complex life and changes of past human societies and to try to communicate this understanding to the present and to each succeeding generation. As Jenkins's comments show, postmodernist philosophy has little insight into historiography and nothing to contribute that clarifies or illuminates its character as an inquiry or a body of knowledge.

Notes

1 William Dray, *History as Re-enactment: R. G. Collingwood's Idea of History* (Oxford, 1995).

2 In my article I refrained from discussing Rorty, who calls himself a neo-pragmatist and has avoided identifying himself with postmodernism. Jenkins, however, places him in the postmodernist camp and there are undoubtedly aspects of his philosophy that connect him with postmodernism.

3 Anthony Giddens, *The Consequences of Modernity* (Cambridge, Eng., 1990), "Living in a Post-Traditional Society," and his remarks in "Replies and Critiques," in Ulrich Beck, Anthony Giddens, and Scott Lash, *Reflexive Modernization: Politics, Tradition and Aesthetics in the Modern Social Order* (Stanford, Calif., 1994); Niklas Luhmann, *Observations on Modernity* (Stanford, Calif., 1998), 3.

4 Charles Taylor, "Rorty in the Epistemological Tradition," in *Reading Rorty: Critical Responses to Philosophy and the Mirror of Nature (and Beyond)*, ed. Alan R. Malachowski (Oxford, 1990), 258.

5 Hilary Putnam, *Realism with a Human Face* (Cambridge, Mass., 1990), 18, 22–25, 139, and *Representation and Reality* (Cambridge, Mass., 1988), 69–70; Susan Haack, *Evidence and Inquiry* (Oxford, 1993), chapter 9, and *Manifesto of a Passionate Moderate* (Chicago, 1998), passim. See also the critical essays by Bernard Williams, "Auto-da-Fé: Consequences of Pragmatism," and Gerald Vision, "Veritable Reflections," in *Reading Rorty*, the latter of which deals with the correspondence theory of truth.

6 See the quotations from Rorty and the comments in Putnam, *Reference and Reality*, 69. In a debate which took place in 1997 between Rorty and John Searle, reprinted in "Rorty v. Searle, At Last: A Debate," *Logos* 2 (1999), 20–64, Rorty defended his opposition to realism and the correspondence theory of truth against Searle's criticisms and support of both.

7 This point is made by Putnam, *Realism with a Human Face*, 109–10.

8 John R. Searle, *The Construction of Social Reality* (New York, 1995), 197.

9 Some of the basic misconceptions in Derrida's view of language which Jenkins tries to defend are clearly examined and exposed in John M. Ellis's *Against Deconstruction* (Princeton, 1989), chapter 2.

7 Response to a postmodernist

Or, a historian's critique of postmodernist critiques of history

Michael C. Coleman

In 2002 I received from Michael Coleman, whom I did not know, an off-print of an article he had just had published by the journal *American Studies in Scandinavia*. I read the article and then went on to read Coleman's 'Gut Reactions of a Historian to a Missionary Text', a critique of Robert Berkhofer's *Beyond The Great Story* which had appeared in *American Quarterly* (50, June 1998, pp. 340–48) as part of a forum which had included Berkhofer (Berkhofer's reply was carried in the same volume). Well, I didn't think much of Coleman's critique and so I suggested to him that I might write a reply. Coleman himself approached *American Studies in Scandinavia* to see if they would carry such a response if I were to write one; they said they would and so I wrote the paper which appears here after Coleman's and which the journal published in 2003. Both papers could be described as polemical and mine at least as 'populist' in intention; there are one or two swingeing criticisms on my part and, I'm afraid, an element of sarcasm. No further communication occurred between us until I asked Michael if he would agree to his article appearing here. He did so without hesitation, for which I owe him a huge thank you. I include the papers here – along with the 'Zagorin papers' – to indicate the type of discussions postmodernism occasioned and, really, still does.

"Thus my current argument," writes Keith Jenkins in his "Postmodern Reply" reply to Perez Zagorin's critique of postmodernism that appeared in a recent issue of *History and Theory*, "is that we might now begin to forget historical discourses of the past and begin to live amid the ample and agreeable imaginaries provided by postmodern-type theorists … "[1] Then Jenkins, who in this article and in recent books stridently positions himself as an advocate of the new way, fires off a dazzling barrage from the postmodernist canon: Roland Barthes, Michel Foucault, Jacques Derrida, Julia Kristéva, and others. These thinkers can, he believes, "generate enough emancipatory rhetorics to eliminate any further kind of foundational or non-foundational past."[2] This "Reply" to Zagorin – "overtly positioned," in Jenkins's own words, "polemical" in mine – is always powerful. And, even to a fairly traditional narrative historian such as myself, it is at times eye-opening and instructive.[3] Jenkins argues, firstly, that Zagorin – and by implication "traditional" modernist historians in general – badly misinterprets crucial postmodernist ideas. And that, secondly, had he understood postmodernism "correctly," Zagorin would have even been more shocked by its implications for history as a discipline which assumes a real past independent of language, a past that historians can at least partly reconstruct through empirical research.

In his "Rejoinder" to Jenkins's "Reply," Zagorin ably defends his position, and needs little help from me.[4] However, I want to use Jenkins's polemic, different perhaps only in degree of zeal from similar attacks on traditional academic history, as an opportunity to constructively critique such attempts by postmodernists to undermine the epistemological assumptions of my discipline. I openly concede that, as believers in the use of clear, "simple" language and of "common sense" explanations, many of us academic historians do need to re-examine our assumptions. Yet I will argue that Jenkins and similar postmodernist proselytisers too often subvert their own arguments. Presenting examples from, especially, American historical studies, I will show that traditional academic history is by no means as static or as "unemancipated" as these postmodernists appear to believe.

Although broadly in agreement with much of Zagorin's "Rejoinder" to Jenkins, I do not accept it all. Zagorin appears to believe more than I in the possibility of historians achieving some degree of truthful reconstruction of the past. I believe only in historical truth as a worthy but unattainable goal; all we can hope for are tentative but demonstrably *credible* constructions. And I feel that even "traditional" historians can and indeed *have* learnt from many of the sub-streams within the broad river of so-called "postmodernism." We especially need to be more reflexive and self-critical in our epistemology, methodologies, and language. We need to jettison what remains of our claim to posses a dispassionate and neutral gaze upon the past, when we are, to use the postmodernist term, always "located" in gendered, cultural, and ideological positions. Our perspectives are always to some degree political. Historians, especially, should develop greater awareness that the supposedly neutral scientific methodology we espouse is itself, as Jenkins validly notes, *historical*; that our "scholarly" approach to evidence and explanation is itself the product of certain modern (perhaps fifteenth to twenty-first-century) assumptions about reality. We have no right to assume that this is the only way of achieving knowledge about the past. And, as Hayden White, most famously, and others have argued, the very stories we construct may unknowingly call upon or fall into narrative structures and patterns deeply engrained in the Western psyche; rather than being "inherent in the evidence," our supposedly original and neutral narratives may actually be "in our minds" first, and then imposed upon that evidence. As historian Karen Halttunen concedes, a major problem "is that we craft our narratives without acknowledging that we do so – *masking the representational as referential*" [emphasis added]. The simplest solution, she believes, "is to practice self-reflexivity, acknowledging the fictive quality of our work and openly revealing our chosen tropes and metanarrative that shape it." Yet simple self-reflexivity may not be enough, she fears. Perhaps the deepest problem is "our unvarying adoption of nineteenth-century realism for all our historical accounts." Only a willingness to experiment with new narrative forms may save us from this stasis.[5]

Yet Jenkins and other critics of more traditional history often violate a cardinal value of their own postmodernism, the need to dissolve binary and polarized thinking. They appear to assume that, *because history cannot objectively reconstruct the past* (how many contemporary historians would claim it does?) *then history is merely one story among many, with no greater claim to credibility than any other kind of story*. I argue here that academic history can – *should* – renounce all claims to objective truth, yet retain its claim to providing us with varying degrees of *credibility* in its constructions of the past. For example, could any scholar or non-scholar seriously claim that the following two "stories" are equally credible or incredible? (1) From the late fifteenth century Europeans began to colonize the Americas. (2) From the late fifteenth century, Aztecs and other peoples of the Americas began to colonize Europe. Analysis of surviving evidence allows traditional historians to draw always-tentative conclusions not about the objective truth but *about the credibility* of such and other stories. By 2001 CE few of us claim much beyond this. In other words, it is not, as Jenkins and such postmodernist advocates would have us believe, an either/or situation. There are infinitely numerous possibilities between (unattainable) objectively true reconstructions of the past and – at the other extreme – the claim that *all stories are equally credible or incredible*. The academic historian's self-assumed task is to help us tentatively decide between conflicting credibility claims in viewing the past.[6]

Jenkins's attempt to sweep history out of serious discourse is, I believe, yet another example of such polarized thinking. There is a further fundamental self-subversion in Jenkins's approach, one not ignored by Zagorin, but demanding more attention – one I have also noticed in the arguments of other self-conscious postmodernists such as Elizabeth Deeds Ermarth and Robert F. Berkhofer, Jr. This is Jenkins's generally unreflexive and highly *traditional* use of history, in an essay that triumphantly declares an end to the modernist discourse of academic history as we have known it for at least two centuries. Jenkins certainly does not pass for an academic historian; Zagorin rightly criticizes him for attacking history while demonstrating little knowledge of how historians actually work.[7] I mean that Jenkins bases his whole argument on an unexamined sense of postmodernism as a complex of ideas developing, indeed coming to luxuriant fruition, in time as understood and periodized by modernist historians.

Most of Jenkins's "Reply" concentrates on issues of language, epistemology, and on his analysis of antirepresentationalism. But towards the end Jenkins openly reveals a breathtaking faith in his own ability to know what happened over vast swathes of Western and even World history. Jenkins believes that Zagorin fails "to comprehend that we are living in a culture wherein it is now too late still to be modern, and where the future is no more containable within the discourses of modernity than the 'modern epoch' was containable within the discourses of 'the medieval.'" Although he admits to stating this argument "baldly," I am still awed at such unreflexive use of old-fashioned, discredited (by Jenkins's standards) history as he effortlessly generalizes across 1,500 years of Western development.[8] And, also noted by Zagorin, such appeal to assumed major historical "truths" to justify a political/ideological argument is surely a classic use of *metanarrative*, supposedly a cardinal sin of modernist historians.[9] This is not the first time I have pointed to such gross inconsistency by evangelists of the new postmodernist/anti-history order.[10] But my criticism goes beyond academic pedantry. A vast metanarrative *is central to their whole triumphalist view of postmodernism*. According to this view, explicit in Jenkins, we in the West passed from "the medieval," to modernity (now almost totally discredited), to postmodernity with its unimagined imaginaries and emancipatory, non-historical rhetoric. Indeed the very term "postmodern" is inherently *historical*.

Nor am I picking one of Jenkins's phrases out of context. Postmodernists, he claims, are much less worried about the future than Zagorin and other espousers of modernity, "given that we have come to an end of *their* 'representationalist' modernity and the end of elements constituting it – like *their* history." One era ends, another emerges: eloquent metanarrative, and not a citation in sight to show how its author came to his grandiose historical conclusion.[11] Suggesting that "we can wave goodbye to history without any nostalgia," Jenkins follows up with history and yet more history. "So strong have (modernist) histories been in the formation of our culture," he continues, "so central their place in the bourgeois and proletarian imagination, that it appears as if history *per se* is a natural phenomenon ... " This, admittedly, is a perceptive historiographical comment; one that historians, steeped in assumptions about the very "normality" of our views about recovering the past, would do well to contemplate. Jenkins follows with another valid criticism that again nicely skewers historians because – inexcusably! – we often forget that our discipline too is situated in history. "It is tautological to say so, but it needs stressing," he writes, "that we have obviously never seen anything like nineteenth- and twentieth-century, Western upper- and lower-case genres ('histories as we have known them') at any other time or place. There have never been, on any other part of the Earth, at any other time, ways of historicizing the past *like that*." Although I am far more modest in my pronouncements on World history and indeed on the history of every other human culture – "there never have been" – I suspect that Jenkins is right. But this is history in the grandest of modernist modes – all in the crusade to invalidate modernist history.[12]

And there is more. He wonders whether "the possibility of emancipation could be rethought after the Enlightenment projects of modernity (projects to try to create in bourgeois and proletarian forms 'human rights communities') could be held to have failed on their own terms ... "[13] Beyond, again, the issue of gross historical generalizing, how can you ever consider the success or failure of Enlightenment experiments (how can you even mention such historical categorizations – metanarratives – as the Enlightenment, bourgeois, and proletarian, which Jenkins does not surround by quotation marks?) while rejecting the very discipline which gave us the concepts through the exercise of empirical analysis of sources? Historians of the Enlightenment and class relations may all have been misled, but that is not the issue. The issue here and throughout his "Reply" is that, while rejecting their very discourse, Jenkins so effortlessly builds his "new" construction upon their construction of that past.

The unreflexive use by Jenkins, Berkhofer, Ermarth, and others of such historical "knowledge" suggests an insoluble problem in the postmodernist crusade against metanarrative. To even accuse modernist history of establishing metanarratives (which it obviously does: the Enlightenment, Progress, the Rise of Science; or, even less flattering to Westerners, Imperialism, the Rise of Race, Fascism, etc), *is in itself to establish yet new metanarratives.*[14] These are just as sweeping, and contain their own ideological agendas (not to speak of personal agendas, such as the drive for academic status); they are no more neutral than the metanarratives spawned by us supposedly less-reflexive traditional historians. Further, if "emancipatory" (a favourite term of Jenkins) means liberation from any kind of oppression, surely it too is nested in its own metanarrative of negative and positive developments and values. I do not argue here for the unthinking perpetuation of historical metanarratives about Progress, or "the Rise of the West," (with their insidious ideological baggage and exclusion of counter-narratives). Postmodernists are right in arguing for highly critical stances towards all such generalizations. Yet, if we are to attempt any understanding of the past and present, even the most modest and tentative understanding, we have to generalize, to employ narrative, and indeed metanarratives – as the writing of Jenkins, Berkhofer, Ermarth, and indeed Hayden White himself have shown. To reject extreme postmodernist attacks on "traditional" history is not, therefore, to ignore the insight of postmodernists that the unthinking building of metanarratives is dangerous; it is to point to the necessity of such generalizing when we contemplate the past, while accepting the need for always self-critical use of all meta- and indeed micronarratives.[15]

Although Jenkins has thus built much of his argument around historical categories and periodizations (metanarratives) supplied by modernist history, he explicitly and derisively rejects this whole academic discourse. "I see no reason why we cannot now gather the strength to rid ourselves of 'the burden of history,'" he writes, "and construct measures of radical emancipation from *current* imaginaries *sans histoire* and especially postmodern ones ... "[16] Disdaining the need to show us what a postmodernist history might look like, and indeed disdaining the very need for any postmodernist history, he arrives at a denunciation that, I have to admit, I savoured despite its contemptuous dismissal of my craft. "From the point of view of emancipatory discourse," he asks, "why hitch your future-oriented wagon to a knackered old horse that answers to the name of history?"[17]

Why indeed? Why does Jenkins himself, along with others such as Ermarth and Berkhofer, hitch his triumphalist, visionary postmodernist discourses to such an exhausted old animal? Do these evangelical postmodernists not subvert their own arguments by doing so? To be fair, Jenkins acknowledges the issue of inconsistency or self-subversion. Noting how critics try to use a "trump card" against postmodernists – that their epistemological scepticism undermines their own claims to valid knowledge – Jenkins notes nonchalantly that they are aware of the inconsistency. Yet "they don't care. Because it doesn't matter … Postmodernists are not weak because they have no foundations because nobody has foundations; we are all relativists now, all postmodern now."[18] A wise person once said that if you ever achieve a logically consistent argument you've left something out. So we should not hold postmodernists to a standard of consistency unattainable by the rest of the human race. But surely we can demand greater consistency of thinkers like Jenkins and other postmodernists, whose books are systematically organized and argued and replete with the formal paraphernalia of academic discourse? History is crucial to the whole postmodernist argument, yet Jenkins heaps contempt upon a discipline/discourse which is actually far more varied, and indeed today more influenced by postmodernist ideas than he is aware. He ends with a near-millennial vision of a world *sans histoire*: "the old upper-case metanarratives of yesteryear are now too decrepit and discredited to be wheeled out again even as farce, while the lower case – which once had limited emancipatory ambitions as expressed in Whig and progressive forms – has long been politically conservative … "[19] And he relishes a future "at the end of the experiment of the modern" – history to the last word almost! – a future full of "new imaginaries – of surprising things to come – [that] may well not include in their number 'histories as we have known them' or, even, histories at all."[20]

As historians have been the butt of much similar postmodernist contempt in recent years, I have sometimes wondered what we (especially the foot-soldiers of the discipline, slogging away in the archival trenches) did to deserve it all. Or perhaps I could reverse the denunciation. Postmodernists validly insist that historians and indeed all scholars need to reflect upon and openly declare their location (as male, white, Western, privileged, or whatever). Of course historians have hardly been ignorant of such issues. For much of the twentieth century they have been aware that "each generation writes its own history" and that, in the famous phrase of Carl Becker, "each man is his own historian." Yet we should concede that, more radically than ever before, postmodernists have exploded the scholarly claim to dispassionate neutrality, the classic Western presumption that the scientist/scholar can somehow remain "outside the experiment." This is surely one of the most valuable of postmodernist contributions: away with fake, omniscient anonymity, with passive constructions and the disguising or erasing of *the scholar as active, located agent*! Therefore I can validly ask postmodernists like Jenkins and Berkhofer to examine *their location* too. Why the animus against a discipline which is itself continually changing, and which, from my reading of historical literature in many fields, is becoming far more aware of the need for self-questioning? Because of academic history's roots in the Enlightenment? But how can postmodernists know of such roots? As far as I am aware, historians do not refer to other disciplines – literary criticism, for example, or sociology or anthropology or philosophy – as "knackered old horses." We are not shouting at them to change their ways and certainly not attempting to banish them from academic discourse, nor are we aggressively evangelizing to turn postmodernists into modernist historians. So, what is it about *you* that makes you so upset by *us*? Turn self-criticism upon yourselves, as you preach at us to do. Most of this resentment against postmodernists like Jenkins is, I admit, defensive. It is the defensiveness of the supposedly deficient "savage" in face of the overweening hubris of the missionary in possession of "the Truth." Because – irony of ironies for those who so publicly denounce believers in modernist "Truths" – Jenkins and other postmodernist advocates radiate conviction that they possess a superior "Truth."[21]

Even if they claim that I have misread them on the issue of reliance upon history and on their own metanarratives (*can* an anti-representational postmodernist claim to have been misread?) it would be difficult indeed to misread Jenkins's contempt for our form of academic discourse and his joyous anticipation of a future *sans histoire*. Indeed, he is as sweepingly confident in his knowledge of the future as about the past. Even if he is right about that future – back in the 1960s and 1970s, I recall, there were times when the Western capitalist order did appear to be the receding wave of the past and socialism in some form the advancing wave of the future – will the world really be a better place without careful academic history? Would we really be more "emancipated" if historians had never attempted to study – and from now on cease to study – the institution of racial slavery in the United States, for example, and the events leading to the actual emancipation of slaves? If by "emancipation" Jenkins means liberation from all kinds of oppression, why can attempting to learn more about the oppression of African Americans in the near or distant past not be emancipatory in his postmodernist sense of the term? This is not to claim that historians have given us *one objectively true account* of such developments. Any scholar who attempts to publish or even reads historical literature knows just how contentious all theories and narratives are; anonymous referees and public reviewers for even fairly traditional history journals endlessly criticise and contest and revise. That, and not complacent stasis, is the way many historians work. But would it be a better, more emancipated world if our knowledge of American slavery came from Hollywood's version of "Gone With the Wind" or from "The Patriot" – or if we just forgot about slavery altogether?[22]

Will the world be better, in other words, without a discipline dedicated to the careful sifting of always problematic evidence and the concomitant questioning of all kinds of popular and hegemonic national/cultural mythology? To take an example from the history of my own country, Ireland: will the future of Northern Ireland be more "emancipated" if academic historians quit the field and leave "history" to postmodernist imaginaries or to the mythmongers on all sides of a divided community? (I'm tempted to admit here that, in Ireland's case, forgetting history might just be a good thing).[23] Of course, many non-academic Irish men and women are quite capable of getting beyond the myths which fuel ethnic bitterness there. But we can surely claim that over the past half century or so, the careful work of academic historians on all sides, many not Irish, *has to some extent broken down the myths and stereotypes and slogans of Irish history* ("England used the Great Famine to exterminate the Irish," etc). I may not agree with all the arguments of these various revisionist schools, but one thing is certain to me: academic history problematizes, asks "how do we know this?" and similar questions which deflate myths of "Other" and "them." It suggests, above all, the *complexity* of historical developments, to the extent that we can know anything about them. Even an occurrence as horrendously evil as the Holocaust calls for more than condemnation from historians; it calls for attempts to understand how it could happen – to seek for complexity again. Will the world be better if academics no longer systematically concern themselves with such things? How can we better learn about them – and Jenkins *et al.* are no help here – except through careful, but always epistemologically humble, empirical research into their origins, development, and later influences? For another thing is also clear to me: people will use history; they will keep telling innocent and/or ideologically loaded stories about the past, irrespective of postmodernist protest. What the world needs, then, is not necessarily more history, but more *good* (myth- and metanarrative-questioning) history.

If Jenkins demonstrates little awareness of how historians work, he demonstrates even less about the explosion of *potentially emancipatory* history that academics produced during the last three or four decades of the twentieth century. The New Social History – leavened, I concede, by postmodernist/poststructuralist/postcolonial concerns with issues such as power and "empowerment" – has attempted to bring the "outs" into historical discourse. By the "outs" I mean ordinary individuals and groups till then ignored by academic historians: colonized peoples, women, slaves, and other such non-Dead White Males. Ironically, Jenkins misses a major issue here: until a few decades ago it appeared that *these groups had no history*! They were *sans histoire* in his sense of being absent from academic discourse. Through the systematic efforts of male and female, white and non-white historians, the "outs" at last have come into history – only to be threatened with expulsion from it again by supposedly emancipated postmodernists! *Will forgetting history be more or less emancipatory for women, African Americans, and other such previously "invisible" groups, whose present struggles are at least partly justified through constructed histories of oppression (generally justified constructions, I believe)?* Of course this is a complex and potentially dangerous issue, and seeking a "usable past" can easily involve the abuse of history and, in some cases, a self-serving cultivation of "victimhood." Yet, if postmodernists oppose racism, patriarchy and all forms of oppression, can they advocate a wilful amnesia about the past in which, even they appear to believe, such oppression occurred?

My own major field, American Indian history, has gone through a veritable revolution in consciousness in these decades. No longer content to see Indian peoples as merely passive victims (or, in older discourses, as "primitive savages,") male and female historians, some of them (regrettably few) Native Americans, have produced a growing body of work in which Indian individuals and groups emerge as active participants in their own histories. These studies show Indians interacting with white Americans and often *influencing historical developments*, rather than passively being influenced by them. In my sub-field of Indian education, historians have attempted to get beyond "top down" studies of assimilationist policy and staff practices at United States government and missionary schools, and to examine from the "bottom up" how Indian children, parents, and communities reacted to and sometimes forced changes in white-imposed schooling. Through the use of correspondence, official records, oral and published interviews, autobiography and other such sources, these historians have sought the voices of Indians young and old.[24] Of course, non-Indian historians must avoid the temptation to "speak for the Other" – I admit to having been culpably ignorant of this whole controversy until, less than a decade ago, I became belatedly aware that postmodernists, postcolonialists, and American Indian people themselves had begun to confront scholars claiming to interpret "them" to us.[25] Many of the conclusions of the New Social History may be overturned by later historians. And some of the initially emancipatory perspectives outlined above may too easily solidify into hegemonic orthodoxies – but is this not true of all emancipatory discourses, including those produced by postmodernists? Also, I have elsewhere argued that New Social History approaches can over-emphasize the creative power of the "outs" and thus underplay the formidably oppressive power of the "ins." Who, during the nineteenth century, held the preponderance of *power* in North America: scattered Indian peoples or the United States government and the expanding white population?[26]

Even if traditional historians cope with such potential problems to their own satisfaction and to that of referees and reviewers, postmodernists may still fault them for the supposedly inherent failings of the whole enterprise. Beyond the issue of "speaking for the Other," historians may essentialize Native American peoples, replacing their kaleidoscopic variety with an ideologically constructed Eurocentric representation of "The Indian." Such studies are still obviously undertaken in the Enlightenment (Eurocentric, hegemonic) tradition of rational empirical research, argued in generally clear and unproblematized language that supposedly mediates directly between reality and researcher or reader. Although Michel Foucualt and Hayden White may receive the odd nod of recognition, the above studies, my own included, are generally little influenced by the famous postmodernist "linguistic turn."

But why should that fundamentally invalidate them or their findings, in the sense of ruling their very effort futile? If, as postmodernists preach, there are no final truths or standards, no canons of any sort, why are such traditional approaches not equally valid or invalid even to postmodernists? The writers of the New Social History or its New Indian History variant claim no final truths, they merely present and contest tentative findings. Further, at least a number of the studies in my own field are produced by Native American men and women, some of whom are major contributors to the new Indian history. They and non-Indian historians powerfully depict both the variety and the changing nature of Indian experiences; even studies focused on particular Indian groups or individual schools leave little doubt as to the great diversity of Indian experiences – and the experiences of white officials and teachers working with them. Also, despite broad agreement on the outlines of United States government educational practices and Indian responses, there is contestation within the field: for example, scholars do not agree on whether theories of biological racism become more prevalent among government officials from around 1900; and, even if they did, to what extent was this reflected in the everyday experiences of Indian pupils? Despite the general use of relatively simple and jargon-free language, these studies do not suggest that the cross-cultural educational experience was itself simple; in one way or another they all convey the complexity, anguish, and sometimes the achievements of those placed in schools constructed by an outside ethnic authority.[27] As regards our unsophisticated, "undeconstructed" use of language – are we really any different from postmodernists? Although they sometimes resort to frightfully difficult language (from the perspective of this plain-speaking historian), and although Jenkins, in particular, delights in proclaiming his commitment to antirepresentationalism, he and they continue to write and to publish with the assumption that at least some other scholars will understand their words and ideas. And (I am not the first to point this out) they all put their own names on their works. When Keith Jenkins allows "Keith Jenkins" to appear under the title of his "Postmodern Reply," he is hardly being antirepresentational.

None of this is to deny the real importance of postmodernist criticisms of traditional history. We have to concede that in the last few decades postmodernists have pushed some of us to ask deeper questions than heretofore about our assumptions and methods and about the very nature of knowledge. Nor have we the right to claim that academic history – broadly understood – is the only valid way to come to grips with the past. But, along with postmodernists, we too have acted under the assumption that "emancipation" involves the opening of the mind, the recognition of previously "invisible" groups, and opposition to racial and other forms of oppression. So surely it is not too much to claim that, at least in some of its concerns and production, the New Social History was and still is a wonderfully *emancipatory* discourse, and the world would have been worse off without it?

To the extent that Jenkins and other postmodernist proselytisers call for reflexivity and self-criticism from historians; to the extent that they decry "radical positivist" claims that historians can objectively *re*construct the past (rather than carefully *construct* a tentative account of it); to the extent that they oppose all forms of academic, scientific arrogance and Western claims to epistemological superiority over "primitive" and non-Western peoples – to the extent that postmodernists like Jenkins call for such things I'll certainly shake his and their hands (if they'll lower themselves to shaking mine). Unfortunately, the world we have inherited throbs with racial, ethnic, national, gender, class, and other contentions. Will we really be better off without men and women from many nations who search for and carefully analyse the surviving evidence relating to such divisions, destined never to get beyond fragile, tentative, complex, but *always contested* understandings of them?

Jenkins, ironically, has answered my question. Sneer as he may at the old horse, he has still hitched his "new" vision to it. And, even more important, he and other postmodernist critics of history *still need that old horse* to pull along the argument that the horse itself is dead. But why "horse" in the singular? I suggest that this further betrays Jenkins's simplistic understanding – and he is not alone in that – of academic history as *a discourse* rather than as multiple, changing, contending *discourses*. To extend the equine metaphor: some of the horses of history, such as radical positivism, may well be ready for the knacker's yard, and I'll help him lead that one there. Others are alive and well, thank you – look at the book reviews, advertisements for new publications, and new article and dissertation listings in history journals every quarter. And still others are beautiful, rearing wild horses, emancipated and emancipating![28]

Notes

1 Keith Jenkins, "A Postmodern Reply to Perez Zagorin," *History and Theory* 39 (2000), 181–200. Quotation, 199. This is a response to Perez Zagorin, "History, the Referent, and Narrative: Reflections on Postmodernism Now," *History and Theory* 38 (1999), 1–24.

2 "Postmodern Reply," 199. Jenkins's book, *Why History?: Ethics and Postmodernity* (London, 1999), is a much-expanded version of the arguments he makes in "Postmodern Reply." In the present "Response" I generally confine myself to Jenkins's essay, but occasionally comment upon the book too. He has also edited *The Postmodernist History Reader* (London, 1997).

Jenkins's adulation of the postmodernist canon of great thinkers is especially striking in *Why History*. He unreflexively utilizes modernist assumptions to inform us that in the last two and a half thousand years "The Western tradition ... produced in that time some fifteen to twenty intellectual giants ... " However, in the last few decades of our own century alone, the group of postmodern intellectuals ("the phenomenon of publicly available intellectual brilliance") has "undermined, reworked and gone beyond the whole of that Western tradition." We "are lucky, *we late twentieth-century lesser mortals* [emphasis added], to be alive in this culture to witness this," *Why History*, 31–2 ... For an excellent critique (review) of this book see Robert Anchor, "On How to Kick the History Habit and Discover That Every Day in Every Way, Things are Getting Meta and Meta and Meta ... " *History and Theory* 40:1 (Feb. 2001): 104–16.

3 In case *I* appear biased in my use of the term "polemical," it is worth quoting Jenkins's description of his book: "This book is written as an extended polemic; it is overtly positioned. It may be impossible to write today in any other way. The idea of writing an objective, neutral, disinterested text, where explaining, describing and 'introducing' something is done from a position that isn't ostensibly a position at all, is a naive one ... The text is thus polemical and partisan ... ," *Why History*, 1. On both counts – that his book is

a polemic, and that all writing is "positioned" – I agree with Jenkins. And I think that his article is equally polemical.

4 Perez Zagorin, "Rejoinder to a Postmodernist," *History and Theory* 39 (2000), 201–9.

5 Karen Halttunen, "Cultural History and the Challenge of Narrativity," in *Beyond the Cultural Turn: New Directions in the Study of Society and Culture*, eds. Victoria E. Bonnell and Lynn Hunt (Berkeley, 1999), 166–7. Many of the essays in this excellent collection bear on the issues I discuss here. For conflicting views on these issues, see also: Geoffrey Roberts (ed.), *The History and Narrative Reader* (London, 2001). Major studies critical of so-called traditional history: Hayden White, *Figural Realism: Studies in the Mimesis Effect* (Baltimore, 1999); and *The Content of the Form: Narrative Discourse and Historical Representation* (Princeton, 1987); Robert F. Berkhofer, Jr., *Beyond the Great Story: History as Text and Discourse* (Cambridge, Massachusetts, 1995); Elizabeth Deeds Ermarth, *Sequel to History: Postmodernism and the Crisis of Historical Time* (Princeton, 1992). For a sense of how practitioners of United States History have incorporated or resisted postmodernist thinking, see many of the essays in Anthony Molho and Gordon S. Woods (eds.), *Imagined Histories: American Historians and the Past* (Princeton, 1998). For example, Linda Kerber, "Gender," esp. 46–53.

6 Other historians have noted such resort to dichotomising: for example, Noel Carroll, "Interpretation, History, and Narrative," in Roberts (ed.), *History and Narrative Reader*, 254ff. Postmodernist critiques of academic history are, of course, only part of a broader attack on the whole empirical tradition of the Enlightenment – indeed on all forms of Western science, "soft" and "hard." For a careful but powerful epistemological defence of Western science against extreme social constructionist views, see Christopher Norris, *Against Relativity: Philosophy of Science, Deconstruction and Critical Theory* (1997). And for a defense of the scientific method in anthropology, see Marvin Harris, *Theories of Culture in Postmodern Times* (Walnut Creek, California, 1999); and see Patricia M. Greenfield, "What Psychology Can do for Anthropology, or Why Anthropology Took Postmodernism on the Chin," *American Anthropologist*, 102:3 (2000), especially 564: "I hope to convince my readers that the babies of Empiricism and Generalization have not been thrown out with the bathwaters of Objectivity, Cultural Homogeneity, Fact, Truth, Otherness, and Science as Apolitical Enterprise. In short, *to accept these latter six assumptions as valid targets of the postmodern critique does not necessarily entail a turning away from empirical methodology; it does not necessarily entail the redefinition of anthropology as literature rather than science*" [emphasis in the original].

7 The same is true of *Why History*. Jenkins examines the work of very few *historians*, apart from Hayden White, David Harlan, Frank Ankersmit, and – Jenkins's special target, supposedly representative of "lower-case" academic historians – Richard Evans. Although in his book Jenkins also effortlessly generalizes across supposed *past* developments in Western history, at no time does he analyse how historians have examined a major problem, such as racial slavery in the Americas. I'd like to suggest a thought experiment: imagine if a historian wrote a polemic against literary critics or philosophers, and hardly touched on the actual work done by such scholars.

8 Jenkins, "Postmodern Reply," 196.

9 Zagorin, "Rejoinder," 203–4. Zagorin wonders too at Jenkins's confident knowledge about *the future*. Zagorin also refers to such postmodernist self-subversions in "History, the Referent, and Narrative," especially 14–15. For an examination of metanarrative, see Margaret R. Somer, "The Privatization of Citizenship: How to Rethink the Knowledge Culture," in *Beyond the Cultural Turn*, Bonnell and Hunt (eds.), esp. 130–2. Somers sees metanarrative as a combination of narrative structure and a positive/negative binary code of social naturalness. Such a combination can establish a metanarrative as a powerful, often unquestioned – indeed *unquestionable* – "gatekeeper of conceptual authority."

10 Michael C. Coleman, "Gut Reactions of a Historian to a Missionary Tract," *American Quarterly* 50 (June 1998), 340–8. This was part of a forum on Berkhofer's *Beyond the Great Story*. I noted nine major ways in which Berkhofer subverted his own argument. I feel that in his forum reply (to me and two other scholars), Berkhofer ignored most of my criticisms:

"Self-reflections on *Beyond the Great Story:* The Ambivalent Author as Ironic Interlocutor," ibid., 365–75.

11 Jenkins, "Postmodern Reply," 187.

12 Ibid., 197–8. Note that all these quotations come from two consecutive paragraphs. Jenkins may be right in his bold claim that, in a century or two, the modernist history discourse may appear as "local, temporary phenomena that postmodernists started taking apart in the late twentieth century." But this statement too assumes a great deal of traditional historical "knowledge." While reading *Why History?* I was similarly struck by Jenkins's broadly modernist assumptions about recent trends in Western history, and I quickly tired of noting particular instances (similar to those from his article quoted in my text above) of his sublimely confident uses of modernist history. See, for example, *Why History?*, 15, 25, 203–4. I feel that Hayden White also uses traditional history unreflexively in his recently published essay collection, *Figural Realism.*

13 Jenkins, "Postmodern Reply," 196–7. I have to admit that at times I found Jenkins's argument in this paragraph difficult to follow.

14 In his review of Ermarth's *Sequel to History*, David Carr made a similar criticism, *History and Theory* 32:2 (1993), especially 182–7. Berkhofer also acknowledges the problem, "Self-Refections," 368–9.

15 On a smaller scale Jenkins also does good old modernist history. He retrospectively examines his mental processes as he began his book, *Why History? Ethics and Postmodernity* (1999). This whole fascinating passage (no irony intended) is *also history* – autobiography, of course, but history no less, as the author contemplates past developments in his own life. It could be classed as New Social History of an ordinary – non-elite – person. Indeed, one could argue that Jenkins's analysis of Derrida's thinking on language and knowledge is also history – the history of ideas, as the Derrida texts that Jenkins examines appeared in the past, if the recent past. And when he accepts Derrida's claim that "history doesn't repeat itself" (190) I again have to ask: how can we know if we can know nothing about the past? The same reliance on historical narrative is true of Jenkins's extended analysis of the writings of other postmodernists; I enjoyed his instructive analysis (again no irony intended) of Hayden White's work over a number of decades, *Why History?*, chap. 5.

16 Jenkins, *Postmodern Reply*, 197.

17 Ibid., 199.

18 Ibid., 195. Hayden White briefly – and in my view inadequately – discusses the issue of self-subversion, *Figural Realism*, 16–18. White also fails to apply his literary critical theories of troping and plot types to his own narratives. Although he too continually resorts to "traditional" history, he can nevertheless be scathingly dismissive of the discipline: "Indeed – at least from a culturalist perspective – history is, if anything, even more constructivist and even more naively so than the versions of reality constructed by the social sciences. No other discipline is more informed by the illusion that 'facts' are found in research rather than constructed by modes of representation and techniques of discoursivization than is history. No other discipline is more oblivious to the 'fictionality' of what it takes to be its 'data.' That is why no other discipline of the human sciences is so resistant to the challenge posed by culturalism to the social sciences. *History is the last refuge of that faith in common sense that culturalism in its postmodernist incarnation seeks to deconstruct*" [emphasis added], "Afterword," *Beyond the Cultural Turn*, Bonnell and Hunt (eds.), 322.

19 Jenkins, *Postmodern Reply*, 198–9. By "Upper-case" history, Jenkins means the discredited metanarratives of modernist consciousness – the Renaissance, Enlightenment, the Rise of the West, Progress. By "lower-case" history he means the more carefully focused contemporary academic practices of the profession, see *Why History?*, 15. Both are deeply discredited in his eyes.

20 Jenkins, *Postmodern Reply*, 200.

21 See, for example, Jenkins's contemptuous reference in *Why History?*, 199: "For there is more at stake in life than the hegemonic continuation of an ideologically positioned set of guild practices reified by their professional beneficiaries into tablets of stone." Having

subjected myself to his article and book in short order, I claim – at the risk of "speaking for the Other" – to sense what it felt like to be an American Indian or other "heathen savage" facing endless denunciation by unreflexively assured missionaries. (And see note 25, below).

22 Not all scholars accept the inherently emancipatory implications of postmodernism. Gerald Holton points to possibly fascist tendencies in postmodernist anti-rationalism, "The Rise of Postmodernisms and the 'End of Science'," *Journal of the History of Ideas* 61:2 (April 2000): 327–41; also, Ramón Flecha, "Modern and Postmodern Racism: Dialogic Approach and Anti-racist Pedagogies," *Harvard Educational Review* 69:2 (Summer 1999): 150–71.

23 Since first writing this somewhat facetious – but despairing – comment, I came upon the following conclusion by Stephen Howe, whose study is generally critical of postcolonial/postmodernist arguments: " ... the main lesson for modern Ireland may be the need, in searching for solutions, simply to dismiss arguments purporting to derive from historical origins and settlement patterns, ancestries and ancestral claims ... ," *Ireland and Empire: Colonial Legacies in Irish History and Culture* (New York, 2000), 237. On the problematic relationships between Irish people and history/myth, see also Brian Walker, *Dancing to History's Tune: History, Myth and Politics in Ireland* (Belfast, 1996).

24 See, for example, Michael C. Coleman, *American Indian Children and the School, 1850–1930* (Jackson, Mississippi, 1993). Recently I have added a comparative perspective: "The Responses of American Indian Children and Irish Children to the School, 1850s–1920s," *American Indian Quarterly* 23 (Summer and Fall 1999), 83–112. This article contains references to recent related scholarship. For a study by a Native American scholar that utilizes the correspondence of Indian parents, school pupils, and white educators to build a powerful sense of the Bureau of Indian Affairs school as a *family* concern, see Brenda Child, *Boarding School Seasons: American Indian Families* (Lincoln, Nebraska, 1998). Child is a Minnesota Ojibwe.

25 I have attempted to address this issue in Michael C. Coleman, "To Speak For/About the Other: Or to Contemplate One's Own (Decentered) Navel?", *In Search of a Continent: A North American Studies Odyssey*, Festschrift in Honor of Professor Markku Henriksson's 50th Anniversary, Edited by Mikko Saikku, Maarika Toivonen and Mikko Toivonen (Helsinki, Finland, 1999), 14–28.

26 Michael C. Coleman, "The Symbiotic Embrace: American Indians, White Educators and the School, 1850–1930," *History of Education* 25 (1996), 1–18. For a more recent expression of this problem, see Susan Pedersen, "The Future of Feminist History," *Perspectives: American Historical Association Newsletter* 38:7 (October 2000): 22–5.

27 On this issue I concur with Henry Ashby Turner, III: "Some advocates of what are now fashionably regarded as more sophisticated modes of scholarship seem to believe that producing an accurate narrative of past events that accounts for their causes is child's play, a simple task unsuitable for great minds. But anyone who has ever undertaken the taxing task of reconstructing a complex chapter of past happenings knows how naive that notion is," "Human Agency and Impersonal Determinants in historical Causation: A Response to David Lindenfield," *History and Theory* 38:3 (1999): 302. I quibble only with the word "reconstruct"; we "construct," I feel.

28 From my own research and from reading/perusing/skimming over twenty history journals each quarter and from reading *thousands* of academic book reviews each year, including many of works far beyond my own fields, my impression is this: historians have continued to do highly varied history in modernist senses of the term; and most, though by no means all, resist postmodernism in their approaches to the past. Along with *History and Theory*, these history journals include among others: the *American Historical Review* (five times a year), the *Journal of American History*, the *English Historical Review, Ethnohistory*, the *Journal of Social History*, the *Journal of Modern History*, the *Journal of Interdisciplinary History*, the *Journal of the History of Ideas, History of Education*, the *Journal of Social History, Church History*, and *Irish Historical Studies*.

8 Against the historical 'middle ground'

A reply to Michael Coleman

This paper is a reply to Michael Coleman's recent article in *American Studies in Scandinavia* ('Response to a Postmodernist: Or, a Historian's Critique of Postmodernist Critiques of History')[1] which, because he's raising in it both *general* arguments against the (apparent) claims of postmodern historians as well as *specific* instances of where I personally seem to have got things hopelessly wrong, is in two parts. In the first I want to address just a few of the more typical arguments which keep appearing against postmodern historians and 'history theorists' which, at this point, ought to come to a halt; they just don't have any purchase any more (if they ever did!). This is not because the postmodernists targeted are no longer paying attention (though most have probably got better things to do than rebut generally ill-informed, swingeing critiques), nor is it because the exchanges which actually do take place have become repetitive, familiar and unproductive (though there may be an element of this as the two 'sides' are said to talk past each other), but because one 'side' of the debate – the postmodern – has won the day, is so convincing that the location and the terms of any remaining worthwhile discussion about the 'nature of history today' can only now take place *within* the framework(s) established by postmodernists and not *between* 'modernists and postmodernists'. If only empirically and epistemologically minded historians, if only Coleman had noticed, they/he would have realised that the reason they may feel they're talking to themselves is because the 'debates' have moved on, leaving them behind. And in the second part of this paper, as already suggested, I want to deal directly with Coleman's specific complaints against me insofar as they are not effectively covered in the general response I will have made in the first.

PART ONE

On generalities

One of the many general complaints made by Colemanists (he is in many ways so typical of mainstream academic historians that the collective noun is not inappropriate) about the sometime engagement between modernist and postmodernist historians (or, as it is often pejoratively put by Colemanists, between historians *as such* and mere 'theorists') is that the two sides take up such extreme and/or uncompromising positions that the resultant polarisation negates the possibility of dialogue: straw persons face straw persons. What would therefore be better (claim Colemanists) is that such unhelpful postures are dropped and, as 'rational' people, we find some common 'middle ground' where, in a mutually respectful and productive atmosphere, 'we' settle our differences and work together for what is surely our joint objective: to consider what constitutes the discourse of history nowadays in ways conducive to the establishment of verifiable historical knowledge so to help the continuation of those vibrant histories contemporary social formations so much need. And I want to say, against this, that such a middle ground no longer exists – and nor should it. And my reasons for saying this involve at least the following ...

Against the middle ground

Because the past (all that has happened everywhere 'before now') and histories (synoptic accounts, interpretive syntheses, etc., which appear at the level of the text) are of a categorically different kind, then to understand what histories most plausibly seem to be we have to necessarily place them under – and read them through – the idea(s) of representation and presentation. And, on the basis that the etymology of representation most plausibly suggests substitutionalism, then we might best understand historians' representations/presentations – histories – precisely as substitutes, as things which stand in for absent objects in a relationship which can only be *metaphorical*: this representation/painting of a vase of flowers *as if* it were a vase of flowers; this text *as if* it was the past or some aspect of the past. And this difference between the two objects so expressed is, again, the difference between two totally different phenomena, and so is a permanent and thus ontological one: there is no way that a historical representation/presentation of the past could ever be 'the past' otherwise it would not be a history; no way that a painting of a vase of flowers could ever be a vase of flowers otherwise it wouldn't be a painting. The only way that the 'before now' can meaningfully enter – transformed – into our consciousness as history, then, is by way of a 'textual' substitution (irrespective of the technical medium) in the mode of metaphor.

Now, all this is pretty basic stuff and fairly well recognised. But the quite devastating logical conclusion of reading things this way is rarely drawn by Colemanists. Not surprisingly. For if it is then at the level of history – at the level of the text which is always more than the level of the statement, the annal, the chronicle – what is definitively ruled out is the possibility that history has ever been, or ever will be, an *epistemology*.

For within the problematic of epistemology, the form(s) and the content(s) which constitute the possibility of epistemological claims (claims to an objectively verifiable knowledge beyond peradventure), that of correspondence and description, are *not* available at the level of the text, at the level of histories. This is because the text (as the embodiment of the figurative, the inescapably aesthetic) is *always* more than – and thus is irreducible to – correspondence and description: the historicised past is always that of the imagined figure.

Again, it is easy to see why this is the case, but a reiteration of some basic points may dispel any remaining doubts. Thus, to get into this via a discussion of singular statements and complete(d) texts, we might say that once the world (and worlds past) has been 'put under a description' (a scheme), then, relative to that description it is possible (by virtue of coherence, consistency and thus correspondence between phenomenal actuality and language which gives us, once language has constituted the actuality of a phenomena as a linguistic 'reality', that problematic of world and relationships we 'know' as 'our' world) – it is possible to make 'true' statements about such a self-referencing reality. Of course. But what holds for statements (albeit perilously on many occasions) *never* holds for texts which, in their ineradicable figural aestheticism, are not objects that can be proven or falsified, made true or false, before the tribunal of knowledge, of epistemology.

The Dutch philosopher of history Frank Ankersmit has explained all this, and its consequences, better than most.[2] For Ankersmit, historians' texts (and by extension texts *qua* texts) consist of many individual statements most of which give an accurate *description* of some state(s) of affairs which took place 'before now'. These 'evidential statements' are extracted from the archive and have about them, when corroborated (on ultimately arbitrary criteria operating by courtesy of a sometime consensus at the 'research phase' of the historian's work) the aura of facticity, a facticity which comes to the surface as *one* element of the text replete with 'current' notions of scholarly apparatus but in ways which suggest that what is being presented here, not just in these statements but in the whole text, is the past – or some aspect of the past – *as such*. And here Ankersmit makes a first qualification. For obviously nobody literally accesses the past *as such*, and nobody nowadays seriously takes the view that history as a discourse is committed to the recovery of the past in some sort of pre-discursive state. The historicised past is clearly 'always already' textual, such that all that there has ever been and ever can be at issue is what can be drawn intertextually from the generic archive, it being these traces which function as the historian's ultimate referent for statements but not, crucially, for texts. Moreover, with the possible exception of areas of the 'before now' with an almost non-existent archival record, the evidential traces and thus the evidential 'true' statements available allow historians to write many more such statements than are ever included in their texts. It is sometimes argued that postmodernists deny that there are any such things as 'facts' and this is accurate in the sense that such 'facts' have to be given that status by much investigation, designation, interpretation, and so on. But, that work done, it is not then a matter of there being no facts but that there are millions of them. Consequently, it is this situation which makes the anti-postmodern stance of such representative Colemanists as Christopher Norris appear absurd. Thus Norris rehearses a near-universal complaint when he writes that there is,

> a certain postmodernist way of thinking about history which goes roughly as follows. History is a fictive construct, a selective, partial, ideologically inflected view of the past. There is no historical truth ... but always a variety of different, competing and strictly incommensurable claims about every significant historical event. Of those aspects of postmodernism I would want to resist, this is the one that most urgently needs resisting for the obvious reason that it opens the way for all manner of 'revisionist' distortions or suppressions of historical fact. The worst example, of course, is the revisionist approach that seeks to play down or to relativise what happened in Nazi Germany and elsewhere during the years of the Holocaust ... [Here] getting things right in the face of competing ideological or politically motivated claims – is a matter of the utmost importance.[3]

Now, this really is a gift. For it would be interesting if Norris (*et al.*) could actually *demonstrate* how any historian writing at the level of the text was not doing something *fictive* (not 'fictional' – a slippage between fictive and fictional appearing regularly in anti-postmodern writing) but *fictive*, in the sense that to create an account of the 'before now' in say, a narrative form when the phenomenon under investigation did not have a narrative form, is precisely what is meant here by fictive; namely, something made up, fabricated, fashioned, shaped, figured, fabular: *fictio*. It would also be interesting if Norris could suggest – given that no account can ever be either logically or contingently exhaustive – an 'account' that is not necessarily a selection. And it would be interesting indeed to know if what is being presented via selective procedures that are not expressible as a universal or algorithmic method (for history knows of no definitive methodology) could escape from being partial and, in the end given no definitive historical method, arbitrary. And it would be amazing if Norris knows anyone who writes histories – including himself – outside of the ethical/moral/ideological/political set of assumptions and desires that give them and him their own distinctive positions, their personal signatures. And it would be not only amazing but absolutely original if Norris could show *exactly* how, at the level of meanings, of interpretive significances which are incommensurable – as in the case of different tropings and emplotments of, to use Norris's own example, the Holocaust – that such incommensurable positions could be resolved by reference to the facts as if value was logically entailed from them; as if it were ever possible to logically transit uni-equivocally from historical syntax to semantics. For the point about revisionism in general is that, whilst there could conceivably be agreement about all the facts of the matter, there can be no entailed agreement about what they might signify. Consequently, until Norris (*et al.*) can show both in terms of a specific instance and general applicability how you derive values from facts, then no matter how much he bemoans the distinction it won't go away. Of course nobody is denying, least of all Ankersmit or me, that it is possible to get at the level of the statement/descriptive phrase regimes, 'facts', and nobody is denying that such evidential phenomena can *constrain* the range of descriptive possibilities such that, for example, the denial of the Holocaust in the light of the weight of corroborated traces is absurd. Moreover – and somewhat in passing – I know of no single postmodernist who is a Holocaust denier – and I doubt if Norris or anyone else does! But what *cannot* follow from all this is that we definitively know what the Holocaust *means*. And it is this 'fact' that gives weight to Ankersmit's point that since the past *per se* has no *intrinsic* meaning of its own in it, then no correspondence between the past and the meanings we ascribe to it are available. Which is also why he thinks that 'representations' are better to be thought of as 'presentations', as proposals for ways of thinking about and thus imagining the shape of things past in the present. For we can now immediately see the problem of trying to verify as objective or true any such proposal given that the past itself does not have in it proposals of its own for any proposal to be checked against. Ankersmit thus concludes his analysis in ways easily rebutting Norris's position: saying 'true' things at the level of the statement is relatively easy – anybody can do that – but saying 'true' things at the level of the meaning-full text is impossible – nobody can do that. And this is why his slogan – the statement is modernist, the text is postmodernist – is so apt. For given that history – to be a history (rather than a list, a chronicle, etc.) is always in excess of the sum of its parts – any historian (Coleman, Norris ...) who remains anti-textural, and therefore anti-postmodern, is just plain passé.

It is for these sorts of reasons that I think Hayden White and Jacques Derrida ought not to be castigated by Colemanists – as they typically are – but rather that their theories about historical representations/presentations be embraced as 'the only game in town'. After the above comments on Ankersmit there is perhaps little need to yet again rehearse White's position on the inexpungeable relativism of all historical readings. But within the literature on White – and I mention this because of Norris's 'oh-so-typical' use of the Holocaust as the 'test case' against postmodern relativism – I want to insist, again in passing, that White has *never* revised his relativist position despite near unanimous claims that he has done so, an accusation which suggests that, in his 'revisionism', he has 'cut the heart out of his philosophy'. And this is important to discuss, I think, because it helps underline the 'relativistic' points I am trying to make so that if Coleman(ists) wish to try and rebut them they know precisely the 'proposal' they have to engage with.

Thus, in his 'Historical Emplotment and the Problem Truth in Historical Representation',[4] White questions whether, with respect to historical emplotments, there are any limits to the type that might properly be used or if 'anything goes'. And his answer is that ultimately 'anything goes'. For we could only presume that 'the facts of the matter' set limits to the sorts of stories/narratives we can tell if we believe that the events themselves have in them a latent story form and a definitive, knowable plot structure. In which case – *if they did* – then we could indeed dismiss, say, a comic or pastoral story 'from the ranks of competing narratives as manifestly false to the facts – or at least to the facts that matter – of the Nazi era'.[5] But of course they don't. For as White says elsewhere 'one must face the fact that when it comes to apprehending the historical record, there are no grounds to be found in the historical record itself for preferring one way of construing meanings over another'.[6]

Thus, why the confusion? White's position seems clear enough. Why is it that historians like Saul Friedlander, Martin Jay and umpteen others have insisted that White qualifies/subverts his relativism here? And the reason seems to be that White suggests that we might indeed be justified in *appealing* to 'the facts' in order to dismiss competing narratives of the Third Reich if they were to be emplotted in a comic or pastoral mode. But – and this is the big but – this attempted 'appeal' could only be an *attempt*; it could never succeed because of the fact value dichotomy. And, in fact, White has himself recently refuted those who have read this attempt as the undercutting of his own long-term relativism. Thus, in his recent article, 'An Old Question Raised Again', he refers to his earlier article to say the following:

> Here I considered the question of whether one could endow the events of the Holocaust with *all* the meaning that the various modes of emplotment known to Western practices of narrativisation provide. And I made two remarks. One had to do with the relation between facts and meanings. I said that when it comes to imputing *meaning* to a given set of historical events the facts *cannot* be appealed to in the same manner they can be appealed to in order to determine the truth-value of specific statements made about specific events. I referred to *meaning*, not *truth*. The second remark had to do with the question of whether the Holocaust could be freely emplotted ... including those [emplotments] of comedy and farce. I did not say that *the facts* precluded the emplotment of the Holocaust as a farce; I said [only] that it would be tasteless and offensive to most audiences to so emplot it. I invoked moral and aesthetic criteria, not facts, as determinative of the choice of the plot structure to be used in the narrativisation of the Holocaust.[7]

For White, then, it remains our moral/aesthetic *choice* to invest the facts with whatever meaning we wish. To be sure, certain investments may be (and indeed are) offensive, but the point remains that offence is not enough to undermine the fact–value dichotomy – and thus inexpungeable moral relativism for ever. And so to Norris and fellow Colemanists I repeat that what they have to do is not to keep on saying that it is ethically/morally repugnant to be able to *logically* emplot the Holocaust 'anyway you like', but to show

how they can actually *logically* expunge such 'inexpungeable relativism' at the level of textual meaning.

And here I move from White to Derrida. For, while as a citizen and a man of the left (and of course as a Jew), Derrida can and does reject Nazism/neo-Nazism/anti-Semitism, etc., in terms of the logic of deconstruction not only are we always able to decide how to make anything ultimately mean whatever we want it to mean but, on the whole, this is considered to be a good thing. And this is because for Derrida *all* ethical/moral/political decisions have to go through the *aporia* of the decision, of 'the undecidability of the decision'.

For Derrida, for a decision to actually be a decision, it must be more than the application of a previous rule or command or legal code. For if I am to do justice to any judgement I might make about an event which comes to me – as events always do – in ways which have never quite occurred before (be they ever so familiar) then this new event *must*, in all its singularity, be judged in ways that are precisely not the reapplication of any previous decision. Because if I were to apply again a decision derived from a previously worked out formula (or from 'the lessons of history' construed as some form of necessity), then I would merely be carrying out an administrative act and thus no decision will have been made. A decision worthy of its name, then, occurs in a situation of radical undecidability, at a moment temporarily outside of all ethics, all morality, and so necessarily involves an element of *invention*. Of course, I can never actually make – nor has anyone ever made – a pure, new decision like that; all decisions have their newness contaminated by one's previous decision-making experience no matter how much one tries to forget it. Moreover, there is a sense in which, when making a decision, I always have to remember at least something for, as Derrida points out, the decision must 'deliver itself over to the impossible decision while taking account of rules and laws' – otherwise it would be so radically 'other' as to be incomprehensible. Yet, nevertheless, it must still be a decision beyond 'all certainty or all alleged criteriology':

> Undecidable – this is the experience of that which, though foreign and heterogeneous to the order of the calculable and the rule, must nonetheless … deliver itself over to the impossible decision while taking account of law and rules. A decision that would not go through the test and ordeal of the undecidable would not be a free decision; it would only be the programmable application or the continuous unfolding of a calculable process. It might perhaps be legal; it would not be just.[8]

From which summary one can conclude that that which has to be avoided at all costs is some sort of evaluative closure. Accordingly, it seems eminently sensible to 'conclude' that it really is excellent news that ethical/moral decisions are always unfixed, always non-totalisable. It is a good thing that there is an unbridgeable gulf between fact and value, that the 'opening' to an ethical/moral decision is always a 'non-ethical opening to ethics', for in these ways the future of 'future decisions' is always open. Accordingly, this way of looking at things allows us to draw together the decisional aestheticism of Ankersmit, the relativism of White and the radical undecidability of Derrida in ways which undercut foundational, meaning-full 'knowledge', and which opens up a space which, as Geoffrey Bennington puts it, 'might reasonably be called political insofar as it makes judgements necessary whilst disallowing any full cognitive grasp or possible programming of that judgement'.

So the challenge to Coleman(ists) is, once again, that they stop wringing their hands over ethical and moral relativism and to show, if they cannot go along with the generous open logic of Derrida *et al.*, both where Derrida *et al.* have got it wrong and, vis-à-vis their own anti-foundationalism, demonstrate how *exactly* foundations can be established and worked. The challenge to Coleman(ists) is that he/they engage directly with the above sort of arguments and rebut them point by point (not by slurs, pejorative slights, *ad hominem* dismissals ...) but philosophically, theoretically. This is an open invitation for Coleman *et al.* to try.

To bring this first part to a tentative conclusion, let me now sum up, in four short paragraphs, the upshot of the preceding discussion before turning to engage with some of Coleman's specific charges against me.

Four conclusions

It can now be seen that critics of postmodern histories *generally* pose to their proposers the kinds of question which are now utterly redundant. Those are questions which, no matter how put, all boil down to concerns about objectivity, disinterest, truth and relativism which, further boiled down, effectively take the following familiar form: if histories are aesthetic, figurative discourses without foundations, then what happens to the pursuit of truth at the end of enquiry? My answer is to say that if the notion of the aesthetic is understood then nobody could possibly ask this epistemological question any longer. There is no point. And this is for the inescapable reason that it is no good expecting an aesthetic mode to answer an epistemological question. For the difference between these two categories is an ontological one: epistemologies and aestheticisations are different not in degree but in kind. And this explains why the break between modernist and postmodernist histories (the first wanting – but not achieving epistemological status – the latter not bothering) is *not,* as things stand, an epistemological break (which seems to allow for the possibility that one day they might be unified and the break 'healed over'), but a permanent because incommensurable difference.

Second, it therefore follows that it's really no good thinking that post-modern insights – into language, representation, narratology, etc. – can be somehow grafted on to modernist histories which might thus allow them to overcome 'postist' critiques and so survive not only intact but strengthened. For this is not possible: the break between modernity and postmodernity is as epochal, and as fundamental, I propose, as that between the medieval and the modern, and it is as inconceivable to think that modernists will be able to long survive in postmodernity (with their vocabularies, lexicons, axioms, etc.) any more than 'the medieval' might survive as if unaffected in modernity: these are differently constituted 'worlds'. It is also, I think, a mistake for academic historians to think that postmodernists want their kind of pseudo-epistemological histories – their epistemological fallacies – to continue, and that they might even want to help them do so. It is understandable that academic historians, mistaking their own time–space-bound *genre* for 'the real thing', can see no alternative to their current practices, but postmodernists can and do and such inventive sightings signal the end of one type of history and the beginning – perhaps – of others, as yet embryonic. Postmodernity offers new births.

Third, from a postmodern perspective, this unavoidable break is a break which, though understandable 'historically' is, *logically*, a break that should never have been made. For if postmodern claims vis-à-vis what is arguably the best way of characterising histories – as aesthetic, figurative discourses – are correct, then it is not that postmodern histories alone are examples of an aestheticisation of the past which then stand over against modernist ones which just happen not to be aestheticisations. *For if history as such is an aesthetic*, then it always has been and always will be; there cannot be histories *qua* histories of any other type. All histories – past, present, future – are thus of the aesthetic type postmodernists raise to the level of consciousness. Which is another way of saying that postmodernist histories are and always have been 'the only game in town'. So that in coming to the *end* of epistemological *attempts* to historicise the past we have, as it were, come home to ourselves. And so let us accept this homecoming, this happiest of thoughts which at this point can be thrown into the wake: *epistemological-claiming histories just ought never to have existed; histories just ought never to have been modern.*

Finally, we can surely now see why we are witnessing the disappearance of 'the middle ground'. For if, as I said at the beginning, one pole of the polar difference between modernist and postmodernist histories collapses such that we are now all postmodern aestheticisers, then there is no middle ground left to occupy. So that to those who still think that history is or could be an epistemology rather than a reflexive, aesthetic, figural, refractive, discursive experiment without foundations – and that to it postmodernism makes no difference – all I can say, finally, is 'think about it'. And then relax; and then go with it. I mean why not … you have nothing to lose but your pasts.

PART TWO

This is not the first time that Coleman has 'replied' to a postmodern historian/theorist. In 1998, in the pages of *American Quarterly*, he attacked Robert Berkhofer's *Beyond The Great Story* ('Gut Reactions of a Historian to a Missionary

Tract').[9] And it is interesting to note that not only have Coleman's arguments not developed over the last four years but that his characterisation of himself as the plain, simple, straight-talking 'real' historian and Berkhofer as some zealous (and thus irrational, confused and fundamentalist) 'missionary', is repeated in his 'historian's' critique of my own deluded, postmodern position: once again the 'real thing' attacks the fake, the quasi-historian, the stupid 'theorist'.

But in fact the 'real thing' is in poor shape, as is its defense, Coleman's arguments – if such they are – being a mix of unsustainable assertions and confusions stirred with *ad hominem* slights and the plaintive cries of an allegedly much-misunderstood, wounded animal. The only real difference between Coleman's two polemical pieces is that in Berkhofer's case he has conveniently tabulated his arguments whereas, in mine, things are just jumbled up. And so, taking a leaf out of his own book, I want to myself tabulate Coleman's points so that I can deal with them one by one: there are six of them.

Objective histories

Whilst Coleman admits that an objectively true history is impossible (p. 50), nevertheless he argues that historians must retain the claim that they can provide 'varying degrees of credibility' in constructing the historical past. Unfortunately, it is not very clear what Coleman means by 'credibility', but if what he has in mind is the production of historical facts of the level of the statement as if 'history' was reducible to that, then all the arguments from Ankersmit apply. And, incredible though it may seem, it looks as if this actually is what Coleman means. For could any scholar, he says, claim that the following two stories are equally credible: '(1) From the late fifteenth century Europeans began to colonize the Americas. (2) From the late fifteenth century, Aztecs and other peoples of the Americas began to colonize Europe.'[10] From which example Coleman argues that, whilst it is one thing to reach *one* objectively true reconstruction of the past, this example shows that the (postmodern) claim that 'all stories are equally credible or incredible' (p. 50) is quite another.

There are several points here. First – and very briefly given what has been said already – it beggars belief that Coleman doesn't recognise – or if he does then *act* on the recognition – that a history is more than the sum of its factive/cognitive elements, and that, therefore, the 'credibility' of cognitive elements does not equate to the credibility of narrative orderings which may include them but which are irreducible to them. But I have to conclude that Coleman doesn't recognise this – otherwise how could he have given the example he has?

But if Coleman's argument won't work – and it obviously won't – then it would seem that postmodernists are right to claim that all narratives are equally credible or incredible and that, therefore, anything goes. And logically this does seem to follow; as we have seen in our discussion of White and Norris, fact and value, syntax and semantics do indeed float free of each other, only contingently (and pragmatically) being 'connected' but never entailed.

Nevertheless, in the above discussion of White and Norris – and indeed Ankersmit – the attention I have given to the 'true' statement (and which I always give) *should* have cautioned Coleman from rushing to the 'anything goes' *logical* conclusion as if there was nothing to take the attitude of 'anything goes' *about*. This 'qualification' of a kind – and it is for many postmodernists 'of a kind' – thus needs to be considered so that the un-nuanced 'version' of Coleman can be corrected.

No postmodernist I know of, then, thinks that a *text* – and by extension the historicised past as *text* – can in the actuality of its existence be *about* absolutely anything, or can be read in complete disregard of 'the words on the page' (or the 'historical syntax'). Rather, postmodernists argue (in the manner of Derrida) that whilst no 'reading' of a *text* can make itself absolutely necessary (hence the logic of 'anything goes'), in fact no existing text can in practice open itself up to just any reading – otherwise the reading wouldn't be about *that* text. No, what texts do is to *appeal* for a *reading*; what the historical past as a text does is to call out for an appropriative gaze, otherwise there wouldn't be a reading but only a passive decipherment – which is very precisely not what a reading is. As Geoffrey Bennington puts it:

> Any reading, however respectful of the text being read … takes place in this [interpretive] opening, and this is why texts are not messages and why the classical conception of communication [Coleman's paradigm of clear, no nonsense prose] is unhelpful discussing them … A text is a text only as at least minimally readable in this sense, and that means it can always be read differently with respect to the way it would (be wished) to be read. An absolutely respectful relation to a text would forbid one from even touching it. The ethics of reading would, then, consist in the negotiation of the margin opened by readability.[11]

In that sense, Bennington's Derrida likens this necessary reading to an *inheritance*. For though inheritances exist (just as a text, just as the historicised past, exists for us … we by no means come from nowhere), and must thus be taken into account, an inheritance just wouldn't be an inheritance (nor a text a text nor the historicised past the historicised past) *if* we didn't *necessarily* pick and choose from it, a picking and choosing which, because one is never sure if the inheritance is complete to pick and choose from, is always itself incomplete: *no picking and choosing, no reading, no interpretation, no appropriation, is ever quite right*. And this is excellent, because it leaves, for example, historical reading as an endless task always before us, thus ruling out any total/totalising/totalitarian closure: the openness of all readings to future rereadings means that this open future guarantees an open past; the past cannot ever be fully settled because the future cannot be fully closed down. As Derrida puts this:

> An inheritance is never fully gathered; it is never one with itself. Its presumed unity, if there is one, can only consist in the injunction to

> *reaffirm by choosing.* You must [*il faut*] means you must filter, select, criticise; you must sort out among several of the possibilities which inhabit the same injunction. And inherit it in a contradictory fashion around a secret. If the legacy were given, natural, transparent, univocal; if it did not simultaneously call for and defy interpretation, one would never inherit from it. One would be affected by it as a cause – natural or genetic. One always inherits a secret which says 'Read me, will you ever be up to it?'[12]

Will we ever be up to it? Will we ever achieve full presence, ever get total knowledge/understanding? Of course not. But the point Derrida is making is that the absence of a 'single unity of meaning' (the objective truth, etc.) does not commit either him or anyone else to a recommendation of meaninglessness, nor does it mean the equivalence of the value of all readings – but rather, as Bennington argues, 'the singularity of each' and the recognition that no one reading will ever be able to claim to have exhausted the textual resources of any text – including the historical past as text – being 'read'.

Jenkins is not an academic historian and therefore ...

This charge is an old chestnut which, in effect, amounts to saying that since philosophers and theorists of history in general – and myself in particular – are invariably not empirical historians of an academic type, then we have no right, given our lack of practical experience, to criticise the methodological and craft practices of the professional historians who have. Against which at least two replies can be made.

First, it is by no means the case that philosophers/theorists of history have no practical experience of doing history – unless one rules out as history the history of ideas, the history of mentalities and intellectual history more generally. But my second and main point against Coleman – one expressed many years ago by R. F. Atkinson when responding to a similar charge against philosophers by Geoffrey Elton – is simply that it is *totally* beside the point if philosophers of history are 'practicing historians' or not. For philosophies of history – like philosophies of science or aesthetics or law – are discursive practices in their own right and do not derive their *raison d'être* from serving another discourse. Consequently, Atkinson correctly argues that philosophers of history are not trying to be historians and that it is therefore 'of no necessary concern to them that their activities help, hinder or otherwise bear upon the practice'. Philosophers interest themselves in history, he adds, 'for their own purposes: the instrumental value, or disvalue, of their investigations to history is wholly accidental'.[13] Atkinson is to the point. If history as a discourse – as a piece of writing – is made up of metaphysical, ontological, epistemological, methodological, ethical and narratological aestheticisations, and if historians make claims to knowledge, then they cannot escape philosophical critiques of each of these constituent elements of their discourse nor the resultant status of their discourse as such. Which means, given that such critiques are leveled against historians' 'practices', that one cannot refute them merely by redescribing the very practice being held to account: a philosophical critique demands a philosophical defence: can Coleman give it?

On metanarratives

For Coleman, postmodernists stupidly contradict themselves when, in 'their crusade [sic] to invalidate modernist history' they themselves not only situate modernity 'historically' but often – and in my case all the time apparently – express such contextualisation by a classic use of the very metanarratives they revile: 'a vast metanarrative', writes Coleman, '*is central to their own triumphalist view of postmodernism*'. Not for the first time, he adds, have I 'pointed to such gross inconsistency by evangelists [sic] of the new postmodernist/anti-history order'; indeed, 'the very term "postmodern" is inherently *historical*'. Accordingly, he concludes, 'the unreflexive use by Jenkins, Berkhofer, Ermarth, and others of such historical "knowledge" suggests an insoluble problem in the postmodernist crusade [sic] against metanarrative. To even accuse modernist history of establishing metanarratives (which it obviously does ...) *is in itself to establish yet new metanarratives*.'[14]

It is incredible to think anyone – let alone Coleman – can be so grossly ignorant of what passes conventionally for a metanarrative and then, secure in such ignorance, accuse postmodernists of not knowing what they are doing. For whilst postmodernists do indeed construct *narratives* about phenomena, a narrative is not the same thing as a *metanarrative* – otherwise why two words? No, for a metanarrative to be a metanarrative it has to have an axiomatically held ground from which deductions are made yet which, being precisely *meta* (meta-physical), is beyond demonstrable proof outside of its own terms which remain unproblematicised: I would hope I don't have to remind Coleman why Hegelian Marxisms, Nietzschean wills to power and Freudian oedipal 'mythologies' are metanarratives. And, of course, insofar as academic history sometimes makes similar claims on 'given' axiomatic foundations, then, in these 'non-refutable' instances, these too are metanarratives. But postmodern *narratives* are not of this type; they are, after Ankersmit, at best proposals about how things might be considered; they are, after Derrida (and I return to this in the last section) always interminably open and revisable, readable and rereadable. Nothing else is being claimed when postmodernists ask people to consider their histories as interesting proposals, and such proposals are not – I mean are they – metanarratives? As to the related question of why, if postmodernists *propose* that we consider that we have come to the 'end of history', 'we' still use historical examples to argue this, well, the reply here is that, just as philosophers *qua* philosophers talk, after Auschwitz (or Hegel) of 'the end of philosophy', and sociologists *qua* sociologists (such as Baumann) talk of 'the end of sociology', so, as a 'historian of ideas', I can, until the actualisation of the end of history in the specific way I talk about this 'end', use 'historical' and other discourses to try and explain this phenomenon. There is nothing paradoxical and certainly nothing contradictory here.

Why do postmodernists hate historians?

In his book, *Historical Representation*, Frank Ankersmit reflects on historians' animosity towards theorists in general and postmodern ones in particular, and he offers the following explanatory 'proposal' for it. 'Deep in their hearts', he writes,

> Historians feel more insecure about the scientific status of their discipline than the practitioners of any other field of scholarly research ... Deep in their hearts historians know that, in spite of all their emphasis on the duties of accurate investigation of sources and of prudent and responsible interpretation, history ranks lowest of all the disciplines that are taught at a university. Since one of the main effects of the historical theorists effort unfortunately is to confront the historian with these sad and disappointing facts ... it is only natural that the historian tends to project frustration about the uncertainties of the discipline onto the theorist. In short, the historical theorist is the historian's obvious target for working off an all too understandable professional inferiority complex.[15]

And above all – and surely Coleman must recognise himself here – that resentment particularly raises itself to consciousness when philosophers of history make claims about the ontological and epistemological status of the historicised past, academic style, 'on the basis of philosophised arguments only, without feeling challenged to find support for the ... assertions in hard historical fact'; thus reducing, with their theorising, 'all the unwearying industry of the historian to mere irrelevant pedantry' or, at least, as producing 'material' they can happily critique out of epistemological existence. No wonder postmodernists are the ones who are hated.

So, in aligning myself with Ankersmit's observations I would *reverse* the direction of the hatred Coleman discusses. 'What', he asks postmodernists, is it 'about *you* that makes you so upset by *us*?' We, he adds, are not attempting to banish postmodern histories in the way postmodernists are trying to end modernity's historicising experiment: 'Turn self-criticism upon yourselves, as you preach [sic] at us to do.' Coleman's language here is desperate, an accusatory language that serves to save him admitting to himself the fact that postmodern theories have won the day and that he doesn't have the philosophical resources to refute them. Postmodernists, then, are not the ones who hate Coleman(ists), rather it is they who are disliked as they point out the shortcomings of 'normal' historical practices and move on to new pastures.

But what about using history for emancipation?

> *Will forgetting history be more or less emancipatory for women, African Americans, and other such previously 'invisible' groups, whose present struggles are at*

> *least partly justified through constructed histories of oppression (generally justified constructions, I believe?)* ... Through the systematic efforts of male and female, white and non-white historians, the 'outs' at last have come into history – only to be threatened by expulsion from it again by supposedly emancipated postmodernists!
>
> Coleman, Response to a Postmodernist, p. 59

Let me begin to answer this quote from Coleman by some quotes from Hayden White who, many years ago, responded to Gene Bell-Villada's critique of himself, a critique that is almost identical to Coleman's pious offering, an offering which, had he been familiar with White's rebuttal (as he perhaps ought to be in his 'concern with theory') might have persuaded him not to bother with this particular protestation. Thus Bell-Villada wrote against White:

> Meanwhile, in the face of a domestic socio-political panorama that begins to look vaguely 'Latin American', plus certain South American 'friendly regimes' that behave more and more nazi-like, the only response that the U.S. 'critical establishment' can come up with is its elaborate paraliterary schemes, its war on referentiality and its preachments that 'History is Fiction, Trope and Discourse'. The families of several thousand Salvadoran death-squad victims may entertain other thoughts about history.[16]

To which White replied that, yes, no doubt the families alluded to do indeed have other thoughts about history than that it consists of fictions, tropes and discourse and, he adds, they would be 'as foolish as Bell-Villada apparently thinks I am if they even entertained such thoughts'. But that is not, he continued, the point of issue. For whilst the histories the Salvadoran oppressed might need ('if they bother to think about history at all') will undoubtedly be about the experiences – both past and present – they have endured, in order to make sense of these experiences they will still have to be troped, made (be fictive) and 'discursive'. Consequently a 'genuine' failure of 'historical understanding' occurs when one 'forgets that history, in the sense of both [previous] events and accounts of events, does not just happen but is made. Moreover, it is made on both sides of the barricades, and just as effectively by one side as by the other.'

In the light of these comments – to which I'll return briefly in a few seconds – I personally have never said (and nor so far as I am aware has White or Ankersmit, Derrida or Foucault, Lyotard or Butler, Kristeva or Ermarth, *et al.*), that people who are oppressed cannot, if they want, frame their resistances historically. And nor have I ever written a text that has not, openly and persistently, urged that histories – if people want them – *should* be written precisely for emancipation and empowerment. Insofar, then, as the 'writing up' of the past into a history (with all the enabling Whitean meta-historical – *not* metanarrative – self awareness that is desirable) that wishes to make a difference in the present and the future is produced and distributed within a socio-economic-political moment where to have a history may help – where to have a history is still deemed necessary – then it would be ridiculous to ignore this: in the fight any weapon. But there are still two caveats to make.

The first echoes White's point that 'legitimate histories' are always available on both sides – or on many sides – of the barricade(s). It would be nice, it would be easy, if the past/history was only on the side of the angels. But of course 'the past' knows of no sides, no angels, the 'past' will go with anyone, be historicised into multiple meanings *ad infinitum*: the fact–value distinction and the *aporia* guarantee this. And second – and this is the position essayed in my *Why History?* to which Coleman constantly refers – I think that, today, we might, in a culture that is arguably so a-historical, 'forget history' and begin to live among those 'posts' that can further emancipation. This is not to say that there are not hundreds of radical and emancipatory histories out there – and Coleman's may be amongst them – but I just don't think they resonate in our culture the way 'postmodernist' works of a radical type do. Amongst the most illustrious of 'today's' intellectuals – say Barthes, Foucault, Derrida, Lyotard, Baudrillard, Rorty, Fish, Butler, Ermarth, Kristeva, Irigary, Cornell *et al.* – *none* are historians. And so I have, precisely *for* the emancipatory purposes Coleman thinks I have ignored, pragmatically 'gone over' to the 'posts' and left, on the whole, historians behind in the way I would argue 'our' culture has.

Last section

In his article 'Deconstructions: The Im-possible', Derrida responds to the request to try and historicise the impact of deconstruction on the USA 'over the last twenty years'. Arguing that no such an account can ever be definitive, objective or true, arguing that every historical representation is always a 'failed representation', he writes as follows:

> Since I cannot here reconstruct all the *topoi* and movements of … the last twenty years, you will allow me to propose, hypothetically, an *emphasis* … The emphasis would concern a past periodisation that I don't quite believe in, that lacks rigour in my opinion, but is not totally insignificant. In other words it would possess, without being rigorously either true or false, a certain appearance in its favour, and an appearance that we should take account of.[17]

'A certain appearance in its favour'. This brief but brilliant encapsulation of 'the short-fall of the empirical', 'the short-fall of the epistemological', *is as good as it gets*. And it's good enough. Good enough in its recognition of the fact that all the decisions that I make in thinking about 'the before now' – metaphysical, ontological, epistemological, methodological, ethical – are always radically undecidable and thus will always be ones about which I must have interminable doubts: no cut is ever clear-cut. The logic of the *aporia* (and if I were to now try and define postmodernism theoretically, I would argue that it is most plausibly the 'era of the raising to consciousness of the aporia') guarantees that our readings have, at best, only a propositional status. But still I must (*il faut*) decide, interpret, appropriate, cut; make-up rules in the absence of rules and then offer up my proposal for a way of thinking about things. And this is the status of my reading of Coleman. I 'know', and I'm happy to know, that I'll never get Coleman 'right'. But I prefer *my* reading of postmodernism and history and Jenkins to *his* reading of postmodernism and history and Jenkins, and I hope, for those who have bothered to read this 'reply', that my side of the story has, at least, that certain appearance in its favour Derrida articulates.

Notes

1 Michael Coleman, "Response to a Postmodernist: or, A Historian's Critique of Postmodernist Critiques of History", *American Studies in Scandinavia*, 34, 1, Spring 2002, pp. 47–64.

2 F. R. Ankersmit discusses most of the issues considered in this reply in his many publications, but never better than in his most recent book, *Historical Representation* (Stanford, Stanford University Press, 2001).

3 Christopher Norris, "Defending Derrida", *The Philosophers' Magazine*, Autumn, 2002, pp. 41–3. This short 'defense' was part of a series of talks on postmodernism held in London in 2002. Norris has written extensively, and repetitively, on the dangers of postmodernism.

4 Hayden White, "Historical Emplotment and the Problem of Truth in Historical Representation", in idem, *Figural Realism* (Baltimore, Johns Hopkins University Press, 1999) pp. 27–42. White's essay has appeared in many places, most 'usefully', perhaps, for this discussion, in Saul Friedlander's *Probing the Limits of Representation* (Cambridge, Harvard University Press, 1992).

5 Ibid, p. 30.

6 Hayden White, "The Politics of Historical Interpretation", in idem, *The Content of the Form* (Baltimore, Johns Hopkins University Press, 1987) p. 75.

7 Hayden White, "An Old Question Raised Again: Is Historiography Art or Science? (Response to Iggers)", *Rethinking History*, 4, 3, 2000, pp. 391–406, p. 402.

8 Jacques Derrida, "Force of Law: The 'Mystical Foundations of Authority'", in idem, *Acts of Religion* (London, Routledge, 2002) pp. 228–98, p. 252.

9 Michael Coleman, "Gut Reactions of a Historian to a Missionary Tract", *American Quarterly*, 50, 2, June 1998, pp. 340–8.

10 Coleman, "Response to a Postmodernist … " op cit., p. 50.

11 Geoffrey Bennington, *Interrupting Derrida* (London, Routledge, 2000) p. 36.

12 Ibid.

13 R.F. Atkinson, *Knowledge and Explanation in History* (London, Macmillan, 1978) pp. 7–8.

14 Coleman, "Response to a Postmodernist … " op cit., pp. 53–4.

15 F. R. Ankersmit, op cit., p. 250.

16 Hayden White, "Literary Theory and Historical Writing", in idem, *Figural Realism*, op cit., pp. 1–26, p. 12.

17 Jacques Derrida, "Deconstructions: The Im-possible", in Lotringer, S. and Cohen, S., *French Theory in America*, (London, Routledge, 2001) pp. 13–32, p. 22.

9 On disobedient histories

In March 2003 I took part in a Round Table at the European Social Science History Conference held at The Hague, The Netherlands on the philosophy of history. I gave one paper (On Disobedient Histories), Rüdiger Graf gave a second (Interpretation, Truth, and Past Reality: Donald Davidson Meets History) and David Lindenfeld gave a commentary (The Twists of The Linguistic Turn). All three papers (mine a somewhat lengthened version of the original) then appeared together in an issue of *Rethinking History* (7.3, 2003, pp. 367–412). In my paper I had argued that we should be happy that historical representations were all 'failed representations' since it meant that no historian could write histories of closure; I used Derrida to help support the argument. Rüdiger Graf rejected this argument in favour of Davidson's defence of truth, objectivity and a type of realism which he claimed avoided its naive forms. Finally, Lindenfeld argued in his papers that my position was incoherent whilst Graf's defence of truth and coherence was equally wanting.

I have not included here the papers by Graf and Lindenfeld even though they obviously hang together with mine. Graf and I wrote our papers independently, and, whilst Lindenfeld had seen both of them in order to make his commentary at the conference, because we hadn't seen each others at the production stage then they don't exactly engage: Lindenfeld did well to bring out common themes. However, I hope that, after looking at the paper here, readers might go to *Rethinking History* for those by Graf and Lindenfeld both of which repay close attention.

> No one has changed the course of History as much as Historians.
>
> Ian Steele

What is really excellent about historians' historical representations is that they always fail. There is no possibility that any historicization of 'the past' can ever be literally true, objective, fair, non-figural, non-positioned and so on, all of which opens up that which has happened 'before now' to interminable readings and rereadings. I want to argue in this article that this professed ability to secure what are effectively interpretive *closures* – the continuing *raison d'être* of the professional historian in even these pluralist days despite sometime protestations – is not only *logically* impossible but also ethically, morally and politically desirable. The fact that 'the past' both as a whole and in its parts is so very obviously underdetermining vis-à-vis its innumerable appropriations (one past – many histories) is to be both celebrated and worked. It is to be celebrated because it is a positive democratic value when everybody can at least potentially author their own lives and create their own intellectual and moral genealogies, that there is no credible authoritative or authoritarian historicized past that one has to defer to over one's own personal history, or indeed to even acknowledge. And it is to be worked because it offers the impossible-to-prevent opportunity for those who still have the desire to articulate past-tensed fictions under the old name of history (for all histories are fictive, it is their value or lack of it that is at issue today) to do so in radical disobedience to the currently stultifying academic/professional *doxa*. The best (and perhaps the only) reason I can think of for saying that we might still need to have refigured histories that are simultaneously reflexive and emancipatory is that they may help to prise open the mental strait-jacket of modernist historical thinking for the benefit of those who have not yet managed to get out of it.

The unpacking of my argument to serve this end is, on this occasion, in three parts. In the first I draw mainly from aspects of the work of Jacques Derrida and in particular his working of the idea of the *aporia* (his main pre-occupation over the past twenty years),[1] to open up history to empowering incompleteness. In the second I move, via the notion of *reading* in Derrida, towards reading/writing the always textualized historicized past in ways deemed ethical/moral. And in the third I suggest a disobedient, refractive attitude towards 'the past' that encourages refiguring histories in ways little practised.[2] I must say straight away that in this third part I do *not* sketch out some sort of 'postmodern' blueprint or template – that would be just too modernist for words. Rather, what I outline might best be called 'favourable dispositions' towards new ways of reimagining historical figures of radical uncertainty; a relaxed attitude towards creative failure. What I am advocating is a critical disrespect towards mainstream historicizations that requires no resolution or consensual agreement as to or about historical problematicizations (which invariably stitches them into the status quo) but which admires the shortcomings of all of them. And which also celebrates, obviously, those refigurings which I just happen to like on the Lyotardian principle of the future-anterior verb: good as they might be they will always turn out 'not to have been good enough'. Nothing ever is. What is finally being recommended here, then, is an attitude that disobeys orthodoxies and which replaces all definitive closures with a suggestive openness, any exhaustive conclusion with an etcetera, and any full-stop with an ellipsis …

On the aporia

Something occurs. Somebody has done something. And I am called upon to make a judgement – an ethical/moral judgement – on the person involved, the person responsible. I have to make a decision about her. This happening, this event which I am to judge, has never happened exactly as it has now (be it ever so familiar), nor will it ever be precisely repeated. It is, in fact, a 'truly' historical event, a singular phenomenon (*sui generis*) such that, to do justice to its particularity, to try and make the right decision about it, I cannot merely reapply any previous decision I have made. For if I did that, if I were to apply a decision derived from a previously worked out code, or law, or a system of ethics or religious commands or 'the lessons of history construed as some form of necessity', then I would merely be carrying out an administrative act (I've used Commandment Three before and this situation seems to be essentially the same and so ...) and thus no decision would have been made – it would have been made 'before me'. Indeed as Derrida insists, if I were simply to draw on a decision the legibility of which was just given, natural, transparent or univocal, then the decision would not be a decision at all but merely the occasion for being affected 'as by a cause – natural or genetic'. And a fake decision of that kind could not be just. In fact, it would be unjust; unjust to the singularity of the event and its agent who has a right to be judged in all her uniqueness uncompromised (unprejudiced) by previous decisions. And so I must start again. Accordingly, the *situational* decision I will make, because it has not been made before, must therefore involve a degree of *invention*. Moreover, the decision I eventually reach and enact cannot – though it appeals to my own sense of justice – be judged 'just' by me simply because I like it. For that would merely be an expression of some kind of liberal individualism, some kind of 'free-choicism' or some sort of egotism on my part no matter how altruistically finessed. In the end, that kind of decision would only be the incorporation of the 'strangeness' of 'the other' into the familiar and the same, the incorporation of the 'not me' into my value system irrespective of theirs, and the reduction of the interests of justice to my own interests. No; for a decision to be both *my* decision (I have no alibis in the form of previous decisions 'which *made* me do it') and yet a decision not reducible to me, then it is 'the other' ('the other in me') who will decide if what is enacted against her is just or not; she will tell me if I am ethical/moral or not. Yet, of course, that judgement on me by 'the other in me' – the *presence* of 'the other in me' – can neither be a *full presence* (for if it were that then I would effectively *be her* and thus my decision would not be mine but hers and so again no decision would have been made by me), nor can her decision about the justice of my decision against her ever be definitive either, simply because she herself cannot merely reapply her previous experience of justice any more than I can – for that would be unjust on me. Consequently, her decision must also involve, if it is her singular decision, her own act of *invention*. Derrida (2001) puts all of this unavoidable uncertainty (the *aporia*) as follows:

> I come now to the decision, without which there would be neither responsibility nor ethics, neither rights nor politics ... [For] a decision, as its name indicates, must interrupt, rend a continuity in the fabric of the ordinary course of history. To be free and responsible ... it must do more

> than deploy or reveal a truth already potentially present ... I cannot decide except when [my] decision does more than manifest my imposition, my power, my capacity to be, the predicates that define me. As paradoxical as it may seem, it is thus necessary for me to receive from the other ... the very decision whose responsibility I assume. When I decide for the other [she] decides as much for me, and this singular substitution of two or more than two irreplaceable singularities at the same time is [both] impossible and necessary. This is the sole condition of the possibility of a decision worthy of its name, if ever there were such a thing.[4]

'If ever there were such a thing'; if ever there was such a decision. For of course there never is. For no one has ever made, or ever will make, a pure, ideal decision like that. For at least two reasons we must note. First, for justice to be done so that the decider acts in ways deemed just and which the person affected also thinks just, the decision must be new. Yet, if this is the case, how do we know if the decision that has been *invented* really is justice, that is, Justice in the upper case? Justice with a capital letter. For that to be a possibility, you would need to have a way of knowing what Justice really is. And that's impossible. Consequently, because no signifier is ever of this transcendental kind, is never literally true in ways that transcend its multifarious material/empirical inscriptions to stand absolutely above and outside them 'beyond the reach of time and chance', then, because we humans can never escape such contingent materiality, any assertion that we can actually posit the ideality of Justice is just that – an assertion. And not only that: the predicates of any such asserted justice are always interminably open to addition, which is to say that if you were to assert that Justice means (has the following predicates) fairness, equality, objectivity, etc., nevertheless you can then always do at least two things. First, you can keep adding further adjectives (predicates) to the list *ad infinitum*, while, second, any such predicates can in turn be interminably problematicized; I mean, what exactly is fairness, is equality, is objectivity? And so in this situation we ought, we Derrideans (and we're *all* Derrideans now, like it or not, know it or not), to try and slough off all of our previous experiences of deciding justly, we ought to attempt to decide *ex nihilo* – but of course we can never do that. For we can never divest ourselves fully of our experience, we are always 'in a text already'. We can never not be contaminated with our past in ways we cannot ever fully know. However carefully we edit, we can never edit ourselves away, be total amnesiacs. In which case every attempt at a new, pure decision is always compromised and so contains an element of injustice or, given the ultimate arbitrariness of our final, never pure decision, an element of *violence*.

And yet, although Justice will always elude us, will always skip free of even our most rigorous thoughts, to act justly, to make the right decision, remains the *motivation* behind all of our efforts. We shall never know what 'real' Justice is any more than we will know what a Woman really is, a Man really is, Humanity really is, Terror really is, Love really is, History really is – like these other names, Justice will remain ineffable, inscrutable, undepictible, *secret*, like the name and face of God. Yet we must (*il faut*) act *as if* we can achieve Justice when, under its name, we decide it all. And we *must decide* (for not to decide involves us in at least deciding that), even though the grounds for our decisions remain eternally *undecidable*. And hence we reach one of Derrida's most famous formulations, that of the 'undecidability of the decision': that the conditions of the possibility of the decision are, simultaneously, the conditions of its impossibility[5] (Derrida 2001). This is the *aporia*, the ineradicable tension between the ideal transcendental gesture and its material inscription that leaves every decision *open* to always further 'failed' decisions: here future freedom to decide is based on the poverty of all our decisions past, present and future.

In this future, as in the present, we must therefore be prepared to live in what might be called the limbo-like *middle-range*. For as Geoffrey Bennington concludes after his own lengthy discussion of Derrida's decision-making (Bennington 2000), if deconstruction (if the *aporia* that is, *perhaps*, deconstruction) always puts us in that tension between the ideality (the metaphysical, transcendental gesture) and its empirical undoing, then deconstruction 'can never predict what the best adjustment of that tension might be'.[6] Placed between two permanently unstable poles on an (infinite) spectrum between the *heuristic* device of an ideality (for the alleged transcendental is only ever a *quasi* transcendental) and equally unstable because contingent actualities of existence, then, at best, any decision is 'like a performative which has both to perform and invent the rules [in the absence of rules] according to which it might, after the event of its performance, be received as happy'.

This is the metaphorical bottom line, and we might as well accept it as 'a fact of life'. Of course, many people seem unable to do this. For some this radical anti-foundationalism gives rise to that intellectual vertigo you might face when you stand before a semantic abyss with nothing to stop your free-fall. For some, living in this way can give rise to the most abysmal of thoughts. But it need not do so. Working on the Derridean principle – which also incidentally forms the 'basis' of the whole of Richard Rorty's thought – that everything can be *redescribed*, it is easy to see that such groundlessness is the most creative, the most joyous, the most liberating of thoughts: anything is possible. For the deconstruction of all fixed terms into what might be called 'semantic weightlessness' (as Derrida puts it, 'the absence of a transcendental signifier extends the play of signification to infinity'), enables us not only to free up those meanings which have become *stuck* in our culture (which have congealed into the normal, the natural, the commonsensical, the reality; which have become literal signs rather than continuing to be thought of as the live metaphors they once so obviously were but which in fact we have now *disavowed*), but also how to think radically otherwise. This is the good news deconstruction brings: the *logical*, *aporetic assurance* that we will always get things wrong and thus be able to intellectually defer for ever total/totalitarian closures.

The postmodern era's vitality – a postmodernism that might be helpfully defined here as the 'era of the raising to consciousness of the *aporia*'[7] – lies in this guarantee of perpetual, perspectival openness. And so does postmodern responsibility. For we now *know* that we have no access to those alibis and excusing reasons that give rise to those alleged mitigating circumstances that displace our sovereign responsibilities; that mitigate what we and we alone decide – always imperfectly but an 'imperfectly' no longer misunderstood – when we make our decisions. Geoffrey Bennington (Bennington 2000) can again be used at this juncture as I begin to pull the above together and move from the end of this first section to the start of the next:

> Deconstruction [he writes] is not a form of hermeneutics however supposedly radical: hermeneutics always proposes a convergence toward a unitary meaning [whereas] deconstruction discerns a dispersive perspective in which there is no one reading. Many readers of Derrida have lost their nerve at this point, fearing a nihilistic consequence which does not in fact follow (others have imagined that Derrida, who spends a lot of time justifying his own reading, must here be caught in a contradiction). [But] the absence of a unitary horizon of meaning for the process of reading [and everything meaningful has to be read] does not commit Derrida to the *recommendation* of meaninglessness, nor does it entail the equivalence in value of all different readings (rather the singularity of each), and indeed the most rigorous textual evidence for readings proposed: but it does argue that no one reading will ever be able to claim to have exhausted the textual resources available in the text being read.[8]

'No one reading will ever be able to claim to have exhausted the textual resources available in the text being read' – including, of course, the past as text; including the texts that write (about) 'the past': histories. The historical text is thus irreducibly open and, in the Derridean spirit being advocated here, must be kept self-consciously, deliberately and reflexively open for new refigurings of, I hope, a radical, emancipatory kind. For in this way we might, as Nietzsche says (a Nietzsche standing full-square behind Derrida and, in different ways, Richard Rorty), outstrip ourselves, dazzle and bewitch ourselves, frolic in new images and so, in transforming ourselves, 'give birth to oneself'. Here is Rorty (1989):

> The hope of the [deconstructionist] strong poet who has found a way to describe the past that the past never knew and thereby found a self which her precursors never knew was possible … is that what the past tried to do to her she will succeed in doing to the past: to make the past itself, including those very causal processes which blindly impressed all her behavings, bear her impress. Success in that enterprise – the enterprise of saying 'Thus I willed it' to the past – is success in what Bloom calls 'giving birth to oneself'.[9]

On reading

Something occurs. I am reading a book in the only way in which it can be conceptually read: as a text. In addition, I am reading it in a deconstructionist way. That is to say, with an awareness that I intend to exploit the fact that no text can make any reading of it necessary, unavoidable, on the basis that 'everything can be redescribed'. Of course, there are many texts that have attempted to remain 'closed books', to effect a definitive closure. Religious books – the embodiment of The Word – aspire to this, as do law books and statutes which attempt to exclude readings other than the one the legislators intended, while Hegel's or Marx's or Freud's works – the works of those greatest of modernist system-builders – are calculated to incorporate all the readings to which they may be held 'to have left themselves open' including, especially, those made by hostile ideologies who attempt to refute them – 'well they would say that wouldn't they?' And, in academic history texts too, more often than not the ambition to *represent* the past means to *settle*, to *solve and resolve* and thus to *control* that which is represented by articulating it through familiar(izing) figures: the peer-respected 'original thesis', the 'interesting debate', the 'fruitful exchange of views', the 'managed controversies' and 'evidentially grounded knowledge'; strategies that fold corrosive scepticism into scholarly caution and empirical facticity, and which limit what is actually the inexpungeable relativism of every historical account by reference to a putative objectivity and disinterested neutrality.

But, as I say, I am reading this text differently, disobediently, in ways it never intended to be read: with an attitude of intentional infidelity. This does not mean (and nobody has ever said it does mean, least of all Derrida) that texts – including the one I am reading – are open to absolutely any reading – otherwise the reading just would not be about *this* text: no text is totally indeterminate with respect to its reading. But there would not be what Derrida calls a reading if texts were not constituted 'as an appeal to a reading still to come'. For in order to be read at all, any text – including Hegel's or Marx's or Freud's – must in principle be open to be read and thereby open to a reading it cannot control in advance: 'if Hegel [for example] is to be read rather than simply repeated, then the chance of a radically unpredictable reading must be open even in the text that is entirely written in order to preserve [forestall] any such reading'.[10] For Derrida, then, 'texts *cry out for reading*' and not just any reading, but one that leaves open an essential latitude or freedom which just is what constitutes reading *as* reading rather than as passive decipherment. Which is why texts are not messages and why classical theories of communication are unhelpful. Consequently:

> It follows that reading has a duty to respect not only the text's 'wishes' (the reading of itself most obviously programmed into itself) but also the opening that opens a margin of freedom with respect to any such wishes, and without which these wishes could not even be registered or recognised.

> Readers recognise these wishes (traditionally thought of as the 'author's intentions') only by opening themselves to the opening which constitutes the very *readability* of the text – however minimal that readability may be in fact – and that readability is, as such, already in excess of those wishes. A text is a text only as at least minimally readable in this sense, and that means it always can be read *differently* with respect to the way it would wish to be read. An absolutely respectful relation to a text would forbid one from even touching it. The *ethics* of reading would, then, consist in the negotiation of the margin opened by readability.[11]

In Derrida, then, there is always a double-reading of any text. The first is a faithful, respectful and detailed explanation or commentary as accurate as possible to the words on the page and to the 'intentions' behind them, followed by a second reading (which is sometimes the only *written* one so that it may look as if the first had not been undertaken – which explains why some think Derrida *does* say you can say anything about *that* text) which opens up those gaps, those *aporetic* tensions which no text can fully suture and into which, when opened up, the text collapses. Thus Derrida never works *on* a text to deconstruct it in the sense of an external *critique*; rather, the text implodes as a result of the opening up of its *immanent* fault lines. And so it is at this point that we arrive directly at history: at the idea of the 'past as a text', at the question of the epistemological status of the history text as standing in for, substituting itself for, the actual past, and thus at historiography as itself the historicized form (generally narrative form) such substitutions collectively are made manifest in. Of course, by the idea of the past as a text no one has ever claimed – and again certainly not Derrida – that the past in all its actuality was literally a text; rather, what reading the past *as if* it was a text draws attention to is that to put the past (the past's traces) into the genre of a history it has to be made readable, textual. But, because the past is not literally a text in its own right/write, then, unlike literal texts (e.g. books, articles), it has no *author* and thus, no matter how much it is claimed to be perceived, obviously no *authorial intent*. Consequently the past *qua* past cannot tell historians which of its parts it would like (it intends) them to study, to pay attention to, to *make* significant or to ignore. The past has no substantive 'anything' of its own; before narrative figuring it has no shape or figure, so that the 'organized substances' of its narrations (*narrative substances*) derive their existence not from the (non-existent) 'form and content' of the past but from the forms of its telling. Historical narratives – with their ultimately arbitrary modes of troping, emplotting and arguing – *embody only their own authors' authorial intentions* with no access to the past *per se* either in part or in whole to check them out against. The past – the past *per se* – thus expresses no rhyme or reason of its own by which to stop 'us authors' speculating *ad infinitum* about possible rhymes or reasons so that different historians' representations are (literally) fabular/fabulous, are fables, that is, imaginative tales without any existence outside of the telling, outside of their tale. Moreover, the dissolution of the notion of a semantics (an intention, a meaning) discoverable or inferable in historiographical tales is, as Hayden White has pointed out so many times, at the same time the dissolution of a *method* by which history in general can be endowed with any sense at all. Consequently, the historian is *liberated* from *having* to say anything about the past: the past *qua* past thus contains nothing we *have* to be loyal to, nothing we *have* to feel guilty about, nothing we *have* to respect, no truths we *have* to find, no problems we *have* to solve, no projects we *have* to complete. For the historicized past we 'bring back' is only ever *our* historicized past: the historicized past is only ever us – back there. Remembered or forgotten as we desire. Of course we cannot *deny* the actual past – both our own and other people's – but we can and perhaps we must learn to *forget* it. In his *Genealogy of Morals*, Nietzsche tried to free men of their capacity to remember on the basis that, freed from their pasts, they could build 'creatively on forgetfulness'. For it is not a matter of human beings needing memory; human beings just have a memory whether they want it or not, the question is whether this capacity to remember becomes a historicized 'threat to life itself'.

Perhaps ... perhaps the era of the postmodern is thus an era in which we can learn to *forget* and to fix our sights on the present and future relieved of much baggage from our past, relieved of 'the burden of history'. For, as I have said, we are free to choose, to *decide*, the inheritance we want. *Otherwise it wouldn't be an inheritance*. Accordingly, the historicized past, the heritage we want 'to come' always remains as a task that lies before us: our historicized past – which may be very little, almost nothing – is always in the future to be read and reread, written and rewritten, over and over again: imperfectly and interminably. Thus says Derrida:

> An inheritance is never fully gathered; it is never at one with itself. Its presumed unity, if there is one, can only consist in the injunction to re-affirm by choosing. You must (*il faut*) sort out among several of the possibilities which inhabit the same injunction. And inherit it in a contradictory fashion around a secret. If the legibility of a legacy were given, natural, transparent, univocal, if it did not simultaneously call for and defy interpretation, one would never have to inherit from it. One would be affected by it as by a cause – natural or genetic. One always inherits a secret which says, 'Read me: will you ever be up to it?'[12]

Will we ever be up to it? No we won't. Will we ever get it right? No we won't. Does it matter? No it doesn't. For it is the secret of the infinite – or the infinite secret – the irreducibility of the 'to come' to the already here, the impossibility of reducing otherness to the same and the familiar, that opens up the present and, if you want it, the past you want to newness. And Derrida always wants to say 'Yes' to newness, to the 'to come': to the perhaps, to the arriver, to the Messianic without the Messiah; to alterity, to difference, to the excess: 'Yes – Come.'

It is, of course, always a risk to take a chance with the 'to come'. It might, writes Derrida, be monstrous. The decision I make about the future-past is thus one about which I must always have my doubts; no cut is ever 'clear cut'. The *aporia* of the decision logically guarantees that I can *never* know for sure if I've got it right. But still I must choose, *interpret*, decide in ways I don't fully believe in, decide in a way that lacks total rigour and yet possesses – perhaps – as Derrida puts it (Derrida 2001), 'without being rigorously either true or false, a certain appearance in its favour'. 'A certain appearance in its favour': this brief but brilliant encapsulation of the 'shortfall of the epistemological' is as good as it gets; this is where we have to start from 'as best we can'.

And so let us take seriously this injunction to start again. And let us do so with Derrida's form of words held self-consciously, self-consciously enough to aspire in our recommendations to nothing more than rhetorical *oratory*. For the figure of the *orator* can, as Hegel classically pointed out, exercise enormous freedom when picking and choosing which bits of the historicized past to use given that the orator's *raison d'être* is the achievement of a practical, pragmatic end: 'the orator is permitted to use historical facts as he wishes, selectively and in response to the end envisaged'. And let us envisage two 'ends'. First, for those still more wedded to the idea of history, let us go with Frank Ankersmit's suggestion *that the best histories are those which are 'so far out' that no historian could possibly accept them and yet be of a kind that no historian can refute*, which stretch us beyond belief! And second – and it is this 'end' that I will essay here – for those less wedded to the continuing importance of history, let us go with an attitude of *disobedience* which we can conjure up, for now, through a combination of 'the postmodern subject', a notion of the intellectual, a notion of commitment, a radical poesis, and a working of the notion of *refraction*. And let me start this recommendation with a short résumé of historical orthodoxy which fixes the context for this refiguring and explains why I think we must indeed 'begin again'.

Towards refraction

Think of a history, then, which exists in the world of the proper, professional, academic historian rooted firmly in the intellectual milieu in which most are rooted, in the realm of 'the real'. Such a history – we should know it well by now – will be reassuringly and communicably realist, obviously, and also, I think, empiricist, factualist, objectivist and, with its privileging emphasis on *the* primary (and thus 'original' and thus 'authentic') sources, heavily documentarist. Such a history will be studied for the past's own sake not ours (own-sakism) and on the past's own terms and not ours (own-termism) and thus non-anachronistically and disinterestedly as opposed to present-centred and ideologically (as if non-anachronistic histories were possible and if disinterest was not yet just another interest), the interpretive flux which still persists even given these strictures to 'truth at the end of enquiry' being accommodated by passing it off as a sign of academic freedom thereby strengthening notions of liberal openness – as if such toleration didn't turn into an intolerant ideology when having to deal with those who challenge not just its putative content but its forms – at which point we meet the accusatory language of 'extremism'. And such a history will pride itself on its robust, no-nonsense language of communicative transparency, though this, ironically, at the very time that it is there only by courtesy of the relative coherence of language as such which, when cured up into a meaningful narrative form gives that very same form – narrative – to the formlessness of 'the before now', the *substance* of this literary artefact – history – thereby being constructed, structured and thus constituted linguistically. Such a history – a modernist history of the academic genre – will scarcely recognize itself as a product of such *narrative substances*, but it is, just as all histories are. And it is histories of misrecognition, like these, that are arguably passé.

And so, let us think again. Let us begin again. And let us think this time in postmodern ways. Let us go with the idea that, if history is *just us back there*, throwing our voice, then that history, like any other history, will inevitably be constituted and understood by virtue of having the selfsame characteristics by which we constitute and understand ourselves. And think now of the kind of characteristics we inhabitants of postmodernity – we postmodernist 'subjectivities in processes' – have, 'like it or not, know it or not'. And think of the possibilities this opens up for a refiguring of 'the before now' beyond modernist figures.

Thus such a 'subject' will see him or herself as constituted performatively so that he or she is constantly being made and remade, read and reread, written and rewritten, incessantly and interminably. Such a subject will see him or herself as always temporarily and spatially positioned and repositioned yet, lacking any fixing, foundational anchor, intrinsic nature or inner meaning, knowable purpose or teleological destiny, then, decentred and fragmented, the sometime product of a reiterated enactment of norms which are radically contingent, he or she will remain an ultimate mystery even to him or herself; everyone has a secret. This is a sometime self held together in what can only be a fictional unity which, it is hoped, will enable enough coping practices to develop such that one can survive in ways deemed variously desirable.

Consequently, this is a self which will understand 'the before now' (just as it understands the present and the future) as sometime appropriable and copable with by virtue of these selfsame features. So that 'the before now' is regarded as sublime in its putative whole and relativistic in its parts, as endlessly readable and rereadable, writable and rewritable, as demonstrably contingent and serendipitous and thus as non-teleological and so of a kind that can only be given a historical shape or a style or a meaning (a figure) via a series of interpretive, perspectival decisions which are ultimately undecidable (here we meet, inescapably, the Derridean 'undecidability of the decision') so as to produce some kind of unity that is clearly a fictional fix, an act of the imagination: indeed, as something clearly *fabular*; that is, to repeat, as something which is told, narrated, having no 'real' existence outside of the tale. As a product that is, quite literally, self-referencing.

And now think of this 'self' in a positive, optimistic way, through the idea of the 'outsider'. That it to say, think of this self as an *intellectual* self which runs the kind of uncompromising critique of the inside, the status quo, which Edward Said in his *Representations of the Intellectual* argues just *is* the role of the intellectual. For Said (1994) the intellectual is a particular kind of person. A person endowed with the capacity for representing and articulating an uncompromising, emancipatory message. A person whose works have a radical, sustained cutting edge. A person happy to raise embarrassing questions, not to take 'No' for an answer, to relentlessly confront dogma and orthodoxy and keep in focus 'those people and issues that are continually forgotten or swept under the rug'.[13] This is a person who enjoys never being fully adjusted, of being beyond the chatty, inconsequential 'reality' inhabited by the natives, of being immune to accommodation; an unco-optable, *disobedient* person. And this is a person who not only accepts the fate invariably meted out by various establishments to this thorn in the flesh – the status of the relative *exile* – but also welcomes it. Who likes being marginal. Who accepts that his or her awkwardness, 'eccentric angles of vision' and unwillingness to follow established paths, gives a freedom and integrity that makes him or her beholden to no one and is ready to accept the consequences of that position: that one can never be settled, never fully accepted, never be entirely comfortable, never 'be at home in one's home'; that one actually relishes being, as Rilke put it, 'a perpetual beginner in your circumstances'.[14] And think of this position as one which allows you to express your beliefs both within the narrower discourse you are primarily engaged in (history) and more generally, politically, and to connect these two things up.

In his *Ethics: An Essay on the Understanding of Evil*, Alain Badiou articulates a way of thinking which helps to make the occupation of this intellectuality an always positive one (Badiou 2001). For Badiou, in the sphere of human action there are just two very different but overlapping subspheres: first, the 'ordinary' realm of established interests and differences, of approved *knowledges* that serve to name, recognize and *place* consolidated identities and, second, an 'exceptional' realm of singular innovations which persist only through 'the *militant* proclamation of those rare individuals who constitute themselves as *the subjects* of a truth [position]; as the militants of their cause'.[15]

How does this *militant* occupation of a 'truth' (or, as I read it here, this militant occupation of a reflexively held 'position') work? How can it be reached? Well, for Badiou, such an occupation can begin only with some sort of *break* with the 'ordinary' by way of what he calls an *event*. Such an *event* has no verifiable content, its happening cannot be proved but only, in the light of *experience*, grasped, affirmed and proclaimed, a position which then persists by virtue of having an attitude of fidelity towards it, of commitment to it, a commitment which 'amounts to something like a disinterested enthusiasm, absorption in a compelling task or cause, a sense of elation, of being caught up in something that transcends {metaphorically} all petty, private or material concerns ... of *holding true* to a principle, person or ideal'.[16] And of having an ethical attitude towards the event too, ethics being understood here as that which helps to literally en-*courage* the subject, to keep going in selfless devotion to a cause. Such *events* are therefore the immediate catalysts that bring to fruition previously developing tendencies, that concretize previous intimations of a position which is then held fast. As Badiou puts it:

> I shall call 'truth' {position} the real process of a fidelity to an event: that which this fidelity *produces* in the situation. For example the politics of the French Maoists between 1966 and 1976, which tried to think and practice a fidelity to two entangled events: the Cultural Revolution in China and May '68 in France. Or so-called 'contemporary' music ... which is fidelity to the great Viennese composers of the early twentieth century. Or the algebraic geometry of the 1950s and 1960s and so forth. Essentially a truth {position} is the material course traced ... from the decision to relate henceforth to the situation *from the perspective of its eventual supplement* ... It is thus an *immanent break*. 'Immanent' because a truth proceeds *in* the situation and nowhere else – there is no heaven {foundation} of truths. 'Break' because what enables the truth-process {reflexive positioning} – the event – means nothing according to the prevailing language and established knowledge of the situation.[17]

This new innovation, this truth, this position which is heterogeneous to the instituted, conventional knowledges of the situation, which '*punches a hole in these established knowledges*', produces a position that is, as it were, *induced* by the *event,* after which one has to rework one's previously *ordinary* ways of being into *newness*:

> It is clear that under the effect of a loving encounter {event} if I want to be *really* faithful to it, I must completely rework my ordinary way of 'living' my situation. If I want to be faithful to the event of the 'Cultural Revolution', then I must at least practice politics ... in an entirely different manner from that proposed in the socialist and trade-unionist traditions. Again, Berg and Webern, faithful to the musical event known by the name of 'Schoenberg', cannot continue with *fin de siècle* neo-Romanticism as if nothing had happened. And after Einstein's texts of 1905, if I am faithful to their radical novelty, I cannot continue to practice physics within its classical framework, and so on. An evental fidelity is a real break (both thought and practiced) on the specific order in which the event took place (be it political, loving, artistic or scientific).[18]

And so, if I want to be faithful to the 'posts' – to post-structuralism, post-colonialism, post-feminism, post-modernism – then *I cannot* remain a structuralist, a colonialist, a feminist, a modernist. I have to break with these, commit an act of infidelity; I have to be loyal to the new. Not loyal, of course, in the sense of refusing to ever reposition myself again (for in Badiou's thought the effort to impose a total or unqualified power is construed as evil). But loyal to the new position that completes the break with the old, loyal to its possibilities, and loyal to the idea of endlessly reworking them save that, with Derrida, one never gives up on that one great, 'underpinning', fictional narrative – that great *fable* of emancipation.

Continue, now, to think further along these lines. And this time think of the possibilities for the interminable refiguring opened up by the *fabular* nature of histories. In his *The Illusion of the End*[19] – which, if it indeed 'punches a hole in reality', which, if it is perceived as indeed empty or void from the perspective of those who dominate the situation, can itself achieve the status of an *event* – Jean Baudrillard argues that the end of the illusion of the end (i.e. the end of the illusion that 'the before now' before historicization had an end *in* it), of the end of what was only ever a simulation of a linear past as history, offers us at least the possibility of imagining what he calls a 'poetic reversibility of events' precisely because of the as yet unexplored possibilities contained in the particular language games we inhabit and yet which we can still think newness through as we seek to go beyond them, break them and break with them (Baudrillard 1994). For today we clearly recognize that it is only the grammar of our language that allowed us to create in the first place grammatical (i.e. coherent) historicizations of 'the before now'; it did not allow us to discover them. Today we recognize that the world always *obeys* our syntax and that 'its' semantics are always only ours. And so think now of a different syntax which may give rise to a different 'orders of things', to new syntactical/semantic figures. And let me follow Baudrillard for a little while as he develops a new poetics of 'history', commenting on it in passing.

For Baudrillard, then, 'the before now' has never unfolded in (say) a linear fashion as part of some kind of inherent structure or in line with some sort of evolutionary or narrative process: the 'before now' knows nothing of our geometries, of our tropes. Linearity is thus an illusion derived from another illusion, namely, that language also unfolds in a linear fashion. Because it doesn't. Linguistically, everything moves in loops, tropes, inversions of meaning. Discursively, linguistically, things relate not logically, but enthymemically, except in artificial (say digital) languages which are, for that very reason, 'precisely not languages'.

In which case, says Baudrillard, might we not freely transpose new language games on to the phenomenon of 'the before now'? I mean, there is obviously nothing to stop us. And not just transpose the major figures of metaphor (metonymy, synecdoche, irony) but also those 'puerile, formalistic games, those heteroclite tropes which are the delight of the vulgar imagination: *anagrams, acrostics, spoonerisms, rhyme, strophe* and *catastrophe*'.[20] In which case, argues Baudrillard, could we not imagine and construct an *anagrammatic* history 'where meaning is dismembered and scattered to the wind, like the name of God in the anagram', or a *rhyming* history which can be read in either direction? Could we not think of 'the before now' organized in the structure of an *acrostic* (where the initial and final letters of lines make different words and sense irrespective and underivable from the words (content) in between)? Or through the form of *strophe* whereby a group of lines are detached from the rest of a poem to form a sense of sense which is underived from the immediate context or the full poem (think microhistories here) – and so on and so forth. Is it ever possible, queries Baudrillard, that such forms, which draw attention to the ways material actuality is organized through language, draw our gaze to that language and to the ways in which it *materializes* into meaning otherwise meaninglessness; indeed, is it possible that such organizing, artificial and arbitrary syntactical grids might allow us to see the world anew and even to confront 'the radical illusion of the world' stripped of our old organizing metaphors and allegories and thus ready to be reallegorized into fresh meanings – a process we know we can *begin again*, over and over? Well, if this were possible then such would be, as Baudrillard puts it, 'the enchanted alternative to the linearity of history', the poetic alternative of refiguring, as reflexively as possible, that which has already been figured into those 'reality effects' we have forgotten are mere effects and think of as reality.

And yet we must be careful that in our possible enthusiasm for the new we never forget that these are merely the effects of the new, that there is no 'reality' here save by virtue of them. Alongside Baudrillard, Elizabeth Ermarth (1992) has cautioned against us becoming immersed, yet again, in 'the depths of the past'. In various articles wherein Ermarth brilliantly considers the possibility of still making history when its modernist apparatus of consensual values of neutrality/objectivity have been undercut, and when its epistemological and methodological fetishisms have been dismantled not just philosophically but 'by the postmodern world', she draws upon the notion of *anthematic* recognition in Vladimir Nabokov's works and on the term *anthemion* which, for Nabokov, refers to those interlaced, flower-like designs where items and patterns arrive and depart from various posting places, recurring without exact repetition and yet which produce a kind of rhythmic iteration where, for Nabokov as for Ermarth, there lie, metaphorically 'beneath' such rhythms, 'tender intervals within which opportunities lie and the sum of which constitutes memory and experience: postmodern experience'. From this perspective the recovery of 'the before now' as striven for in modernist histories – 'the attempt to keep the whole world in mind' as Ermarth puts it – is increasingly difficult not least in a multicultural and multinational world bereft of both foundational *grand* and *petite* narratives, such that the *anthematic* alternative seems not just an attractive but an almost unavoidable alternative. For in this construal, says Ermarth:

> The unprecedented and unrepeatable event is the potential beginning of anthematic development, each a specification of a systematic potential, each with its own pattern and possible future. The sum of such anthematic development over time constitutes the continuum of an individual

> life. Anthematic emphasis falls precisely on the present moment, *not* as a transfer site between past and future, but as the growing point of an unpredictable anthemion of a life. Each sequence has its own possible *grammars* and specifications, its own past and trajectory.[21]

Drawing on the first chapter of Nabokov's novel, *Transparent Things* (Nabokov 1973), and in doing so adding to the concept of *anthemion* that of *refraction*, Ermarth tells how the narrator warns the *novices* of the book – *novice historians in this case* – to avoid sinking into the depths of the historicized past, modernist style, and to remain very precisely on the surface of things. Thus Nabokov writes:

> When we concentrate on a material object, whatever its situation, the very act of attention may lead to our involuntary sinking into the history of that object. [But history] novices must learn to skim over matter if they want to stay at the exact level of the moment. Transparent things, through which the past shines!
>
> [Of course] man-made objects, or natural ones, inert in themselves but much used by careless life ... are particularly difficult to keep in surface focus: novices [easily] fall through the surface [of the now] humming happily to themselves, and are soon reveling with child-like abandon in the [history] of *this* stone, the [history] of *that* heath. I shall explain. A thin veneer of immediate reality is spread over natural and artificial matter, and whoever wishes to remain in the now, with the now, should not break its tension film. Otherwise the inexperienced [history novice] ... will find himself no longer walking on water but descending upright among staring fish.[22]

To which Ermarth glosses Nabokov thus:

> The powers required to pursue history destroy the past by sinking into it; allowing the past to *refract* through 'transparent things' requires a discipline as miraculous as that of walking on water but nevertheless possible for the [historian] novice ... who learns by staying at the exact level of the moment, letting the past shine through. 'Things' no longer function as they did in the objectifying grammars of modernity; 'things' are not 'objects' but instead, the occasions, the carriers, the sites where new acts of attention can be performed, where memory [experience] inflects and reinflects again; an imaginative awareness engaged in the process of creating the unique and unrepeatable poetry of a life.[23]

Let me now gloss Ermarth and work her comment that our attitude towards historicization should be *refractive*. Thus, let us imagine the past as a medium of different density which we can only ever enter obliquely in the present: what we see under and through the 'surface' is never quite in the right place;

there is always a *dislocation* (as when we see a stick in a glass of water).[24] And so let us see historicizations of the past as precisely *fractures*, as breaks between the now and the then which can never be – nor should we ever bother about them ever being – healed up into a full, unbroken meaning. And let our *attitude* towards historical orthodoxy be *refractory*; that is, *cantankerous, contentious, difficult, disobedient, disputatious, disrespectful, headstrong, intractable, obstinate, unruly*: let us embody our *Thesaurus*. Let us stay on the surface and skim. Let us trick with our tropes, plot and emplot, figure and refigure in poetic arrangements that resist codification and the death-knell of orthodoxy … let us be – whatever we want to be …

For those who can think in this way, the postmodern way of Baudrillard and Ermarth, it now becomes inconceivable to think of a historical consciousness that remains sunk in the depths of the realist/epistemological mindset of modernist historians – however *reflective*. Postmodernism, to this way of thinking, is not some sort of fashion, nor some kind of typical 'critical discourse' that can be ignored or recuperated back into modernity in the guise of 'pluralistic interpretations' once its excesses are shed: for postmodernism *is* its excesses; *postmodernism is everything modernity just cannot ever be*. Postmodernism for me, here, is the getting of an attitude, a militant, radical disposition, that undercuts not only the content but also the grammatical, fictional forms of modernist histories without a hint of apology or nostalgia and offers in their place – *if you still want them* – in its new grammars and acts of attention, new ways of rendering up 'the before now' as yet unconceived of. *Modernist histories and historians fade away and disappear here*. So that to those modernists who think that history is still an epistemology rather than a reflexive, aestheticizing, figuring, grammatically promiscuous, *refractive* discursive experiment *sans* foundations – and that to it postmodernism makes no difference, has no 'relevance' to the twenty-first century, all I can say finally is, think about it. And then relax. And then go with it. And then unite. I mean, why not? You have nothing to lose but your pasts.

Notes

1 Derrida has spelt out the idea of the 'undecidability of the decision' in many places, but most accessibly in two short essays and an interview. Thus, see his 'Remarks on deconstruction and pragmatism', in C. Mouffe (ed.) *Pragmatism and Deconstruction* (London: Routledge, 1996), pp. 77–88; 'Deconstructions: the impossible', in S. Lotringer and S. Cohen (eds) *French Theory in America* (London: Routledge, 2001), pp. 13–32; 'The deconstruction of actuality', *Radical Philosophy* 68 (1994). See also Ernesto Laclau's comments on Derrida's undecidability in his 'Deconstruction, pragmatism, hegemony', in Mouffe, pp. 47–68.

2 The third section of this paper is taken, essentially, from the last chapter of my book, *Refiguring History: New Thoughts on an Old Discipline* (London: Routledge, 2002).

3 On Derrida and 'invention', see 'Deconstructions: the im-possible', in Lotringer and Cohen, *French Theory in America*.

4 Ibid., p. 27.

5 Ibid., *passim*.

6 G. Bennington, *Interrupting Derrida* (London: Routledge, 2000); see the collection of essays/chapters that make up Part I of Bennington's text ('Pedagogics'), pp. 5–58.
7 Postmodernism has many different definitions; in this article I have decided to think of it as 'the era of the *aporia*'. By that, I mean that this is an era when all the decisions we take – political, ethical, moral, interpretive, representational – are ultimately undecidable (*aporetic*). That our chosen ways of seeing things lack foundations and that, as far as a discourse such as history is concerned, it is essentially to be thought of as an aesthetic – a shaping, figuring discourse – and *not* as an objective, true or foundational epistemology. Indeed, perhaps the era's greatest achievement is to rid us of the idea – so central to modernist historicizations – that history is, at the level of the text, an epistemology.
8 Bennington, *Interrupting Derrida*, p. 11.
9 R. Rorty, *Contingency, Irony, and Solidarity* (Cambridge: Cambridge University Press, 1989).
10 Bennington, *Interrupting Derrida*, p. 138.
11 Ibid., p. 36.
12 J. Derrida, *Spectres of Marx* (London: Routledge, 1994), p. 16.
13 E. Said, *Representations of the Intellectual* (London: Vintage, 1994), p. 9.
14 Ibid., p. 46.
15 P. Hallward, 'Introduction to A. Badiou, *Ethics: An Essay on the Understanding of Evil*' (London: Verso, 2001), p. viii.
16 Ibid., p. x.
17 Ibid., p. 42.
18 Ibid.
19 J. Baudrillard, *The Illusion of the End* (Cambridge: Polity Press, 1994); see especially Baudrillard's last two (very short) chapters in which he outlines his new 'poetics of history'.
20 Ibid., pp. 120–2.
21 E. D. Ermarth, 'Beyond "the subject": individuality in the discursive condition', *New Literary History* 31(3) (summer 2000), pp. 405–20. Ermarth has developed her ideas – discussed at length in her *Sequel to History: Postmodernism and the Crisis of Representational Time* (Princeton, NJ: Princeton University Press, 1992) – in various places. See her 'Ph(r)ase time: chaos theory and postmodern reports on knowledge', *Time and Society* 4 (1995), pp. 95–110; 'Time and neutrality: media of modernity in a postmodern world', *Cultural Values* 1 (1998), pp. 355–67. Ermarth has written a brief but incisive intellectual/autobiographical essay ('Beyond history') for *Rethinking History Journal* 5(2) (2001), pp. 195–215. Ermarth is, I think, one of the very few writers who takes the end of modernity's histories for granted and who is interested, above all, in 'the possibilities for writing histories once the consensus apparatus supporting modernity has been dismantled? This is the question currently engaging me' (p. 212).
22 V. Nabokov, *Transparent Things* (London: Weidenfeld & Nicolson, 1973), pp. 1–2.
23 Ermarth, 'Beyond "the subject"', p. 417.
24 Frank Ankersmit has pointed out in a correspondence that the reference to 'staying on the surface' and skimming is similar to Walter Benjamin's 'approach' in his *Arcades Project* where 'Benjamin suggests that the historian does, or should relate to the past in the way the Baudelarian dandy [and *flaneur*] relates to the metropole. The real secret of the metropole is not some hidden "essence" but what lies on the surface and is, precisely because of that, perceived only by the dandy [and *flaneur*] since he has no hidden agenda guiding his perception of the city.'

References

Badiou, Alain (2001) *Ethics: An Essay on the Understanding of Evil*, London: Verso.
Baudrillard, Jean (1994) *The Illusion of the End*, Cambridge: Polity Press.
Bennington, Geoffrey (2000) *Interrupting Derrida*, London: Routledge.

Derrida, Jacques (2001) 'Deconstructions: the im-possible', in S. Lotringer and S. Cohen (eds) *French Theory in America,* London: Routledge.

Ermarth, Elizabeth Deeds (1992) *Sequel to History*, Princeton, NJ: Princeton University Press.

Nabokov, Vladimir (1973) *Transparent Things*, London: Weidenfeld & Nicolson.

Rorty, Richard (1989) *Contingency, Irony, and Solidarity,* Cambridge: Cambridge University Press.

Said, Edward (1994) *Representations of the Intellectual*, London: Vintage.

10 Modernist disavowals and postmodern reminders of the condition of history today

On Jean-François Lyotard

For many years I had been reading Jean François Lyotard – at least since the publication in English (in 1984) of *The Postmodern Condition.* But apart from a chapter in *Why History?* (1999) I had not written on him. This paper's more immediate impetus, however, was reading Sande Cohen's tribute to Lyotard (who died in 1998) – 'The "Use and Abuse of History" according to Jean François Lyotard' – which appeared in *Parallax* (6, 4, 2000, pp. 99–113), and which made me rethink Lyotard and history somewhat differently. Just as importantly, perhaps, was that reading Cohen's paper made me go back to Cohen's own works (which I had read only intermittently before I'm ashamed to admit) and which explains my general introduction to Cohen's texts in a paper also in this volume (pp. 270–294).

Looking back on some formative influences, I think that Lyotard, along with Derrida, Baudrillard and Nietzsche, have been crucial to me. Lyotard's fantastic imaginative writing and the sheer inventiveness of his ideas are really breathtaking, and I am all too painfully aware of how the paper here absolutely does not do him justice.

Within our culture, here in the anglophone West, in England, history – and especially history as a professional academic discipline and as an edifying discourse – is still generally regarded as 'a good thing'. We really cannot, so the familiar story goes, live our lives uninformed by our own personal history and the history of the social formation to which we 'belong'. To live outside of history – to live without memory (and in this construal these two ontologically quite distinct concepts are invariably conflated) – would be to suffer a form of debilitating amnesia. Without previous reference points our personal and public lives would be without – or at least without much – direction, point, rhyme or reason. But with history, with our stories about 'the past' and with our own personal recollections intact, we can locate ourselves securely, stitching ourselves into networks of previous significance and so imagine what we might, with luck, become.

And the study of history – of this kind of history – brings with it other important benefits. The fact that people similar – though not identical – to us walked and talked where we walk and talk means that, despite our multifarious *historical* differences from them, we can *all* be made sense of by invoking a common humanity so as to help develop what are proposed as being common, essential values. Values of toleration, of empathy, of sympathy; values lending weight to all manner of 'understandings' and, on occasion, to justifiable outrage. Here is a shared discourse, then, for both comparison and compassion that helps produce – as it shuttles back and forth between the present and the past (the 'before now') – the construction of what are our own composite and mobile identities, but identities all the same. And even more particularly, more locally as it were, here in England now, history is deemed essential at the 'benchmarked' level of generic aptitudes, attitudes and skills. Here, 'doing history' can help develop our stiff-upper-lipped commitment to objectivity, fairness and 'truth at the end of enquiry'. Here we can refine – through methodological practices and the application of an empirically grounded reason hopefully unsullied by too much theory – those ethically informed habits of mind which, sharpened (as they say) on the whetstone of historiographical debate, help us to become reflexive practitioners and responsible professional colleagues, paragons, in fact, of humane, liberal virtue.

Of course there have been and there still are various well-recognised problems with all of the above. Some historians and some theorists, for example, have and still do insist on studying *their* 'past' for themselves and on *their* terms rather than on the past's own terms. Others have tried to insert deconstructive variants of scepticism and relativism into an otherwise objectivist discipline that has tried to resist them as best it could and with some success, recuperating these phenomena through the valorisation (in the case of scepticism) of proper scholarly caution and (in the case of relativism) a wistful, peer-approved pluralism. Accordingly, these sometime irritants suitably neutered, the benefits of a relatively unconcerned historical consciousness are still considered obvious. Here the discipline of history presents itself both within universities and across those extramural media that saturate our culture and which we meet everyday in our televisual virtualities and in the street, as self-evidently worthwhile; I mean, how could we possibly survive without history?

And yet, of course, we should be suspicious of all of this. For when any kind of thinking establishes itself as the doxa, when it trips right across a social formation, when its naturalness and its knowledge claims are quite literally taken for granted, are hegemonic, then we can confidently say that we are in the presence of an insidious political *ideology*.

Now, I have to admit that I am constantly surprised at the residual strength of what is so obviously an example of special pleading when this type of history manages to pass off its peculiar practices as of a universal kind, not least because we all 'know' that no discipline, no discourse, can fail to express the particular interests that empower and inform it, and that such interests rest on no establishable, universal foundations. When so many of us are aware that, while the 'before now' has many things in it, two of the things it has never contained are 'the past' or 'history' (such that the desire to 'go back to the past' or to 'find a history' is to mistake mere figures of speech for 'the real thing'), then the fact that these linguistic entities are still assumed to actually 'be out there' seems incredible. And again, when so many of us are aware that histories are literary artefacts made possible only if the 'before now' is itself textualised so opening it up to countless readings – and when we recognise that such readings can never exhaust the textual resources available – then we can only listen in amazement to objectivist-talk and truth-talk. And whilst it is indeed the case that historians' writings demonstrably contain cognitive, empirical and thus epistemologically renderable entities (the evidential facts, the corroborated singular statement, the description) as texts irreducible to these sometime checkable parts, then histories *qua* histories are impossible to definitively demarcate from fiction and myth such that, once again, one can only watch in amazement as academic historians try to turn their fabular tales into something that has the status of an epistemology.

Now, it seems to me that there is already enough in these early tip-of-the-iceberg remarks to begin to problematicise the *doxa* beyond the usual suspects of scepticism and relativism. And yet it seems fairly obvious – otherwise the *doxa* wouldn't still be the *doxa* – that these sorts of objections, at least on the surface, can simply be ignored, shrugged off. Somehow, these criticisms seem not to really matter very much; the show still goes on much as before, such that we might have to make a suggestion to account for this. And so it will be my suggestion, my argument, that what we are facing here is the phenomenon of *disavowal.*

For when academic historians are aware – albeit dimly perhaps – of these more penetrating problematicisations beyond recuperation yet choose to ignore them, when they decide, consciously or semi-consciously, to go about their practices *as if* such 'theoretical' objections do not concern them, then we are inevitably talking about avoidance, about a constitutive disavowal. That is to say, that when it is abundantly clear that history as a genre of literature is necessarily the *product of rhetorical figures and devices*, when its realism is unavoidably the realism of the figure, then what defines academic history and shapes it as an empirical, epistemologically striving discipline is precisely *its reluctance to face these facts*. Academic history thus constitutes itself in denial. To forget to remember and to work the presence of figural language in all histories which by definition mark them from beginning to end – indeed, which creates the very idea of a 'historical beginning and end' (for 'actuality' knows of no such things) is thus an act of repression, a repression that has structurally locked up within it (otherwise it would not be repression) its unfailing return – *the return of the repressed* which, again being impossible for history to raise to full recognition since to do so may signal its ruination, haunts it, in some cases this spectre taking on such a magnitude that attitudes towards it become neurotic, pathological.

This attitude is obvious, I think, in the anti-postmodern texts (for it is postmodernism that I am beginning to talk about here) of such historians as Geoffrey Elton and Gertrude Himmelfarb, Arthur Marwick and Keith Windschuttle, while, in more nuanced ways, it patterns the work of such people as Lawrence Stone, Willie Thompson, Martin Bunzl, C.B. McCullagh, Bryan Palmer, Richard Evans, Mary Fulbrook *et al.* These are the producers of writings that are all – to a greater or lesser extent – *obsessive*, a concern for 'history' sometimes spiralling into fantasies that postmodernism unrestrained might lead us to have to fight the Second World War all over again to concerns about the very future (in another universalising gesture) of culture and civilisation 'as such'.

And so I think – to draw these preliminary remarks together – that today, modernist, epistemologically striving academic history is facing various post-modern articulations that do indeed threaten its future – this is what its defender's defence attests to – and that these articulations are a good thing! And so, to briefly develop a medical metaphor myself, it might be useful to think of previous criticisms of academic history that have lived under the names of scepticism and relativism as criticisms that can be fairly easily lived with, accommodated. These were and are analogous, if you like, to varieties of the common cold or to a minor tummy-bug. Modernist academic historians – like you and I with reference to those minor ailments – have got used to these, have built up a certain immunity against them such that they can be recuperated back so as to strengthen the 'discipline of history' by allowing them to become positive features: here, in welcoming diverse viewpoints, new perspectives and multi-levelled readings, history can flaunt its open and tolerant attitude towards possible contamination as it folds these potential 'problems' into a benign, well-inoculated pluralism.

But the criticisms emanating from postmodernism with its notions of, say, the *aporia*, undecidability, incommensurability, the *differend*, the event, the figure, the trace, difference, the symbolic, anamnesis, and so on, are not of that kind. These are not components of a critique which leaves the old history intact though now more wary of some of its claims, but shows how the history we have is constituted by refusing to acknowledge an excess which ensures, without exception, that all historical representations are *failed* representations. These names are not equivalent to the common cold but are more like uncontrollable viruses which carry with them intimations of fatality. And this, the lethal potentiality of postmodernism, is what history must – on pain of death – disavow.

So, *modernist disavowals and postmodern reminders* – words in the title of this paper – are the things I now want to develop in a way which treats the possible end of academic history not as a sad lament or a cause for alarm but as a form of liberation, a kind of life after death. Simply put, my argument will be that postmodern ways of dealing with the 'before now' – if you want to bother with it at all – embody new ways of being healthy, new ways of putting a spring in one's step. And to help me think some of this through, I want to draw on various writings by Jean-François Lyotard as someone who – hopefully without too much 'distortion' – can be made relevant to my own arguments here.

In the Foreword to the English edition of *The Postmodern Explained to Children* (Lyotard 1992, p. 7), the translators pose the question: 'What would happen if thought no longer had a childhood?' Their answer, which is also

Lyotard's answer, is that there would be an acceptance of conformity, a deadening of thought, and that it is postmodernism that, contrariwise, insists that what thought has to do is to:

> Set out without knowing its destination … leave itself open to the unfamiliarity of whatever may occur to it, and make [up] rules in the absence of rules. The [resultant] postmodern text will [thus] be in advance of itself: it will be writing written in the *what will have been* of the future anterior [verb].
>
> (ibid)

Consequently, though Lyotard in *The Postmodern Explained* never explains the full implications of postmodernism to children or to anyone else (how could he, given that no thought is ever 'fully fashioned'?), he is, nevertheless, able to show how and why it is necessary to think 'childishly'. For childhood is, he writes, 'the season of the mind's possibilities and of the possibility of philosophy'. A child is born totally future-orientated, quite literally pre-mature. It has no conscious anterior to hold it back, no habitual baggage to weigh it down. It just likes to play. It just has to make things up as it goes along – experimentally. Analogously, postmodernism is also future-orientated. Postmodernists are those people who we might grow up into if we can escape being governed by the past or by the beckoning termini of teleology or by preprogrammed schemas. Postmodernism is the chance to iconoclastically go beyond existing rules – and rulers – in hopefully emancipatory and democratising ways. As Lyotard explains:

> It should be made clear that it is not up to [philosophers] to *provide reality* but to invent illusions to what is conceivable but not presentable. And this task should not lead us to expect the slightest agreement between 'language games' – Kant – naming them the faculties, knew they were separated by an abyss, and that only a transcendental illusion (Hegel's for example) could hope to totalise them into a real unity. But he also knew that the price of this illusion is terror. [Well] the nineteenth and twentieth centuries have given us our fill of terror. We have paid dearly for our nostalgia … for a reconciliation of the concept and the sensible. The answer is: war on totality. Let us attest to the unpresentable, let us activate the *differends* and save the honour of the name.
>
> (ibid., pp. 24–5)

It is obvious from this quote, I think, that Lyotard's work is thoroughly political ('I have always,' he writes in *Just Gaming*, 'given myself as an excuse for writing a political reason') (Lyotard and Thébaud 1985, p. 17). As we shall see below, Lyotard is haunted in what he calls *immemorial* ways by the 1930s and by the Holocaust/Auschwitz, and by a fear of a future totalitarianism – and hence his war against totality, closure. In his book *The Inhuman*

(Lyotard 1991, p. 73), Lyotard claims – and if postmodernism ever needed a credo to defend then this might be it – that 'being prepared to receive what thought is not prepared to think is what deserves the name of thinking'. And the way he does this sort of thinking himself is through the ultimately arbitrary separating and linking together (for there is no definitive method available) of what he calls different phrase regimes (denotative, interrogative, prescriptive, cognitive, speculative) as constituted through a whole battery of ideas that together variously make up Lyotard's work: ideas of (say) performativity, the event, the excess, the sublime, the sign, the figure, the unpresentable, genres of discourse, incommensurability, anamnesis and the *differend* which, when applied to history, combine to effect a root-and-branch despoiling of all forms of representation (of presentation) from meta to *petit* narratives, such that his writings serve to accelerate what has been called 'the unemployment of the dialectic', the unemployment of the synoptic account, the definitive version, the great story, the narrative gesture and all 'hermeneutics of meaning'.

If it is obvious, then, that Lyotard's thinking is politically motivated, it seems equally obvious that no form of historical writing escapes unscathed from his criticisms. Lyotard's arguments are bad news indeed for epistemologically minded historians working in whatever period, or from whatever perspective or in whatever sub-genre they fancy. For Lyotard's criticisms problematicise *all* the formal properties *all* histories have, not least when they are presented – as they invariably are – in the shape of narratives.

This narrativisation of the non-narratable 'before now', which began in the earnest realism and empiricism of the nineteenth century, has since proven to be a seminal moment which unwittingly stored up for it problematics that are only now being fully appreciated. If only it had been realised that history's ostensible coherence – with its meaning-laden beginnings, middles and ends, its structures, patterns, contexts and watersheds, its directional switching points which ensure that the past rolls right up to us – was never a 'found' coherence but always a coherence issuing entirely (and I mean *entirely*) from the applied forms of the narrative genre itself. If only it had been understood that, while the temporal organising of events into a diachronic series can only ultimately make sense if there is a last sentence that makes all the preceding ones significant, no such last sentence has ever been found and it beggars belief to think it could ever have been imagined. If only it had been seen that the substance of history was only ever a 'narrative substance' and that narrative orderings are always aesthetic figures no matter how many 'mirroring', 'reflecting' or other mimetic metaphors are used to ostensibly legitimate the impossible trick of turning the imaginary into the real. If only the *fictive* nature of all historicisations of the 'before now' had been celebrated before historians plunged into the enveloping darkness of their epistemological tunnel, then things could have been so different, right from the start. But, of course, without these misrecognitions, this constitutive blindness, there would have been 'no start to start'. Consequently, Lyotard's reminding us all of this, his insistence in the radically circumstantial, contingent and unfathomable singularity of life, his insistence on the *sui generis* nature of things, his insistence on the fact that the 'before now' is utterly indifferent to whatever reading it has conferred upon it in the absence of any capacity to present its own and hence the problematical status of any notion of correspondence (however attenuated), well, all of these things should be deeply disturbing to the practices of those historians not intellectually sleep-walking.

The American historian Sande Cohen (Cohen 2000, pp. 111–12) makes this same point:

> Lyotard's reflections on historiography turned the latter into a zone of such intense contestation that his work has simply befuddled the vast majority of historians – but they prefer it that way ... Lyotard's writings ... as experimentation with subjectivity, this to the point where one might 'invent illusions to the conceivable which cannot be presented', of this, historiography wants to know nothing.

Yet there is a qualification to be made to Cohen's judgement. For while Lyotard's ideas do indeed befuddle historians when they know all about them, most historians do not. Although historians may well have heard of Lyotard and have perhaps a passing acquaintance with 'the postmodern condition' he has helped to make visible, Lyotard's own intellectual world is one which few of them have ever bothered to actually enter. And with good reason. For what Lyotard reminds them of if they do and which they need to disavow is simply that, after Lyotard, history as we have known it 'really is history'; intellectually passé.

So, how can we enter Lyotard's discourse and, if we have a mind to, re-emerge not in despair but glowing with health and ready to go? Well, I think a threefold approach may be best. Thus, first – and at the risk of a homogenisation of Lyotard's varied works caused by the fact that my reading is largely a reading through Lyotard's *The Differend* (Lyotard 1988a) – I want to link together some of the names already mentioned (event, figure, incommensurability) in ways which might help produce a sort of general overview of Lyotard's 'position' within which history may then be located. In Part one I work in from the general to the particular before going on, second, to say something more specifically historical by focusing on an 'event' Lyotard himself focuses on: the French Revolution of 1789 *après* Kant. Third, I want to suggest very briefly what 'history' – if the sort of acts of remembrance Lyotard likes still need that old name – might look like after Lyotard; here I draw on his notion of the *immemorial*.

PART ONE

It was Kant who, at the beginning of modern critical thought, tried to firmly locate the *sublime* outside of the *phenomenal* world, outside of theoretical reason, in the noumenal realm, any seepage flowing back into the phenomenal being coped with by transforming it through, and placing it within, the productivist economy of 'the beautiful'. Contrariwise, Nietzsche and Heidegger put the sublime back into the phenomenal, thus disrupting every fixed boundary between the phenomenal and the noumenal, the inside and the outside, the knowable and the unknowable, dissolving at a stroke the *bar*, the *cut*, instituted precisely to fix the ontological difference between the *real* and the *unreal*. As a consequence of which the 'inside' was immediately problematicised by its awareness of an 'outside' at least 'as real as *its* real', by its grasp that the phenomenal real was not the name of an empirical given (some kind of objectivist reality) but was always only the effect of the metaphysical desire for a definitiveness (a full presence) that could never be secured.

Analogously, history as such – history as a discourse which is the only way the 'before now' can be recalled – is never an empirical given, some kind of fixture, but, again, the always temporary outcome of the metaphysical attempt at definitiveness, at inclusivity, the attempt to 'cut history down to size' by excluding its inevitable excess. Accordingly, it is Lyotard's deconstructionist task (as it is Derrida's and Baudrillard's) to open up the inside – because what is on the inside hurts people – to a potential otherness (to difference, to the 'to come', the arriver, radical alterity, the fatal), always remembering, of course, that this 'other' is not some kind of 'thing' waiting in the wings as some sort of alternative, but is that something, or nothing, or everything, that is incapable of being thematised or ontologised but which is, nevertheless, 'hauntingly there', a 'there' dependent for its 'potential' on the temporary placing of the *bar*. This – the (as yet) unpresentable – is not, then, another version of what is 'lacking' or 'missing' from representation, but rather those potentialities/othernesses unable to be yet fully *historicised*. And so it is Lyotard's hope to destroy the existing bars which frame and constitute reality/history, not to replace them by some definitive 'cut' of his own but to welcome the unsuturing of everything stitched up so that new things can be invented in advance of the rules that will, retrospectively, confer a fleeting legitimacy on them subject to the future anterior verb which guarantees that whatever will be created 'will not have been good enough'.

So, moving from these generalities to more detail but still within the first part of what I want to say vis-à-vis the construction of Lyotard's general position, how are these general aims worked out? Here I have chosen to start arbitrarily (if not randomly) with Lyotard's notion of the *event*, not least because, in his *Lyotard: Writing the Event* (Bennington 1988), Geoffrey Bennington has argued for the 'centricity' of this 'idea' in Lyotard's work(s).

Nothing that happens, then, no *event*, can be made sense of out of context, but no context permits saturation. Consequently, the effect of this – namely, the radical singularity of an event, its *sui generis* nature – invites invention. Necessarily. For two reasons. First, because from the happening, the 'eventhood' of the event – the 'it happens' as Lyotard puts it – no meaning (what Lyotard calls the 'what happened') is ever entailed. As Lyotard puts this concisely: 'There are events: something happens which is not tautological to what has happened' (Readings 1991, p. 57). And, second, because any decision that is made as to how to link phrases or sentences together, any decision to phrase the relationship between a cognitive phrase (it happens) and a speculative phrase endowing meaning (what happened) (i.e. to phrase a fact–value relationship), or to phrase 'it happens' and 'what happened' in the form of a cognitive phrase and a prescription (to phrase an is–ought relationship) is, in the absence of any conceivable entailment, without any logical rule connecting *incommensurable* cognitive and speculative/prescriptive 'phrase regimes', an 'undecidable decision' and thus one which calls for a radically new judgement, or what Lyotard calls a *transcendental* judgement. By which is not meant a judgement that actually comes from a 'real' transcendental source (for example, God), but, because God is dead, is a decision grounded only in the contingency of the decision itself. Lyotard being concise again: 'When I say "transcendence" it means: I do not know who is sending me the prescription in question' (Lyotard and Thébaud 1985, p. 69).[1]

Seen from this perspective – the perspective of the event as a radical singularity – the event can become what Lyotard occasionally calls a *tensor*, that is, something which refuses/disrupts all attempts at assimilation into an ongoing *genre of discourse* (philosophy, literature, politics, history, and so on), a disruption the more easily achieved if one stresses the event's *inanity* (its singular senselessness). Here the event (and a single sentence can be an event, Lyotard's texts can be an event; 1789 or Auschwitz can be events), here events take on the semblance of being absolutely empty – signifiers-in-waiting as it were – as they open themselves up to re-signification *ad infinitum*.

Events, then, can potentially deconstruct the rules/rulers of meaning. But it's not just that. For, as Bill Readings puts it in his *Introducing Lyotard* (Readings 1991, pp. xviii–xix):

> For Lyotard it is not simply the case that there are events that deconstruct the rule of meaning; one [also] has to judge how to judge them. One must do something with events, speak after by linking phrases to them, despite the fact that events offer no criteria as to how we might do it or how well we might do it.

Thus, while the linking of phrases and sentences is a *necessity* (everything has to be phrased somehow – even silence) what phrase or sentence (or silence) comes next is utterly contingent. And while genres of discourse (philosophy, history, and so on) attempt to reduce such contingency as they try to enforce certain linkings as more appropriate and habitual/necessary than others (otherwise they wouldn't be doing their job as *genres of discourse*), for Lyotard *justice* is precisely the attempt to respect the contingency of each linking as the corollary of respecting the singular eventhood of each phrase, each sentence and thus each 'actual' event. Accordingly, the occasion of linking phrases from different/heterogeneous/irreducible phrase regimes (cognitive, interrogative, imperative, speculative) can only be the subject of a singular act of *reading*, a reading which rests precisely on ethical (and thus political) decisions of the undecidable type. Lyotard again being concise: 'We do not interpret, we read' (Readings 1991, p. xix).

The act of reading is thus raised to a crucially important level. For Lyotard, the act of reading is a listening out for events and a refusal to submit them to any existent rule of meaning, whether that meaning refers to their content (interpretation) or to their conditions of possibility (theory). Of course, everybody reads things all the time, but not everybody reads deconstructively, since not everyone reads in order to make events *Events*. Lyotard (Lyotard 1988b, p. 18) is fairly concise:

> There are many events whose occurrence doesn't offer any matter to be confronted ... they come to us concealed under the appearance of everyday occurrences. To become sensitive to their quality as actual events, to become competent in listening to their sound underneath silence or noise, to become open to the 'It happens that' rather than 'What happens' requires at the very least a high degree of refinement in the perception of small differences ... without mediation or protection of a pre-text [pretext].[2]

Reading is thus the *performance* of rupturing events out of all residual contexts and predictable contexts-in-waiting, a task that will be further facilitated by the use of one of Lyotards hardest working names; namely, that of the *figure*.

The notion of the figure first emerged extensively in Lyotard's *Discourse/figure* of 1971 where the (perhaps binary) opposition between discursive meaning and rhetoric is one of the many things articulated since when it has been variously updated. For Lyotard in general, discourse organises its 'objects of knowledge' as a system of signifiers defined in terms of their position relative to other signifiers, this network/grid placing a bar between the included real and *its* outside. Against this, the figure refuses all grids, all concepts, it being the figure which opens up discourse to that 'outer' otherness that is always (potentially) within it. In that sense of 'becoming', the figure *qua* figure is literally nothing. It is not a thing, a concept; rather the figure is a kind of energy, a force, a power latent within discourse, a power capable of exceeding all thematisation and so creating that potential semantic *space* within which newness 'could come'. And this is something that discourse can never eradicate – though it can try to forget it, disavow it – the 'it' being that no discourse can ever be fully literal, and hence true. Insofar as history does have a kind of truth in it, in the end it is the truth of fiction. Bill Readings (Readings 1991, p. 71) also being concise: 'There is no discourse free from figures – the dream of literal discourse, if it were possible, would be the *litotes* of figurality.'

This is, of course, brilliant news for Lyotard. To live with contingency, to accept a radical incommensurability between things, to live within/in-difference forever opens things up in ways which can never be totalised, never closed down. And, of course, incommensurability again brings into 'the open' not only the fact that the practices that constitute history as an epistemology rest on a demand that can never be justified by appeal to things (it happened), but also that such incommensurability is, as it were, for ever guaranteed by the *differend*, a name that trails after it, for Lyotard, the names of *justice*, *ethics* and *politics*. For it is this 'openness' which makes it likely that the antagonisms of the social (class, gender, ethnic; methodological, aesthetic, epistemological) will produce via their pragmatic existence incommensurable judgements that precisely constitute the conditions producing the *differend*.

So, what is Lyotard's *differend*? Lyotard explains it thus (Lyotard 1988a, p. xi):

> As distinguished from a litigation, a differend would be a case of conflict between (at least) two parties, that cannot be equitably resolved for lack of a rule of judgement applicable to both arguments. One side's legitimacy does not imply the other's lack of legitimacy. However, applying a single rule of judgement to both ... as though it were a litigation would wrong (at least) one of them (and both of them if neither side admits this rule).

Consequently, the task of politics is not compromise or consensus; it is not to attempt to reduce *differends* to litigation. For Lyotard, freedom – and hence justice – can be preserved only if the *differend* is preserved, *injustice* being precisely the infringement of specific phrases/games by other phrases/games with reference to a unifying master game, to a metalanguage and/or to a metanarrative. Lyotard again (Lyotard and Thébaud 1985, pp. 66–67):

> Absolute injustice would occur if ... the possibility of continuing to play the game of the just were excluded. That is what is unjust. Not the opposite of the just, but that which prohibits that the question of the just and the unjust be, and remain, raised.

Of course there may be a contradiction or at least a paradox here. By prescribing that no 'language game' (especially a prescriptive one) should dominate the others, one seems to be doing precisely what it is claimed one must never do: namely, dominating the other games by 'the game of games' that insists that they all continue playing. But Lyotard's way around this is by invoking (as Sam Weber does in the very essay where he raises the problem in Lyotard and Thébaud 1985, pp. 101–20) Nietzsche's idea of a general *agonistics* whereby the condition of possibility of agonistics is not prescribed as a principle of inclusion – namely, as the singularity proper to each game – but as a *ludic* gesture shared by *all* games: as Lyotard puts it in his *Just Gaming* (Lyotard and Thébaud 1985), this is just what 'just' gaming is all about. Freedom, then, lies in the proliferation of *petit* language games, each with their own pragmatics and each in their heterogeneity resistant to homogenisation, to monolithic closure. Consequently, on this account *politics* is not the putting into place of a perfect polity deducible from a first or single principle (for there is no first principle; there is always more than one), nor is it the bringing of politics under a concept or theory; rather, because no speculative/prescriptive phrasing is ever certain, then politics is only happening when:

> there is something to institute. There is no politics if there is not … everywhere in the society, a questioning of existing institutions; a project to improve them. … This means that all politics implies the prescription of doing something else than what is.
>
> (Lyotard and Thébaud 1985, p. 23)

And so extending, or rerouting, all of this back to history, two observations may serve to facilitate this. First, we might observe that from the viewpoint of 'consensual' historians it would be nice – but it would be wrong – to think that what Lyotard is saying (or, as historians might say, '*all* that Lyotard is saying') may be reduced to some type of pluralism. For this is not the case. For pluralists, different games (different positions, different interpretations, different perspectives) pertaining to the same area of enquiry simply give rise to a number of interesting/fascinating/alternative 'points of view' from which one might choose one, fairly indifferently, pluralism cashing in on the idea of liberal tolerance as underwritten by the reassurance that, in the end, 'we are all historians' and we all want to raise the level of historical consciousness for – guess what – liberal openness. But, of course, this tautology, this circular closure, is to precisely ignore (disavow) Lyotard's view that this sort of consensus is the silencing of those figures that will wreck every consensus (at this point Lyotard's own work takes on the role of an event-full figure) … and which prizes, to break that avoidance, the *polemical* (*agonistic*) nature of freedom. Which means, second, that all reading and writing (including historical writing) is inevitably polemical.

Of course, polemicism is often looked down on in academia – it is somewhat unseemly, adversarial, the stuff of extremists/sectarians. But Lyotard's point is that it is *logically* impossible for there not to be a condition of *polemos* whenever there are no grounds upon which agreement *has* to be reached. Which, logically, is always. Perhaps on this occasion Derrida, in his *A Taste for the Secret* (Derrida 2001, p. 12), puts it better than Lyotard. He writes:

> There is *polemos* when a field is determined as a field of battle because there is no metalanguage, no locus of truth outside the field, no absolute or historical overhang … in other words the radical historicity of the field makes the field necessarily subject to multiplicity and heterogeneity. As a result, those who are inscribed in the field are necessarily involved in a *polemos*, even if they have no special taste for war.

PART TWO

All right. So much for this general type overview of aspects of Lyotard relevant to the needs of this paper. Against which I now want to turn to a historical event which illustrates some of the above generalities and which firms things up a little history-wise; namely, the French Revolution of 1789 *après* Kant.

In a paper of 1982 (Lyotard in Benjamin 1989, pp. 393—411) ('The Sign of History' – which incidentally has the same title as the last chapter of *The Differend* and covers similar ground but which I prefer on this occasion), Lyotard makes the point that, in his *Critique of Judgement*, Kant marks a distinction between two modes of presentation. First, for what he calls a determinant judgement, i.e. when one is dealing with a descriptive phrase, then either these phrases are 'experience phrases' (empirical concepts) and 'intuition presents them with objects as examples', or they are 'knowledge phrases' and 'intuition presents them with objects as schemata'. But, second, when we are dealing with ideas (of, say, the world, God, literature, history) then, although we are capable of forming ideas of these, we *cannot* present definitive objects to correspond to them, so that any presentation has to take place indirectly, by analogy, with an *as if* as a putative referent. For there is literally nothing to present: we can think of the universe or the world or history *per se* or '1789', but we can never actually present examples or schemas of them that are checkable. We are thus locked into the realm of speculative reason, ideas of reason. Moreover, says Lyotard, although Kant privileges judgement when it comes to the possible unification of the Faculties (a potential of phrases that can be subjected to rules and their presentation), in the end judgement (prescription) has no determinate rules either. Consequently, the sovereignty of reason, the sovereignty of that finite reason which is the only resource humans have in a world bereft of God's final judgement, cannot deliver the goods – cannot deliver the judgement of 'the good'. And hence that sometime feeling of isolation in a universe bereft of knowable meaning, that anxious feeling of being in semantic free fall that sometimes rises, like damp, from the pit of a nauseous stomach via sweaty palms to that intellectual dread of which nightmares are made and from which the only escape is by a death that is, ultimately, the very cause of our angst. This is the sometime feeling of the sublime. Of course, this is not the only way to read the sublime. For knowing nothing for certain, there being nothing that 'thou shalt not do', then we are free: everything is permitted. Has there ever been, asks Nietzsche, such a brilliant opportunity as this – such an open sea? And though Lyotard's Kant is much more 'afraid', this is how Lyotard himself reads the sublime. For on the back of the sublime via the *aporia* of the decision rides a welcoming of the fact that, despite being freed up for choice, and never knowing if we have ever made the really right choice, nevertheless, this keeps choices, decisions, open for ever. Here is Lyotard (in Benjamin 1989, pp. 398–9) starting to bring all this home to history:

> The importance of the philosophy of the beautiful and the sublime in the ... *Third Critique* lies both in the de-realization of the object of aesthetic feelings, and in the absence of a real aesthetic faculty of knowing.

> The same holds, perhaps even more radically, for the historico–political object, which as such has no reality, and for any political faculty of knowing which must remain inexistent. The only things that *are* real (i.e. of which intuitions can be presented) are phenomena ... The series [which] makes up the history of humanity ... is never itself given. The series is not given, but is the object of an Idea and thus [unpresentable].[3]

Historical discourse, *as if* it was ever capable of being knowledge, is therefore based on confusing that which can be presented as an object for a cognitive phrase and that which can be presented only indirectly – analogously, metaphorically, figuratively – in other words, it confuses examples and schemas with *analoga*: the past actuality as such does not give us much to go on when writing history. Consequently, when trying to say 'what happened', any judgement depends on our being able to construct as referents actually unpresentable phenomena (structures, patterns, trends, cause–effect relationships) that never existed in the 'before now' or anywhere else except in those very constructions, those very referents, which mask the fact that they *are* unpresentable. There is thus – to use Carolyn Steedman's phrase – 'a double nothingness' in historical representation, namely, 'it is about something that never did happen in the way it comes to be represented (the happening exists in the telling or the text) and it is made out of materials that aren't there [those *inferred* structures that act as real referents] in an archive or anywhere else', a nothingness that we take to be, nevertheless, 'a sign of history' (Steedman 2001, p. 154).

'A sign of history'; what does this mean specifically for Lyotard? Well, take the French Revolution of 1789. A real revolution – apparently. Yet a revolution is just an organising idea, an act of the imagination, the placing of events under a speculative name as distinct from some/all of its presentable elements in the form of singular statements and which can, given its unpresentability, be only capable of acting as a sign, analogously. But a sign of what? Of the end of the old regime? The concrete beginning of republicanism and the glory of France? The enactment of liberty? The harbinger of terrors to come, of totalitarian democracy? Or, as Kant thought on the basis of his reading of what the 'disinterested spectators' of the 'revolution' – in their sympathy and enthusiasm for it beyond personal interests in the light of a potential consensus (a *sensus communis*) in favour of 1789 as embedded in a general surmise of historical progress allowing 1789 a retrospective significance – a sign of progress?[4] Could 1789 be one of these, or all of these, or none of these? Could it be a sign as yet unassigned? I mean, says Lyotard, is there anything 1789 *could not be a sign of* and, by extension, anything that any of the phenomena that make up 'the past' could not be signs of? I mean, how could we know? A useless question, as if an aesthetic figure could answer an epistemological query; as if there wasn't that ontological abyss between the Faculties.

And yet, having said that, critics have pointed out that Lyotard may himself be drawing from his 'heterogeneity is inescapable' conclusion the sort of closure neither he – least of all he – nor anyone else should draw. Is the inescapability of heterogeneity a definitive sign of history? Indeed, could this conclusion be the 'end-point' of a metanarrative of Lyotard's own? And while I think the answer is no, explaining why this is so might allow me to draw several conclusions of my own vis-à-vis history after Lyotard.

At first it seems that Lyotard (in Benjamin 1989, p. 408) is very clear about this now:

> 'There is progress': the critical judge can legitimate this phrase every time he can present a sign to be a referent to this assertion. But he cannot say *when* such 'objects' will present themselves because historical sequences forming a series only give *data* to the historian and *never* signs. ... And, as for the philosophy of History ... it is an illusion born of signs being [taken for] a semblance of examples or schemes.

Only data then, never signs. And yet, he goes on, is it possible that this failure to find signs is itself a sign, albeit a negative one, for demonstrating the end of metanarratives and the permanency of *petit* narratives? And he says, perhaps unbelievably, 'yes', maybe it is. For Lyotard argues that because all events can potentially be raised to the level of *tension* – to a level where they can be torn free from the then dominant discourse and call out for a refiguring figure – then, because we now know that while all such events liberate judgement, we also know that all such judgements must take place without a criterion and that, and I quote, 'this feeling becomes in turn a sign of history'. To which he adds (Lyotard in Benjamin 1989, p. 409):

> However negative the signs to which most of the proper names of our political history gives rise [Auschwitz, Budapest, May 1968] we should nevertheless have to judge them *as if* they proved that this history had moved on a step in its progress. ... This step would consist in the fact that it is not only the Idea of a *single* purpose which would be pointed to in our feeling, but already the Idea that this purpose consists in the formation and free exploration of Ideas *in the plural*, The Idea that this end is the beginning of the *infinity of heterogeneous finalities*.[5]

Is Lyotard, after all, Hegel? Is ludic heterogeneity, *dissensus,* the definitive end of history of which late twentieth-century events are definitive signs? Of which 'postmodernism' is a definitive sign? And, as I have said above, I think the (charitable) answer is no. For it seems to me that any establishing of heterogeneity is 'based on' a logical, not a historical 'proof'. For while it may well be the case that the latter part of the twentieth century may indeed be periodised as, say, postmodern – in that this registers both a phase in the development of capitalism and the widespread raising to consciousness of the *aporia* (such that if I were to try to define postmodernism now I would say that it is precisely 'the era of the raising to consciousness of the *aporia*') –

this *aporetic* condition of thought has *logically* always been there, albeit not nearly as extensively recognised, discussed and accepted (and here my earlier remarks on the logical conditions necessary for *polemos* make this same point). Thus, in that sense, it could be sensible to say that, logically, we have always been '*aporetic*', always postmodern. And it is this 'point' that now enables me to draw several conclusions about the condition of history today *avec* Lyotard.

First, it suggests that, if history has always been aporetic, undecidable, polemical, if it has always been constituted by rhetorical figures and devices, then it is obviously the case that there have never been histories of any other kind. So it is just not the case – as is suggested by Marwick and Evans *et al.* – that there are modernist, epistemological histories that stand over against postmodern histories which happen to be aestheticisations of the 'before now', and that you can (pluralistically) choose between them, but that *all* histories are of the aesthetic, postmodern type. That modernist histories are as much the product of rhetorical devices as every other history is. In which case we might conclude (with Stanley Fish) that 'postmodern'-type histories have always been 'the only game in town'.

This, I think, is the major point Lyotard's study of history makes which, rephrased, might be put thus: that epistemologically striving histories were just an enormous philosophical mistake; that it would have been better if history 'had never been modern'. Allied to which major point are two important minor points to note.

First – and for this I am much indebted to Sande Cohen's excellent article (Cohen 2000) on Lyotard as indeed I am for point two – if names semi-dissolve into the more fluid ambiguities of the 'reading of signs', 'then the historian's *research* is no guarantee of objective sense … but only another *medium* of cultural filtering'. In this way, then, Lyotard relegates the *research phase* of the historian's work to the cognitive, a cognitive that can never be, unaided by the rhetorical figure, 'history'. And, second, this primacy of the rhetorical – of the speculative and the prescriptive as the basis for the only way meaning can ever be made – confirms the importance of emotion (of feeling, desire, will) in the conferring of historical significance. Cohen:

> As Lyotard reads Kant, historical connexion as such is thus established on the basis of sublime feelings – the formlessness and potential unfigurability of events … presupposes a capacity of the subject to experience history as [both] *sense and confusion*. [Thus] the very form of narrative is inseparable from possible links to confusion … One makes mistakes in interpreting, experiencing, and making signs. [Which is] to say the medium of any such linkage can be only that of feeling, and that once this is acknowledged, the *dialetical, cognitive and moral claims of history vanish*, since those … can only be rendered in good forms that annul [disavow] the experience of the sublime.
>
> (Cohen 2000, p. 110)

PART THREE

Now, I said towards the start of this paper that in its *third part* I wanted to raise the question of what 'history might look like' after Lyotard. I mean, is it possible to think historically after Lyotard? Lyotard himself thinks yes, a yes that he articulates under the name of the *immemorial*. And so I now want to look – in what is the third part of the paper – at this notion of the immemorial, very briefly, and then to conclude.

Referring in his *Heidegger and The Jews* to Adorno's remarks in the latter's *After Auschwitz*, Lyotard says that to reduce the horror of the Holocaust by putting it under concepts – to make it an empirical object of cognition – would be to drown out the screams of its victims (Lyotard 1988a). If history could remember the Holocaust cognitively it would therefore have forgotten it. Thus, to respect the impossibility of 'coming to terms with' and 'understanding' the now silence of the Holocaust's victims, we have to have a history – *a remembrance* – that will testify to that horror without 'representing it'. It is an 'ethical necessity' for Lyotard that the Holocaust haunts us; that is, as he puts it, that it cannot be remembered but that it cannot be forgotten either. This event – and perhaps all events – must be *immemorial,* that is, something that cannot be fully recalled or fully obliterated. Auschwitz obliges us to speak to enable this event to remain an event so that its singularity is not lost in historical representation; the immemorial acts as a sort of figure for historical consciousness, an impossible figure. As Lyotard puts it:

> What really preoccupies us ... is this 'past' which is not over, which doesn't haunt the present in the sense that it is lacking; missing. It neither occupies the present as a solid reality nor haunts the present in the sense that it might indicate itself even as an absence, a spectre. This 'past' is not an object of memory in the sense of something which may have been forgotten and must be remembered. ... This 'past' is therefore not even there as a blank, an absence, *terra incognita*, but it is still there.[6]

Here history – if this immemorial remembrance still is history – becomes the place where it is recognised that there is *always* something that cannot be said. That there is that productive but always unbridgeable abyss between the 'it happens' and 'what happened', such that Geoffrey Bennington (Bennington 1988, p. 148) has commented that, insofar as Auschwitz *reminds* us of the limits of the cognitive phrase, then 'Auschwitz is the realist of realities'. Auschwitz, he adds, signals the limit of historical competence.

And yet, queries Bennington, if this is the lesson we can all draw from Auschwitz, what happens to that happy heterogeneity which forbids this kind of all ... 'all of us'? How can we agree, why must we agree with Lyotard (and Adorno), that something *new* happened in the Holocaust? Can't we read the Holocaust, *must* we not read the Holocaust, differently to this in order to save the *differend*? And I think that there probably is a slippage in Lyotard's thinking at this point – though probably a slippage he knows about.

And yet I would want – because I like Lyotard – to end on a more generous note, by saying that what Lyotard is arguably doing here is asking us to remember – is reminding us – not that we must remember the Holocaust or anything else come to that, but that if and when we do remember we remember that we do so imperfectly. That we remember that we always fail to read things right and that this is the very best of things. This is the *logical* outcome, I think, of Lyotard's war on totality and against that certaintist mentality that might fuel future Holocausts. And this is to face the future – a future without foundational certainty – with optimism. And it is this which also, I think, allows Lyotard to be what he probably always was – a Nietzschean adventurer. For as Nietzsche wrote (Nietzsche 1910, p. 167):

> In fact, we philosophers and 'free spirits' feel ourselves irradiated as by a new dawn by the report that the 'old God is dead'; our hearts overflow with gratitude, astonishment, presentiment and expectation. At last the horizon seems open once more. Granting even that it is not bright, our ships can at last put out to sea in face of every danger; every hazard is again permitted to the discerner; the sea, *our* sea, again lies open before us; perhaps never before did such an open sea exist.

This, it seems to me, is the sea on which Lyotard was always sailing – and on which I think we might remember to join him as and if we need to create 'future pasts'.

Notes

1 When I say 'transcendence' I take over a term used by Lévinas, and also by Kant when the latter says that that which obligates is absolutely beyond our 'intelligence' (p. 71).

2 Lyotard continues: 'It is not a matter of concentrated attention. On the contrary … the right way … is to pay this discourse "equally floating attention". In order to take on this attitude you have to impoverish your mind, clean it out as much as possible, so that you make it incapable of anticipating the meaning, the "what" of the "It happens". … Thus, to encounter an event is like bordering on nothingness. No event is at all accessible if the self does not renounce the glamour of its culture, "its wealth, health, knowledge and *memory*"' (p. 18).

3 Geoffrey Bennington (1988, p. 163) makes the following point about the shortfall of the empirical when he writes: 'A historical discourse which remains within the cognitive genre will never establish an order in history, and a discourse which takes the idea of such an order as its "guiding thread" will not operate according to the rules of establishing reality, but by analogous presentations which are for Kant proper to "dialectical" sentences, i.e. those taking ideas as their referent. If the discourse of order assumes it can proceed by direct presentation, then it falls into the transcendental illusion: in Lyotard's formulation, acting *as if* it were referring to phenomena, when in fact it is referring to "*as if* phenomena".'

4 On Kant and 'progress' and 1789, Lyotard writes: 'The French Revolution, for example, committed a monstrous amount of injustices, crimes, murders, and ended with the Terror. It nevertheless received everywhere an enthusiastic reception. … This enthusiasm

constitutes an event ... which is the sign ... that mankind is in progress toward the better' (Lyotard 1988b, p. 41).

5 On 'progress', Lyotard also writes: 'One can say that the more numerous the disputes, the arguments ... to convince and persuade others, the more developed the repressibility to the moral idea is ... so it would not be absurd to sketch out something like progress in this field to the extent that more and more situations previously considered to be natural and above suspicion ... become objects of judgement and deliberation' (Lyotard 1988b, p. 39).

6 Lyotard, quoted in Readings, 1991, p. 62. I am indebted to Readings's somewhat brief but penetrating remarks on the Holocaust here.

References

Benjamin, A. (ed.) (1989) *The Lyotard Reader*, Blackwell: Oxford.

Bennington, G. (1988) *Lyotard: Writing the Event*, Manchester University Press: Manchester.

Cohen, S. (2000) 'The "Use and abuse of history" according to Jean-François Lyotard', *Parallax*, vol. 6, no. 4, pp. 99—113.

Derrida, J. (2001) *A Taste for the Secret*, Polity Press, Cambridge.

Lyotard, J.F. (1988a) *The Differend*, Manchester University Press, Manchester.

—— (1988b) *Peregrinations: Law, Form, Event*, Columbia University Press, New York.

—— (1991) *The Inhuman*, Polity Press, Cambridge.

—— (1992) *The Postmodern Explained to Children*, Turnaround, London.

Lyotard, J.F. and Thébaud, J.L. (1985) *Just Gaming*, University of Minneapolis Press, Minnesota.

Nietzsche, F.W. (1910) *The Joyful Wisdom*, Foulis, Edinburgh.

Readings, W. (1991) *Introducing Lyotard*, Routledge, London.

Steedman, C. (2001) *Dust*, Manchester University Press, Manchester.

11 Ethical responsibility and the historian

On the possible end of a history "of a certain kind"

In 2003 the journal *History and Theory* put out a call for papers for their 2004 theme issue on 'Historians and Ethics', papers which were asked to address such questions as: 'do historians *as* historians have an ethical responsibility and if so to whom,' and, 'do historians have such ethical commitments whether they like it or not?' In his short introduction to the 2004 issue, the Executive Editor of the journal, Brian Fay, wrote that 'It is clear from our experience in putting this issue together that these questions hold great urgency at the present time: the journal received more submissions for this Theme Issue than for any other in our history.' From the papers that were published, only Elizabeth Ermarth's *Ethics and Method* and my own considered, as Fay put it, 'the moral implications of history considered especially in the light of what postmodernism tells us it is or ought to be as a discipline'. Since 2004 *History and Theory* have published several other papers centrally concerned with history and ethics though, unfortunately, few that have come from a postmodern position construed sympathetically.

Introduction

In the call for papers issued by *History and Theory* in 2003 with regard to Julian Benda's old concern as to the role of the intellectual in society (and in this case the role of the historian as intellectual), the basic question suggested as anchoring the theme of the proposed issue of the journal was: "do historians as historians have an ethical responsibility, and if so to whom and to what?" This paper is an attempt to answer that question.

Of course it has to be said immediately that there is no definitive approach to a question such as this. But one way of considering it is to read it quite literally and then pose to it certain questions that might enable it to be analyzed. These questions are: what would intellectuals look like if they looked *as if* their work were governed by a sense of ethical responsibility; next, is there something particular or peculiar about historians that gives them a special kind of ethical responsibility that is to be exercised by virtue of being a historian *beyond* that of the ethically responsible intellectual as such and, if so (as the call for papers has it), to whom or to what might that responsibility – *ought* that responsibility – be directed?

Articulated in this way, what is immediately striking is the impossibility both of privileging historians *qua* historians above intellectuals *qua* intellectuals and of arriving at anything other than a relativistic response to such queries. In the end, this relativism might be expressed thus: since we can only ever be ethically responsible relative to the way in which we stipulate ethical responsibility, we can do no more than direct what we have so defined to whomever and whatever we just happen to prefer for reasons we just happen to like; there is no knowable, universal notion of ethical responsibility that somehow compels our subordination to it. Further, we can never definitively say what history is, what its ethical purposes really are and, therefore, what a historian's ethical purposes really are as if such purposes, such responsibilities, were somehow an inherent property of history and historians and which consequently laid on them an inescapable imperative along the lines of a logical entailment, namely, that from the fact of being a historian what one ought to do is entailed. Accordingly, the impossibility of fact value (of is-ought) entailments seemingly guarantees endless free-play, such that it appears as if "anything goes." At the very least it certainly seems that there cannot be, *pace* Benda, any kind of "higher ground" or foundation or absolute operating in the vicinity and, therefore, any way of making ethical responsibility more than a matter of non-cognitive taste.

In that sense it looks as if we have already reached what might be called "the bottom line" fairly quickly. And so, a conclusion of sorts having been reached, maybe we should stop at this point: each to his or her own. For, in the end, no matter how nuanced our nuances, how fine our finessing, this relativistic outcome seems inevitable. But then … but then suppose we decide not to stop but to push on. Suppose we do finesse. Will it make a difference? Well, perhaps in the end it won't, or at least, it won't very much. Yet, by adding certain complications, by facing up to and working through certain problematics, it might be possible to become more at ease with – or indeed *celebrate* and *champion* – at least "a certain kind of relativism" for "a certain kind of historian" that is worth considering as it is "raised to the level of consciousness." Indeed, it may be that we can actually sketch out some characteristics of an ethically responsible historian that we can – or at least I can – subscribe to (though it may well be, as my subtitle suggests, that such characteristics signal the end of "a certain kind of historian" too …). Anyway, be that as it may, this is the task I have set myself, a task that is developed in two parts. In the much longer first part I address the question – in the way I've already indicated – of what those might look like if they were driven by a sense of ethical responsibility. Here, from a large number of theorists – or in this context a large number of intellectuals – I could have drawn upon, I have decided on this occasion to rely mainly on and discuss Alain Badiou's *Ethics: An Essay on the Understanding of Evil*; Jean-François Lyotard's *The Differend* (not only because the idea of ethical responsibility runs throughout this text but also because, in every chapter of it, the phenomena of the Holocaust and Auschwitz are discussed, "events" that recent historiography has been much engaged with and which *History and Theory*'s call for papers suggested that contributors might like to consider); and, finally, Edward Said's *Representations of the Intellectual.*[1] A certain reading of Jacques Derrida and Richard Rorty also has a constant if largely "absent presence." In the second part, I look at the question of whether being a historian involves a special kind of ethical responsibility peculiar to historians and, if so, to whom and to what should it be directed. I end by raising the question of whether being the kind of intellectual I have portrayed is the kind of being that presently constituted historians can also be yet still remain historians "as we have known them." I'm afraid I reply negatively.

On the ethical responsibility of the intellectual

In his book, *Ethics: An Essay on the Understanding of Evil*, Alain Badiou develops a way of thinking that he claims helps human beings to become ethically responsible *subjects*. This claim rests on his argument – taken as axiomatic – that "the social" (the "sphere of human activities") is divided between two distinct but, nevertheless, interconnected sub-spheres: the "ordinary" everyday world of established interests, of approved knowledges and opinions that serve to produce, name, place, and conserve "consolidated identities," and an "exceptional realm" of "singular innovations or truths" that can persist "only through the militant proclamations of those rare individuals who constitute themselves *as the subjects* of a truth, as the militants of their cause."[2] How does this militant occupation of a truth (or, as I prefer to think of it, utilizing Badiou's *own* alternative to truth, an *innovative position*) work; how can it be reached? For Badiou, such an occupancy can only begin with some sort of break with the ordinariness of the everyday by experiencing what he calls an "event," an event with both individual and social dimensions.

Individually, Badiou argues, humans are just animals, but animals with the capacity to become *subjects*; that is to say, "that at a given moment everything he [*sic*] is – his body, his abilities – is called upon to enable the passing of a truth along its path. This is when the human animal is convoked [*requis*] to be the immortal he is not yet."[3] What might constitute these truth-inducing circumstances? For Badiou, they are the conditions that provide the occasion for those extraordinary happenings, those *events*, after which nothing can still run the same; happenings that tear apart the commensensical parlance of the everyday (wherein "every animal gets by as best it can") and expose "individuals" to the possibility of making an (ungrounded) decision that will transform them into ethical subjects:

> We must suppose, then, that whatever convokes someone to the composition of a subject is something extra, something that happens in situations as something that they and the usual way of behaving in them cannot account for. Let us say that a *subject*, which goes beyond the animal (although the animal remains its sole foundation) needs something

> to have happened … that cannot be reduced to its ordinary inscription in "what there is." Let us call this *supplement* an *event*, and let us distinguish multiple-being, where it is not a matter of truth (but only of opinions), from the event, which compels us to decide a *new* way of being …
>
> From which decision, then, stems the process of a truth? From the decision to relate henceforth to the situation *from the perspective of its evental supplement*. Let us call this a *fidelity*. To be faithful to an *event* is to move within the situation … by *thinking* the situation "according to" the *event*. And this, of course – since the *event* was excluded by all the regular laws of the situation – compels the subject to *invent* a new way of being and acting in the situation.[4]

This "evental" experience that constitutes the emergence of a new subject can be put more socially (more historically) in Badiouian language. The everyday world of routines and opinionated opinions is structured according to the interests of those (this is the Gramscian/Althusserian aspect of Badiou) who dominate "the state of the situation" and who are constantly (if imperfectly) vigilant against situations becoming *events* in ways irrecuperable by the *status quo*. Indeed, for Badiou, in the unexceptional ordinariness of everyday life, hegemonic order is "effectively absolute" – indeed, so absolute as "to be beyond any precise measurement or determination."[5] Accordingly, and in line with the "mortal animal" becoming an "immortal ethical subject" (in that for Badiou, although the ethical transformation is always a singular experience of the *event*, that experience, and the resultant ethic, is potentially universalizable and/or potentially "immortal"), access to this realm of innovatory truths is achieved – as might be expected by now – "by *fixing* the domination of the state over the situation and in *evading* this domination." This whole truth-making procedure is thus both wholly subjective (it is founded only on the subject who experiences it "performatively") and, simultaneously, a condition productive of a potential truth for everyone. As Badiou's translator and explicator Peter Hallward puts it: "A truth is innovation *en acte*, singular in its location but universal in its 'address' and import. Inaccessible to the classification of the state, the truth comes to pass as a universal-singular, particular to but unlimited by the contents of the situation in which it comes to exist."[6]

An *event*, then, though absolutely crucial for Badiou, is yet an *event* with no particular content. In fact, Badiou insists, the *event* has nothing verifiable about it; its happening is not a matter of "the facts," of the cognitive; its significance cannot be "proven" but only, in the light of one's experience of it, grasped, acclaimed, and proclaimed, a new-born truth that persists by virtue of one having toward it an attitude of *fidelity*, an unswerving loyalty to it that amounts to "something like a disinterested enthusiasm, absorption in a compelling task or cause, a sense of elation, of being caught up in something that transcends all petty, private or material concerns … of *holding true* to a principle, person or ideal."[7] It also consists in having an *ethical* attitude towards this *event*, ethics being understood here as that which literally *encourages* the subject to "keep going," to "not give up on your desires." Such *events*, then, are the immediate catalysts that bring to fruition developing tendencies and concretize previous intimations of a position that, once gained, is then held fast. As Badiou puts it:

> I shall call "truth" the real process of a fidelity to an event: that which this fidelity *produces* in the situation. For example, the politics of The French Maoists between 1966 and 1976 which tried to think and practice two entangled events: the Cultural Revolution in China and May '68 in France. Or so-called "contemporary" music ... which is fidelity to the great Viennese composers of the early twentieth century. Or the algebraic geometry of the 1950s and 1960s and so forth. Essentially a truth is the material course traced, within the situation ... from the decision to relate henceforth to that situation *from the perspective of its eventual supplement* ... It is thus an *immanent break*. "Immanent" because a truth proceeds *in* the situation and nowhere else – there is no heaven [foundations] of truths. "Break," because what enables the truth-process – the event – means nothing according to the prevailing language and established knowledge [for them it is just a *void* to be avoided].[8]

This innovation, this truth, this new *power* that "punches a hole in reality ... in established knowledges," produces a position that is, as it were, *induced* by the *event*, after which one has to rework and forget one's previously held, ordinary ways of being:

> It is clear that under the effect of a loving encounter, if I want to be *really* faithful to it, I must completely rework my ordinary way of "living" my situation. If I want to be faithful to the event of the "Cultural Revolution," then I must at least practice politics ... in an entirely different manner from that proposed by the socialist and trade-unionist traditions. And again, Berg and Webern, faithful to the musical event known by the name of "Schoenberg," cannot continue with *fin-de-siècle* neo-Romanticism as if nothing had happened. After Einstein's texts of 1905, if I am faithful to their radical novelty, I cannot continue to practice physics within its classical framework, and so on. An evental fidelity is a real break (both thought and practiced) in the specific order within which the event took place (be it political, loving, artistic or scientific ...).[9]

And so if I want to be faithful to, say, the "posts" – to post-structuralism, post-Marxism, post-feminism, post-colonialism, postmodernism – then I *cannot* in good faith remain a structuralist, a Marxist, a feminist, a colonialist, a modernist; I have to break with my old love for a new one, commit an act of infidelity, break it off. I have to be loyal to the new. Not loyal, of course, in the sense of never moving my "position" again – for in Badiou to effect such a "closure" on myself (and others) is to commit an act that he terms *Evil* – but loyal to the new in the sense of developing it while remaining committed to it, and even open to the possibility of someday breaking off with it even while being faithful to it.

Now, this reference to *evil* in the above paragraph is, on my reading, Badiou's way of qualifying or denying that relativism that I think is implied by everything I have said (by everything I think Badiou has said) so far; it is Badiou's attempt to be the promulgator of a "relativism of a certain kind." For given how things stand at this point – that *events* have no verifiable content, that *events* are experienced by a singular subject who becomes that subject only through that experience, that that which breaks with the conventional is immanent to the evental situation and, perhaps above all, that the examples given of events throughout Badiou's text seem on the surface at least to be so diverse ("St. Paul's militant concept of apostolic subjectivity … the Jacobin or Bolshevik fidelity to a Revolutionary event … two lovers' conception of themselves as amorous subjects, rooted only in a fidelity to the ephemeral event of their encounter; an artist's or scientist's fidelity to a creative line of enquiry … "[10]) – then it really does look as if anything "radical" can be included. If Badiou can include as *events* the Bolshevik Revolution, then why not the Nazi takeover of power? If he can include Jacobins, then why not Stalinists? If May '68, why not the *events* producing the truth-claims (which are certainly meant to apply universally by the holder(s) of them) of an Osama Bin Laden or a George Bush? Does it not look as if anything could be included?

But, as indicated already, Badiou's answer to this question is actually an unqualified *no*, a no that is argued for on the basis of a series of discriminations between types of events and types of outcome that are deemed to be either ethical or evil. This discriminatory apparatus is made up of three parts that, together, form the basis for an arguably acceptable concept of ethics as subordinate to the development of truths. For lurking within Badiou's positive maxim, "'Keep going!' Continue to be this 'some-one,' a human animal among others, which nevertheless finds itself *seized* and *displaced* by the evental process of a truth,"[11] there lies what he calls three "perversions," three "paradoxes" that, *dependent* on his notion of truth, would seek to destroy it:

> It is at the heart of the paradoxes provoked by this maxim that we discover the veritable figure of Evil (which in this way is dependent upon the Good, i.e. upon truths) in its three forms: the *simulacrum* (to be the terrorizing follower of a false event); *betrayal* (to give up on a truth in the name of one's interest) and the forcing of the unnamable, or *disaster* (to believe in the total power of a truth).[12]

Consequently, it is by identifying and refuting examples of these *evils* that Badiou is able to claim that only certain events are "real events" as opposed to fakes (to simulacrum-type events), and that thus allows Badiou to construct the image of the ethically responsible intellectual he wants and which I think

I (and others) can use. So, how does Badiou's idea of *evil* work to achieve what he takes to be this non-relativistic end?

Slicing somewhat arbitrarily into Badiou's preliminary but complicated observations on the nature of evil, my reading begins at that point in his argument where he is reminding his readers that the "dimensions" of a truth involve three components: the *event* (that which brings to pass something other than current opinions and instituted knowledges, an "unpredictable supplement, which vanishes as soon as it appears"); *fidelity* ("the name of the process: it amounts to a sustained investigation of the situation under the imperative of the event itself; it is an immanent and *continuing* break"); and *truth* as such ("that is, the multiple, internal to the situation, that the fidelity constructs, bit by bit; it is what the fidelity gathers together and produces").[13] These three dimensions are then posited as having their own ontological characteristics out of which could emerge – as their dialectical opposite – the distinctive ontological characteristics of *evil*. Thus, for example, the characteristics of the event are that it is both *situated* ("it is the event of this or that situation") and *supplementary* (it is detached from "all the rules of the situation") in ways that *void* the normal; that is to say, an event is a genuine event if to existing ways of "being in the world" it makes no sense, so that from this perspective it goes unnoticed, is just a hole, a meaningless nothing, a "void" of no significance.[14] Next, the ontological condition of *fidelity* is such that continuing loyalty to it is never inevitable or necessary. What remains permanently undecidable is whether the "disinterested interest" it presumes on behalf of the becoming subject who participates in it is sustainable, or whether it will degenerate into mere self-interest, it being because of this ineradicable uncertainty "that there is a place for an ethic of truths."[15] And, finally, the ontological characteristic of a truth that does emerge from the event is its *power:* "we should say that the truth … heterogeneous to ordinary knowledges … forces new knowledges, the verb 'to force' indicating that the power of a truth is that of the break, of the violation of established knowledges." Accordingly – and pulling all of this together – it is by virtue of these three "dimensions" (the convocation by an *event* of the *void* of a situation, the uncertainty of *fidelity*, and the forcing of new knowledges by a new *truth*) that the phenomenon of *evil* depends – an *evil* that now has its own "names" each with their own ontological characteristics:

> to believe that an event convokes not the void of the earlier situation, but its plenitude, is Evil in the sense of *simulacrum* or terror;
> to fail to live up to a fidelity is Evil in the sense of *betrayal*, betrayal in oneself of the immortal that you are;
> to identify a truth with total power is Evil in the sense of *disaster*.
> Terror, betrayal and disaster are what an ethic of truths … tries to ward off … And [it] is certain that there can be Evil only in so far as there proceeds a Good.[16]

How, in a little more detail, does this work? Let us examine each evil in turn.

With regard to the evil of simulacrum and terror, the criterion operating to distinguish between the "real" event and the fake is that the genuine event must call forth and name the "*void* of the situation" by which a mere happening takes on the mantle of the *event*; otherwise it remains only a simulacrum. Thus, says Badiou, as he expands on this, when the Nazis talked about the "National Socialist Revolution," when they borrowed the names of "revolution" and "socialism" from those great modern *events* of the French Revolution of 1792 and the Bolshevik Revolution of 1917, then it looked as if, by association, it too was a "voiding" break, just like them. *But it wasn't.* For while the elements named by the Nazi seizure of power may look event-like, in fact that seizure was distinguished not by the vocabulary of a void, but by a vocabulary of *plenitude*. This seizure was not an *event* at all but the mere *simulacrum* of one, since it did not bring about the *void* of the earlier situation but rather its *fulfillment* (plenitude); not the universality of that which is sustained "by no particular characteristic," but the absolute particularity of a community "itself rooted in the characteristics of its soul, its blood, and its race." Thus, because the Nazi seizure of power was essentially a "continuity with the before" and not a break with it, since it conceived itself as a German revolution "faithful only to the alleged national substance of a people," then "right from the moment the event is named ... it is radically incapable of any truth whatsoever": "When a radical break in a situation, under names borrowed from real truth-processes, convokes not the *void* but the 'full' particularity or presumed substance of that situation, we are dealing with *a simulacrum of truth*."[17]

And that's not all. For not only is the Nazi takeover not an event, but fidelity to it – fidelity to a simulacrum – has as its "content" potential war and massacre: these make up the "evil reality" of a mistaken fidelity. Badiou:

> [F]idelity to the simulacrum – that appalling imitation of truths – presumes nothing more about those they designate as the enemy than their strictly particular existence as human animals. It is thus this existence that will have to bear the return of the void. This is why the exercise of fidelity to the simulacrum is necessarily the exercise of *terror*. Understand by terror, here, not the political concept of Terror, linked (in a universalisable couple) to the concept of Virtue by the Immortals of the Jacobin Committee of Public Safety, but the pure and simple reduction of all to their being-for-death. Terror thus conceived really postulates that in order to let the substance be, nothing must be ... In sum, our first definition of Evil is this: Evil is the process of a simulacrum of truth. And in its essence ... it is terror directed at everyone.[18]

It is now easy to see how the utilization of an event that "voids," and, contrarywise, of the *simulacrum* that doesn't, allows Badiou to approve of – as the bearer of ethical responsibility – only certain types of happening. Thus on the one hand we have real (voiding) events after which nothing runs the same again – the Pauline Conversion, Einstein's 1905 texts, 1792, 1917, May '68 – while on the other we now understand why evental *simulacra* are not voiding breaks but continuations, rearticulations, re-emphases, reforms, fulfillments – thus Hitler, Stalin, Pol Pot, the Berlin Wall, 9/11 …

While it is evil to give oneself completely to the simulacrum of an event, it is also an evil not to give oneself entirely to "the real thing." Hence Badiou's second evil is precisely to "give up on your desires," to "sell out" on those genuine events that demand your disinterested interests: this is the *evil* of *betrayal*.

Betrayal: a lack of continued will; a giving-in to adversity, the succumbing to the siren-calls of the everyday, the conventional, the safe, is thus an ever-present danger. It's not easy, this going beyond the animal to become the subject of a new truth. Everyone, writes Badiou, is familiar "with the moments of crisis faced by a lover, a researcher's discouragement, a militant's lassitude, an artist's sterility … Opinion tells me … that the fidelity to which I am faithful looks very much like – too much like – this or that certified Evil, [which] is always a possibility, since the formal characteristics of this Evil (as simulacrum) are exactly those of a truth."[19] So it is that the defect of the ethics of a truth at some undecidable point of a crisis ("I must go on – I can't go on" … the undecidability of a Derridean-type *aporia*) thus presents itself as a possible betrayal. *Betrayal*, then, is "the second name … of the Evil made possible by a truth."[20]

The third evil is a qualification to that very act of fidelity to a truth: too zealously pursued, such fidelity would silence those who would question it by insisting on its absolute correctness. The outcome could lead to totalitarianism. Badiou poses the problem starkly: "The question we must now ask ourselves is this: does the power of a truth, in the situation in which it pursues its faithful course, have the potential to be total?"[21]

His answer is yes. Why? Because truth (like opinion) is concerned with determining and naming the "elements of the situation" since its process is nothing other than their examination *from the perspective of the event*. Yet because such constitutive elements, such variables, are always ultimately of "an infinite number," then we can never fully account for them all. Consequently, if, driven by a zeal for the truth, one imagines that *all* the elements can actually be accounted for, that there is nothing else left to say, then one has fallen for the delusion that *a* truth is *the* Truth.

> We can now define what the *total* power of a truth would be: it would imply the ability to name and evaluate *all* the elements of the objective situation from the perspective of the truth-process. Rigid and dogmatic (or "blinded"), the subject language would claim the power, based on its own axioms, to name the whole of the real, and thus to change the world.[22]

This is serious. For such a truth feels compelled to "eliminate opinion," and this is *evil*. The attempt to impose the total power of a truth "ruins that truth's very foundation," for there are no truths like that:

> There is no History other than our own; there is no true world to come. The world as world is, and will remain beneath the true and the false. There is no world that might be captive to the coherence of the Good. The world is, and will remain, beneath Good and Evil ... Its sole being lies in the situated advent of a singular truth. So it must also be that the power of a truth is also a kind of powerlessness.[23]

"The power of a truth is also a kind of powerlessness." This is crucial. For a truth must not silence others who "are not in the truth," must not "absolutize a truth":

> Every absolutization of the power of a truth organizes an Evil. Not only does this Evil destroy the situation (for the will to eliminate opinion is, fundamentally, the same as the will to eliminate, in the human animal, it's very animality (i.e., its being)), but it also interrupts the truth-process in whose name it proceeds since it fails to preserve, within the composition of its subject, the duality of interests (disinterested-interest and interest pure and simple).[24]

No one, then, has the power to name *all* the "elements of the situation." At least one element – one variable – must remain that is inaccessible to "truthful nomination," and that element ("I shall call this element the unnameable of a truth" ... the non-immortality of a truth) must remain speakable by someone else (some "other") in opposition to the potential totality of a truth. Evil is thus "in this case ... to force the naming of the unnameable. Such, exactly, is the principle of disaster."

And so, finally: "Simulacrum (associated with the event), betrayal (associated with the fidelity), and the forcing of the unnameable (associated with the power of the true): these are the figures of Evil, an Evil which becomes an *actual* possibility only thanks to the sole Good we recognise – a truth-process."[25]

I hope that it is now clear where ethical responsibility lies for Badiou. It lies in distinguishing "voiding" breaks from simulacra, and in keeping going against all "opinionated" recuperations of that new truth issuing from the event save that that truth must not silence all opposition to it in case it should take on the mantle of an *absolute* truth that would brook no resistance: no one can name the "name of names."

This capacity to keep open even truthful discourse, to keep dissent open, to not silence in the name of an impossible totality even in the teeth of the necessity to remain loyal to one's desires; to keep "opposition speech" going in the face of one's most highly encouraging truth – all these anti-totality/totalitarian positions constitute the whole point. Badiou's writings are born in the shadow of the totalitarian nightmares of the twentieth century, a shadow that must never again be visited upon us. It is this anti-totalizing/anti-totalitarian urge that also animated both Jean-François Lyotard's *The Differend* and Edward Said's notion of the "intellectual as exile."

What I want to stress about Lyotard's notion of the *differend* is that it arguably offers a way of measuring the extent, the degree, and the type of *freedom* within any given social formation, a freedom that, in turn, allows him to construct the idea of an ethically responsible intellectual as someone who insists on its maintenance and, indeed, its extension. For while in everyday life we humans seem to get along by settling our differences relatively amicably, or by letting each other get on with "our own thing" (generally subject to some or other consensus-seeking principle of reciprocal liberty or whatever ...), there sometimes arises a fundamental antagonism, a massive disagreement, a polarization of beliefs such that a "final vocabulary" of a person or an ideology is one on which its proponents refuse to compromise and which, counterposed against an equally strongly held alternative final vocabulary, results in a stalemate that can only be broken if one or other of the "sides" either gives way or if a climb-down is "unjustly" enforced. This uncompromising, principled stalemate is the situation of the *differend.* As Lyotard explains:

> As distinguished from a litigation, a differend would be a case of conflict, between (at least) two parties, that cannot be equitably resolved for lack of a rule of judgement applicable to both arguments. One side's legitimacy does not imply the other's lack of legitimacy. However, applying a single rule of judgement to both in order to settle their differend as though it were merely a litigation would wrong (at least) one of them (and both of them if neither side admits this rule). Damages result from an injury which is inflicted upon the rules of a genre of discourse but which is reparable according to those rules. A wrong results from the fact that the rules of the genre of discourse by which one judges are not those of the judged genre or genres of discourse ... The title of this book suggests ... that a universal rule of judgement between heterogeneous genres is lacking in general.[26]

Does this mean that in cases of fundamental disagreement anything goes? Does it mean that every antagonist, having the right to speak (and enact what is spoken about) can speak (and do) anything they like? Does it mean that, say, a Nazi enunciation of anti-Semitism, declarations of intent with regard to ethnic cleansing, the exploitation of vulnerable minorities or other types of "hate speech" (or, from the points of view of the Nazi, ethnic cleanser, and exploiter, "correct speech"), are permissible? After all, if injustice, for Lyotard, is being unable to speak, then in what name do we have a legitimate right to take away the freedom to speak without those from whom that right is taken away (legitimately) resisting? Is there no criterion operating here (for Lyotard is well-known for his animosity towards all totalizing, metanarrative closures, and hence his championing of free-wheeling heterogeneous/incommensurable language-games and phrase-regimes that never "link" in ways that are *necessary* such that the next phrase is entailed – despite the fact that "genres of discourse" (history, literature, philosophy) link all the time in ways "faking" normativity and naturalness)?

Lyotard's answer to this question as to the existence of a kind of non-relativistic criterion is … "yes" … yes there is such a criterion that, baldly stated, goes like this. The freedom to propound a view in opposition to a counter-view is allowed – no matter how contentious or extreme it might be held to be – *if*, and only if, were it ever "hypothetically" to win and be enacted, it would not then *close down* future *differends* opposing it or any other *differend* such that the game(s) of the *differend* could not be played. Lyotard puts this very clearly in *Just Gaming*:

> Absolute injustice would occur if the pragmatics of obligation, that is, the possibility of continuing to play the game of the just, were excluded. This is what is unjust. Not the opposite of the just, but that which prohibits that the question of the just and the unjust [of what is just and unjust] be, and remain raised. Thus, obviously, all terror, annihilation, massacre, etc., or their threat, are, by definition, unjust. [For] the people whom one massacres will no longer be able to play the game of the just and the unjust. But moreover, any decision that takes away, or in which it happens that one takes away, from one's partner in a current pragmatics, the possibility of playing or replaying a pragmatics of obligation – a decision that has such an effect is [also] unjust. But of course one must imagine this effect, these effects … [27]

So, taking our cue from Lyotard, let us do a little imagining. Let us imagine the "just and the unjust" in relation to the Holocaust and to Auschwitz – Lyotard's *own* test cases. For Lyotard, the point about the Holocaust/Auschwitz is not that there is a *differend* between the Nazi SS and the Jew, *but precisely that there isn't*. Of course, *if* there were to be an exchange involving the final vocabularies of the Nazi SS and the Jew over the justice of the Holocaust/Auschwitz, it is clear that a *differend* would be operating. The final vocabulary of the Nazi SS and the Jew – vocabularies arguing, on the one hand, for the extermination of the Jew, and, on the Jewish other, for their lives, could not be resolved by any third-party equally unacceptable to both sides: here a *differend* is firmly in place. But as Geoffrey Bennington (in his quite brilliant reading of *The Differend* in his *Lyotard: Writing the Event*) has pointed out, in fact a *differend* is actually absent with regard to the Holocaust/Auschwitz: "Between the SS and the Jew there is not even a *differend*, because there is not even a common idiom (that of a tribunal) in which a damage at least could [even] be formulated."[28] And the reason for this is that the Jew is held to have no right to a voice: *the Jew is not allowed to speak*. To the sentence uttered by the Nazi SS to the Jew: "You shall die – that is my law," the Jew cannot reply: "I shall not die – that is my law," for the Jew cannot reply at all. Thus the Jew is immediately the victim of an injustice, a *wrong*, that of being unable to be a party to a *differend*. The Jew is silenced; annihilation awaits. Consequently, because the Nazi SS do not allow a *differend* even to exist, then, for Lyotard, they themselves should not have been allowed to speak in the first place – or ever. For only those who agree to allow *differends* to continue interminably are allowed to play the game – the game of "just" gaming.

In this context, the significance of the Holocaust/Auschwitz is not about the question – so debated by empirically-minded historians – of whether, or how, or why, the Holocaust/Auschwitz "happened." For Lyotard, the real significance to be registered here is not what can be empirically demonstrated, but that the Holocaust/Auschwitz *are the names of a silence*. This is a silence/silencing that cannot be more or less adequately dealt with by phrases of a cognitive/factual kind. That is to say, if one is to respect the annihilation of the Jews (and those "others" silenced with them), then one must respect that silence. No amount of empirical detail, no amount of new "evidence" or old evidence newly raked-over, no witness or testimony can ever represent the screams, the terror, the stench of death, the utter fear and dread of the victims. One can only register that silence and its enormity by letting it speak "for itself"; it is not possible ever to fill in the detail of – ever to effectively challenge at the empirical level a Holocaust denier like Faurisson over – the death camps. What can only speak against a "revisionist denier" like him is that silence – in volumes. It is, therefore, the memory of that silence – a silence that we cannot ever fully "know" or comprehend – that ensures that, though this "event" is something we cannot ever fully remember, we cannot ever fully forget either: it is, as Lyotard puts it, an *immemorial* event.

Referring in his *Heidegger and "the Jews"* to Adorno's remarks on silence in the latter's *After Auschwitz*, Lyotard suggests that to "reduce" the terror of the Holocaust by "putting it under concepts" – to make it an empirical object of cognition – would indeed be to drown out the screams of its victims: if history could remember ... if history could dot every "i" and cross every "t", if everything could be accounted for and folded away finished ... then it would have been forgotten. Thus, to respect the impossibility of ever "coming to terms with" or "understanding" the now silence of the Holocaust's victims – to keep its meanings open – we have to have a remembrance that will indeed testify to that horrendous silencing precisely by *not* "representing" it. It is an ethical responsibility – it is the *historian's* ethical responsibility – to ensure that the Holocaust/Auschwitz forever haunts us.

For Lyotard this "event" gives weight to his suggestion that *all* events, actually, are immemorial. That "the past" both in general and in its particulars can never be fully known. That no amount of empirical work can ever entail its definitive significance; that there is no necessary connection between cognitive and speculative/prescriptive phrase-regimes or genres. Consequently, as Bennington argues, for Lyotard the Holocaust/Auschwitz is *a sign of history*, a sign, among other signs, of the limits of the empirical/cognitive genre, of the limits of any history that suffers from the delusion that it is an epistemology:

> So if "Auchswitz" suggests, almost emblematically, that the historian needs to be attentive to that which cannot be presented according to the rules of the cognitive genre, then, on this account, "Auschwitz is the realest of realities." As a sort of emblem, Auschwitz signals the limit of historical competence: but this limit is implied in the structure of "reality" in general ... historians are at the mercy of a Faurisson if they imagine that justice consists solely in the application of cognitive rules in such cases. If history were merely a question of such rules, it is hard to know how Faurisson could be accused of injustice.[29]

This reference by Bennington to the limits of historians' competence to *say* everything, when coupled to the remarks immediately preceding the above quotation to the effect that *all* history must be immemorial (that is, never fully recallable empirically), raises the question whether the ethically responsible historian – who perhaps wants to give a voice to the hitherto voiceless; to give a voice to all those who have been relatively or absolutely silent both in the "actual past" and/or in the historiography – actually needs to make the unheard heard in order for them to be remembered. For if E. P. Thompson's framework knitters and liberty-seeking artisans, if men and women of color, if members of the working class, if various other minorities, have effectively and variously lived silently outside of history/historiography, then isn't the registering of their silence/silencing, isn't an investigation of the dimensions and means by which those silences have been achieved enough for us to be able to remember them? *Maybe there is no need to fill their silence with empirical noise.* Thus, for example, for Lyotard the greatest "wrong" done to the working classes under capitalist mode(s) of production was that they were (and are) variously deprived of the ability to legitimately phrase their labor power as anything other than a commodity to be exchanged for a wage; and that the knowledge of this *wrong*, this silencing is all you need to know in order to make this point.

> Marx in 1834: "a class with radical chains, a class of bourgeois society which is not a class of bourgeois society, a sphere which has a universal character by its universal suffering and claims no particular right because no particular wrong but wrong generally is perpetrated against it." This wrong is expressed through the silence of feeling, through suffering. The wrong results from the fact that all phrase universes and all their linkages are or can be subordinated to the sole finality of capital. [Consequently] the silent feeling that signals a differend remains to be listened to. Responsibility ... requires it. This is the way in which Marxism has not come to an end, as the feeling of [a not yet heard] differend.[30]

For Lyotard, the basis of thought, the basis of ethical responsibility, then, revolves around the *logical* inability ever to close down the *differend* even if on occasion (under the Nazis, for example) this is attempted and achieved in "actuality." It is thus Lyotard's aim, *contra* totality, to establish, as an ethically responsible intellectual, a condition of permanent *dissensus* (a condition for which he thinks postmodernity has established the conditions in current social formations), as the name for that heterogeneity and incommensurability of genres of discourse that he considers the basis for that freedom that must never be surrendered, namely, the freedom to be able to find the idiom to phrase, and participate in, a *differend*.[31]

The place of Edward Said in my composition of an acceptable, ethically responsible intellectual is to accept the *outsider* status that thinking in the ways of Badiou and Lyotard – against the tide of opinion – might well bring to the person who thinks as they urge. In his *Representations of the Intellectual* Said tries – among other things – to square a particularly difficult circle: to be both an organic intellectual (après Gramsci) when he speaks on behalf of the Palestinians, and a quasi-universalist when he speaks "for us all" – a feat achieved, I think, by simply wanting for the Palestinians what he wants for everyone (self-determination, emancipation, empowerment, freedom …). But if this is perhaps too easy a solution to what some have seen as at least a paradox if not a contradiction marring Said's book, it is not a discussion I wish to dwell on here. Rather, it is the role of the intellectual as a *necessary* outsider (necessary because one cannot be an intellectual if one is not an outsider) that is germane here, an outsider on whom Said confers the name of the *exile*.

For Said, intellectuals are a particular kind of person. They are those who are not (merely) experts, nor technocrats, nor specialists, nor necessarily academics, and certainly not accomplices of the *status quo* (as he thinks so many "experts" directly or indirectly are). "Nothing in my view," he writes,

> is more reprehensible than those habits of mind in the intellectual that induce avoidance, that characteristic turning away from a difficult and principled position which you know to be the right one, but which you decide not to take. You do not want [shades of the Evil of an enticing opinion après Badiou] to appear too political; you are afraid of seeming controversial; you need the approval of a boss … you want to keep a reputation for being balanced, objective, moderate; your hope is to be asked back, to consult, to be on a board or prestigious committee, and so to remain within the responsible mainstream … for an intellectual these habits of mind are corrupting *par excellence* … .[32]

Said's intellectual, then, is a person with the capacity for presenting an uncompromising emancipatory message. A person whose work(s) have a radical, sustained cutting edge. A person happy to raise embarrassing questions, not willing to take no for an answer, to relentlessly confront dogma and orthodoxy, and to keep in focus "those issues and people that are continually forgotten or swept under the rug." This is a person who *enjoys* never being fully adjusted, of existing happily beyond the chatty, inconsequential "reality" inhabited by the natives; of remaining immune to accommodation: an uncooptable, *disobedient* person. This is a person who not only accepts the fate meted out by various "professionals" and "establishments" to this thorn-in-the flesh – the status of the relative *exile* – but who also welcomes it. Who likes being marginal. Who accepts that her or his awkwardness, eccentric angles of vision, and unwillingness to follow established paths give a freedom and integrity that makes her or him beholden to no one, and ready to accept the consequences of that position: that one can never be settled, never fully accepted, never be entirely at ease; that it is part of being ethical, part of morality, not to be (as Adorno put it) "at home in one's home." To be sure, says Said, a condition of marginality might seem to license a sort of irresponsibility or flippancy. But it need not – these are evils to look out for. Nor does he have in mind "the free-floating intellectual" whose "technical competence is on loan or sale to anyone." No, what he is finally saying is this:

> that to be as marginal and as undomesticated as someone who is in real exile is for an intellectual to be unusually responsive to the traveller rather than to the potentate, to the provisional and risky rather than to the habitual, to innovation and experiment rather than the authoritatively given *status quo*. The *exilic* intellectual does not respond to the logic of the conventional but the audacity of daring, and to representing change, to moving on, not standing still.[33]

Now think of this person as one who expresses her or his position both within the narrow discourse in which she or he is primarily engaged (in this case history) and, more generally, politically, and who connects these two things up but always with the former subordinated to the latter. Said's intellectual *qua* intellectual has bigger fish to catch than some or other version of the past "for its own sake."

At this point I think it possible to answer the question of what intellectuals might look like if they looked as if they were driven by a sense of ethical responsibility. With the provisos essayed by Badiou under the name of evil, such intellectuals would be compelled by a particular cause or concern to which fidelity and perseverance are the sustaining powers. They would almost certainly find themselves engaged in innumerable *differends*, as resistance to their voices that speak "justice and truth to power" would seek both openly and covertly to nullify or silence them while they themselves pledged – on criteria taken from Lyotard – not only to keep the *differend* open but to use every opportunity to expand it to those currently wronged, an extension justified in the names of heterogeneity, difference, and "the other" (*dissensus*) as opposed to homogeneity, the same, and closure. These intellectuals would accept the necessity, were their own desires to be fulfilled, of a critical reflexivity vis-à-vis precisely those desires lest they should succumb to, on the one hand, the pull of the always beckoning consensual "center," and, on the other, to totalizing intolerance. All this, of course, would be informed by an awareness of that *aporetic* undecidability of the decision that animates Derrida, and by an ironic (yet responsible) attitude that they would have towards their own, Rorty-like, never-final "final vocabulary." For they are people who have radical, ineradicable doubts about their own "final vocabulary" because they have been impressed by other vocabularies. They realize that arguments phrased in their present vocabulary can neither underwrite nor dissolve those doubts, and they recognize that their vocabulary is not nearer to "reality" than others; that they and it are not somehow in touch with a power not themselves.[34] They are intellectuals – like Said's intellectual – who are never "finalized," never "fully-fashioned," because they are aware of the contingency and foundationlessness of everything – including themselves and their own "position" – a position they hold to, however, until convinced by others that it is "not right." They also hold unflinchingly to two "fables" of their own: the Derridean fable of emancipation ("we must never give up on the great story of emancipation"), and the Rortyan, ironical belief that "cruelty is the worst thing we do":

> I use "ironist" to name the sort of person who faces up to the contingency of … her most central beliefs and desires – someone sufficiently historicist and nominalist to have abandoned the idea that those central beliefs and desires refer back to something beyond the reach of time and chance. Liberal ironists are people who include among those ungroundable desires their own hope that suffering will be diminished, that the humiliation of human beings by other human beings may cease.[35]

Given the contingency of our "human condition," a condition wherein "everything can be redescribed" interminably, the portrait of the ethically responsible intellectual I have all too briefly sketched is radically provisional. Nevertheless, the kind of theorizing about ethical responsibility gleaned from a Badiou, a Lyotard, a Said, a Derrida, and a Rorty can provide me sufficient characteristics to allow me to draw up an idea of an ethically responsible intellectual that I can perhaps begin to live by and – on some of my very occasional better days – even begin to live up to. Maybe others can too.

Ethical responsibility and the historian

Badiou, Lyotard, Said, Derrida, and Rorty: not a historian among them. Should we be surprised? Not really. Because in a way it seems obvious that, if I want to construct an ethical position, then I should go to ethical/moral philosophers to do so. If I want to think about the idea of the intellectual, then I should go to those who have written widely and wisely about this. This is not to say – and I want to underline the fact that I am not saying it – that historians do not constantly invoke ethical and moral judgements, and, occasionally, raise them to the level of consciousness such that it is patently obvious that they are doing so. It is certainly not to say that historians are not intellectually sharp, analytical, erudite, and often highly reflexive as to the status – including the ethical/moral status – of their work(s). But I think it does say that the historian *qua* historian – or better still, in this *History and Theory* context, professional historians *qua* professional historians – are not in a situation where, by virtue of their "historical knowledge," they have something *extra* to say about ethical responsibility as opposed to raising both general and particular "examples" of different situations in the past where ethical decisions have been taken at the time and/or where, in the "present," historians are constantly making them. I also think that the strictures so embedded in the "training" of historians and the profession's "maxims of prudence" within which most mainstream historians arguably work (with their valorization of empirical methods, objectivity, and "truth at the end of enquiry"; with their injunction to ensure that their unwieldy academic bulk does not – and should not – get in the way of trying to present the past both "for itself" and on "its" own terms; with their warnings to avoid the pitfalls of anachronism, hindsight, and other manifestations of present-centeredness; with their constant reminders to shun partisanship and commitment to an overt position that would vitiate and even threaten their "professional calling" – all this being said in addition to criticizing anything that smacks of too much – or even any – theory) also ensure that the role of the overtly committed intellectual position as I have penned it here makes it both an inappropriate and unlikely one for such historians to occupy.

Consequently, it is in this sort of "context" that the question as to whether (professional) historians *qua* (professional) historians have a duty over and above that of the intellectual as such has to be answered (in these general terms) negatively: "no they do not." I thought – and dismissed the idea on reflection – that one way of conceiving this "not" would be to try to construct an answer to the question of "to whom and to what" ought the ethically responsible historian be responsible by keeping my answer *within* the framework and borders of professional orthodoxy. That is, by arguing that the shibboleths guiding (professional) historians gave them an ethical responsibility toward their particular objects of enquiry – the past in general and in particular – both in terms of a scrupulous adherence to their methods of enquiry (the "research phase" of the historians' "craft"), and to a rigorous and reflexive attention to their modes of representation within various narrative genres. But I was not much convinced by this, not much impressed that these things – which in themselves I am not castigating in any way whatsoever (save to add the reminder that there is, of course, no such thing as a single historical method, nor any way of making those aesthetic figures that we call "narratives" and which constitute historical representations at the level of the text susceptible to "truth" or "objectivity" claims couched in terms of epistemology) – are enough to turn even the most brilliant scholarship into an intellectual commitment – to turn what are in the end *mechanisms, means*, and *procedures* into matters of ethical substance and commitment of a Badiou/Said/Lyotard type. "History" can or could, of course, be used as a means to such an end, but it is not "in and of itself" currently constituted as that type of discourse at all.

What I am finally trying to say here, then, is that the substance of intellectuality après Badiou *et al.* comes from a place (most) professional historians *qua* professional historians neither come from nor are going to: a concern for present and future *justice* for all human beings of the kind that intellectuals – like Badiou, Lyotard, Said, Derrida, Rorty – *have taken as the animating core of their entire* (and not just their professional) *lives*. Accordingly, the answer to the question of "to whom and to what" should historians be ethically responsible is, for me, tantamount to saying that they should ditch all those things that make them resistant to becoming partisans of a "truth," and, "freed from the burden of history," should take up the cause of human emancipation in ways that determine the way they write their histories. They would not diminish, but rather enlarge, their calling by answering a call that comes not from the past at all but directly from ethics.[36] But I am aware that answering a call like this may well result in the end of "a certain kind of history," and, of course, the end of "a certain kind of historian," too ...

Notes

1 Alain Badiou, *Ethics: An Essay on the Understanding of Evil* (London: Verso, 2001); Jean-François Lyotard, *The Differend* (Manchester, Eng.: Manchester University Press, 1988); Edward Said, *Representations of the Intellectual* (London: Vintage, 1994).
2 Peter Hallward, Introduction to Badiou's *Ethics*, viii.
3 Ibid., 40.
4 Ibid., 41–2.
5 Ibid., ix.
6 Ibid.
7 Ibid., x.
8 Ibid., 42.
9 Ibid.
10 Ibid., x.
11 Ibid., 91.
12 Ibid.
13 Ibid., 67–8.
14 Ibid., 69.
15 Ibid.
16 Ibid., 71.
17 Ibid., 73.
18 Ibid., 77.
19 Ibid., 79.
20 Ibid., 80.
21 Ibid.
22 Ibid., 83.
23 Ibid., 85.
24 Ibid.
25 Ibid., 87.
26 Lyotard, *The Differend*, xi.
27 Jean-François Lyotard and Jan-Loup Thébaud, *Just Gaming* (Minneapolis: University of Minnesota Press, 1985), 66–7.

28 Geoffrey Bennington, *Lyotard: Writing the Event* (Manchester, Eng.: Manchester University Press, 1988), 153.

29 Ibid., 148. For Lyotard, of course, these limits to historians' competence are a good thing. Lyotard's reasoning goes as follows: To know everything, to be absolutely certain, to have nothing left to say, is to have closed down any further discussion. But in history – as in other discourses – this endpoint is never reached, simply because it is always possible to make the "known facts" *mean* otherwise; there is no fact–value entailment. Consequently, because neither all the facts nor any definitive meaning of them can ever be fully ascertained, then, rather than being completed and thus finished with, the phenomena under discussion remain permanently open. They are thus "immemorial," that is, not fully remembered and yet not fully forgotten either, because there is always "more to say." And thus disputes (and probably *differends*) stretch interminably into an "open future." It is excellent news that historians' representations are always failed representations, that historians always "get it wrong."

30 Lyotard, *The Differend*, 171.

31 In the literature this conclusion, that with *dissensus* we have reached "the end of history" – and that Lyotard has therefore constructed his own metanarrative – is not a sustainable criticism of him, despite its ubiquity. I have given a detailed argument as to why this is the case in a [then] forthcoming article, "Modernist Disavowals and Postmodern Reminders of the Condition of History Today: On Jean-François Lyotard," in *Rethinking History: The Journal of Theory and Practice* 8:4 (2004).

32 Said, *Representations of the Intellectual*, 74.

33 Ibid., 47.

34 Richard Rorty, *Contingency, Irony and Solidarity* (Cambridge, Eng.: Cambridge University Press, 1989), 73.

35 Ibid., xv.

36 This reference to the "burden of history" refers, of course, to Hayden White's famous 1966 essay "The Burden of History" in *Tropics of Discourse* (Baltimore: Johns Hopkins University Press, 1978). (Originally published in *History and Theory* 5 [1966], 111–34.) It also recalls, as an approximation to an ethical history, Foucault's notion of history as "histories of the present" that *effectively* cut into the past to bring back that aspect of it that is useful politically. It is regrettable, I think, that historians have not much taken White and Foucault to heart.

12 'Once upon a time'

On history

In 2005 I gave a somewhat belated Professorial Inaugural Lecture at the University of Chichester. The paper, which has not been published 'publicly' before, was one I found difficult to write because the audience was made up of historians, history theorists, members of other departments in the university, people generally associated with it, and so on. The difficulty was thus that of trying to say things to historians in ways they hadn't completely heard before whilst not 'losing' the rest of the audience (the majority) that would find most of what I was going to say too 'internalist'. In the end I went for an 'intellectual autobiography' type of approach that might be judged to have been too personal and even confessional rather than professional, but I include it here because it helped me to think about why I think of history in the way I do, and that that might be vaguely interesting to others. In part the Lecture drew on some points I had made in an earlier article which had appeared in *Rethinking History* – in their 'Invitation to Historians' 'feature' – where historians are asked to address the question of why they are the historians they are ('After History', *Rethinking History,* 3, 1, 1999).

I ought to say, right at the very start, that this lecture takes the form of a 'kind of' intellectual autobiography, a lecture which I want to begin in what is, perhaps, too literal a way, by thinking about what a Professorial Lecture in History might be like: what might this thing call on the lecturer to do? Well, with regard to the professorial element this seems straightforward; it suggests to me that such a lecture might allow the said professor to openly *profess* what he or she believes in in terms of the discourse of history and/or some aspect of it. But with the notion of *inauguration* things can become more complicated. Because, whilst inauguration generally means a beginning of things, it also suggests things done long before. Whilst a professorial lecture is indeed a very precise starting point – it is there to mark publicly the appointment of a new professor – the things that this new professor will profess are, generally, pretty old. Indeed, it is precisely on the basis of these 'old things' that one has been appointed to a Chair in the first place. Consequently, professing in a professorial lecture what the lecturer – in this case me – might be happy to profess suggests a certain 'looking back'.

There is, of course, no necessity operating here; it's not essential that I look back. Moreover, even if it might be useful to do so on occasion (an occasion like this ...) the past *per se* doesn't give me much to go on if I want to turn it into a historical story. I mean, it's not as if the 'events' of the past have already got the shapes of stories in them which I can 'find'. Which means that any story that I tell is inevitably the product of a particular type of theorisable labour constitutive of which are a series of decisions that relate at best contingently to that 'once actuality' I have to somehow figure (out) as my 'real referent'. And not only that – and this point is important to make now because I shall be discussing it later – it may well be that, as a culture, we have come towards the end of historicising the past altogether such that, if in the future we still need to raise aspects of it to the level of consciousness, then the *form* of its raising may well be of a kind that finds few if any resonances in 'history as we have known it'. But these remarks are already opening things up in the way I thought they might, are already pushing things on too fast. For I really only wanted to use these early reflections on a 'professorial inaugural lecture' to 'set the scene' for this one; to indicate where I'm going to go in it and how I mean to get there. And what I want to do in this respect is conventional. I want to begin by way of an impressionistic recall of those aspects of my life that I think about when I need to think about them with regard to why I now consider history in the way I do. I then want to look at my current thinking about history and what I call 'temporal studies', concluding by suggesting how this thinking may determine any future work I might 'conjure up' and which, once 'conjured up', I am then prepared to profess.

Now, this idea of 'conjuring up' historical work, of 'conjuring up' history (and I shall stay with the term history not temporalisation for the moment) suggests a kind of trick, a sort of sleight-of-hand, is taking place. The suspicion is that in the productive labour whereby the past is transformed into something it never 'in itself' actually was – namely a history – something magical occurs. And I think this suspicion is correct. For as Carolyn Steedman has recently reminded us, the grammatical tense of the 'historical' is not the future perfect or the past-historic of English-speaking historians, but the syntax of the fairy-tale: 'Once upon a time' is the rhetorical mode, the generally unspoken and, for most historians, the generally unassumed starting-point that then figures their historicisations throughout. 'Once upon a time, in the Summer, in the August and September of 1914 ... ', or 'Once, long ago, in 1361, on a hill overlooking Rouen, there lived ... ', etc., etc., such that the peculiar literary *genre* called history has always had about it – and always will have about it – the aura of magical realism.[1] In strictly formal and stylistic terms, histories are always constituted through a whole battery of rhetorical devices and stylistic figures which ensures that they are always cut, shaped and 'made up', bespoke style, to suit all shapes and sizes, all requirements, unfailingly: almost uncannily historians always return from their visits to 'the past' with the histories they want. Such histories as these, as Steedman puts it, are thus intimately connected to those stories 'in which a girl flies, a mountain moves, the clocks run backwards and where [and this is the historians' particular contribution] the dead walk among the living'. If the archive, if history is a place of dreams, she adds, then it permits this one above all others: 'of making the dead walk and talk'; of making them appear again, quite magically 'all around us', even though they are not there – nor ever will be.[2] Of course there is a sense in which neither I nor anyone else can ever leave their 'past'. My past always stays inside me; in me and nowhere else is the boy of eight or nine or ten I once was – I'm still him, just grown older. But I cannot ever literally be him again, any more than a remembering culture can be what it remembers again. We remember, we forget, we select – consciously and unconsciously – in ways that guarantee that all our representations are partial and failed representations. In our concocted inheritances we process through a mix of tropes and emplotments the things we apparently want to remember – and we can never remember everything – otherwise it just wouldn't be an inheritance. Otherwise our histories need not begin in the mode of 'Once upon a time'. But in fact they always do, and that beginning inflects them until they arrive at their equally arbitrary destination, at which point they pronounce those equally magical words: 'The End'.

Once upon a time, then, in the late 1940s and early 1950s, I grew up in a working-class home on the edge of a small village in the middle of rural Derbyshire. I lived for the first fifteen years of my life in a one-up, one-down cottage with no indoor toilet, no running hot water, no electricity. I can remember still the hissing sound made by the gas that escaped through the holes in the mantles that dimly lit our rooms, and bedroom windows which in winter were thick with ice – on the inside. And where (and remember that, whilst all of this may well be 'rural', this is still a place located in the very middle of an England that had been industrialising for over a hundred and fifty years and which was one of the most advanced economies in the world), where, nevertheless, our milk was delivered daily in churns carried on the top of a horse-drawn cart. And yet, despite these relative privations, I think I enjoyed an almost idyllic childhood. I had no intellectual ambitions and nobody pushing me to get any, and so I just played, generally out of doors and in all weathers, in neighbouring woods and fields and lanes. I attended a local primary school with no idea of what education might be for and thus managed – to be honest without any effort whatsoever – to fail my 11+, thence to go on to the local 'secondary mod'. I attended this infrequently. So far as I recall I never did any homework or a single spot of revision, only to emerge suitably rewarded, at age fifteen, without a single educational qualification to my name from a school that didn't put any pupils into public examinations anyway.

And so, somewhat romantically (and those of you who can spot the mode of emplotment of a story a hundred yards away will already have recognised that this one is cast in the mode of a romance), the question I now want to address is: how did I begin to get out of this situation?

I don't believe in monocausal explanations – I mean who does? – but if I were to single out the major vehicle for my move away (and it was quite literally a vehicle) it would have to be the acquisition, at age eleven, of a new bicycle. It wasn't a racing bike, but when I heard of a nearby cycling club I adapted it as best I could, I joined the club and, by working illegally after school, had managed by the age of fourteen to have enough money to buy the real thing: a Mercian Campionissimo. I began to seriously train and, from the age of sixteen, to seriously race in events throughout the Midlands. I don't know if how I spent my youth was misspent, but there were no discos or pubs for me, only long training sessions punctuated by races.

But the significance of this – which I can see clearly now – was that my cycling took me out of the village and away from my hanging-around friends, on long summer training rides and weekend trips to races, so that I began to escape, to quite literally see new horizons and to develop ambitions unrestricted by those that had, by my mid-teens, become all-too-familiar. I felt I had to get away, and the literature which accompanied cycle-racing and which focussed on the continent (the first 'literature' I had ever really read) suggested where I should get away to. I dreamed of becoming a professional racing cyclist; of living in Europe; of following in the tracks of Brian Robinson, Tommy Simpson. Until, that is, at age eighteen, when I crashed in a road race and, in the winter that followed, lost not only what form I had but I also began to seriously entertain the possibility that, despite quite a lot of local success, I just wasn't going to make it. Little did I know that the decision I struggled to make was my first real experience of a Derridean *aporia*. In the event I decided I would immediately stop wasting my time cycling, but I would go to Europe. And so I sold my bikes, gave up my menial day job and left, aged nineteen, to spend the next two years hitch-hiking across East and Western Europe and Scandinavia, working infrequently as necessary then moving on. It was just another chance to play. But around the age of twenty-one I returned home to face another decision: what was I to do more long-term? I looked around for a job that I thought might allow me a considerable amount of freedom and so, after some consideration, I plumped for teaching. But there was a snag: I had no qualifications. I thus decided to take five 'O' levels (the then minimum requirement for teacher-training) but my local F.E. College only ran two-year courses and that seemed a lifetime. And so I bought a correspondence course that promised me 'rapid results' – it was after all supplied by the Rapid Results College of London – and so I took my 'O' levels in eight months, miraculously passed them and, aged twenty-two, entered teacher-training college.

I liked it a lot. I read History as my 'main subject' and P.E. as my 'subsid' (so I could still run around and play), but I now began to study really hard to leave three years later with a Distinction. But I didn't want to leave. My teaching-practices in school had been OK, but they'd also made me realise that I would prefer to lecture in something like a college or, more ambitiously, a university. Another decision was called for. I decided to teach for a year and then take a degree. Thus, in 1969 I went to the University of Nottingham to read Medieval and Modern History transferring, in 1972, to the Department of Politics where I began to research for a PhD.

Now, in a moment I shall be continuing, but first I want to back-track briefly so that I can explain how I gradually became involved with historical theory.

When I entered higher education I thought of historical knowledge as the accumulation of lots of facts about what had 'really happened in the past', and so I was totally thrown by my first contact with multiple interpretations of the same 'event' through reading various volumes in the 'Problems of European Civilization' series published by D. C. Heath (the so-called 'Heath Series'), all of which brought together in single volumes different readings of the same 'topic'. I didn't understand. I mean, my thinking went, there was only one past so why couldn't professional historians all agree as to what had actually happened? Yet, looking back, I think that this was when I first realised that the past and history are totally different things, are ontologically distinct. That prior to historicisation 'the past' isn't history at all and that (thanks to the fact–value problematic) the 'facts of the past' cannot logically entail one and only one reading of them. But I think there was also another reason why this interpretive 'free-for-all' so disturbed me initially, because when I say I didn't understand why historians couldn't all agree on one 'interpretation', I really mean that I couldn't understand why they couldn't agree with mine – at that time a naive but committed Marxist one.

I'm aware that there is no necessary connexion between being working class and being on the political left, but there was a connexion for me. When I first read E.P. Thompson's *The Making of the English Working Class* in the late 60s I thought that this was a way of understanding the past all humane human beings should agree with. That they didn't – and the dawning realisation that they couldn't (given the way class/ideology broadly governs readings) brought home to me the positioned nature of *all* readings – including my own. And so, henceforth, I never again felt the power that 'academic' historians gave to 'the facts' or to what 'really' or 'objectively' happened; I never felt the desire 'to study the past for its own sake on its own terms', seeing the 'sakes' and 'terms' they allegedly found being ones they had projected back there for their own sakes and their own terms in the first place. Put tautologically, I realised fairly quickly that we are the semantic source for whatever the past might be meaningfully historicised as. I was (I still am) on the political left; I did (I still do) like Marxist (now post-Marxist) analyses best. But I never again thought this preference could be written as truth, nor that history and truth ever went together. I saw that all historicisations were just like mine – ethico-political *investments* – and that my own politicised history was therefore not something to cover up as if it constituted some sort of unsightly blemish but was something I could be open about so that at least my own position wasn't – to use the jargon of the day – 'mystified'.

But what I'm beginning to say here in a roundabout way, is that by the late 60s I was already becoming receptive to a sort of relativistic postmodernism 'before the letter' – or at least before the letter had reached me. In the 60s, of course, postmodernism was embryonic, but when it grew stronger in the 80s and 90s I was already prepared for it, not least for the reasons I've been outlining. But there was something else, a single event that began to turn me towards the postmodern and towards theory.

I can pinpoint this event precisely. Though nowhere near Damascus – actually I was in a bus travelling from Derby – I can still remember the shock of seeing the words 'the death of God' on a page of the book that I had bought earlier that Saturday afternoon: Albert Camus's *The Rebel*. It was, as they say, a germinal moment. For what Camus's text did was to transport me, almost overnight, to an intellectual world I had scarce dreamed existed. This was a world of rebellion, of existentialism, of phenomenology, of the absurd, of the sublime, written with an intensity and a range of references that bewildered me. Who were, and what did St Just, de Maistre, Max Stirner, Baudelaire, Turgenev and, above all, Nietzsche say? And then there was the blurb on the back cover of the paperback:

> Slave camps under the flag of freedom, massacres justified by philanthropy or a taste for the superhuman, cripple judgement. On the day when crime puts on the apparel of innocence [then] it is innocence that is called on to justify itself.[3]

I hadn't thought like this before. And then there were the section headings: The Sons of Cain, The Dandy's Rebellion, Fastidious Assassins, Nihilistic Murder, Rebellion and Style. What did they mean? Though perhaps pathetic and certainly melodramatic to say so – not least now – I felt I had to find out. But again I had a problem. My reading of Camus took place whilst I was still at training college and though it helped turn my attention towards 'theory', not much of this was taught in schools. And so this is perhaps the more intellectual reason that pushed me towards University.

At first the University of Nottingham seemed the wrong place to have gone to, but it turned out to be just right. For *three* reasons. *First*, I certainly learned a lot of history in the 'proper' academic, empirical way, and this served only to turn me, disobediently, even more towards theory. *Second*, I had the time to pursue the reading occasioned by Camus. By the early 70s I had read most of his works: I now knew who St Just and de Maistre were; I read existential and phenomenological texts and I read, above all, Nietzsche. I was also – in a sort of flanking movement – to start benefiting from that tremendous effort by New Left Books to translate into English a group of 'Western Marxists' who, in their sometime relativism, scepticism and pessimism, inadvertently helped prepare me for the end of that 'Classical Marxism' I'd initially known. Thus my bookshelves began to be filled with texts by Lukacs, Adorno, Horkheimer, Marcuse, Benjamin, Colletti, Althusser, *et al.* And, *Third*, in reading Politics as my 'subsid', I met for the first time a 'real' political theorist, J. S. McClelland.

McClelland, whose 800-page *A History of Western Political Thought* was published recently[4] was, in the early 70s, a newly appointed lecturer from

Cambridge where, under the supervision of George Steiner, he had just finished his PhD. A supremely arrogant man, I suffered his intimidatingly difficult Special Subject on Marxism and then, in 1972 on finishing my degree, started to research for my PhD. under his supervision, completing my thesis (*Ideology and Science in the Political Thought of Nietzsche, Freud and Sorel*) in 1975. McClelland, strangely in a way, still remains an influence on me. Anyway, I was now a bit of a political theorist, all I needed was a job.

That wasn't to be. The number of political theory lecturing posts I saw advertised *c.*1974–78 numbered just two. I applied unsuccessfully for both of them, and thus spent the years 75–78 teaching on a part-time basis in schools, colleges and at the University of Nottingham until, in 1978, I took up a post in the History Department here.

Here two things were responsible, I think, for shifting my interests from political to historical theory. First, though appointed to teach European History, my experience in schools also saw me take over the Secondary History PGCE in 1981. This was a course which over the next fifteen years brought me into contact with graduates from virtually every university in Britain and pushed me towards thinking much more about 'the nature of history'. And what struck me here – with notable exceptions – was how underdeveloped any theoretical thinking was in my students. Most had managed to gain very good degrees from prestigious universities in a 'discipline' whose metaphysical, ontological, epistemological, methodological, aesthetic and ethical/ideological constituents remained a mystery they showed little inclination to probe: why keep theorising about history they used to moan, 'let's just do it'.

Yet this seemed to me an appalling indictment of British history degrees and was totally unacceptable (and, insofar as it still exists remains totally unacceptable). And so I began to deliberately teach in more theoretical ways influenced by my own growing interest in historical theory and particularly my interest in the American history theorist, Hayden White.

I first read White's 1973 text, *Metahistory*, in the mid-70s and I didn't understand it.[5] I'm ashamed to say I neglected White until the mid-80s when I bought a copy of his *Tropics of Discourse* (1978). Until then my reading in the philosophy/theory of history had been frustrating; even the foremost journal in the world – *History and Theory* – seemed dull in those days. Nor were the standard introductory texts on the 'nature of history' much better: Bloch, Carr, Elton, Marwick, Tosh *et al.*, were so ordinary. Consequently, my rediscovery of White through a reading of his *Tropics* was a godsend, as was my further 'discovery', at about the same time, of White's European counterpart, Frank Ankersmit, and the anti-foundational, neo-pragmatist philosopher, Richard Rorty. Accordingly, it was this reading which provided the basis for a whole series of articles I wrote during the 1980s and which I drew upon for my first book, *Rethinking History* (1991).[6] Designed as a polemical intervention, it was deliberately opposed to the kinds of history I *knew* most young historians were exposed to as I tried to blend together the ideas of White with theorists by then identified by the prefix 'post', all of whom were capable of being located heuristically under the name of 'postmodernism'. Accordingly, it was this mongrel-mix of theorising which allowed me to weave together historical discourse and postmodernism in ways which – at least in some small degree – hadn't much been done before. Subsequently, and following in the wake of *Rethinking History*, in 1995 I developed certain new considerations in a second book, *On 'What is History?': From Carr and Elton to Rorty and White*, following this in 1997 with *The Postmodern History Reader*.

I am now moving after this jog down memory lane (the first part of my lecture if you recall) to the second wherein (again if you recall) I want to sketch-out how and what I think about history (and temporality) today. And here, crucial to my present position, is a change of emphasis and attitude from the concerns essayed in my first three books to those which underpinned the next I was to write and which provides much of what I would now want 'to profess'; that book was called *Why History? Ethics and Postmodernity*, and it came out in 1999.[7]

By the time I came to write *Why History?* I had developed a series of assumptions that now acted as axioms informing my work. The main one was that, after reflection, I took it for granted that we lived in postmodernity; that we lived *after* modernity. Of course modernity and postmodernity are difficult to pin down, but my working premise was that we had come to the end of the 'experiment of modernity'; that is, that those post-Enlightenment experiments of trying to establish in bourgeois and proletarian forms 'human rights communities' had failed on their own terms amongst the genocides, the gulags and the death camps of the twentieth century. And that postmodernity was the 'whatever it was' that came after the breakdown of this experiment, postmodern*ism* being that condition of postmodernity raised to the level of consciousness more generally and, more specifically, to theoretical levels.[8] And I regarded this as 'a good thing' in that I thought that the radical postmodernism I liked managed to keep alive – despite everything the twentieth century had thrown at it – that 'great fable of emancipation' which Derrida urged we should never give up; that hope of an 'Enlightenment to come' which, though so different from its eighteenth-century forerunner, might still allow a desirable newness to enter the world. And – another and – in order to help this 'to come' to come, I construed postmodernism as being, in important part, about clearing the decks of all those old discursive assumptions that might prevent a new emancipatory Enlightenment, such that postmodern theory so considered acted as a kind of 'critical retrospective' of the Western Tradition (and especially the Western Tradition in its late-modernist forms) as its constitutive elements were sifted through to see if, amongst all the clutter, anything could be retained that might still be useful for that 'new social to come'. Very little was.

It was for this reason, I argued in *Why History?*, that this postmodern retrospective was very much about deaths, was very much about endings: postmodernism as a kind of 'post-mortem'. There is a long list of such deaths and such endings in the various literatures: the death of God, the death of man, the death of the subject, the death of the author, the death of centres; the end of metaphysics, the end of the phallologocentric tradition, the end of onto-theology, the end of epistemology, the end of ideology, the end of progress, the end of literature, the end of philosophy after Auschwitz and, among many other endings, the end of history, too. And it was this idea, of the end of history, that now claimed my attention in *new ways*.

Now, in its main thrust the idea of the end of history applied primarily to those great metanarrative structures (Hegelianised Marxisms for example) that had claimed to somehow 'find' a direction, a purpose, a meaning: the expression of an essence or a teleology *inherent* in the contingencies of previous phenomena. And of course postmodernism spoils all of this; postmodern anti-essentialism and anti-foundationalism empties out *all* intrinsic meanings and *all* values from everything – nothing *intrinsic* is left anywhere – which means that any such putative meanings, etc., are always imposed from 'the outside'. And, once everything is opened up to the outside – to *extrinsicality* – then there is no stopping: the outside simply goes on and on or, as Derrida put it, 'the absence of a transcendental signifier extends the play of signification to infinity'. Either way, bereft of all things intrinsic, the past could now be historicised (i.e. made meaningful) in any way anybody liked. In that sense the past could now be seen as being utterly promiscuous; it would go with anybody – Marxists, Tories, empiricists, racists, feminists, structuralists, phenomenologists – anybody could have it. And why not in these democratic days beyond the author, beyond unquestionable authority, beyond the authorised version and authoritarian *fiat*. But all of this was disturbing, to say the least, to old believers in intrinsicality, believers stretching right across the traditionalist left–right ideological/discursive spectrum. For them the idea was not easy to swallow that history could be absolutely anything you wanted it to be. No metanarrative could survive this evacuation of intrinsicality intact – but then, no academic history could survive it intact either.

In fact, however, very few academic historians realised just how devastating one of these endings – the end of epistemology – was when it was applied not only to metanarratives but to their own *genre* of history. Of course the end of empirically based, epistemologically assured history – the 'essence' of the professional/academic *genre* – is a massively complicated practico-theoretical area to consider but, simplifying massively, the argument I put at length in *Why History?* can be summarised thus.

Academic historical discourse certainly does contain empirically testable elements related to past events at the level of, say, singular statements and sentences that 'correspond' to singular or clusters of singular evidential sources, well-corroborated 'facts', etc. But history as a discourse, history at the only level at which it can actually be a history – at the level of the text – is constituted by things ontologically unconnected and thus irreducible to such empirically verifiable, 'epistemological' elements. For historical texts as complex narratives have to have – simply to be historical narratives – all the elements common to narratives *per se*. That is, they have to be troped and emplotted and sustained by various modes of argumentation; their articulation depends upon textual poetics, rhetorical devices, compositional strategies, intertextual understandings, variable/contingent theories and methods and personalised theses, etc., which infuse such texts with life and which, though not totally ignoring the empirical/epistemological elements are massively underdetermined by them: there are many things in the archive but they don't include any of these things; the very means of 'making history'. In the end, therefore, a history is best seen as a figure, a shape, an act of the imagination: an *aesthetic* and thus, as an aesthetic, unaccountable to the court of the epistemological. Consequently, academic historians – just like metanarrative historians – are not only able to impose any reading they like on the past but they simply *have* to given that the past has no figure 'to call its own'.

And, of course, there is another point here that is seemingly unsuspected by anti-postmodern, academic historians. Which is that the end of history as an epistemology is, logically, an end that should never have occurred. Why not? Because no empirical/epistemological history has ever really existed. For if postmodern claims regarding the best way of characterising histories – as aesthetic/figurative discourses – are correct (which they are), then there have never actually been histories of any other type. That is, it is not as if there are 'now' aesthetic historicisations of the past that stand over against modernist empirical/epistemological ones which are not aesthetic phenomena at all. For if history *per se* is an aesthetic discourse then all histories always have been and always will be of the type postmodernism raises to consciousness: strictly speaking, logically speaking, no empirical/epistemological history and no empirical historians have ever existed on the face of the earth. So that, in coming to the end of 'epistemologically striving' histories and historians of whatever stripe, we have, as it were, come home to ourselves. And I think we all *ought* to accept this homecoming which at this point I threw into the modernist wake, namely, that such epistemologically striving histories are just an aberration, that it would have been better if histories had never been modern. It is no surprise, given this message, that few academic historians liked the postmodern messenger.

Now these things – or at least some of them – I had 'known' long before writing *Why History?* But it now began to occur to me – *and this is where the change from my earlier position took place* – that the end of viable modernist histories (histories made problematic by being unable to live up to the very criteria they had themselves erected) may call into question the role of histories as such – including 'viable' postmodern ones – vis-à-vis that project of emancipation Derrida had urged us never to forget. For, whilst in earlier works I had argued for the end of problematical metanarrative and academic histories in the name of postmodern replacements which might help keep that Derridean project alive, I now began to wonder if that project actually needed *any* history at all – viable or not.

For when in writing *Why History?* I ran my eye over the greatest critical theorists the world has arguably ever seen, an incomparable generation of theorists running from the mid-1960s to the late 90s – theorists who had deconstructed in the space of but thirty years the whole of the Western Tradition – something immediately struck me. Here is a list of some of them: Roland Barthes, Michel Foucault, Gilles Deleuze, J. F. Lyotard, Jacques Derrida, Jean Baudrillard, Gayatri Spivak, Judith Butler, Ernesto Laclau, Alain Badiou, Richard Rorty. And I think that what immediately strikes you when you look at this list of critical intellectuals is simply this: that not one of them is a historian. And when I extended this list to include twenty then thirty then forty theorists, there still wasn't a historian amongst them. And when Hans Bertens and Joseph Natoli did the same in their *Postmodernism: The Key Figures*,[9] out of the fifty-three theorists they included only one was a historian: Hayden White. Consequently I began to think – to cut a very long story very short indeed – that if Butler and Rorty could provide just about all the emancipatory analyses and rhetorics needed without being historians, if Rorty *et al.* could do without history, then maybe we all could.

And so in *Why History?* I developed these arguments to conclude that perhaps we now have no need – in the sense of *really need* – to have histories at all – not even postmodern ones. That, to put it bluntly, when it comes to emancipation whether we have a historical consciousness or not is *an option*. Of course traditional historians working in old modernist *genres*, and radical and/or postmodern ones working in a differently constituted *genre* that suits them, can obviously continue to do so relative to their own lights. But in terms of urgent emancipatory *praxis* – the only light I was using in *Why History?* and am still using as the primary criterion to assess the worthwhileness of any backward glance – such work may not be much to the point in a culture that is now, arguably, so post-historical in its postmodernity, that is, now too late still to be modern.

However, all this raises the question – the question governing this lecture in fact – of what I am now able to *profess* in terms of history as we come, as a culture, toward its possible/probable end. I've known for a long time what I *couldn't* profess. I couldn't profess modernist histories in either metanarrative or academic *genres*; towards those I had long had that attitude of incredulity Lyotard had reserved for metanarratives alone.[10] But, as I've already explained, previously I'd filled the vacuum created by their 'going' by those postmodern histories, emancipatory-style, that I'd championed. Yet now the full realisation that absolutely brilliant theorists could do just about everything emancipatory that was necessary without being historians raised the question of why bother with history at all. *And yet … I was reluctant to let history go completely*. Could it therefore be refigured, I wondered, in ways which might still make it available for a future thinking of a radical politics if the need for it should (occasionally) arise? And I decided that perhaps it could. Consequently, to refashion history for that possible need is what has preoccupied me over the last few years and continues to do so. In *Refiguring History: New Thoughts on an Old Discipline* (2003), in parts of *The Nature of History Reader* (co-edited with my friend Alun Munslow in 2004)[11] and in maybe a dozen or so articles and papers written over the past five or six years, I have tried to rethink the 'old past' not so much as history at all but under the name of *temporal studies* on the basis that although we can live 'outside of history' (i.e. outside of history as a very particular type of essentially Western discourse) we cannot live outside of time (besides, so radioactive is history with old connotations, despite postmodern meltdowns, that I no longer find it useful to think through such an old name). Accordingly, working on new ways of figuring time, though radically incomplete and just conceivably barking-up-the-wrong-tree altogether, nevertheless, constitutes a developing position I think I can profess. And, since I consider this rethinking as good for more than just me, in a quasi-universalising gesture I couch my advocation of it in the plural: this is how we *all* ought to think about 'temporal studies'. And so in the third and final part of this lecture I now want to briefly describe the basic premises of this position: there are *five* of them.

First, I want to insist that, freed from 'the burden of history' (a phrase of Hayden White's), we should privilege the cause of human emancipation in ways governing *entirely* the way we should read/write temporal studies. That we should answer a call that comes not from the past at all (the location of the 'traditional historian's calling') but directly from ethics, from politics; from the present and the future. And I can only re-echo as reasons the ones Derrida gives for this subordination of 'the past' to politics. For never before, he wrote in *Specters of Marx*,

> have violence, inequality, exclusion, famine and thus economic oppression affected so many human beings in the history of the world and of humanity. Let us never forget this obvious, macroscopic fact, made up of innumerable sites of suffering [that] no degree of progress allows one to ignore that never before, in absolute figures, have so many men, women, and children, been subjugated, starved or exterminated on the Earth.[12]

Second, that to this end we should have an unswerving ethico-political commitment. And here, though he fits uncomfortably alongside certain postmodern positions, I think we might draw profitably on the work of the French philosopher, Alain Badiou, to help us to do it.

In his book *Ethics: An Essay on the Understanding of Evil*, Badiou sketches out a way of thinking whereby human beings can become ethically responsible *subjects*: can become 'subjects of a truth'.[13] This claim rests on his argument – taken axiomatically – that 'the social' (the 'sphere of human activities') is divided between two distinct but nevertheless interconnected sub-spheres: the ordinary, everyday world of established interests and practices which constitute the commonalities of everyday life wherein we live fairly automatically and unthinkingly, and an 'exceptional' realm of 'singular innovations' or 'truths' which come into existence and persist only through 'the militant proclamation of those rare individuals who constitute themselves as the subject of a truth, as the militants of their cause'. How, then, can we become these rare subjects, these militant occupiers of a truth?

Well, for Badiou such an occupation of a position can only begin with a *break* with the 'ordinary' by way of working through an *Event*, an event which has nothing verifiable about it, but is something which, in the light of one's positive *experience* of it, can only be grasped, affirmed and proclaimed; an affirmation that then persists by virtue of adopting an attitude of *fidelity* towards it, a commitment which, as Badiou puts it, 'amounts to something like disinterested enthusiasm, absorption in a compelling task or cause, a sense of elation, of being caught up in something that transcends all petty, private or material concerns … of holding true to a person, principle or ideal'. And of having an ethical attitude towards the event too, ethics being understood here as that which literally *en-courages* the subject to 'keep going', to not backslide, to maintain a selfless devotion to a cause. For Badiou, events are thus those catalysts that rip such developing subjects out of the social. The *Event* thus constitutes a break between different modes of life. Badiou writes:

> I shall call 'truth' the real process of a fidelity to an event; that which this fidelity *produces* in the situation. For example, the politics of the French Maoists between 1966 and 1976 which tried to think and practice a fidelity to two entangled events: The Cultural Revolution in China and May '68 in France. Or so-called 'contemporary' music … which is fidelity to the great Viennese composers of the early twentieth-century. Or the algebraic geometry of the 1950s and 1960s, and so on. Essentially a truth is [to be traced] … from the decision to relate henceforth to that situation *from the perspective of its supplement* … It is thus an *immanent break*. 'Immanent' because a truth [emerged out of] the situation and nowhere else … Break because what enables a truth-process – the event – means nothing according to the prevailing languages and established knowledge of the situation.[14]

This new truth which *voids* the conventional 'state of the situation', thus produces a new position which, *induced* as it were by the 'evental break', then necessitates a re-working of one's previous way of being into newness. In that sense, says Badiou, the 'evental break' is *poetic* in its thinking outside of and/or beyond conventional ways of 'curing things up into meaning': 'When the situation is saturated by its own norm, when the calculation of itself is inscribed there without respite … then one must be *poetically* ready for the outside-of-self. For the nomination of an event – in the sense in which I speak of it, that is, as an undecidable supplementation which must be named to occur … *this* nomination is *always* poetic. To name … a chance, an incalculable, one must draw from the *void* of sense, in default of established significations, to the peril of language. One must therefore *poeticise*, and the poetic name of the event is what throws us outside of ourselves.'[15] Here is a final quote from Badiou, concretising all of this:

> It is clear that under the effort of a loving encounter (event) if I want to be really faithful to it [then] I must completely rework my ordinary way

> of 'living' my situation. If I want to be faithful to the event of the 'Cultural Revolution', then I must at least practice politics ... in an entirely different manner from that proposed by the socialist and trade union traditions. Again, Berg and Webern, faithful to the musical event known by the name of Schoenberg, cannot continue with *fin de siècle* neo-Romanticism as if nothing had happened. After Einstein's texts of 1905, if I am faithful to their radical novelty, I cannot continue to practice physics within its classical framework, and so on. An evental fidelity is [thus] a real break (both thought and practiced) on the specific order in which the event took place (be it political, loving, artistic or scientific).[16]

And so if I want to be faithful to 'postist' thought – to post-structuralism, post-colonialism, post-feminism, post-Marxism, postmodernism and to the ethics of emancipation, then I cannot remain a structuralist, a colonialist, a feminist, a Marxist, a modernist, an old moralist; I have to make a break, commit infidelity, just as the occupation of a new notion of temporality means I have to break with 'old history'. I have to be loyal to the new. Not loyal in the sense of not repositioning myself again and again 'within the truth' (for in Badiou the attempt to achieve a total or unqualified truth betrays its always only *axiomatic* status and is thus construed as *Evil*), but loyal enough to the new to break with the old; loyal to its sustained possibilities and loyal to endlessly rearticulating them save for not forgetting that over-arching demand for human emancipation.

Third, this kind of commitment must inform and be grafted on to a way of thinking 'temporality' that expresses 'ourselves', that expresses postmodern subjects-in-process (slightly different subjects vis-à-vis Badiou's but ones which can be made to complement them), subjects 'other' to that archetypal Cartesian subject that was so 'central' to modernity.

Thus, let us go with the idea that if the past, however conceived, is always made in the conceiver's image, is always just us – back there – throwing our voice, then *our* past will be constituted and understood by virtue of having the self-same characteristics by which we constitute and understand ourselves ... this is the only way that the past can become familiar to us: when Cezanne paints a landscape, he doesn't try to imitate it; rather, he tries to paint a Cezanne. So think now of the characteristics we postmodern subjects have – like it or not, know it or not – and think of the possibilities these could open up beyond modernist closures.

Thus such a subject (in process) will be constituted 'performatively' so that she is formed and reformed, read and reread, written and rewritten contingently and incessantly. Such a subject will lack any foundational anchor, intrinsic nature or purpose, knowable meaning or destiny such that, radically decentred and fragmented she will remain a mystery even to herself. This is a post-Cartesian subject held together in a totally fictive unity which, at worst, will enable her to at least cope with existing life and, at best, become 'subject to a truth'.

Consequently, this 'self' will understand the past (and the present – and the future) in precisely the same ways, endowing it with her own characteristics. Thus *her* past will be sublime in its putative whole and relativistic in its parts, a past susceptible to endless combinations and recombinations, readings and rereadings, writing and rewritings; as radically contingent and thus as non-teleological and so of a kind that can only be ascribed a temporal shape or figure via a series of undecidable decisions (so that here we meet the inescapable Derridean *aporia* of the 'undecidability of the decision') so as to produce a fleeting unity – a history, a temporal fix – that is clearly an act of the imagination, indeed as something recognised as entirely *fabular*, that is, as something which is told and which has no meaningful existence – or indeed existence *per se* – outside of the telling. This is a past which 're-exists' if and only if we 'call for it', 'call on it'; an always imperfect discursive calling (because it never was such that it is told).[17] And these fabular/fabulous/magical acts of recalling and retelling open up the past for reformulations otherwise than modern. This is a vast area to consider and for reasons of time I refer to just one way of imagining a 'new poetics of the past'.

Fourth, then, in his *The Illusion of The End*,[18] Jean Baudrillard argues that the end of 'the illusion of the end', that is, the end of the illusion that the past (or time) has an end *in* it, offers the chance to explore the endless possibilities contained in the language games we do and/or could inhabit. For today we recognise that it is only the coherent grammars of our language(s) that ever allowed us to create coherent historicisations of the past in the first place; it did not allow us to 'discover them'. Today we recognise that the world and worlds past *always* obey our syntax, that 'their' meanings, 'their' semantic expressions, are always ours. That history's ostensible coherence – with its meaning-laden beginnings, its middles and ends, its structures, patterns, contexts and watersheds, its directional switching-points which ensure that the past rolls right up to us, bang on time – was (and is) never a found coherence and direction, but always a coherence coming entirely – *and I mean entirely* – from the applied forms of syntactical/semantic fashionings embedded within the narrative form itself: no sequence of events ever possess the formal attributes of the stories we tell about them. And so let us now think, as Baudrillard urges us to think, of different syntactical forms which will give rise to new semantic figures.[19]

For Baudrillard, then, the past has never actually unfolded in, say, linear fashion 'in line' with some kind of evolutionary process; the past knows nothing of our straight lines (or our circles, or whatever); it just doesn't organise itself to suit our geometry. No, linearity is an illusion derived primarily from another illusion, namely, that language also unfolds in linear forms. For of course it doesn't. Linguistically everything moves in loops, tropes; things relate enthymemically not logically. In which case, asks Baudrillard, might we not transpose new language/aestheticising games onto the past, new temporalisations? And not just by using those major figures of metaphor (metonymy, synechdoche, irony), but also those 'puerile, formalistic games, those heteroclite tropes which are the delight of the vulgar imagination: anagrams, acrostics, spoonerisms, rhyme, strophe and catastrophe'. In which case could we not imagine an *anagrammatic* temporal fashioning 'where meaning is dismembered and scattered to the wind like the name of God in the anagram'; or organised through the form of a *strophe* whereby a group of lines are detached from the rest of the poem to form a sense of sense underived from either the immediate context or the full poem (think micro-histories here), and so on. Well, if this were possible then such would be, as Baudrillard puts it, 'the enchanted alternative to the linearity of history', the poetic alternative of refiguring that which had already been refigured into the 'reality efforts' we have forgotten are just effects and think of as reality *per se.*

Thus, *fifth* and finally, we must ourselves never forget that our new realities, our new 'temporal fixes', are just such 'reality effects' and that they don't put us in touch with 'reality', with 'actuality' *plain.* Alongside Baudrillard, Elizabeth Ermarth has cautioned us against becoming immersed, yet again, in the 'depths of the past', urging us to stay on the surface of things, skipping lightly. In various works wherein she considers the possibility of still making something out of the past when modernist values of neutrality, objectivity and empiricism have been undercut and epistemological fetishism dismantled not just philosophically but 'by the postmodern world', Ermarth draws on the notion of *anthemion* in the works of Vladimir Nabokov, a notion which, for Nabokov, refers to inter-laced, flower-like designs where items and patterns arrive and depart from various places without exact repetition or direction and yet which produce a kind of rhythmic iteration.[20] Such anthemic patterns – all surface phenomena – inflect sequences rather than plot them, wander multidirectionally rather than progress; they turn digressiveness into a principle: all straight lines are twisted. Things rhyme and alliterate rather than evolve, each specification is a new semantic creation; each site the possibility of multiple awareness and palimpsestuous play in the production of a complex and arbitrary figure – a figure that is just a figure, *not* a representation. From this paratactic perspective the recovery of the past as striven for in modernist histories, 'the attempt to keep the whole world in mind' in a neat and orderly and 'progressive' fashion in order to factor-out all that might 'look random or chaotic if recorded by, say, a giant world-historical camera', becomes not only impossible but positively undesirable.[21]

Drawing on Nabokov's novel *Transparent Things*[22] – and in doing so adding to the notion of *anthemion* that of *refraction*, Ermarth re-emphasises how the narrator warns the *novices* of the book – novice *and* experienced historians in our case – to avoid sinking into the depths of the past, modernist-style, and to remain very precisely on the *present* surface of things. She writes:

> The powers required to pursue [modernist] history [actually] destroy the past by sinking into it; allowing the past to *refract* through 'transparent things' requires a discipline as miraculous as walking on water but nevertheless possible for the novice ... who learns by staying at the exact

> level of the moment, letting the past shine through. [Here] 'things' no longer function as in the objectifying *grammars* of modernity; 'things' are not 'objects', but instead the occasions, the carriers, the sites where new acts of attention can be performed; where memory inflects and re-inflects again; an *imaginative* awareness engaged in the process of creating the unique and unrepeatable poetry of a life.[23]

And let me now gloss Ermarth and especially her comment (suggestion) that our attitude toward historicisations, toward temporalisations, should be *refractive*. Thus, let us imagine the past as a medium of different density which we can only ever enter obliquely from the present: what we see through and under the surface is never quite in the right place, it never quite 'corresponds'; there is always a mismatch, a break, a dislocation (as when we see a stick in a glass of water). And so let us see temporalisations of the past as precisely fractures, as breaks between the past and the present which can never be – nor should we ever bother about them ever being – healed up into a full, unbroken meaning, it being precisely in these breaks and gaps that the space for all manner of things can be imagined.[24] And let our attitude towards all historical orthodoxies be *refractory*, that is, cantankerous, contentious, difficult, disobedient, disputatious, disrespectful, intractable, stubborn, obstinate: let us embody our *Thesaurus*. Let us stay on the surface and skim, trick with our tropes, plot and emplot, figure and refigure in poetic arrangements that resist codification, incorporation, and the stasis of orthodoxy. Whatever temporalisations this type of thinking may produce one thing is for sure: they will not look much like histories as we have known them – or even histories at all.

For those who can think in this way, the postmodern way of Derrida, Badiou, Baudrillard and Ermarth … and of Lyotard and Said, Butler and Laclau, *et al.*, it now becomes inconceivable to continue thinking in terms of a historical consciousness sunk in the depths of the realist/empiricist/epistemological mindset of modernist historians. To this way of thinking postmodernism is not – to the chagrin of so-called 'proper' historians – some kind of fashion or some kind of 'critical discourse' that can be ignored and/or recuperated back into modernity in the guise of 'pluralistic interpretation' and with an 'added attention to language'. For the difference between modernist epistemological histories and postmodern aesthetic temporalisations is a difference not of degree but of kind, is an ontological one. And this explains why the break between modernist and postmodern histories/temporalisations is not an 'epistemological break' (which seems to allow for the possibility that one day they might be 'joined up' and 'healed over') but a permanent because incommensurable difference. Modernists who thus bemoan the 'extremism' and the 'excesses' of postmodernism just don't get it, just don't understand that the break between modernity and postmodernity is – in the long term – as epochal as that between the medieval and the modern: these are just different worlds. From which perspective postmodernism just *is* its excesses; *postmodernism is everything modernity cannot ever be.* Postmodernism is thus, for me, the getting of an attitude, a militant, disobedient disposition that stresses the grammatical, fictive forms of historicisation without a hint of apology or nostalgia, and offers in their place – if anyone still wants them – new ways of rendering up the past as yet unconceived of: modernist histories fade away and die here. Yet this ending is precisely the possibility of beginning again. And this 'beginning again' is, I think, what I can profess and try to make attractive to others so that they too might try to reinvent themselves. And why not? After all, they have nothing to lose but their pasts.

Postscript

I was going to end at this point. I planned to speak for an hour and, give or take the odd minute or two, I think I've done that. But I want to add a very short postscript, a little bit of script post the script I've just read to underline two things which have acted as the organising *motifs* of this paper.

First, I think it is obvious that for me (if not for others) 'postmodern deconstruction' – let me put it that way – is wholly optimistic: it both clears the decks and it intimates how things might be refigured.[25] This optimism is the kind of optimism you *can* find in Nietzsche – to whom I always seem to hark back. I would hope that nobody – absolutely nobody – would actually want to live in Nietzsche's own ideal polity (least of all Nietzsche), but in his deconstruction, his destruction of 'the Western Tradition', he prefigures so much that is postmodern. Here he is in a passage from *The Joyful Wisdom*, being optimistic:

> In fact, we philosophers and free spirits feel ourselves irradiated as by a new dawn by the report [that has finally reached us] that the old God is dead. Our hearts overflow with gratitude, astonishment, presentiment and expectation. At last the horizon seems open once more. Granting even that it is not yet light, our ships can at last put out to sea in face of every danger; every hazard is again permitted ... this sea, our sea, again lies before us; perhaps never before did such an open sea exist.[26]

This is the sea, I think, on which all of us, irrespective, are now cast adrift; an unfathomable sea we need to get used to navigating on without – as Derrida put it in *The Other Heading*[27] – a course set too rigidly in advance. For a culture to be on the move with 'otherwise than a heading' means to hold itself more radically open to the future, to what is 'to come'. Here history is not – and temporality certainly is not – a course set in advance toward a foreseeable, anticipatable, masterable future; rather we all have to sail without much of a course, on the prow of something new, 'other than a heading'.[28]

Second, it is therefore not certain where we might one day eventually arrive, where we might 'end up'. But I hope without too much *sentimentality* – for what is being suggested here, despite my phrasing, lexicon and register on this occasion, is a politics[29] that will probably be as difficult as any politics we have ever yet known – that it might still be possible to achieve, 'otherwise', those 'human rights communities' that, promised by modernity, were dashed in and by its own exigencies. It would therefore be 'nice' if, one day in the not too distant future, in a Derridean-type of future 'to come', a future storyteller's backward glance could allow a story to be told of that achievement *after* the experiment of modernity and *after* the postmodern retrospective we are living through. That story would begin with the words that *all* stories just have to begin with irrespective of the discursive object they discourse about: with the words, 'Once upon a time … '. But this time it would be nice if this story could *end* with the words which only the very, very best stories end with: 'And so they all lived happily ever after'.

'The End'.

Notes

1 Steedman, C., *Dust*, Manchester: Manchester University Press, 2001, p. 150.
2 Ibid., p. 150.
3 Camus, A., *The Rebel*, Harmondsworth, Penguin, 1962. Certain parts of this part of the lecture appeared in a slightly different form in 'After History', *Rethinking History Journal*, 3, 1, 1999, pp. 7–20.
4 McClelland, J. S., *A History of Western Political Thought*, London: Routledge, 1998.
5 White, H., *Metahistory*, Baltimore: Johns Hopkins University Press, 1973. See also, White, H., *Tropics of Discourse* (1978), *The Content of the Form* (1987) and *Figural Realism* (1999), all Johns Hopkins University Press. Although over the years White has been much criticised I subscribe almost entirely to his 'Narrativism'. Thus I take it as read, as White says, 'that no given set of events figures forth apodictically the kind of meanings with which stories provide them … no one and nothing *lives* a story' (*Tropics*, p. 111); that 'the meaning, form, or coherence of events, whether real or imaginary ones, is a function of their narrativisation' (*Figural Realism*, p. 74); that 'one must face the fact that when it comes to apprehending the historical record, there are no grounds found in the historical record itself for preferring one way of construing its meaning over another' (*The Content of the Form*, p. 67); that the only 'grounds' for choosing 'one perspective on history rather than another are ultimately aesthetic [and] moral (*Metahistory*, p. xii) … and so on and so forth. I also agree with White that it is more important to change the form – especially of a discourse like history where 'form is more important than content for the definition of orthodoxy' than the content of history if discourse is to be 'refigured' – as I argue later in this paper.
6 Jenkins, K., *Rethinking History*, 1991 (2nd edn 2003); *On 'What is History?': From Carr and Elton to Rorty and White*, 1995; *The Postmodern History Reader*, 1999, all London: Routledge.
7 Jenkins, K., *Why History? Ethics and Postmodernity*, London: Routledge, 1999.
8 If I were pushed to *now* define postmodernity I would do so as the 'era of the raising to consciousness of the *aporia*'. By 'era of the *aporia*' I mean that this is an era when all the decisions we take – political, ethical, moral, interpretive, representational, figural, etc. – are ultimately undecidable (*aporetic*); that our chosen ways of seeing things lack foundations and that, as far as a discourse like history is concerned, it is essentially to be thought of as an aesthetic – a shaping, figuring discourse – and not as an objective, true or foundational epistemology. Frank Ankersmit has been particularly important in this appreciation of the limits of epistemology as against the aestheticisation of history where, of course, epistemology can make no claims. See Ankersmit, F. R., *History and Tropology,* Berkeley: University of California Press, 1994; *Historical Representation*, Stanford: Stanford University Press, 2001; *Sublime Historical Experience*, Stanford: Stanford University Press, 2005.

9 Bertens, H. and Natoli, J., *Postmodernism: The Key Figures*, Oxford: Blackwell, 2002.

10 Lyotard, J. F., *The Postmodern Condition*, Manchester: Manchester University Press, 1984, *passim*.

11 Jenkins, K., *Refiguring History: New Thoughts on an Old Discipline*, London: Routledge, 2003; Jenkins, K. and Munslow, A. (eds) *The Nature of History Reader*, London: Routledge, 2004. See also, Jenkins, K., 'On Disobedient Histories', *Rethinking History Journal*, 7, 3, 2003, pp. 367–85; 'Modernist Disavowals and Postmodern Reminders of the Condition of History Today: On Jean-François Lyotard', *Rethinking History Journal*, 8. 3. 2004, pp. 365–85; 'Ethical Responsibility and the Historian: On the Possible End of History "of a Certain Kind" ', *History and Theory*, 43, 4, 2004, pp. 43–60.

12 Derrida, J., 'Specters of Marx', *New Left Review*, 205, 1994, p. 50. See also *Specters of Marx*, London: Routledge, 1994.

13 Badiou, A., *Ethics: An Essay on The Understanding of Evil*, London: Verso, 2001. Badiou is currently being busily translated into English: see especially: *Theoretical Writings* (eds: Brassier, R. and Toscano, A., London: Continuum, 2003); *The Century*, London: Verso, 2003; *Infinite Thought*, London: Continuum, 2005. Peter Hallward's *Badiou: A Subject to Truth*, Minneapolis: Minnesota University Press, 2003, is already a classic text. The question of the 'ethics of history' is one long debated. In 2004 *History and Theory* devoted its theme issue to 'Historians and Ethics' (43, 4, 2004), whilst both Frank Ankersmit and Kalle Pihlainen return to this area repeatedly in interesting ways. See, for example, Ankersmit as cited in note 8 (above); Pihlainen, K. *Resisting History*, Turku: Turku University Press, 1999; 'Understanding and Commitment ... ' *Clio*, 34, 1, 2004–5, pp. 59–82.

14 Badiou, A., *Ethics*, ibid., p. 42.

15 Badiou, A., *Infinite Thought*, op cit., p. 75.

16 Badiou, A., *Ethics*, op. cit., p. 42.

17 By discursive here, by history as a discourse, I mean that it is a particular type of production wherein the historian's possible objects of study are identified, various methods and procedures are considered and applied, and where an ostensibly proper manner of talking about such objects are contrived. The result is a 'poetics of historical knowledge' where poetics is meant in the sense of the 'making' or 'inventing' or 'fabricating' of a 'discipline' that it then tends to disavow.

18 Baudrillard, J., *The Illusion of The End*, Cambridge: Polity Press, 1994.

19 Ibid., pp. 120–2. See especially Baudrillard's last two (very short) chapters wherein he outlines his 'new poetics of history'. In some ways Baudrillard's poetics is not unlike paratactical history. Elizabeth Ermarth's *Sequel to History* – noted in relation to some of her other work in note 20 – also uses parataxis pretty much throughout to undercut all notions of connectivity, linearity and smooth (hypotaxic) meanings. And, of course, once time is remembered not as 'flow' but as memories of juxtaposed, jumbled-up places, spaces and events, the effect of bouncing back and forth between present, past and future, fluctuating for presentist reasons, then 'smooth' chronology gives way to parataxis in general such that paratactical 'history' is, ironically, perhaps 'closer' to 'real' historical memory than conventional, 'straight' history. The relationship of postmodernism to history and literature is too vast a field of analysis to go into in this paper; an indication of its scale might be seen by comparing/combining, say, Amy Elias's *Sublime Desire: History and Post 1960s Fiction*, Baltimore: Johns Hopkins University Press, 2001, with Peter Hallward's *Absolutely Postcolonial: Writing Between the Singular and the Specific*, Manchester: Manchester University Press, 2001.

20 Ermarth, E. D. See especially her *Sequel to History*, Princeton: Princeton University Press, 1992, and, among her articles: 'Beyond "The Subject": Individuality in the Discursive Condition', *New Literary History*, 31, 3, 2000, pp. 405–20; 'Beyond History', *Rethinking History Journal*, 5, 2, 2001, pp. 195–215; 'Ethics and Method', *History and Theory*, 4, 43, 2004, pp. 61–83. Ermarth is, in fact, one of the few historians and theorists who has seen the implications of the epochal nature of postmodernity for *traditional* history and the possible need to go beyond it. Thus she writes: 'Historical method, as it is almost universally understood in the West, rests on the common-denominator values that characterise

modernity. Historians treat these values as if they were universally valid and rarely acknowledge them. Postmodernity … which cannot be profitably explained away or trivialised, characteristically denies the possibility of any such universal common denominators. This challenge poses a problem for historians that goes to the heart of their enterprise … It is [therefore] way past time to consider and deal responsibly with the critique of modernity that poses so many challenges to historical writing. That critique has increasingly made standard historical writing seem about as quaint an undertaking as painting realistic landscapes: laudable, appealing, reassuring no doubt, but relatively useless in terms of cultural renewal' ('Ethics and Method', pp. 61–2). Ermarth's essay addresses the question of precisely what alternative methods, if any, might be available to historians wanting to not only rethink 'historical' writing for postmodern conditions but also wanting to produce a 'postmodern calling and engagement arising from the effort to square our enlightened and political assumptions with our actual cultural conditions … assumptions … that may still be renewable for changed conditions' ('Ethics and Method', p. 62).

21 Ermarth, E. D., Ethics and Method, pp. 78–83 *passim*.

22 Nabokov, V., *Transparent Things*, London: Weidenfeld & Nicolson, 1973, pp. 1–2.

23 Ermarth, E. D., 'Beyond "The Subject"', *op. cit.*, p. 417.

24 This 'working the gaps', etc., is not only possible but absolutely unavoidable if history is to be produced at all from a past that is not remotely historical. In *Dust* (*op. cit.*) Steedman argues that there is a 'double nothingness' in the historical account, analysis, narrative, etc., i.e. in history *per se*. What are these two absences? They are these. *First*, there is the question of what is the historical (the historians) *referent*. And here it has to be understood that historical writing does not refer *directly* to the past, nor to the stuff of the archive, nor to the traces of the past. Rather, what is referred to are anterior entities – structures, processes, statistical runs, trends, influences, movements, contexts, meanings, etc., – which never existed in those formats and which are thus brought into existence through *inferences* (abduction) from various 'traces', it being, however, not the traces themselves but what they indicate/suggest about the past that become the things to which historian's statements refer, and it is these inferences that fill the gaps imaginatively. *Second*, it is therefore, as Steedman puts it, solely the historian (and those acting *as if* they were historians) 'who make the stuff of the past (everything) into a structure or event, happening or a thing through the activities of thought and writing; that they were never actually there, once, in the first place, or at least not in the way a nutmeg grater [actually] was, and certainly not in the way "they have been told"' (p. 154). And thus the 'double-nothingness' in the writing of history: history is 'about something that never did happen in the way it comes to be represented (the happening exists in the telling or the text); and it is made of materials [the inferences …] that aren't there, in an archive or anywhere else' (p. 154).

Jacques Rancière has made a similar point with beautiful simplicity: 'There is history because there is an absence … The status of history depends on the treatment of this twofold absence of the "thing Itself" that is no longer there [the past is past] and that never was … because it never was such that it was [and is] told'. Rancière, J., *The Names of History: On the Poetics of Knowledge*, Minneapolis: University of Minnesota Press, 1992, p. 63.

25 This optimism is based on an analysis of postmodernity which may, of course, be outdated. Although many of the characteristics Gilles Lipovetsky puts under the name of 'hypermodern' might still fit under the name of postmodernity as I read it, the kind of analysis he conducts makes a 'to come' of a Derridean type highly improbable. At the same time, however, Lipovetsky's 'pessimistic side' offers no solace to those who might still see a 'necessity' for history. If anything history *per se* is even less necessary for him, whilst 'new temporalisations' seem to scarce cause a ripple of interest. See G. Lipovetsky, *Hypermodern Times*, Cambridge: Polity Press, 2005. See also his *The Empire of Fashion: Dressing Modern Democracy*, Princeton: Princeton University Press, 1994. There is also, of course, a vast literature which tells me why I should not be optimistic about the possibility of postmodernism being the harbinger of radical socio-political changes of an emancipatory kind at all since postmodernism is complicit and in collusion with capitalist necessities, i.e. is

the socio-economic-cultural logic of capitalism. This reading, which is variously influenced not least by the work of Fredric Jameson (and especially his *Postmodernism, or, the Cultural Logic of Late Capitalism,* London: Verso, 1991) is articulated by such people as David Harvey, Terry Eagleton, Christopher Norris, Alex Callinicos and many others, and comes from a 'left' much more disillusioned with 'politics' than I am and which I think takes much too short a view of things, is, ironically, not historical/temporal enough.

26 Nietzsche, F. W., *The Joyful Wisdom*, Edinburgh: Foulis, 1910, p. 167.

27 Derrida, J., *The Other Heading: Reflections on Today's Europe*, Bloomington: Indiana University Press, 1992, *passim*.

28 Derrida, J. and Caputo, J., *Deconstruction in a Nutshell*, New York: Fordham University Press, 1997, pp. 117–18. I am grateful to Mark Mason for drawing my attention to Derrida's *The Other Heading* and Caputo's discussion of it. See Mason, M., 'Exploring "The Impossible": Jacques Derrida, John Caputo and the Philosophy of History', *Rethinking History Journal* (forthcoming, 2006) [10, 4, Dec. 2006, pp. 501–22].

29 In matters of political analysis I have in general terms long subscribed to the view forwarded by Ernesto Laclau; see his *Hegemony and Socialist Strategy* (written with Chantal Mouffe), London: Verso, 1985; *New Reflections on the Revolution of Our Time*, London: Verso, 1990; *Emancipations*, London: Verso, 1996; *On Popular Reason*, London: Verso, 2005. See also Butler, J., Laclau, E. and Zizek, S., *Contingency, Hegemony, Universality*, London: Verso, 2000. These analyses are not discussed at all in this paper but they stand behind and inform its general political position.

13 Postmodernity, the end of history, and Frank Ankersmit

In 2000 Robert Burns (Goldsmiths College, University of London) organised a series of ten seminars on the philosophy of history (broadly construed) to run throughout the academic year 2000–2001 at The Institute of Historical Research, University of London. The seminar, as I write now in its ninth year, has been – thanks in huge part to the efforts of Robert Burns, who has organised and chaired most of the meetings as well as being involved in the organising of several associated one-day conferences – an enormous success and, so far as I know, is the only philosophy of history seminar to meet regularly anywhere in the world.

The paper here was the one that I gave to the first meeting of the seminar in October 2000, and is taken from *The Philosophy of History,* edited by Alex Macfie and published by Palgrave in 2006, a volume containing over a dozen of the papers given at the seminar – a seminar which Alex, like myself, has hardly missed more than a couple of meetings of in the last eight or nine years. I mention the seminar more than my paper here in order to sing its praises; since 2000 it has met over 80 times, has attracted speakers from all over the world as well as encouraging 'home-grown scholars', and takes place in an atmosphere best described as 'intellectually engaged'.

Introduction by Alex. L. Macfie

In the following chapter – the first of the talks given at the Philosophy of History seminar, set up at the Institute of Historical Research, London, in October 2000 – Keith Jenkins, a leading British philosopher of history and exponent of what might be described as the postmodern approach to the philosophy of history, explains how he came to the view that we should more or less abandon not only modernist history (both upper-case – Hegelian, Marxist – and lower-case – traditional, academic) but also history as such. At the same time he explains the part that various ideas, advanced in the work of Frank Ankersmit, the noted Dutch philosopher of history, played in persuading him to arrive at this conclusion. By the postmodern approach to the philosophy of history Jenkins means the approach, promoted in the last fifty years or so by a number of mainly French and American philosophers and historians, including, in particular, Sartre, Foucault, Derrida, Lyotard, Baudrillard, Hayden White and Rorty. What these philosophers argued is that it is not possible to discover anything in the world that provides a firm foundation for thought, nor is it possible to identify essence and reality. As Jenkins remarked, in the introduction to his *The Postmodern History Reader* (1997, p. 4): 'We must accept that we live and have always lived amidst social formations having no legitimating ontological, epistemological, methodological or ethical grounds for beliefs and actions beyond the status of an ultimately self-referencing (rhetorical) conversation.' It was this approach, in Jenkins' view, that gave rise to the postmodern age, the age in which, whether we like it or not, we live. For a concise and readable account of Jenkins' philosophy of history, as it developed in the following years, see Keith Jenkins, *Refiguring History* (2003).

This chapter more or less represents – give or take the odd nuance – the way I think about the status of history in what I want to call (despite the fact that some people think we've gone beyond them) these 'postmodern' days. It is not based on current research, though it does contain a little updating. Basically, however, it derives from the work I did for a book Routledge published in 1999 – *Why History? Ethics and Postmodernity* – a book wherein I came to the conclusion that, under the impact of all those 'isms' that travel under the sign of postmodern, we have possibly come to 'the end of history' and that this is 'a good thing'. That there really is no reason why we cannot now wave goodbye to what is an utterly contingent phenomenon and live happily among the agreeable imaginaries of recent/current postmodern thinking, a postmodernism shorn of *all* historical and *all* ethical foundations and which can arguably give us all the intellectual resources we need to think in future-orientated and – hopefully – in emancipating and democratizing ways.

Now, in reaching this 'end of history and it's a good thing too' conclusion, I used in the book three philosophers to help undercut what I called *upper-case* (metanarrative) histories (say, various Hegelianized Marxisms, various 'Progressivisms'), namely, Derrida, Baudrillard and Lyotard, and, to similarly subvert *lower-case* (academic, professional) history, two theorists of history, Hayden White and Frank Ankersmit. And – and I mention them here although I won't be referring to them again – I also drew on the works of Elizabeth Ermarth and David Harlan to help sketch in what it might be like to live beyond 'modernist' histories and, maybe, beyond history as such. And what I want to do in part of this chapter is to say just a little bit about the contribution to this argument about postmodernism and the 'end of history' by Frank Ankersmit – perhaps one of the less familiar theorists upon whom I drew.

The chapter is divided unevenly into *two* parts. *First*, and in a very general way, I want to say a little bit about how I came to the view that we might have reached the end of modernist histories ('histories as we have known them') and, maybe, history per se. And, *second*, I want to look at two aspects of Ankersmit's theorizing that are germane to that thesis. In the first aspect I outline what I take to be the main critique he levels at the epistemological status of, in particular, professional, academic history, namely, the failure of the historians of that *genre* to generally work the vital distinction between the historical statement and synoptic accounts/narratives and to rethink the classical distinction between analytical and synthetic 'truths', the upshot being that, together, these two arguments establish that history per se cannot ever be an epistemology. While second – and finally – I link what Ankersmit sees as some of the fatal implications of his anti-epistemological arguments back to my own position regarding the end of history under the impact of the postmodern.

When I came to think about writing *Why History?* I began with the question in mind as to what we might now need in terms of imaginaries – in terms of acts of the imagination – such that the possibility of emancipation could be rethought after the Enlightenment modernist projects (after those experiments to try and bring about in bourgeois or proletarian forms 'human rights communities') had arguably failed on their own terms. I took it as a plausible hypothesis that the phenomenon of postmodernity and postmodernism can best be thought of as coming *after* modernity (although I know there's much debate about this) and that 'postist' thought can be profitably construed as representing not least a kind of *retrospective* of modernity in such a way as to at least *raise* the questions of what, vis-à-vis emancipation, we are to do now, and what, if anything, we need from the past appropriated through modernist (and other) historicizations to help us to do it. In posing these questions I originally came up with a positive answer, not least because I had long had in mind – to the extent that it almost seemed common sense – George Steiner's observation that it is not the literal past that determines our present or our future save, possibly, in a genetic sense, but 'images of the past', images that, as selective as any other *myth*, give each new era its own sense of identity, of regress and of new achievement such that, as Steiner put it, 'the echoes by which a society seeks to determine the reach, the logic and the authority of its own voice, come from the rear' (Steiner 1972, p. 13). But I am no longer convinced by this. For postmodern theorizing may well have made us appreciate – as never before – that the *myths* that may take us from the present into the future may well be *of* the present and *of* the future. That perhaps we don't need – and never have needed – to measure ourselves against what are always obviously highly selective appropriations of the past, but also that such practices are positively restrictive in their smothering cloyingness – in their 'reality'. Consequently, there seems no reason why we cannot now gather the strength to unburden ourselves of the dead-weight of the historicized past and construct measures of radical emancipation from current, postmodern ones, which, fabricated and articulated in the future-anterior verb tense, we recognize will always 'not have been good enough', will always be problematic.

Now, in a way this is not the sort of argument I had much run before. One of the reasons why I had previously gone along with postmodern-type ideas and postmodern-type histories was because their anti-foundational deconstruction of modernist upper- and lower-case *genres* at least offered (and in a way still offers if you're interested) the chance for radical historians to legitimately historicize the past in more generous ways (for example, in post-structuralist, post-feminist, post-colonial, post-Marxist ways), the result being the construction of potentially reflexive histories which, openly partisan, signalled (and signed) their sometime 'confessional' standpoints; these are, if you like, 'histories that have come out'. And I thought, and I still think, of such reflexive histories as an advance over modernist ones, which claimed (and claim) – in varying degrees when pushed – not so much to be *creating* histories of the past but of somehow *finding* them in it, it being histories of the former, reflexive type that I had tried to advocate as appropriately as I could in previous work. But for a range of reasons I discuss in *Why History?* I no longer feel this position really faces up to the challenges issuing from postmodernism, challenges – risks and chances – that I think should not be resisted but exploited.

This realization – that thanks to the non-historicized imaginaries we can glean from postmodernism we can now wave goodbye to history – came to me most vividly when I got to thinking seriously about the insistent demand made by traditional historians right across the left–right ideological spectrum for postmodernists to come clean and explain 'what exactly would a postmodern history look like?' You can see the thinking behind this demand. So strong have (modernist) histories been in the ideological formation of our culture, so central their place in those bourgeois/proletarian 'experiments of modernity', that it seems as if history per se is a natural phenomenon. I mean, why not? There is always a past, so what could be more natural than that there should always be historicizations of it? Accordingly, it is this which arguably explains both why it is still very much an expectation (an expectation some postmodernists share) that, after the end of modernity and modernity-styled histories, we might well expect to see, as a constituent of postmodernity, postmodern-type histories, and why the perceived threat of such histories superseding modernist ones makes defenders of them (Marwick, Himmelfarb, Fulbrook, Bunzl, McCullagh, Thompson, Stone, Elton, Richard Evans *et al.*) rush to the barricades in case such new histories situate themselves in the spaces created by the now withering hegemonic bulk of the old *genres*.

But, of course, history is not a natural phenomenon and there is no reason why such a peculiar practice should always be around. By definition, in a culture nothing cultural 'is of a natural kind'; consequently, no discourse being anything but a contingent fabrication, then, there is no reason to think that the past (the 'before now') – if it is to be recalled at all – need to be so through historicizing expressions just because it recently has been. For, actually, timings-of-time have been (and are) articulated 'historically' in only very specific kinds of social formation. It is tautological to say so, but it needs stressing, that we have obviously seen nothing like nineteenth- and twentieth-century, western upper- and lower-case *genres* ('histories as we have known them') at any other time and place: that there has never existed, on any other part of the earth, ways of historicizing time like *that*. Rather than being natural, then, such histories are both unique (historians like telling people 'history' is made up of unique events) and ephemeral (they are even better at telling them that everything is temporal/temporary) and there is no reason to exclude modernist histories from these broad – but true – commonplaces. Consequently, there is no reason why, in 'postist' social formations beyond modernity, postmodernism need drag modernity's very odd ways of historicizing the past with it. For despite the current postmodern meltdown of modernity so radioactive with old modernist connotations is 'history' that to think radically new ('to make up new rules in the absence of rules' *après* Lyotard), it is arguably a distinct handicap for the imagination to think through such a *passé* category. Accordingly, if a postmodern politics is to begin to set agendas, to now cast any part of it in familiar historical *genres* is, I think, both unnecessary and undesirable.

For while there are, as I read it, two sorts of recognizable histories still around – albeit in an arguably moribund existence – the old upper and lower cases, the old upper-case metanarratives are now too archaic to be wheeled out again even as farce, while lower-case histories – which had once had limited emancipatory ambitions as befitted their sometime articulation of an advancing bourgeoisie – have long been conservative, have long withdrawn from the world to become studiously own-sakist, studiously non-worldly 'academic'. Thus, broadly speaking, nothing much in the way of an emancipating discourse can be expected of them. And so it is for these reasons, as I have said, that it has looked (and looks) to some, as if postmodernism will have to *invent* its own genres given the emancipating *uselessness* of the other two – and hence the anxious query as to 'what will it look like?' Better the enemy you know. But why need 'it' look like anything? Why need it exist? I mean, if postmodern critiques have shown that the past will go with anybody, if it will obey any 'reading', if it will support everybody in general but nobody in particular, if, moreover, the status of *all* historical knowledge beyond the statement and the chronicle (and history is *always* beyond the statement and the chronicle) has been fatally wounded by postmodern-type scepticisms, relativisms and neo-pragmatisms anyway, then not only is the question indeed raised as to what a viable postmodern history would look like but the question of why bother with one at all looks positively compelling. From the point of view of emancipatory discourse, what possible use is such a deeply problematicized and *passé* discourse any more?

Thus, I think that it can at least be argued that we can now forget history (especially modernist ones but maybe history per se) and live amid the imaginaries provided by postmodern-type theorists (say, Barthes, Foucault, Deleuze, Derrida, Lyotard, Baudrillard, Irigary, Kristeva, Spivak, Judith Butler, Laclau, Sande Cohen, Stanley Fish, Richard Rorty, Elizabeth Ermarth … and these are just a few of the bigger names), theorists who can generate enough by way of emancipatory rhetorics such that we no longer need any kind of historicized foundational or non-foundational past. Of course, such theorizing may need to refer on occasion to what you might call the 'philosophy of history', but such a referral need not be dependent on –

any more than it is now actually – the kinds of historical accounts provided by, say, traditional historians. Besides, it's counter-intuitive to argue – though historians habitually do it – that we will *always* need a history to place ourselves in the present and to think (*après* Steiner) the future. For such arguments are counter-intuitive in the simple sense that postmodern theorists do very well indeed without either modernist or postmodernist histories. Some of the most brilliant thinkers of our current condition – for instance those I've just listed – are able to write book after book, article after article, without any of them being practising historians. Accordingly, my argument is that if Derrida and Rorty can do it then we all can. To be sure, traditional historians working in either case – and postmodernists working reflexively in any differently conceived *genre* that suits them relative to their own lights – can obviously continue doing so. But in terms of emancipatory *praxis* – the only light I am using – such work is, I suspect, not much to the point in a culture that is now too late still to be modern, in a culture that is so radically post-historical in its postmodernity. Here a *post histore* future that is not tied to an old past, here a way of unshackling yourself from old constraints, seems exciting. We really don't need the past any more – I don't think we ever much did.

That is my very general argument, then, with regard to postmodernism and the end of history, and what I want to do now is to explain how Frank Ankersmit may help us to see how *his* type of postmodernism (for Ankersmit is actually one of the very few card-carrying postmodern historians there are) helps undercut – for me at least – lower-case history *especially*. I take it as read – obviously – that towards metanarratives we can now only have, *après* Lyotard, an attitude of incredulity, but it is my argument here that the collateral impact on lower-case history caused by the collapse of metanarratives serves only to extend that sense of incredulity to lower-case histories too: metanarratives, *petite* narratives, they're all the same, they're all fictive, all acts of the imagination. As Hayden White has commented, the historicized past is, of course, a place of fantasy.

So, let me now turn to Frank Ankersmit, an Ankersmit who, to some extent, stands on the shoulders of Hayden White – as Ankersmit acknowledges. But Ankersmit – Professor of Intellectual History and Historical Theory at the University of Groningen, the Netherlands, author of many books in Dutch and, in English, most notably, *Narrative Logic* (1983) and *History and Tropology* (1994) as well as numerous articles in such journals as *History and Theory* – Ankersmit is not some sort of pale reflection of White.[1] No, Ankersmit is original in his own right, particularly in his theory of statements, narrative substances and representation, theorizations that shift attention from the research/archival aspect of the historian's work to the shaping, aestheticizing, troping, proposing, performative 'textual' aspect of historicizations of the past, a shift *he* thinks most 'proper'/professional historians have been loath to contemplate, let alone much understand and follow.

Now, Ankersmit details the ideas behind 'statements and texts' and 'narratives substances' and 'representation' in enormous detail in *Narrative Logic* and *History and Tropology*, but the gist of his arguments can perhaps best be approached on this occasion via two essays – Reply to Professor Zagorin, which appeared in *History and Theory* in 1990, and The Linguistic Term: Literary Theory and Historical Theory (the first chapter of *Historical Representation*).[2]

Ankersmit's Reply to Professor Zagorin opens – vis-à-vis his arguments with regard to *statements and texts* with the statement: 'At the start of our line of march from modernism to postmodernism we find the historical text', a line of march which can be summarized thus.

We can say about historical texts two things. *First*, that such texts consist of many individual statements, most of which give an accurate or 'true' *description* of some state of affairs that existed in the past. These 'evidential' statements are 'found' in the itself 'historical' archive and have about them – when corroborated – the aura of facticity. This is straightforward, though Ankersmit notes the significance of such facticity, which, emerging out of the research phase of the historian's practices, comes to the surface of the text replete with all the scholarly apparatus of professional history (footnote piles, etc.) such that it lends to such 'facts' the deceptive aura of 'the real' (reality effects), which in turn tends to suggest that what is being represented here is the past as such ('for', and I quote, 'though the fact can only ever have a linguistic existence as a term in a discourse, it is as if this literary existence were merely a "copy" of another existence situated in the extra-structural domain of "the real"'). But since Roland Barthes's *Discourse of History* – from which that quote comes – nobody really takes the view of history as a discourse committed to the recovery of the past in some kind of prediscursive state: the historicized past is 'always already' textual (Barthes 1967). For, as Tony Bennett has commented – complementing both Ankersmit and Barthes – all that ever has been and ever will be of issue in historical discourse is what can be drawn intertextually from the generic record and archive, it being this (itself discursive construct) that functions as the historian's referent in that it constitutes the last court of appeal for the *veracity* of historical statements (not texts – statements): here, so to speak, the historian hits base – but always a base *in* discourse (Bennett 1990). And it is Ankersmit's first point that while this 'court of appeal' exists (albeit if always problematically) at the level of the singular statements (or the chronicle) it does *not* exist where it matters most – at the level of the text: the historicized past may always be textual but it is never literally *a text*, which means it has no actual 'author' and hence no actual authorial intent and hence no 'discoverable' or 'inferable' meaning. Which means, says Ankersmit, that history as a discursive practice never has been and never will be an epistemology: that objectivity and truth – cognitive criteria – are, therefore, not finally at issue (and cannot ever be at issue) at the level of the historical text.

Thus, Ankersmit's *second* point is that, with the possible exceptions of some areas of the past with almost non-existent traces, the evidential traces and, thus, the evidential 'true' statements available to most historians allow them to write many *more* true statements about the historical past than are actually found in their texts. It is sometimes argued – it is a typical seminar topic – that here are no such things as historical facts as such, and this seems true in the sense that 'facts' have to be given that status by much interpreting investigation, designation, etc. But, that investigation/designation done, the result isn't that there are then no facts but that there are millions of them. Consequently, the situation facing the historian is not one of non-existence or scarcity but of abundance. Accordingly, the historian's problem then becomes that of the selection, the distribution; the 'weighing up' and the *giving* of significance (which is never already there) always to just some of 'the facts' in always problematical combinations/colligations *relative to* – *relative to* – a whole range of interests that combine them in always unsutured (i.e. always indeterminate and, thus, arbitrary/contingent) contexts. Thus, as Ankersmit says:

> Of all the statements historians could have made about the relevant parts of the past, they carefully select *qua* descriptive content and *qua* formulation the statements they will ultimately decide to mention in their texts – one might thus say that the writing of the historical text requires of historians a *politics* with regard to the statement, and that the *text* is the result of this *politics*.[3]

And the reason why historians are careful about *their* statements is because such statements, when considered together, determine the picture of that part of the past they wish to present to their readers as a *proposal* about how to figure out that past. And now we see immediately the problem of trying to verify as 'objective' or 'true' any resultant picture/presentation/proposal so produced, for such synoptic proposals (generally in narrative form) are of a different *kind* – not different *degree* but different *kind* – from singular statements such that their *proving* is an impossibility: a history is not simply a long sentence. For while it is the case that individual statements of a *cognitive/descriptive* kind can indeed be checked (albeit *relative* to the way they have been put under a description) against a discrete evidential trace to see if they *correspond*, proposals/presentations of the past can never be so checked simply because, as noted, the past does not have *in* it proposals of its own prior to this combination for this combination to be checked against. And since, Ankersmit argues, what is most crucial in the writing of historians is not to be found at the level of the individual statement but at the level of the proposed presentation – in that it is this that stimulates historiographical debate and, thus, determines over time the ways we come to *imagine* the historical past – then I think we have to concur with Ankersmit's (and Hayden White's) point that history per se is always as much *invented/imagined* (the combinations, the proposals, the presentations, the inferences the figures and so on) as *found* (the 'facts', etc.) and that the resultant historicizations are thus 'inexpungeably relativistic', aesthetic, non-cognitive, positioned and so on.

Thus, Ankersmit is able to draw two conclusions from his discussion: *first*, that the text's statements refer to and describe part of the evidential past and can be said – again vis-à-vis the way they have been put under a description – to be true or false and, *second*, that they individuate the 'picture of the past' historians wish to convey to readers who, as readers, bring to the resultant text their own multifarious 'reading and working positions' such that interminable, interpretive, intertextuality is the result with, at the level of the text, nothing to stop it. Accordingly, Ankersmit is able to conclude by pointing out that saying *true* things about the past's traces at the level of the statement is easy – anybody can do that – but saying true things about the past's traces at the level of the text is *categorically impossible* – nobody can do that. For texts are not – sadly it seems for some – cognitive, empirical, descriptive epistemological entities but speculative, propositional invitations to *imagine* the past *in infinitum*: on this reading the statement is 'modernist' and the text 'postmodernist'.

OK. So much for statements and texts. And so let me now move on to the other 'concept' I want to talk about here, namely, the idea of *narrative substances*. So what are *narrative substances* and how do they further help to subvert the epistemological status of historical discourse?

Well, perhaps the best way to get into this is via Ankersmit's discussion (in 'The Linguistic Turn: Literary Theory and Historical Theory') of W.V.O. Quine's classic 1951 article *Two Dogmas of Empiricism*.[4] In this article, Ankersmit explains that the two dogma's Quine queried were the empiricist belief in some fundamental cleavage between truths that are *analytic* – i.e. truths independent of the facts – and truths which are *synthetic* or *precisely* grounded in fact, in empirical 'actuality'. Of course, Quine was not, Ankersmit notes, arguing against the 'conventional' meaning of the terms *analytic* or *synthetic* truths, but against the empiricists' claim (two 'dogmas' of empiricism after all) that truth is reducible to one or other of these two. The *dogma* Quine thus critiqued was that which claimed that there are no other *sources* of truth, that empirical (synthetic) truth can always be distinguishable from the analytical and that never the twain shall meet. Consequently, the gist of Quine's critique was that not only are there true statements that actually do fit into these two categories (such that a combination of analytical and synthetic statements is absolutely *necessary* if meanings are to be produced) but also, and more importantly, that this *necessary* combination of the analytical and the synthetic means, against empiricist objectors, that discourse *always* runs together synthetic statements about 'reality' and analytical statements arising self-referentially out of linguistic practices in ways undercutting any claims that history (for example) is an (empirical) epistemology – thus re-articulating the claims of Ankersmit and White – that history is as much imagined (the linguistic/the analytical) as found (the empirical/the facts, etc.).

Now, what exactly does all this mean? Ankersmit gives quite a lot of examples in his paper from which I take two and add one of my own to try and make the point.

Ankersmit's first example is Newton's law according to which *force* is defined as the product of mass and acceleration. Here we might say that the statement is empirically 'true' (a synthetic truth) because it is in agreement with the observed behaviour of physical objects. But we can also say that it is a conceptual/analytic truth (true by definition irrespective of the way the world actually is) and thus '*not*' of the world. And, for Ankersmit, Newton's law – its meaning – is paradigmatic of the way meaning per se gets *put* into the 'reality' of *our* world, namely, through the necessary use of both the non-worldly, imaginary analytical concepts of force, mass, acceleration and the empirical (insofar as we understand the now 'empirical' to be the manifestation of previous usages/practices). And precisely because this necessary, analytical component is true *irrespective* of the way the world is, then this act of the self-referential imagination means that meanings are, once again, as much imagined (the analytic) as found (the synthetic). Consequently, and turning to history, historical knowledge is never just of the cognitive, empirical, synthetic kind; the 'historical' evidence never fully *dictates* the analytical categories by which it is invested with significance so that, always a mixture of the imaginary and the actual made real via the mediations constituting reality effects, the empirical basin for historical knowledge – for objectivity and truth at the level of the *abductive* narrative – collapses: history is *not* an epistemology. Of course, says Ankersmit, one can see why historians are attracted to the idea that 'historical evidence' *does* dictate which presentation the historian should propose about the past. For only on this assumption could one run the argument (as Marwick or McCullagh or Himmelfarb or Evans do) that nothing much happens in the journey from the evidence to the text. But, of course, this is completely wrong. For in historicizing the past – in the way it is figured, troped, shaped, narrated, in the way that it is the product of rhetorical devices, *everything* happens as description becomes presentation and the 'referent collapses into presentation', a process leaving us with the insoluble task of trying to tell where precisely *presentation ends and reality begins, or where reality ends and presentation begins*. Either way an epistemology that *thinks* it can tell drops out of the frame.

All this can be very easily illustrated by two historical examples. The first is from Ankersmit. Think, says Ankersmit, of a study of the Renaissance or the Enlightenment. There, just as with the Newton example, it's the case that such a study contains both the empirical/synthetic basis for a specific view of these 'phenomena' as well as a proposed definition of them. As Ankersmit puts it:

> Lots of historians have written books on the Renaissance stressing different aspects of the past and this is why they come up with different definitions of the Renaissance or the Enlightenment. And, if this is how they decide to define the Renaissance or Enlightenment, then all that they have been saying about it must be (analytically) true since what they have said about it can analytically be derived from the meaning they want to give to the terms Renaissance and Enlightenment. It is thus a conceptual 'truth', just as Newton's law can be interpreted as a conceptual 'truth'.

> Consequently, we cannot distinguish between truths *de dicto* and truths *de re*, and so the kind of criteria that are decisive for 'meaning' are not reducible to questions of truth or falsity. For here it is essentially a decision about which set of 'truths' we might prefer when we are looking for the best account of the relevant parts (for us) of the past. Here, truth is not the arbiter of the game, but its stake so to say.[5]

A second example. Take the 1960s in Britain. And let us say that a whole range of historians agree on its description; on the *facts* of the 60s. And then they have to address how to present it. Was it, say, a decade of trauma or years of banality? Or joy? Or was it *really* a lazy decade, or was it, *really*, the Swinging 60s? Here the way the years of the 60s actually were remain exactly the same, are synthetically/empirically *finite*. But the ways they are made into the stuff of historical narratives are infinite – I mean, how could you ever definitively *know* that the 60s really were swinging rather than snoozy? And hence, for Ankersmit, the *substance* of historical narratives, his *narrative substances*, are constituted precisely through the use of such proper names as the Enlightenment, the Renaissance, the Swinging 60s, the Seventeenth Century Crisis, the Industrial Revolution, etc. conceptually, analytically, by definition irrespective of the actual conditions of the past. And Ankersmit draws all this together in a really crucial paragraph:

> Such notions as the Renaissance, etc., should thus be seen as the *analytical* names of *narrative substances*, and thus, as far as reference is concerned, they must be denied the capacity to refer to anything outside of the text: they refer *only* to *narrative substances*, that is, a set of statements contained by the text. For what prevents such narrative substances from referring outside of themselves is because the Renaissance, say, didn't actually exist to so refer to. Similarly, the Enlightenment is a concept performatively produced by *colligating* the text's *internal statements* and thus there is nothing outside them for them to refer to. Which means that narrative substances are only ever analytically 'true' *via* the text's internal statements and never externally (synthetically) true because there is no Enlightenment 'out there' for them to correspond to *before* the narrative substance creates it as a collective/proper noun for *its* set of statements.[6]

Of course, concludes Ankersmit – and this is responsible for the way terms like 'the Renaissance' are sometimes held to refer to 'actuality' – if a narrative substance becomes widely accepted by historians then it sometimes looks *as if* there was really a Renaissance 'out there' and that it has been *discovered*. But all that is actually going on here is the widespread acceptance of a *proposed* way of thinking through an analytical category. Nothing else. From which position Ankersmit draws two specific results from his arguments.

First, because there is no past ever given to us *plain* against which we can compare differently *imagined* Renaissances to see which one *corresponds* to the past per se, then the past per se has *NO* role to play in historical discourse. From the point of view of historical knowledge, a referential past is a useless notion. 'Historically speaking', texts as combinations of the synthetic and the analytic are all we have, and we can therefore only compare texts against texts. Intertextuality – not the past per se – is the always problematic, interpretive bottom line. And, second, and finally for Ankersmit, this radical undecidability is an integral part of his way of understanding political freedom and future possibilities. That is to say, that for freedom to exist there must be choices: opportunities for decisions. For if there was only one interpretation of the past then it would no longer be an interpretation but *the* truth. And this would then have to be accepted save for those happy to be dissenters – and be prepared to be treated accordingly: here truth begets *closures* – of all kinds: 'regimes of truth' après Foucault. Politically, then, it is not the laid-back relativist who one ought to be afraid of but people, or institutions, or states, who claim to know the truth of things at the actually irreducible level of interpretation. And so in this way the freedom of interminable interpretation leads to a politics of hegemony without foundations. This is a point Ernest Laclau has seen perhaps even better than Ankersmit and I conclude with his point that, today, in these postmodern days, the

> metaphysical discourse of the West is coming to an end and philosophy in its twilight has performed a last service for us: the deconstruction of its own terrain and the creation of the conditions of its own impossibility. Let us think, for example, of Derrida's undecidables [his aporias]. Once undecidability has reached the ground itself – once the organisation of a certain camp is governed by a hegemonic decision – hegemonic because it is not objectively determined, because different decisions were also possible … the realm of philosophy comes to an end and the realm of politics begins. This realm will be inhabited by a different type of discourse … which constructs the world on the grounds of a radical undecidability.[7]

Let me now, briefly and finally, turn to the way I think Ankersmit links all of this up to postmodernism and to the argument about the end of history I began with and how his theories of statements and narrative substances and representation provide some interesting 'grounds' for such a connection.

In his Historiography and Postmodernism, published in 1989 in *History and Theory*, Ankersmit argued that 'autumn' has come to Western, modernist historiography. What does this mean and how does this seasonal analogy work? The short answer is via his 'tree' analogy.

Compare, says Ankersmit, history to a tree. And here the metanarrative tradition of Western historiography has focused on the trunk, using it to define, as it were, its essence. Historicism and modernist scientific writing of the 'more lower case' (with their attention to what 'the past essentially was') were situated much more on the branches of the tree but, nevertheless, from this position they still remained focused on what held the branches together, on the inferred 'reality of the trunk'. As Ankersmit puts it:

> Just like their speculative predecessors, both the historists and the protagonists of so-called scientific historical writing still had the hope ... of ultimately being able to say something about the trunk after all ... Whether it was formulated in ontological, epistemological, or methodological terminology, historical writing since historicism has always aimed at the reconstruction of the essentialist line running [objectively] through the past or parts of it.[8]

And this is what postmodernism has changed. And what it has changed is the direction and the object of the modernist's *gaze*. It has redirected it away from the trunk and the branches (and one might add the twigs and the stem) to the *leaves*. Within this postmodern view of history the aim is no longer integration, or synthesis, or totality, or objectivity, or a dialectical truth. In the anti-essentialist, anti-foundational, aesthetic, aporetic, nominalistic perspectivalism of the postmodern, *if* we want to privilege anything then we can and must only privilege the *leaves*.

Which brings Ankersmit to his main point. For it is a characteristic of leaves that they are relatively loosely attached to trees and that, when autumn comes, they are blown off and away by the wind. Thus:

> For various reasons, we can presume that Autumn has come to Western historiography. In the first place there is, of course, the postmodernist nature of our own time. Our anti-essentialism ... has lessened our commitment to science and traditional historiography. The changed position of Europe in the world since 1945 is a second important consideration ... The trunk of the tree of Western history now strikes us as merely being part of a whole forest. The *metarécits* we would like to tell ourselves about our history, the triumph of Reason, the glorious struggle for emancipation of the nineteenth century workers' proletariat, are only of local importance and for that reason can no longer be suitable metanarratives. The chilly wind, which ... arose around 1900 simultaneously in both the West and the East, finally blew the leaves off our historical tree in the second half of this century.[9]

Now, all this is fine and agreeable so far as it goes, but it might be useful to add a little to Ankersmit's tree analogy/metaphor. For while I think we now well know that there never has been anything but the leaves, it's not so much that they've blown off some sort of tree. That is too presumptuous. For arguably there never was a tree. There never was a trunk. Nor branches. Nor twigs. Nor stems. All there has ever been are leaves. And we have no idea where they have come from, or what they mean, or why they exist(ed). They're just, as it were, 'lying around', being blown hither and thither in the autumn wind. Coming and going. And from their phenomenal existence we have inferred, on the basis of causal logic (behind every deed a doer; behind every effect a cause, etc.) *fantastic* essences, meanings, teleologies, objectivities and truths to explain what we have apparently been and are – and will be – both at the level of the parts and at such putative wholes as we have been able to imagine. We have, in our raking together of the leaves, in the various piles we have tried to put them in, read into them, much like we have read into the leaves in our teacups, all manner of fortunes. But today, as we dissolve all of this into contingency, into the 'undecidability of the decision', the aporia and the aesthetic, the aleatory and the ludic, into that relativism and singularity that just *is* the human/ethical, moral condition, we are left with the only radical illusion there is: the radical illusion of 'the world', of the (apparent) leaves. This is also, incidentally, Nietzsche's challenge: to accept this as our lot (*amor fati*) with joy, and to give to this apparent meaninglessness of existence an imagined *urgency* that can still – even after the failure of the experiment of modernity to build human rights communities – animate us after 'the end of history'.

Now, there is clearly something of this 'end of history' argument in Ankersmit's works, but by way of bringing this paper to a fairly sharp close I think that in the end Ankersmit still has a 'nostalgia' for a historical past and, thus, for a 'continuing' history – albeit for him one of the leaves and maybe other arboreal bits and pieces – as he makes very clear in the final chapter of *History and Tropology* (for example, in his liking for microhistories, leaf histories and, more recently, in his discussions of trauma and the sublime). But the question is, what is this nostalgia, etc., for? What, really, is the point – particularly from the perspective of working towards an emancipatory *future* beyond the experiment of modernity where the trick might be, as Hayden White has put it, not to get into history but to get out of it – of getting out from under yet another pile of 'artificially collected' dead leaves. And so at this juncture I would want again to start running my own 'end of history' argument. But as I've already done that – and there's no point in 'history' repeating itself – this may well be as good a place as any for me to stop; to come to an end myself … as it were.

Notes

1 F. R. Ankersmit (1983), *Narrative Logic*, F.R. Ankersmit, *History and Tropology* (1994).

2 F. R. Ankersmit, 'Reply to Professor Zagorin', *History and Theory*, vol. 29, no. 3, 1990. The paper I used in 2000 was unpublished, but appeared as chapter I of Ankersmit's *Historical Representation* (2001). I thank Frank Ankersmit for allowing me early sight of his paper.

3 Ankersmit, 'Reply to Professor Zagorin', p. 277.

4 Ibid., *passim*.

5 This quote, from Ankersmit's early version of the first chapter of *Historical Representation*, is slightly different from the published version. See Ankersmit (2001), pp. 32–3.

6 Again, see Ankersmit, *Historical Representations*, pp. 32–6, *passim*.

7 E. Laclau, *Emancipations* (1996), p. 123.

8 F. R. Ankersmit, 'Historiography and Postmodernism', reprinted in *History and Tropology*, pp. 162–81, esp. p. 176.
9 *Ibid.*, pp. 176–7.

References

Ankersmit, F. R. (1983), *Narrative Logic*, The Hague, Martinus Nijhoff.
—— (1994), *History and Tropology*, Berkeley, University of California Press.
—— (2001), *Historical Representation*, Stanford, CA, Stanford University Press.
—— (2005), *Sublime Historical Experience*, Stanford, CA, Stanford University Press.
Barthes, R. (1967) *The Discourses of History*; reprinted in K. Jenkins (ed.) (1997), *The Postmodern History Reader*, London, Routledge.
Bennett, T. (1990), *Outside Literature*, London, Routledge.
Jenkins, K. (1997), *The Postmodern History Reader*, London and New York, Routledge.
—— (1999), *Why History? Ethics and Postmodernity*, London and New York, Routledge.
—— (2003), *Refiguring History: New Thoughts on an Old Discipline*, London and New York, Routledge.
Laclau, E. (1996), *Emancipations*, London, Routledge.
Steiner, G. (1972), *In Bluebeard's Castle*, London, Faber.

14 The end of the affair

On the irretrievable breakdown of history and ethics

In 2005 I was asked to give a paper at a conference on history and theory to be held at the University of Greifswald, Germany, in 2006, and I wrote an earlier draft of the paper that appears here for that conference. That version was published in *Wahre Geschichte: Geschichte Als Wahre* (edited by C. Kühberger, C. Lübke and T. Terberger and published by Rahden/Westf, Verlag Marie Leidorf GmbH) in 2007. I also gave another version of the paper as part of a seminar series at the University of Limerick, again in 2006. To some extent the paper was meant as a more polemical rethink of the relationship between history and ethics and so is a 'sort of" short supplement to my article of 2004 which appeared in *History and Theory* (reproduced pp. 188–207).

One of the things historians always seem to claim is that a historical understanding is necessary for everything, including ethics, and that an ethics informed by history is of a better kind. I have never followed this logic. For it's possible to read brilliant moral and ethical philosophers without any visible display of their knowing 'the history of moral/ethical thinking' or any other history at all in ways historians might feel sufficient. Moreover, though histories are ethical (political) through and through, views of 'history' are not necessarily entailed from ethics nor ethics entailed from history. And it's this latter point that I try and make in this paper.

The relationship of modernity to postmodernity – the relationship within which I wish to locate this paper on history and ethics – is a difficult one to pin down. But one way, just one way of doing it, is to see postmodernism as directing a series of radical critiques against the 'experiment of modernity', against that post-Enlightenment experiment of trying to establish, in bourgeois and proletarian forms, 'human rights communities' on a global scale, an experiment that arguably failed on its own terms amidst the genocides, the gulags and the death-camps of the twentieth century. And that postmodernity was and is – to use Elizabeth Ermarth's phrase[1] – the 'whatever it was' that came *after* the breakdown of that experiment, postmodern*ism* being that condition of postmodernity raised to the level of consciousness more generally and, more particularly, to theoretical levels (Ermarth 2004, p. 68). On this reading postmodernism is thus, in important part, about clearing the decks of all those modernist assumptions that might prevent a new emancipating/

empowering enlightenment 'to come' – an enlightenment 'otherwise' than that of its eighteenth-century forerunner – such that postmodernism so conceived can be regarded as a critical retrospective of the 'Western Tradition' (and particularly the Western Tradition in its late-modernist forms) as its constituent elements were sifted through to see if, amidst all the clutter – all the damaged 'goods' – anything might be salvaged that might still be useful for this new social 'to come'. Very little was.

It is this, I think, that explains why – before too many positive proposals about how to figure new possibilities such that things might begin again *after* modernity and *after* the postmodern retrospective we are arguably living through – postmodernism is very much about deaths, is very much about endings: postmodernism as a kind of 'post-mortem'. There is a long list of such deaths and such endings in the various literatures: the death of God, the death of man, the death of the subject, the death of the author, the death of centres; the end of metaphysics, the end of the phallologocentric tradition, the end of onto-theology, the end of epistemology, the end of progress, the end of ideology, the end of poetry and philosophy after Auschwitz, the end of foundational ethics and the end – amidst even more endings – of history, too.[2]

These last two endings – of foundational ethics and of history – go together, I think, not least because, historically speaking (though not logically speaking since logically the fact–value and is–ought problematics *ought* to have ensured that they were never definitively related in the first place), they had, in practice, long been 'long-term partners' to the extent that, for many, it appeared (and for some it still appears) as if their mutual attraction – even their mutual fidelity – would last forever. But postmodernism – postmodernism as the raising to consciousness of the *aporia*, of the undecidability of the decision, of a corrosive anti-essentialism – has put an end to all of that.[3]

Now, in its main thrust the idea of the end of history (and of 'historical ethics', as it were) was applied primarily, of course, to those great metanarrative structures (Hegelianized Marxisms for example) that had claimed to somehow 'find' a direction, a purpose, a meaning, the expression of an essence or a teleology and thus of an ethical value *both* in the contingencies of previous phenomena *and* in the writing about them – histories. And of course postmodernism spoils all of this. Postmodernism's anti-essentialism and anti-foundationalism empties out *all* intrinsic meanings and values from everything: nothing *intrinsic* is left anywhere. Which means that any putative intrinsic meanings and values are always an imposition from outside. And, once everything is opened up to the outside – to *extrinsicality* – then there is no stopping; the outside simply goes on and on or, as Derrida somewhere expressed it, 'the absence of a transcendental signifier extends the play of signification to infinity'.

Either way, bereft of anything intrinsic, 'the past' (the 'before now') is now available to be historicized (i.e. made meaning-full) in any way anybody likes. In that sense the past is now seen as being overtly promiscuous; it will go with anybody, obey any 'order': Marxists, Whigs, empiricists, racists, feminists, structuralists, phenomenologists, postmodernists – anybody can have it. And why not, one might say, in these democratic days beyond authoritarian fiat: beyond *the* author, *the* authorized version, *the* 'word'. But all of this was (and still is) disturbing, to say the least, to old believers in intrinsicality, believers stretching right across the left–right ideological spectrum. For them the idea was not easy to swallow that history could be absolutely anything you wanted it to be. No metanarrative could survive this evacuation of intrinsicality intact, but, then, no 'academic' history could survive it intact either.

Yet, in fact, few academic historians fully realized (and some still do not) just how devastating one of these endings – the end of epistemology – was when it was applied not only to metanarratives but to their own particular genre of history. Of course, the end of empirically based, epistemologically assured history – still the 'much valued' *essence* of the professional/academic genre – is a massively complicated practico-theoretical area to consider. But, massively simplifying, the relevant bits of countless arguments and expositions can be briefly drawn together and put as follows.[4]

Academic historical discourse certainly does contain empirically testable elements related to past events at the level of, say, singular statements and sentences that 'correspond' to singular or clusters of singular evidential sources, well-corroborated 'facts', etc. But history as a discourse – history at the only level it can actually be a history: at the level of the text – is constituted by things ontologically unconnected and thus irreducible to such empirically verifiable 'epistemological' elements. For historical texts as the complex, ubiquitous narratives they are simply have to have, just to be narratives, all the elements constitutive of narratives per se. That is, they simply have to be troped, emplotted and sustained by various modes of argumentation; their articulation depends upon textual poetics, rhetorical devices, compositional strategies, intertextual readings, variable/contingent theories and methods and personal theses, etc., which infuse such texts with life and which, whilst not ignoring the empirical/epistemological elements, are massively and logically underdetermined by them. There are many things in the archive, but they do not include any of these things – the only means available to *make* a history. In the end, therefore, history is best seen as an act of the imagination, a fictive product; a figure, a shape, a way of carving-up 'the past' that the past 'itself' has no way of determining not only 'once and for all' but at all. Consequently, academic historians, just like metanarrative historians, are not only able to impose any reading they like on the past but they simply *have* to given that the past has no figure 'to call its own'.

And there is another, generally overlooked point that relates at this juncture to my earlier comment that the end of history is, though historically understandable, logically an ending that should not have occurred. For if postmodern claims regarding the best way of characterizing history per se (as an aestheticizing, figurative discourse) are correct – which they are – then logically there cannot ever have been histories of any other kind. That is to say, it is not as if there are 'now' aesthetic historicizations of the past (say postmodern-type ones) that stand over against, say, 'modernist' empirical/

epistemological ones which are not aesthetic phenomena at all. For if history as such is just an aesthetic discourse then all histories always have been and always will be of the type postmodernism raises to consciousness. Thus, logically speaking, no empirical/epistemological histories and no empirical/epistemological historians have ever existed on the face of the earth. So that in coming to the end of epistemologically striving histories and historians of whatever stripe we have, as it were, come home to ourselves. And I think we should accept this homecoming, should recognize that it was just an enormous category mistake to have ever thought of histories as being not of an aesthetic but of an epistemological kind, that it was just a mistake to make histories in ways which were 'modern'. In other words – and finally – what I am saying is that the difference between modernist empirical/epistemological and postmodern aestheticizations of the past is an ontological one, and that it is this which explains why the break between the modern and the postmodern is not an 'epistemological break' (which seems to allow for the possibility that one day they may be united on modernist terms in the guise of multiple interpretations and with an added attention to language, etc.) but a permanent because incommensurable difference.

Yet, although all of this seems pretty clear-cut to me, it is not surprising, given this postmodern message, that few academic historians liked the postmodern messenger. For if it is no longer possible to give primacy to those empirical/epistemologized elements modernist historians think guarantee, pretty much, their historical knowledge and understanding, and if any ethical 'lesson', or none, can be drawn from the study of the past, then concerns about the 'barbarians at the gate' and all that stuff become understandable.[5] Consequently, concerns about a paralysing nihilism, a licence-to-do-anything relativism and an individualism-gone-mad-solipsism (which imply that 'we' are now unable to withstand the challenge of fundamentalist extremists such that we might have to fight the Second World War all over again) are rehearsed endlessly. What about truth, objectivity, the facts; what about professional integrity, peer-review safeguards, honesty, disinterestedness, neutrality and the study of the past for its own sake; what of our ethical obligations to the dead – to the past per se? How many more times is Gadamer going to be hauled out to save us, with Collingwood on stand-by? How many more times is a Bakhtinian dialogism going to be invoked as a provisional foundation that treads a middle road between 'strait-jacket grounding and absolute openness'?[6] How can we 'wed', yes *wed*, 'two seemingly incompatible ideas: that history is not true but that it is still reasonable'? Can we not all at least be neo-pragmatists of a neo-realist type, believers in warranted assertability, or just accept as 'true' 'arguments to the best explanation'? And I think all these concerns and 'solutions' are just unnecessary. For what these and all other attempts that try – in the end – to sustain modernity's old empirical/epistemological concerns against the 'excesses' and 'extremism' of a fully fledged postmodernism just do not get, just do not understand, is that postmodernism just *is* its excesses, just *is* its extremes: *postmodernism is everything that modernity cannot ever be*. For the break between modernity and postmodernity is, in the long run, I think, as epochal a break as that between the medieval and the modern. These are just different worlds and we do not have to try and live in both of them. There is no need for nostalgia here; we can be thoroughly postmodern.

With regard to 'history and ethics' in general, then, I agree entirely with Hayden White's view that, placed as we are:

> ... before the alternative visions that history's interpreters offer for our consideration, and without any grounds for preferring one vision over another [then] we are drawn back to [ungroundable] moral and aesthetic reasons for our choice of one vision over another. ... The aged Kant was right. In short, we are free to make of the past what we will [relative to our] own moral and aesthetic aspiration.[7]

This radical *decisionism* – 'make of things what you will' – is now in the air we breathe and there is no other air. And so we might as well breathe in. The axiom of this decisionism is, of course, the old fact–value/is–ought problematic, the undecidable aporia, the lack of any necessary entailment. To be sure there is a sense in which, in advocating decisionism, I may seem to be contradicting myself by drawing from this 'fact', this 'is' (this decisionism) a value, an ought (that is, we *ought* to embrace this decisionism). And maybe on the surface of things I am. But I'm *not* drawing this conclusion because it is entailed, but because I just like this way of reading things and think maybe I can defend it: I know my decision to do so is ungrounded. And I am comfortable with this because some of the theorists I admire most – Foucault, Lyotard, Rorty, Laclau, Butler, Baudrillard, Badiou, Derrida – are ethical to their very 'core' without that 'core' being founded in anything other than an ethico-political preference. There is no time here to go into detail as to how Lyotard *et al.* are highly 'ethical' on the basis of nothing other than, I think, a bottom-line relativism. But if I were to make some brief points relative to all of this in the case of just two people on this occasion – Badiou and Derrida – this is how they would go: I use them to 'support' my argument.

The figure of the Event – Event in the upper case – is the axiomatic linchpin that holds together the radical philosophy of Alain Badiou (Badiou 2001, 2003). In various texts Badiou develops a way of thinking whereby human beings can become 'subjects of a truth'.[8] This claim rests on his argument – taken axiomatically – that 'the social' is divided between two distinct but, nevertheless, interconnected spheres: the ordinary world of established interests and occurrences that constitute normal everyday life wherein we operate fairly automatically, repetitively, and an exceptional realm of singular innovations or 'truths', which come into existence and persist only through the 'militant proclamation of those rare individuals who constitute themselves as subject of a truth, as the militants of their cause'. How do these rare subjects, these militant occupiers of a truth, get made?

Well, for Badiou, such a making can only begin with a break with the ordinary 'state of the situation' by working through an *Event*, an event that has nothing verifiable about it but is something which, in the light of one's positive experience of it, can only be grasped and affirmed, an affirmation that persists by adopting an attitude of *fidelity* towards it, a commitment amounting to 'something like disinterested enthusiasm, absorption in a compelling task or cause, a sense of elation, of being caught up in something that transcends all petty, private or material concerns ... of holding true to a person, a principle or ideal'. And of having an ethical attitude toward the Event, ethics being understood here as that which literally *en-courages* the subject to keep going, to not backslide. For Badiou, Events are catalysts that rip such (potential) subjects out of their usual situation, constituting a break between different modes of being-in-the-world:

> I shall call 'truth' the real process of a fidelity to an event; that which this fidelity *produces* in the situation. For example, the politics of the French Maoists between 1966–76 which tried to think and practice a fidelity to two entangled events: the Cultural Revolution in China and May '68 in France. Or the so-called algebraic geometry of the 1950s and '60s, and so on. Essentially a truth is [to be traced] from the decision to relate henceforth to the situation from the perspective of [its] *supplement* ... It is thus an immanent break, 'immanent' because a truth [emerges out of the] situation and nowhere else ... 'break' because what enables a truth process – the event – means *nothing* according to the prevailing languages and established knowledge of the situation.[9]

This new truth which *voids* the conventional thus produces a new position, which, induced by the 'evental break', thus necessitates on the 'basis' of a foundationless fidelity a reworking of one's previous way of being into newness. In this sense, Badiou argues, the evental break is *poetic* in its thinking otherwise: 'When the situation is saturated by its own norm', he writes:

> ... when the calculation of itself is inscribed there without respite, when there is no longer a void between knowledge and prediction, then one must be ready for the outside-of-self. For the nomination of an event – in the sense in which I speak of it, that is, as an *undecidable* supplementation which must be named to occur ... this nomination is *always* poetic. To name a supplement, a chance, an incalculable, one must draw from the void of sense, in default of established significations ... One must therefore poeticise, and the poetic name of the event is what throws us outside of ourselves ... [10]

This throwing ourselves outside of everything which has hitherto made sense to us and which the Event and its subsequent happenings now make 'null and void' is nothing but an 'incalculable', then, the outcome of a chance encounter, an encounter that *can* give birth to a new, sustainable subject. There is no higher order, nothing transcendental to guarantee this, there is only the chance to break out, to make 'something out of nothing'; out of the null-set; a *singular* breakout which carries with it, however, a promise of being a true break for everyone: a generic truth. As Peter Hallward (Hallward in Badiou 2001) has put it, 'A truth is innovation *en acte*, singular in its location but universal in its "address" ... Inaccessible to the classifications of the state, the truth comes to pass as a universal singular, particular to but unlimited by the state of the situation in which it came to exist.'[11]

So much for Badiou's 'ethical subject', then, so now, how does history and how does ethics come out after an engagement with Derrida? Let me hazard the following.

In Derrida's work in general, *différance* seems to say it all. *Différance* is the unresolvable tension between the idealized transcendental gesture (that inescapable metaphysical postulate/axiom) and the necessity of 'empirical'/material inscription. Every sign wants to say what it 'really' means, to refer unequivocally to its referent. This is the desire that motivates the sign; this is the idealized gesture of the transcendental. However, for the sign to operate it must be irreducible to one context; it must be repeatable, it must be *iterable* in 'other' contexts – otherwise it just would not be a sign. Consequently, the possibility of (potentially endless) inscription, of reiteration, guarantees the 'impossible to attain purity' (the pure 'presence') of the transcendental gesture: the empirical/material endlessly undoes all such 'closures'. Here is the site of Derrida's aporetic tension, namely, that while we can always 'think' the transcendental gesture, that gesture is never *realizable* in the sign at any given moment. So, history, say, is thus at once constituted both by the transcendental gesture – that promise to deliver a fully knowable history per se – and the material particularly that denies that promise. The idealized gesture is thus always 'to come', it never arrives, there is no 'last instance', no definite history ever; all historical representations are failed representations. History-in-practice, then, as a transcendental desire – the desire for a true/objective/epistemological/definitive account of the past, both in general and in its particulars, is thus an impossible desire, a myth of satiatedness that can never be achieved. Historical discourses as such are thus governed entirely (and I mean *entirely*) by an undoing, untying, unwelding *différance*. For the aporetic tension between the transcendental and the material/iterable (incidentally undoing any notion that Derrida is an idealist), the site of all deconstructions, is itself indestructible. In a familiar phrasing, the very condition of possibility for the thinking and the doing of history is thus also, simultaneously, the condition of its impossibility. And this 'impossible possibility' is the same for ethics: here the possibility of a truly ethical decision is, quite precisely, the impossibility of that decision.

For when making an ethical decision, because the thing one has to decide about is never exactly the same as any previous thing (or any future thing), then the demand that the decision that is made be a *just* decision (the transcendental gesture motivating Justice), the demand that the decision that is made does justice to the 'thing's' singularity, is the very 'thing' that make justice per se – an unconditional justice – impossible. Here the demand for a particular just act is the demand for continuous invention and incalculable calculation: there is no final judgement. For if one simply reapplied a previous judgement to a new situation (be it ever so familiar – perhaps), then this would merely be the application, the reapplication of a commandment, of a code, an administrative act that requires no 'decision' at all. Paradoxically then, aporetically then, it is precisely the fact that no judgement is definitive, that no judgement is ever fully adequate, that makes the demand for justice interminable. Bereft of all foundations, lost without logical entailment, forced to decide when one does not *know* exactly how to decide, then it is precisely here, in indifference, that ethics comes into its own. Ethics only exists when one does not *know* what to do – yet when one must do something – and take responsibility for it: there are no excuses, no alibis. The making of the undecidable, singular, ethical decision is thus our fate, our destiny. And for Derrida – as for Badiou and, for what it is worth, for me too – this is, I think, 'a good thing' in that it prevents, logically, all attempts at ethical closure. In the end, as Badiou comments, 'the objective of postmodern philosophy is to deconstruct the idea of totality',[12] to deconstruct any idea of 'a final solution'.

Let me now, very briefly, draw things to an inconclusive conclusion.

In the light of the above discussion, what seems to me to be amazing is not that history and ethics should be seen as being permanently separate but that they should ever have been deemed to have 'really' got together in the first place in an arrangement that was not anything other than the most casual of affairs. For a relationship between an ultimately unknowable, inexpungeably relativistic history and an undecidable ethics never seemed the best candidates from which to weld a long-term union. This is *not* to say, of course, that history and ethics have not always been, inescapably, thrown together, have not always been interconnected. For they have been. History has always been ethically/politically/ideologically *driven and governed*, and ethics has never escaped historicity. Obviously. But the always pragmatic understandings reached have never settled down on bases beyond the *ludic*, the aleatory, the contingent and thus, in the end, the arbitrary. And there are those who feel that, bereft of a real relationship, bereft of an absolute commitment, a position ultimately premised on a radical relativism means that we are on that slippery slope toward nihilism and solipsism which I mentioned earlier. But the point is that absolutes just do not help us in any of this, for absolutes, as Richard Rorty has put it, are 'also useful to the bad guys'. 'Bad guys' like absolutes. Or, at least, *putative* absolutes. For it is not as if there actually are some people who really do possess real absolutes and other, weaker people who are left with relativism, because there are no absolutes around for anybody to have: we are all relativists now. Consequently, having a position the articulation of which is its only ground is the best any of us can do. In the final pages of *Contingency, Irony and Solidarity* (Rorty 1989), Rorty writes that the 'fundamental premise [axiom] of the book is that a belief can still regulate action, can still be thought worth dying for, among people who are quite aware that this belief is caused by nothing deeper than contingent historical circumstances'.[13] This is as good as it gets, and this 'as good as it gets' will just have to be 'good enough'.[14]

Notes

1 Ermarth 2004, p. 68.
2 Badiou 2005. Badiou writes: 'In particular, postmodern philosophy proposed we dissolve the great constructions of the nineteenth century to which we remain captive – the idea of the historical subject, the idea of progress, the idea of revolution, the idea of humanity and the idea of science. Its aim is to show these great constructions are outdated; that we live in the multiple, there are no great epics of history or of thought; that there is an irreducible plurality of registers and languages ... so heterogeneous that no great idea can totalise or reconcile them' (pp. 32–3).
3 Postmodernism has [had] many definitions; I find it useful to think of it as 'the era of the *aporia*', an era when all the decisions we take – political, ethical, interpretive, representational, etc. – are ultimately undecidable, aporetic – that our chosen and favourite ways of looking at things lack foundations.
4 Much of the argument that follows owes much to the brilliant work of Frank Ankersmit; see, for example, his *History and Tropology* (1994), Berkeley, University of California Press; *Historical Representation* (2001), and *Sublime Historical Experience* (2005), both Stanford, Stanford University Press.
5 See Richard Evans's 'Introduction' in his *In Defence of History* (1997), for the 'barbarian threat'. Evans speaks for many, I think, in the history profession.
6 Elias 2005, pp. 159–72. With regard to empiricism, by the way, Collingwood's anti-empiricism/anti-epistemological position is surprisingly straightforward. 'The past', he writes, 'is never a given fact' which the historian 'can apprehend empirically'; rather our 'knowledge' is 'always mediate and inferential or indirect, never empirical' (p. 282).
7 White 1973, p. 433.
8 Badiou's texts are being busily translated into English. See especially: *Theoretical Writings* (2003); *Ethics: An Essay on the Understanding of Evil* (2001). Peter Hallward's *Badiou: A Subject to Truth* (2003) is an excellent introduction.
9 Badiou 2001, p. 42.
10 Badiou 2005, p. 75.
11 Hallward 2001, p. viii.
12 Badiou 2005, p. 33.
13 Rorty 1989, p. 189.
14 Since writing this paper, *History and Theory* (2005) has published an exchange between D. Moses and Hayden White under the title 'The Public Role of History' (vol. 44, no. 3, pp. 311–47). See also, in the same issue, C. B. McCullagh's review of Roy Harris's *The Linguistics of History*, pp. 441–55, relating, as it does, to matters of ethics and 'truth'.

References

Badiou, A. (2001) *Ethics: An Essay on the Understanding of Evil*, London, Verso.
—— (2003) *Theoretical Writings*, London, Continuum.
—— (2005) *Infinite Thought*, London, Continuum.
Collingwood. R. G. ([1946] 1994) *The Idea of History*, Oxford, Oxford University Press.

Elias, A. (2005) 'Metahistorical romance: the historical sublime and dialogic history', *Rethinking History*, vol. 9, nos 2/3, pp. 159–72.

Ermarth, E. D. (2004) 'Ethics and methods', *History and Theory*, vol. 4, no. 43, pp. 61–83.

Evans, R. (1997) *In Defence of History*, London, Granta.

Hallward, P. (2001) 'Introduction', in Badiou, *Ethics: An Essay on the Understanding of Evil*, London, Verso, p. viii.

—— (2003) *Badiou: A Subject To Truth*, Minneapolis, University of Minnesota Press.

Rorty, R. (1989) *Contingency, Irony and Solidarity*, Cambridge, Cambridge University Press.

White, H. (1973) *Metahistory*, Baltimore, Johns Hopkins University Press.

15 'Nobody does it better'

Radical history and Hayden White

In 2006 I was asked by Frank Ankersmit if I would write a paper for the *Festschrift* he was putting together (with Ewa Domanska and Hans Kellner) to celebrate the 80th birthday of the American Historian and Theorist Hayden White. About the same time, Alun Munslow also asked me if I could write a paper for White's birthday for a special issue of *Rethinking History*. In the event, I hadn't the time to write two separate essays, and so I asked Frank and Alun if I could write just the one paper which could appear in both places. They agreed. The paper here is from *Rethinking History* because in the event it came out first (in early 2008); the Ankersmit volume (*Refiguring Hayden White*) is due to be published later in 2009.

As I say in the paper, Hayden White is, for me, an intellectual hero; his *Metahistory* (1973) was germinal for my thinking and I have come to accept pretty much every position he holds on historical theory. But, because White has been written about so much, to say anything really new about him was hard. So the essay here is split into two very uneven parts. In the first, long part, I try to sketch out some of the main characteristics of a radical history, one that I could hold to if I had still to have a history and expressed at the level of various presuppositions/axioms, etc. And then, in the second part, I try to say how much the first part owes to White – which is pretty much everything.

I want to begin this article for Hayden White – an article inconceivable without White and therefore an article indebted to him – by sketching out, in its very much longer first part, what I take to be the necessary conditions of possibility for the production of radical (and let me stress the word *radical*) histories – by which I mean histories which, from the point of view of the current 'state of the situation' are deemed of no significance. What do I need to be able to think these things, and what are some of their consequences? And in Part two, I want to explain how I see all of this relating back to White.

PART ONE

Without further preliminaries, then, let me repose the question governing this first part: what are the necessary conditions of possibility for the production of a radical history ... ? And here I want to take a step back so that I can identify as my starting point certain *ontological* presuppositions which, acting as *axioms*, will then allow me to build a history thereon, axioms and the resultant history both being, on this occasion, presented in tabular form (and thus somewhat skeletally, impressionistically).

(1) I take as my originary axiom the existence of matter: of materiality, of 'actuality'. I take it that the 'stuff' we call, for example, the world, the universe, etc., is really out there and is therefore not the product of my current mental state. Of course I cannot prove this; I cannot get out of my head to check if there is something outside of it, but my premise is that there is. In that sense I'm a *realist* but a realist of a certain kind, namely, a *transcendental realist* – by which I mean that not only does such stuff exist (and has existed previously and will exist in the future), but that it transcends each and every attempt in each and every social formation to reduce it to their inhabitants' experiences, vocabularies, lexicons, abstractions, etc., such that they might think that they really do *know* it. For it seems apparent that the actuality of 'existence' skips free of every (definitive) anthropomorphism. Yet, at the same time such transcendental realism does not commit me to *metaphysical realism* (namely, that we can know the way things are independent of the way we access them). Rather, my type of realism commits me to precisely the opposite. Insofar as we can present examples of our intuitions via various representations, such intuitions/representations cannot escape the exact circumstances of their production; cannot shrug off the pressure of time and chance, and so are thus *radically* contingent (radically meaning here forever irreducible to definitive meanings). In other words, I hold the view (with Richard Rorty) that whilst the 'world' is 'out there' *meanings* are not; that whilst the world is 'out there' *truths* are not, since meanings and truths are in sentences and sentences are not 'out there' (Rorty 1989, 5). There is therefore a radical break – an *ontological* break – between the 'actuality' of the world (all that 'stuff') and so-called reality, such reality being created/constituted by our human discourses which are 'about' but which do not knowingly correspond to that to which they 'refer'. Indeed, it is these discourses – broadly construed – which alone *make* the world variously meaning-full, and we know of no other common reality than that thus constituted.

(2) This reduction of any 'knowledge' we 'may think we have' of the world (past, present, future) to the contingencies of knowledge production, distribution, reception, etc., means – as already noted but now rearticulated slightly – that we can never have access to the actualities of 'stuff' plain, pure. That such 'worlds' as ours are always just that, ours, and are thus *inescapably* human, 'inescapably' meaning here that just as, say, giraffes or eagles have giraffe and eagle worlds – have their own species-bound 'readings' of the stuff of actuality, never cognisant of human readings of the same phenomena – so, locked up in our own human readings, we have no access to giraffe and eagle 'reality'. Nor is there some form of neutral actuality/reality that offers a way of adjudicating between different species readings in the hope of finding a trans-species 'real reality'. Thus we human animals ('just one more species doing its

best') are indeed just doing our best to pragmatically live out a life unknown to other species and which is for all of us – both them and us – ultimately unfathomable.

(3) Such irreducibility of the actuality of the stuff of our 'worded world' to our human sensations, experiences, concepts, categories, schemas, analogies, etc., whereby we try to transform our 'experiences' of the 'concrete' into the 'concrete in thought', the inadequacy of every representation to fully capture the objects 'subjectified' by our gaze (to gain subject–object identity, full-presence, etc.), means that, when carrying out our meaning-making operations, we cannot but become (on the back of our transcendental realism) *inter-subjective idealists*, namely, that it is we who make our actuality 'real' by endowing attributes to stuff which thus real-ises 'it'. This is a way of still thinking of 'actuality' – after all these years – along the lines of the old Kantian 'thing in itself'; as that ungraspable (noumenal) *excess* which thwarts ('for all we know') all our efforts to make things identical to us, the same as us. I therefore hold, axiomatically, that the stuff of existence exceeds our every limit, transverses all our boundaries, escapes our most definitive closures, making both our experiential actions and our thoughts unremittingly and inescapably *open*: *ludic*, aleatory, heuristic and thus, once again, radically contingent. And here we might recall some recent and well-known formulations of this excess: Camus' absurd, the sublime of Lyotard and White, Badiou's multiples, Lacan's Real, Derrida's undecidables, Kristeva's semiotic, Baudrillard's symbolic-semiotic spiral, and so on. Of course, we must not for a moment think of such formulations as ever being adequate to the excess. For the excess, the *sublime*, is not a delimited object or thing; it is not something which we knowingly 'lack' and which, if found, would allow us to fulfil our (sometime) human desire for completion, closure, totality. For the sublime is forever unpresentable, is something unable to ever be historicized, is precisely non-ontologizable – otherwise it just wouldn't be sublime – and is therefore just a further dimension of our human imagination which posits that beyond our every closure there lurks an 'undoing outside' which, despite all our attempts to disavow or negate or just plain forget, hauntingly persists to remind us that beyond all the 'somethings' we have made out of 'nothing' (making 'something out of nothing' is the story of our lives) is the sense of that (constitutive) nothing that can spell *ruin* for even our very best *representations*. Thus, to my growing list of axioms – to my transcendental realism, inter-subjective idealism and the undoing sublime – I add radical *anti-representationalism* together with, at this point, a certain type of *nominalism*, a (metaphorical) naming process which, because of its unavoidable *violence*, forcefully welds together the ontological (and the ontic) to the political and thus to what I take to be (axiomatically) just one expression of the (power) political: *history*. And in articulating this interconnection I have found it useful to think of this production of meaning as having (after Jacques Derrida) *three* levels.

(4) To make (to realize) a meaning, to bring meaning into the world is ultimately an act of violence – a violence of 'writing' that can be called *first-*

level violence. Since there is no one-to-one natural correspondence between word and world, no literal entailment of signifier to signifier and thence to the putative signified and thence to the putative referent (putative since the referent is now collapsed back into representation – into signs), then to get the actuality of the world into a 'language' it never asked to be put in is to always establish both a power and a metaphorical relationship (that tree as if it really was a tree, that past as if it really was history ...). Yet, accurate as this is, Derrida thinks that the notion of a metaphorical relationship still runs the risk of carrying (naive) realist overtones, in that it may suggest that there is (already) a meaningful 'reality', some solid ground(ing), to which the sign-system refers – albeit figuratively. But obviously there isn't. Consequently, the founding concepts of meaning are instances not of metaphor generally but the (metaphorical) trope of *catachresis*: a violent production of meaning, an imposition, an abuse. Derrida:

> I have always tried to expose the way in which philosophy is literary, not so much because it is metaphor but because it is *catachresis*. The term metaphor implies a relation to an original 'property' of 'meaning', a 'proper' sense to which it indirectly or equivocally refers, whereas *catachresis* is a violent production of meaning, an abuse which refers to no exterior or proper norm (Kearney 1995, 172).

Yet, whilst this violent call to meaning is, of course, a necessary one if any meanings are to be produced at all – since this violent imposition is the very condition of the possibility of meaning – Derrida is concerned to show how this naming process can never achieve what it would like to achieve – namely, literal full-presence. And for him it is precisely *différance*, as the irreducible tension (*aporia*) between what he calls the 'idealized transcendental gesture' and the necessity of empirical inscription, that is the site of its unavoidable undoing.

Now, how can this undoing be developed in what is termed the level of *secondary violence*; well, *différance* again says it all.

For Derrida, every sign wants to say what it 'really' means. This is the sign's motivation, the idealized gesture of the (quasi) transcendental – to achieve full-presence and so forth. Yet, for the sign to operate as a sign it must be irreducible to one context, it must be repeatable (albeit always slightly differently) in other contexts (*iterable*), otherwise it just wouldn't be a sign. Consequently, the necessity of empirical inscription guarantees the logical impossibility of the purity of the transcendental gesture. Nevertheless, the 'myth' of the transcendental (universals, absolutes ...) remains the animating force behind the signs of, say, Justice, Law, Ethics, or History, such that it is here that the *aporetic* tension inevitably resides. For while the originary violence of the sign enables us to think the transcendental gesture, that gesture is never realizable at the empirical level. Consequently, Justice or Law or Ethics or History are always only accessible at the level of the empirical/

iterable (as justices, laws, ethics, histories ...) and yet are irreducible to them. Historical discourse then (now concentrating on 'history') cannot ever escape indeterminacy; cannot escape *différance*; of being always both the idealized gesture *and* iterable – that is, being always open to new inscriptions, meanings, to interminable redescriptions. The fulfilment of any idealized gesture is thus permanently delayed, will always be 'to come' yet will never arrive: there is no 'last instance', no 'last word', no closure, no 'final solution'. We shall never know what History/history 'really is' – that will remain a secret like the name and the face of God. Its putative aim – the truth-full reconstruction of the past – is thus an impossible 'myth', yet one which continuously energises historians' productions. We shall, courtesy of *différance*, never know what the nature of history is any more than we shall know The Law, Justice, Ethics or God; we shall never know the past 'in and for itself', for its 'own sake'.

Now, it is precisely this 'fact' (and if there is a fact this is it) that Derrida thinks we have tried to forget, to disavow. And it is this refusal to remember the violent, contingent and thus arbitrary relationship of words and things in favour of literal truths, permanent categories, invariable essences and non-relativistic ethics that goes under the name of *secondary violence* – the violence of forgetting.

This 'mind-world' of secondary violence – of 'realism', of representationalism, of ethical imperatives – is the one most of us habitually inhabit: this is 'reality', this is what we 'take for granted'. And it is these repressed actualities which Derrida and others wish us to recall by deconstructing via *différance* those protective, fictive shelters of secondary violence which, if I can put it this way, the overwhelming thrust of the Western Tradition (of which modernity – and the (violent) modern nation-state – was its swan-song) erected as barriers against 'the other(s)'. I mean, all those 'infinite fixes', those rigid designators, those binary oppositions, those various/sometime white, ethnic, gendered, onto-theological fantasies which, embodied in phallologocentric articulations, have included amongst their vehicles numerous histories, not least those finding sometime expression in upper-case (metanarrative) and lower-case (certaintist/academic/professional) forms. And Derrida as I read him – along with other radical post-structuralist/postmodern historians – is concerned to remove all and every remaining, privileging carapace insofar as they have tried (and try) to help legitimate reasons excusing acts of *third-level violence*, that is, the everyday empirical violence of exclusion, rape, murder, war, genocide. At which point the deconstructionist drive works *backwards* from third- to first-level violence – for it can now be shown that level-three violence is not of a *necessary* kind but is just the arbitrary outcome of its catachretic founding, thus opening it up – de-realizing reality – to 'alternative realities' which could be – which *ought* to be – explicitly liberating, empowering and uncompromisingly emancipating for those people needing these things: most of us. This is not to say that any such 'new reality' will not be 'arbitrary', will not be another simulacrum, but the deconstructionist hope is that this world might be a better one than the one we inhabit now. This is a hope for a 'less violent' world based on the interminable revisions of its *axioms*, an 'open' world that, recognizing its undecidability, its provisionality, refuses all closures. Ernesto Laclau has seen the unavoidability of this better than most:

> The metaphysical (logocentric) discourse of the West is coming to an end, and philosophy in it twilight has performed a last service for us in the deconstruction of its own terrain. Let us think, for instance, of Derrida's undecidables. Once undecidability has reached the ground itself – once the organisation of a certain camp is governed by a hegemonic decision – hegemonic because it is not objectively determined, because different decisions were also possible – then the realm of philosophy comes to an end and the realm of politics begins. This realm will be inhabited by a different type of discourse … which … constructs the world on the 'grounds' of radical undecidability (Laclau 1996, 123).

This is the sort of politics the radical historian is committed to.

(5) And so I come now to some of the details of that radical history which might (possibly) be used to help realize such emancipating goals by *building* on the above set of 'open' axioms a sort of *superstructural* history that might transform and supersede the 'normal' historian's 'traditional calling' by responding to a call that comes not from the past at all but directly from ethics, from politics. Radical historians, unlike 'normal' ones, don't go to work to understand the past on it own terms and for its own sake; radical historians don't work on behalf of the people who lived in the past: they work for us.

So to the question of how to proceed to the establishment of the necessary conditions for the production of such a radical history, my answer, on this occasion, is *dialectically*. That is to say that I want to show, initially, how the conditions of possibility for a closed, empirical/epistemologically striving *non-radical* historian – for a historian that attempts to establish assured historical knowledge, understanding and meaning – *cannot* ever be met: this acts as my *thesis*. Of course traditional historians of whatever stripe – the majority of the history profession, say – are not unaware of some of the factors which deny them surety, intuit that their type of history has epistemological (and/or even scientific) ambitions it lacks the means to deliver. But more often than not it's 'business as usual', and as such troubling thoughts are brushed under the carpet or, if raised to the level of consciousness, are articulated as 'problems' to solve, 'challenges' to overcome and 'difficulties' to work through, as they 'come to terms with the past'. And it is my argument – my *antithesis* – that such limits and difficulties are not seen by radical historians as problems at all but as *opportunities* for newness. Radical historians thus turn the weaknesses of 'proper history' into strengths, celebrate the fact that historians' representations (including theirs) are *always* failed representations, that historians *qua* historians always get the past wrong and that it is these 'facts' which become the basis for a new *synthesis* which, discarding the desire for closure, builds uncertainty on uncertainty. At which point old (modernist) empirical/epistemologically striving histories in whatever case – histories which can never achieve closure nor prevent interminable openness – hopefully 'drop out of the conversation' as radical (postmodern) histories take their place. There is no need for any nostalgia here – modernist histories have had their day in the sun – and thus there is no need to keep a foot in both camps in some middle-ground, conserving consensus: we can all become thoroughly postmodern. So let me now give some substance to this position, beginning by outlining my *thesis*, that is, by sketching out the irremovable obstacles to the establishment of any empirical/epistemological history of closure. And let me retabulate as I work through six relevant areas.

(1) First there is the problematicising contamination – the interpretive bulk – of the author. Frank Ankersmit sets the scene and triggers off a train of thought. Ankersmit:

> We have historical writing in order to compensate for the absence of the past. So whereas in the case of pictorial and political representation the represented has a logical priority to it representation, in the case of historical representation the reverse is the case, namely, that the represented – that is, the past – depends for its (onto)logical status on its representation. No representation, no past (Ankersmit 2006, 328).

No representation no past: exactly. And, because such representations by no means come from nowhere, then it is the 'writers' of history, historians (and those acting as if they were historians), who have a prior 'logical priority': no representation no history, is (tautologically) 'correct', as is, no representor, no representation.

Representors – historians – come in all shapes and sizes to the production of the historicized past but none come innocently. Historians are affected by all kinds of suasive desires and material everyday pressures that are not left behind when they enter the study – by ambitions, jealousies, careerist aspirations; by institutionalization, duplicities and disavowals; by niggling worries, acts of gratitude and support and various incompetencies, and so on – that cannot avoid unevenly, singularly influencing and conditioning the practices and the products of the author-historian. History is a contaminated discourse which cannot be purified of the tensions and ambiguities – never fully knowable – of situation, circumstance, authorization, legitimation, play; any 'genealogy of history', as Sande Cohen puts it, by any half-thorough account, must demonstrate such 'mixed origins' which no appeal to the archive, the sources, the data, the facts and objectivity, can negate or transcend (Cohen 2000, 100). These are the circumstances which variously and unmeasurably infuse the historians' texts with life and which, whilst not ignoring the empirical/epistemological components of historicizations, are underdetermined by them.

(2) In which context the next question is what, more precisely, is this historian's referent and its status? Could it be the past per se? Well no, since that no longer exists. Moreover, even if it did, the (*idea* of) the past is far too complicated to become a fixed object of enquiry. For there is never a solid, 'real' past that acts as the common/neutral past for everyone – any more than there is a common/neutral time it exists 'in'. Rather, many different levels of many pasts and presents and many perspectival 'timings of time' congeal and become unstuck, sometimes rapidly, sometimes slowly, and these affect how someone/they/we choose, as Cohen puts it, 'to initiate, to accept, to reject the data of experience, interpreting and assessing inner and outer relations'. Present habits and memories, continues Cohen,

> incessantly weave themselves into degrees of pastness in the form of powerful memories mixed with obsessions blended with attempts to self-distract, joined with new projects of forgetting, so that there is no neutral present's relation to the past – as. Remember that the present 'is' no more objectively nor subjectively real than the past, as both are embroiled in the other in terms of actualization in any present … we are constantly dismantling and assembling the present; we are constantly dissembling the present to have a different effect/affect of and with the past.
>
> (Cohen 2006, 248–9)

No stable referent here then.

So can the historian's referent be the *traces* of the past, the (always already historicized) archive, as widely construed as one wishes? Well no. Because although historians refer to the archive and to, say, the documents therein and the 'facts' that may be generated out of them in terms of singular statements that 'correspond' to singular or clusters of singular 'evidential sources', and so on, and though they *reference* these things copiously in footnotes, these things are still not their *referent*.

So what can it be? And the answer is simply that the historian's referent is 'nothing' but the product of their *inferences* based upon their existential (personal, ethical, public, ideological …) condition, their previous/current 'dealing' in the field, their modes of prefiguration which work up the 'material' they variously have to make it into an object capable of analysis, and their constitutive 'research' concerns, theses, and so on which, in never stable interconnections, *cause* some of the traces they find/produce to become activated as relevant sources and thence as *evidence* for any arguments they happen to be running (for the 'past itself' doesn't have in it any arguments or problems which historians solve – only historians have arguments as they seek to establish their reading over others). And that on these bases they then *infer* a past – either simple or complex – which now *fits* their data, their position, their inferences. And this inferential process *cannot* work in reverse, no matter how much pleading to the contrary. For historians cannot *know* the past – especially that part of it which they are putatively 'finding' for the first time as they seek the holy grail of 'originality' – and then search for the sources to correspond to it, thus confirming it as 'knowledge'. Rather, the process is that of using 'this and that' from which a past to conform to 'this and that' is inferred. And this inference, now the historicized past and which constitutes the figural 'content' of their texts to which they refer – this is their *referent*, a referent, let us note and underline, which is 'always in thought': no one can knowingly ignore Roland Barthes's strictures on this (Barthes 1997, 120–23).

(3) But note now some further aspects of the epistemic status of this referent. Note *four* things. Note, first of all, that this is a referent which cannot ever have the status of truth or definitiveness – it's only an inference after all – and nor can it be objective. For not only is it self-referencing, but other self-referencers (historians) going to, say, the same archives and working on even the same traces/sources can and do infer very different pasts; indeed, history (as historiography) is composed of such 'interpretive differences' that no appeal to the facts as other historicizations (inferences) can close down. And, of course, lurking in this area is the old fact–value problematic that ensures that, whatever the inferred relationship between phenomena and meaning, that relationship is never entailed: 'the past' can be read and 'made to mean' any way you like.

Note, second, the fact that inferences are always arguments means, again, that truth and so on cannot ever come into it.[1] For, as we all know, arguments are never true or false; arguments can only be valid or invalid so that, no matter how many times 'forgetful' historians slip the notion of an argument 'that's true' into their 'discussions', a true argument, like another old favourite, the true interpretation, is an oxymoron. Note, third, that because the historian's referent is inferential, then the kinds of things inferred – structures, processes, trends, watersheds, statistical runs, influences, movements, explanations, meanings, and so on – were never actually there in the first place, or at least, not in the way Nelson's Flagship *Victory* was once there. There is thus, as Carolyn Steedman has put it, 'a double nothingness' in the writing of history. History is about something that never did happen in the way in which it comes to be represented (the happening exists in the telling, in the text), and it is made of materials (the inferences) which are also not there – in the archive or anywhere else (Steedman 2001, 153–4). Jacques Rancierre has made the same point: 'There is history because there is an absence … [and] the status of history depends on the treatment of this two-fold absence of the "thing itself" that is no longer there [the past is past] and that never was … because it never was such that it was [and is] told' (Rancierre 1992, 63). And note fourth and finally that the logic of inference is the logic of *probability*, which is to say that the historian's logic is not that of the *syllogism* (although syllogistic reasoning can appear in parts of the historian's text), but rather the logic of the *enthymeme*, a form of logic which cannot lead to definitive conclusions – and thus closure – but can only be to the occasion for the expression of an 'undecidable decision', an *aporetic* choice. For enthymemes always involve a calculation of probabilities and a judgement, and leave things open so that one can always argue contrary-wise: 'both sides of the case'. Consequently, history as a probable/possible reading – and this is the status of *all* histories – is always neither rigorously true nor rigorously false; at best it can have to recommend it 'a certain appearance in its favour'. This, a measure of the shortfall of any epistemological claims for histories, is as good as it gets.

(4) On this account, history has all the elements that fulfil the classic criteria for something to be of a rhetorical kind – namely, a method 'to invent subjects and arguments, to organize discourse, and to make good judgements' (Olmsted 2006, 1) – and is therefore the type of phenomenon Aristotle called *illusio* which, because it deals with things contingent and opaque, can only be demonstrated or 'proved'. On this reasoning, history cannot ever be a science. For since history has no definitive object of enquiry (the 'past' looked at 'this way and that way' may be imagined but definitive examples of it cannot be presented), nor any definitive (universal) method of enquiry, then such a discourse, as Martin Davies has put it, 'belongs properly to the realm of rhetoric' since this is of a kind that, 'not dealing with "any one definite class of objects" is "merely a faculty for furnishing arguments"'. Moreover, since history and politics also have an instrumental, ideological intention, their aim is rhetorical: they are concerned to 'discover the real and apparent means of persuasion' (Davies 2006, 55).

Since history, then, thus deals only with contingencies (accidental facts, antecedent possibilities, metonymic extrapolations …) and proceeds by means of enthymemes (rhetorical induction) that can only provide a lesser standard of proof than 'logic' offers, then history will remain interminably open, always waiting for the next interlocutor to arrive. One always comes along.

(5) Which means, still pursuing this line of thought, that as *illusio*, as inferential acts of the imagination, historical representations and consciousness (of this and that) are both fictive (that is, fabricated, made up, fashioned) and, as the product of rhetorical devices and stylistic figures, of an *aesthetic* kind. And such aesthetic figures are not, of course, subject to epistemological checks at the level of the text: an aesthetic cannot answer to epistemology. Of course, as already noted, empirical/epistemological elements can and do (once things have been 'put under a description') operate at the level of singular statements and so on, but a discourse with a story to tell in the form of a *narratio* is always a manifestation of that mixture of the 'found' (the sources, etc.) and the imagined (the inferences) wherein, between these two unstable poles, one is always in a radically indeterminate 'middle range'. This is indeed a past as much imagined as found or, more precisely I think, *more* imagined than found: the aesthetic overdetermines the 'empirical'. Always.

And the radical historian likes this overdetermination, likes the essentially aesthetic nature of *all* histories. For it is not, incidentally, as if there are some histories (say modernist ones) which really are of an empirical/epistemological kind 'all the way down' and that these can be set against aesthetic histories (say postmodern ones). Rather, the point is that all histories – just to be histories – always have been and always will be of an aesthetic type; all histories are of the type the radical/postmodern historian raises to the level of consciousness: rhetorical/aesthetic histories are the only game in town. Thus, logically speaking, no empirical/epistemological histories, and no empirical/epistemological historians, have ever existed on the face of the earth. Traditional historians of this type are generally quite proud and normally not at all defensive when they are called 'empirical historians' – indeed, many insist on being so called. But in fact no such specimen has ever been found and it beggars belief to think that they could 'ever have been imagined'. RIP.

(6) And so I come directly to the area which Hayden White has pretty much made his own over the last forty years or so: narrativity. To be sure, right from the start White has been much criticized by various history establishments across the left–right ideological spectrum – what do you expect if you insist history is a kind of fiction-making – and many historians and some theorists continue to critique, disavow or just plain ignore him. There are some very silly people around. And, of course, I am aware of these critiques, just as I am aware that White has made some (minor) adjustments to his position over the years. And I recognize that White isn't – nor would want to be – the closing/last word on anything. Nevertheless, all that said, I think the radical historian can subscribe – I subscribe – *entirely* to White's decisionist/impositionist/relativistic position on narrativity. Thus I take it as read, for example, 'that no given set of events figure forth apodictically the kind of meanings with which stories provide them … no one and nothing *lives* a story' (*Tropics of Discourse*); that 'the meaning, form, or coherence of events, whether real or imaginary ones, is a function of their narrativism' (*Figural Realism*); that 'one must face the fact that when it comes to apprehending the historical record, there are no grounds found in it for preferring one way of construing its meaning over another' (*The Content of the Form*); that the only grounds for choosing one perspective on history rather than another are ultimately aesthetic and ethical/political: 'the aged Kant was right, in short, we are free to conceive history as we please just as we are free to make of it what we will' (*Metahistory*). And I sign up to all these *axioms*, just as I sign up to most of the detail whereby White establishes the *metahistorical* nature of *all* history productions vis-à-vis the ubiquity of tropes, emplotments, argumentative governing and ideological positioning; I mean can you imagine a history that is not troped, not emplotted, not governed by argumentation and not suasively/ideologically intended? Could one exist? Now that *is* a rhetorical question.

And I subscribe to all of this because I also sign up to what I think of as White's radical 'philosophy of history'. That the past is sublime in its 'whole' and problematic in its parts; that at the level of meaning (not truth but meaning) historical narratives are inexpungeably singular/relativistic; that scepticism about historical knowledge/meaning is a necessary counter to dogmas everywhere; that 'the past' has no legitimate gatekeepers who can tell us what we can and cannot do with it (least of all academic historians); that no one owns the past nor has a monopoly of how to appropriate it; that the interminable openness of the past to countless readings should be celebrated and democratized in the hope that we might, disobediently, seriously entertain those creative historical 'distortions offered by minds capable of looking at the past with the same seriousness as ourselves but with different affective and intellectual orientations'; that this should alert us to the conserving nature of now pre-eminent narrations that tidily lock up events in case their willingness to be relocated is exploited radically and which absorb experimentation in the name of a fake pluralism; and that the essence of a radical history is its future-orientated politico/ethical thrust. White:

> I take ethics to be about the difference between what is (or was) the case and what ought to be (or ought to have been) the case in some department of human comportment, thought, or belief [opening] up a space in which 'something has to be done'. This is quite different from morality that, on the basis of some dogmatism, insists on telling us what we *must and must not do* in a given situation of choice. The historical past is 'ethical' in that its subject matter (violence, loss, absence, the event, death) arouses in us the kind of ambivalent feelings, about ourselves as well as the 'other', that appear in situations requiring choice and engagement in existentially determining ways.
>
> (White 2006, 338)

And this existentialism, this 'humanism' with a performative rather than an essentialist subject – an old *topos* in White's work – is also invoked in the cause of permanent openness. Commenting that Camus had once written that, in trying to find out whether or not life had to have a meaning to be lived and that his conclusion was that 'it will be lived all the better if it has no meaning', White writes that 'we might amend the statement to read: it will be lived all the better if it has no single meaning but many different ones' (White 1978, 50).

And I think, finally, that radical historians should always wear these kind of sentiments where White has always worn his: openly, explicitly, on his sleeve. White cannot have the last word for radical historians – for he is not the only voice which *ought* to be heard. But I think he deserves to have the first.

Now, history as I have presented it here could be seen as being in bad shape; it's difficult to imagine how this particular Humpty Dumpty could ever be put together again. On the 'top' of my 'open' axioms it has contaminated writers, an object of enquiry it can neither access nor definitively present; it has a referent that is inferred and therefore imagined, which is another way of saying that, given that inferences constitute history, then history is imagined. Moreover, it has no definitive, shared method; it is a mode of discourse of a rhetorical kind, a product of argumentation and figuration: an aesthetic *illusio*. In its presentation as *narratio*, history has to have – simply to be a narrative – all the elements common to narrative per se; that is, it has to be troped and emplotted and sustained by argumentation, its articulation depends on textual poetics, rhetorical devices and figures, compositional strategies, intertextual readings, variable/contingent theories and methods and personal theses which are expressed by, and expressive of, the circumstances of the author. None of these things are 'found' in the past, but these are the conditional elements of any history. This is the way history just is for all of us – these are 'its necessary conditions of possibility'. And this condition is not *denied* but *accepted* willingly and reworked by radical historians. Radical historians *like* this history; they can live with it, use it, experiment with it and, insofar as we still need histories at this point in time, direct it towards emancipation and liberation. (By which I mean the making possible of that which is considered impossible: to put an end to consensus.) And, of course, radical historians recognize that history just is impossible to close down, not just 'once and for all', but at all. A history of this kind – and these are some of its consequences – means the end, surely, of every metanarrative edifice and all those academic histories of an empirical/epistemologically striving type; towards both of these *genres* we must have that incredulity Lyotard reserved for metanarratives, as well as working in opposition to all those who would work to prevent what, in the end, radical historians like: the fact that historicizations of the past can be anything you want them to be. This raises, of course, all kinds of dangers; it's always a risk, always a chance, to exist without something like foundations: some future historicization may well be monstrous. But it's not, I'm afraid, the case that this is a 'risk worth taking' *as if* it were an option; it's a risk that is unavoidable: we have come, let's hope for better rather than worse, to the end of the illusion of the possibility of closure in such a manner that it seems incredible that (to reuse one of White's epigrams again) not only have such histories been imagined in the past but that they have actually been found. Radical historians hope that such absurdities will not be repeated in the future even as farce – and certainly not as tragedy.

PART TWO

I now come to what I hope by this point is obviously yet just another rhetorical question: what has all of this got to do with Hayden White? For the answer is simple: *everything*. To be sure, in the above argument I have occasionally had in mind influences gleaned from what are by now old favourites: Marx, Nietzsche, Collingwood, Althusser, Barthes, Foucault, Lyotard, Derrida, Rorty, Laclau, Baudrillard, Badiou *et al.*, as well as mid-term or newer ones: Frank Ankersmit, Arthur Danto, Elizabeth Ermarth, Judith Butler, Sande Cohen, Martin Davies *et al.*, a few of whom I have referenced. But the point is that I 'got into' most of these people because of Hayden. And by this I don't mean that he introduced me to or helped me to think better or differently about things, but that he has been involved in my intellectual formation – he figures as *the* point of departure for my thinking about history that my subsequent journey remains indebted to. For it was Hayden who, almost single-handedly, turned me from the old Marxist I once was to the post-Marxist I think I may have become, and from the old normal/empirical/modernist historian I was by 'training' into the postmodern person I would like to be. Of course, it's not his fault – nor anyone else's – that I have turned out the way I have – a populariser of postmodern history – and I don't expect Hayden to necessarily agree with anything I have done under the influence – however attenuated – of his brilliant writings, including this paper. No. All I am saying is that he occupies a special place in my thinking, and I want to write just two final paragraphs on this.

I first read Hayden's 1973 text *Metahistory* in the mid-1970s and I didn't understand it. I'm ashamed to admit that I neglected him until the early 80s, when I bought a copy of *Tropics of Discourse* (1978), after which I went back to *Metahistory*, rereading it through the later volume of essays. After that, Hayden became my critical guide through the types of history that then constituted the 'historical theory' field, a field that, compared with Hayden's work, seemed myopic, sterile and, often, just plain dull. Indeed, Hayden's theorizing – coupled with the fact that he seemed to say everything so unerringly 'right' and in a style that was at once so analytically powerful and so memorably epigrammatic (such that looking over his texts now I can hardly read them since they are so underlined and contain so many marginal comments) – well, these texts were so different from anything else I had read that they just seemed to come from nowhere. Accordingly, it was Hayden's theorizations which became my touchstone, a way of looking that gained increased momentum with my further reading of his various books and papers as they appeared. I've never looked back, nor have I really looked elsewhere; my thinking about Hayden's texts fused with other reading such that there is a sense in which 'reading White' has taken on the mantle of a Badiou-like *Event*: an immanent, transformative break after which things just never ran the same and to which I have remained faithful; an act of fidelity to a certain 'truth' which, like all fidelities, necessitates reflexive, critical development but which has only served to strengthen my original commitment. Why not say it, Hayden is an intellectual hero of mine.

The final paragraph. When I first read Hayden – over thirty years ago now – I never thought that I would meet him. But over the years – on his occasional visits to London, at various conferences in Europe and England, over the telephone and, more latterly, via email, I have got to know him a little. And on every occasion when we have met (even when he rebuked me for 'falling asleep' whilst on a panel …), he has been unfailingly kind and supportive. A complex mixture of laid-back modesty and forceful assertiveness with more than an edge, a man who doesn't suffer fools gladly and yet who is incredibly generous to his often far from generous critics (*many* of whom are very foolish indeed), there is a moment – I relate it somewhat anecdotally – that has stayed in my mind in a way which typifies Hayden for me. In 1997, when passing through London, he agreed to an interview. Published in 1998 in a slightly edited form as 'A Conversation with Hayden White' (Jenkins 1998, 68–82), our discussion, which lasted for about three hours, was finally brought to a close when I asked him about criticisms of his work: was he happy to live with them, even the unjust ones? And his reply was as follows:

> My attitude about the books and articles I have written is that you write them, you send them out and if people can use the stuff that's fine. If they want to use it in a distorted form, if they want to adapt it, let them do it. That's what intellectual work is all about, if they don't like it, let them reject it, do it better. Collingwood used to say, 'I don't engage in polemics.' He used to say if you don't like my ideas do them better. It's no good getting angry about things, these are ideas which we are trying out in as interesting a way as we can. And I agree with that.
>
> (Jenkins 1998, 82)

And I just want to conclude by saying that actually, for me, 'nobody does it better ... '[2]

Notes

1 For a brilliant essay on argumentation see, Bennington 2001, 34–56 (with a reply by Derrida).

2 A slightly different version of this article will appear in a *festschrift* for Hayden White (edited by Frank Ankersmit, Ewa Domanska and Hans Kellner) in 2009 (*Refiguring Hayden White*), published by Stanford University Press.

References

Ankersmit, F. 2006. "Presence" and myth. *History and Theory* 45, no. 3: 328–36.

Barthes, R. 1997. The discourse of history. In *The postmodern history reader*, ed. K. Jenkins, 120–23. London: Routledge.

Bennington, G. 2001. For the sake of argument (up to a point). In *Arguing with Derrida*, ed. S. Glendinning, 34–56. Oxford: Blackwell.

Cohen, S. 2000. The "use and abuse of history" according to Jean-François Lyotard. *Parallax* 6, no. 4: 99–113.

—— 2006. Essay on Lyotard. In *History out of joint*, ed. S. Cohen, 182–202. Baltimore: Johns Hopkins University Press.

Davies, M. 2006. *Historics*. London: Routledge.

Glendinning, S., ed. 2001. *Arguing with Derrida*. Oxford: Blackwell.

Jenkins, K. 1998. A conversation with Hayden White. *Literature and History* 7, no. 1: 68–82.

Kearney, R., ed. 1995. *States of mind*. Manchester: Manchester University Press.

Laclau, E. 1996. *Emancipations*. London: Verso.

Olmsted, W. 2006. *Rhetoric*. Oxford: Blackwell.

Rancierre, J. 1992. *The names of history: On the poetics of knowledge*. Minneapolis: University Press of Minnesota.

Rorty, R. 1989. *Contingency, irony, and solidarity*. Cambridge: Cambridge University Press.

Steedman, C. 2001. *Dust*. Manchester: Manchester University Press.

White, H. 1978. *Tropics of discourse*. Baltimore: Johns Hopkins University Press.

——. 2006. The public relevance of historical studies: A reply to Dirk Moses. *History and Theory* 44, no. 3: 333–8.

16 Sande Cohen

On the verge of newness

In 2006 Sande Cohen – who I had briefly corresponded with previously – kindly sent me a copy of his *History Out of Joint* (Baltimore: Johns Hopkins University Press, 2006) and I was, as they say, 'blown away by it'. Now, I had read all of Cohen's previous books but, because of other interests at the time, had been unable to use them. Reading *History Out of Joint* suddenly made me realise what a mistake I'd made, and so I went back and read them again, along with a few essays by Cohen which I had. The result was a compounding of my experience of being 'blown away'; Cohen's writings are, for me, absolutely brilliant. Yet, although Cohen was by no means unnoticed in the history world, popular he was not; on every reading list he was not. But I thought he deserved to be.

This background partly explains this paper. The other part goes like this. I asked the Editor of *Rethinking History* journal, Alun Munslow, if I could guest-edit an issue on Sande Cohen. Alun agreed. I then got in touch with Sande and explained what I wanted to do; would he give this his blessing and maybe write a paper for the issue? He said yes on both counts and the issue came out (with essays, in addition to Cohen's and mine, by Martin Davies and Mark Mason) in late 2008. Not only that, Sande came to London to give a paper at the IHR (University of London) Philosophy of History seminar in late 2007 (see my comments on the seminar on p. 239) and proved to be as brilliant a speaker as he is a writer. Cohen is a genuine intellectual, a formidable theorist and right about so many things concerning 'historical culture' that I urge everyone who reads this to read Cohen: it could be a life-changing experience.

No one comes from, or writes from, nowhere. Everyone has a position, a set of core beliefs which, held with varying degrees of flexibility and reflexivity as at least axioms, broadly govern the way *their* world is *made* to make sense to *them*. And Cohen is no exception, except perhaps for the fact that, amongst historians, he is so overt about the historico-political position he occupies: no one could wittingly mistake Cohen's distinctive voice for anyone else's. So what is Cohen's general position: the voice which articulates his desires and, I imagine, his hopes for their realization?

Well, I see no reason not to locate Cohen where he locates himself, as a man of the existential left with anarchistic tendencies (opposition to all received authorities and dogmas) (Cohen 1986, 12). From whence one of his aims is to deconstruct – to fracture, to block, to jam the codes – and thus go beyond the existing ways in which Capital (especially Capital but also every other social formation which indentures the vast bulk of their populations to various intensities of exploitation) – is *affirmed* by naturalizing, mythologizing and therefore ideologizing discursive practices such as to make existing arrangements appear to be, 'realistically', the only possible way things can and should be, 'forsaking all others'. And Cohen's kind of deconstruction (of a non-flamboyant, non-Derridean kind) (ibid., 12), this fissuring, this cracking open, is done in the hope that it might *reveal* (let me use this word for now), unformed and untapped as it might be, the realm of a bottled-up *excess*, a kind of Lyotardian and/or Deleuzean creative energy that might figure-forth genuinely new 'lines of flight', genuinely new possibilities relatively uncontaminated by the old. And although this may be too programmatic for Cohen's taste, it might nevertheless be useful, illustratively, to briefly compare his position to that of Alain Badiou who, in his *The Century* (2007, 178), builds his 'formalized in-humanism' on Foucault's radical anti-humanism, an anti-humanism which, following in the wake of the (interrelated) deaths of both God and the figure of the 'old humanistic man', unfolds a space wherein it is possible to think differently as radical anti-humanism builds on the theme of godless man as an opening, a chance, an endlessly receding horizon of possibilities uncluttered with the weight of too much previous baggage. We now need, writes Foucault, 'to think without immediately thinking that it is man who is thinking'; to think 'in the void left by man's disappearance' and so '*begin* to think' (ibid., 173). And to think, returning now to Cohen, not least beyond those (contingent) 'historical' timings of time by cultural clocks all-too-familiar to us as they frame what we do and do not 'have time for'. And to think through a range of concepts (dispossession, discrepancy, the differend, eternal recurrence, repetition and difference, lines of flight, the Event …) and through a range of names designated by Nietzsche as 'wicked'; those 'wicked thoughts' which, disobedient and responsive to no reactive coding mechanisms, no affirmative agendas, open up a future beyond the daily tread-mill grind 'the past' has seemingly led up to. Here 'the past' (the 'before now') perhaps at last fulfils its destiny as, fading away in the receding mists of time, it gets placed where all things 'past their time' *ought* to be placed: behind us. Here history is trumped by a future not shackled by the present and the past but freed from them by a positive 'will-to-forget': 'Anticapitalism', writes Cohen, 'is not compatible with any form of historicism' (1986, 10); his analyses isolate 'those history functions that … promote the myth that history is a condition of knowledge' (12).

Now, in the light of just these few early remarks, I want to take it as an *axiom* for my own reading of Cohen that he holds as a major constituent of his overtly expressed political position the long held thematic that we should, put at its strongest, effectively 'forget history' or, in a weaker version, should say, for example, 'that historical representation is just material for discussion – we wish to test ourselves with it instead of stepping into its comfort zones'

(2006, 261). And I say 'long held thematic' because I think that Cohen has remained faithful to four *axioms* (he calls them hypotheses) which he first presented in book form in *Historical Culture* (1986). Now, the details of how these four axioms receive many rearticulations constitute, perhaps, the interpretive bulk of this paper but, still in prefacing mode, an outline of them might help us to orientate ourselves to Cohen's general way of thinking and to the style of its expression as he analyses history in general and – his main focus of attention – academic history/history culture in particular.

I take Cohen's *first* axiom, appearing *inter alia* and to be accompanied by three numbered axioms in *Historical Culture*, to be that the actuality of the past (*res gestae*) is best understood as being riven by class (and related) conflicts which, read over the long term enable him to claim – with and through Lyotard – that the West was (and is), wherever it was (and is), destructive: 'always a slaughter bench' (Cohen and Lotringer 2001, 293). In the 'face of Enlightenment controls that do not disturb capitalist reproduction, Lyotard and others proposed that one might think of the West as a colossal *monad*, devouring the future' (293). History (*historia rerum gestarum*) ensconced as it is in academia, is complicit here:

> As a prose culture, academic discourse does not promote forms of knowing that threaten the accumulation of surplus value, the constant of capitalist exploitation. From this angle, it is an open issue whether academia has been a disaster upon culture, projecting upon the social endless idealizations of literature, technology (expertise), and so on, while mass illiteracy has speeded up. The function of most systematic academic codes of signification is to muffle and contain, displace and reduce, pseudo-synthesize and thereby recode multiple social-intellectual contradictions, dispelling the latter's intellectual force … 'painlessness' for the mind, as Nietzsche put it. Exploitation of labour is ceaselessly remade the most universal constant of society and {yet} appears in innumerable academic formulations as normal.
>
> (Cohen 1986, 15)

It is such reasoning that leads Cohen to succinctly state his *second* axiom: that history discourse is inextricably bound up with the complexities/contradictions of previous and current class struggles which, in its academic forms, locates it unevenly but persistently on the side of dominant hegemonic forces as a reactive/affirmative discourse: 'my … hypothesis {axiom} concerning academic history is this: by imposing the form of story, academic history reproduces a culture of {ostensibly} common language, common society, or common reality in the face of uncommon language (codes), class society, and uncommon realities (chasms between cultural worlds)' (Cohen 1986, 16). Academic history culture thus overwhelmingly steers the apparatus of cultural containment, fostering intellectual channels of transmission that exclude loss of meaning and direction (cultural vertigo), and the 'decoding of value' (loss of values). Western culture legitimates and privileges 'its' culture by historicizing it: histories include and exclude, ordering and bossing the past around, forcing it into required shapes; histories give pedagogical advice (all those lessons), ensuring that 'no "living" struggles are recognized until compared and reduced to an exchange "with the past"' (Cohen 1993, 85), all of this displacing attention to what is actually going on.

Out of which arguments axiom *three* emerges, an axiom that underlines the theoretical (and practical) limitations and intellectual incoherence of both narrative representations and the 'historical' methods used to produce them. For although Cohen can *imagine* the idea of history as a coherent and valid activity, as soon as he actually reads histories he finds himself 'plunged into multiple semantic, logical, psychological, theoretical and other such ideations', and therefore 'complications', such that he thinks he can argue that 'there is no way the historian's narrative can acknowledge – and remain a narrative – the gaps and codings of gaps between their utterances and some "collective subject of narration"' (Cohen 1986, 13). It is thus no surprise that history texts self-destruct under close methodological and linguistic examination; no text can survive intact a close reading. The finished 'book form', which appears so solid, so accomplished, so true, is simply a cover for yet another failed representation. For history is made up, after all, of a schizoid-making hotch-potch of contingent factors which defy methodological controls and epistemic surety. By (say) depleted traces, chance survivals and archival opportunities; by cultural pressures, ideological preferences, multiple guesses and hunches, hazardous extrapolations, inferential problematics, enthymemic logic, arbitrary structurings and emphases, etc. – not to say narrative devices of trope and emplotment, argumentative and polemical pressures, compositional forms, rhetorical fancies, all of these and more mixed and remixed with personal abilities, ambitions and desires, levels of attention and concentration, peer and publishing pressures, personal-to-holder theses and so on and so forth, elements combining/recombining in never stable interconnections so to produce histories ('history effects') as *illusio* which, since they have no fixed object of enquiry nor definitive method can, as Aristotle pointed out long ago, only furnish materials for inconclusive argumentation of a rhetorical, aesthetic type. And so it's stretching credulity to breaking point to think that from such 'mixed origins' such a concoction could ever have been held to constitute a 'discipline', let alone the sometime ambition to be a science. In which case it is difficult to see how anybody came to let such a phenomenon gain any influence, to have ever taken its epistemic claims seriously for a moment. Moreover, *none* of the above 'factors' – all of which are factors inherent in *every* history as they help constitute the 'conditions of possibility' of such a discourse (not least Cohen's and mine) – are found in the past; none are discoverable in that famous 'archive'. And, talking of the archive, Cohen notes that although historians are prepared to go to the wall to defend archival research (as the 'source' of that 'facticity' and that 'being there' which ostensibly constitutes the epistemic/'moral' bulwark against scepticism and relativism), not a single instance of doing archival research has ever been presented: 'to present the act of research one would have to have a *literary record of the sensations of reading and thinking about* these documents, that is, an immediate presentation that is not "research", not the vaulted act of research itself' (Cohen and Lotringer 2001, 295). Who knows what actually goes on during those unrecorded decision-making processes historians 'have in mind' between the sharpening of their HB pencils?[1]

Thus I think that Cohen has some pretty good reasons for asserting axiom *four*; namely, that there is no primary object or complex that warrants calling forth the signifier history since it 'does not coincide with any semblance or purport other than its articulated sign functions' (Cohen 1986, 21), Cohen going on to 'formally' define history as

> A concept of last resort, a floating signifier, the alibi of an alignment with obligatory values. It pertains to no signified at all; depending on how the past is positioned, it can preclude confusion of temporal coordinates, preserve the imaginary idea of collective relations, substitute when for where, or dismiss present intensities. 'History' must be radically severed from 'past': the former is always calibrated with cultural contradictions, whereas the latter is much more fluid a notion. 'Past' is involved with both active and involuntary memory, but 'history' can only project the simulation of the remembered.
>
> (ibid., 329)

Consequently, the ostensibly binding ties affected by history through its closures are now recognized as interminably unstable, 'open' to ruination. And so it really is a question for Cohen (and for all of us) of just how 'history culture' remains so (apparently) resilient when surely no one can really believe in its quite arbitrary ways of carving up time and space, its contingent emphases, its rankings, periodizations and so forth, as it blithely (and apparently innocently) goes about what Cohen sees as its *primary* function in capitalist social formations: *removing new claimants from the future by historicizing them away in ways precluding the legitimation of their claims*. Language is fantastic – it can make things (and people(s)) appear and disappear – and so can histories. Purged of disturbingly awkward differences, then, academic history becomes a major bulwark against unwanted change, against 'potential' chaos and the potentially chaotic (I mean, if the 'happenings' of the past and the present were recorded as by a 'giant world-historical camera' (Ermarth 2004, 78),[2] then things would appear chaotic, so why are there no histories of chaos, chaotic histories? By what magical methods does chaos melt down into smooth, cool historicizations?). Well, the reasons/explanations are not difficult to find: not anyone can have the past (and thus be on the high-road to the future); there have to be safeguards (all those peer-approving mechanisms of the profession) against the idea that the past can be read 'any way you like', against that old relativist bogey-man. Only 'workable pasts' need apply for current employment. And so one might well expect to find inscribed on the graves of most academic historians thriving in the closeted atmosphere of those 'debates' and 'controversies' that make academic life and history so 'enjoyable', the legend, in life as in death: 'do not disturb'.

Cohen wants to disturb. For him every historical representation seems to be a cover for something. No matter how seamlessly put together the past and present and future are, they are always 'out of joint', never self-identical, never definitive, always the mere occasion for 'other' readers, 'other' readings to come along. For if, as Cohen (rightly) argues, all that one has available in making temporality and duration 'historical' are traces, are polysemic *signs*, then 'the historian's research is no guarantee of objective sense, of common being, but only another *medium* of cultural filtering' (Cohen 2006, 11). Agitation and disturbance thus become Cohen's strategy; to release the present and the future from the dead weight of the past his aim. The future is *not* the property of the past, so that Cohen's drive is to undercut the way capitalism 'naturalizes' its worst privation: the way it 'locks up time' (Cohen 1993, xviii). Cohen's gaze is fixed firmly on alternative futures: things *can* be done differently there.

But isn't all of this, one could say, in all its radical, possibly revolutionary way, just too simple, too hyperbolic, too wrong-headed, too conspiratorial, too romantic and so just, well, so utterly unrealistic? What will we *actually* do with all that freedom to be what we have not yet been, but *ought* to be? Well, yes of course. Relative to the current 'state of the situation' and the ideological processing mainstream academic historians produce to make it appear as if they and the past were just made for each other, what Cohen is suggesting makes little sense. Keyed into contemporary culture in the ways in which history is, Cohen's analyses seem far-fetched and his possible alternative well, just anarchistic – it looks as if what he is suggesting is a way of producing 'another Beirut' as he puts it; another Iraq we might say. And, yet ... if we think about our world for only a moment, can we really remain so complacent about how things are? For if we – we overwhelmingly over-stuffed inhabitants of the West – if we think, as we wobble down our shopping malls, trolleys loaded with thousands of surplus calories, if we think as we settle down on our settees with our pizzas to watch on television, nightly, fellow human beings huddled in refugee camps dying for lack of basic hygiene and aspirins with yet another genocide and manufactured famine around every other corner (as Cohen notes as an example, one-third of the world's population – over two billion people – have no daily, reliable source of potable water), along with urban deprivations of various kinds blighting inner cities globally – well, if we think anything at all as we watch such 'spectacles', then cannot we ask why on earth historians, who oft aspire to 'understand the world in which we live', cannot actually try to think about changing it. Cannot historians, as privileged intellectuals, do something other than think backwards? I mean, the present day is rarely *damaged* by mainstream academic historians. Well, speaking generally – and *excluding* from this somewhat blanket condemnation radical historians and others who do very much see these and other manifold injustices as infusing their writings/actions with life – Cohen does seem to have had enough, ethically/politically speaking, of our narcissistic backward glances and our precious career trajectories, enough of our thinking, commonsensically, that 'historically' the future will be (to use a Martin Davies phrase) just 'the same old thing'. As I read him, Cohen thus stands, if he stands anywhere, 'on the verge of newness'. And I think he challenges us all to think why we shouldn't join him even at the expense of seeing 'history as we have known it', and maybe history as such, *disappear*.

From history to nihilism

Cohen's critique of the locations/functions of historical culture in advanced social formations – and especially contemporary capitalism – doesn't come, as one *could* have expected, from the Marxist left, but from a Nietzschean informed analysis of it as nihilistic, an analysis he gives, for example, in the three sections that constitute much of his Introduction to *Academia and the Luster of Capital* (1993): 'Memories of an Ex-Historian', 'Society without History' and 'Capitalism after Nietzsche'. And I want to use these sections to bridge the gap between the above prefacing remarks and the sections that follow this one, since they allow me to position Cohen as being an essentially *binary* thinker.

Like Nietzsche, then, Cohen takes it that there is no intrinsic value, no residual meaning – or none that is ever 'discoverable' – in anything, not least history. And he therefore asks, so where does meaning (representations/simulacra) come from and who benefits by it, bypassing the 'historical' answer which generally grants priority to pre-selected subjects of narration and hegemonic ways of figuration and territorialization in ways suggesting that the past and history are synonymous, commodifying the historicized past as a convenience (food) for capital to feed off in favour of the view that, given the lack of any given meaning then the opportunity is there to create alternative readings which don't intravenously drip into the body politic but would be rejected by it. In this way strange new *priorities* could emerge. These are priorities which are explicitly ahistorical and argumentative and which would 'help one to forget narrative persuasion in an active manner – such that one draws more distinctions, erects even more elaborately complex differentiations, and activates singularities, all the while aware of the tremendous attractive energy of narrations to come, already sent from somewhere else' (Cohen 1993, xiii). These are thoughts 'out of joint' with the times, untimely, unseasonal thoughts, Nietzsche's 'wicked thoughts', thoughts with an escape velocity from our current conditions: 'everything is permitted' thoughts. Accordingly, since such thoughts cannot be thought in the languages of the past, of tradition ('and yet we do not find ourselves in this present') there thus arises the need for new languages without memory, without history, *against* representation. The production of a language such that 'a body or a word does not end at a precise point', that resists absorption into old idioms so to form passages to elsewhere, an elsewhere with only beginnings and where every sentence leaves off with an etcetera; no full stops …

Consequently the chapters in *Academia* (1993), like those in *History Out of Joint* (2006) some 13 years later (and perhaps like all of Cohen's writings), are essentially Nietzschean. In what more specific sense? Well, for example, Cohen articulates his preference for Nietzsche's *active* nihilism over history in general and academic history in particular by essaying his objections to Marxism, a historical phenomenon through and through. For, though a thinker of the left, Marxist thought is just *too* historical for Cohen. It presents itself as the only *true* rival to capitalism since it conceives of itself 'as the only claimant worthy of the "whole of history" … and the latter's "journey"'; here an 'altogether speculative "knowledge of history" is transposed or displaced onto the political-cultural realm as "critical theory" or "unity of theory and practice" or "historical awareness", phrases devoted to judging claims (to represent, to mean)', as if it were the real grounds for an ontological and epistemic fix (1993, xvi).

Against this, what makes Nietzsche a more useful writer about the cultural/ideological relations that help to define capitalism as nonhistorical and (important for Cohen's 'binarism') nondialectical, is that Nietzsche is able to argue that Capital is nihilistic and not 'historical' at all; that it just is without value gradations based on foundations or essence(s), just is nonteleological, just is randomness codified. Stripped down to its bare-bones (bare-life, perhaps) contemporary existence just is capitalistic and capital just is exploitive and conflictual, conditions masked by all manner of 'historical contextualization', all those 'necessary relations', those 'stages of development' (going where?) … which make history a reactive/affirmative, complicit discourse. It is therefore one of Cohen's tasks to nihilize capital, to rip it out of time. Here capital is 'not one with the category of labour, or even of assigned values (division of labour), but is instead associated with the success of nihilism': nihilism is the 'origin of modernity and not the fairy tales of progress, growth, development, result, end' (1993, xvii), a nihilism that is now particularly reactive: *passive nihilism*. For if capitalism's supreme goal is, as Deleuze says, 'the production of lack – for only by increasing production can production be the screen of what we don't have – then a critical intellectual *perspective* cannot be attached to the virtues of intellectual translation and mediation, opposition, negation, synthesis, hope, restoration, melancholy' (Cohen 1993, xix) … or history. For Cohen, then, historical culture is one of the key ways in which the contingencies of life can appear meaningful/necessary; yet, *none* of the compelling problems we confront today are inherently 'historical'. Which is why the suspension (at least) of history is now on the agenda: *contra* Fredric Jameson's famous phrase, history *doesn't* hurt; *life* hurts.

Cohen's axiom that capitalism just is nihilistic and that this can be worked advantageously *sans histoire*, depends at this point on a distinction between reactive/affirmative/*passive* nihilism, and active, *creative* nihilism. Thus, thoughts (and experiences) are reactive when they exclude uncomfortable and potentially uncontrollable sense; to be reactive is to place future possibilities within 'realistic limits' set by the past; to be reactive is to limit the number of concepts in contention, to shy away from *agonistics* as permanent openings to hegemonic/counter-hegemonic conflicts and disagreements that need to be heard, instead of managing and massaging them into an ostensible consensus, their strangeness/unwelcomeness snuffed out as they become neutered by those famous 'liberal tolerances'.[3] Well, Cohen wants nothing of this, yoking to his readings of Lyotard and Deleuze Jean Baudrillard's verdict that the 'contemporary scene sets up a *symmetry* between "productive criticism" and a world that absorbs and even benefits from negativity: "hypertrophy, a world that cannot manage to give birth. All these memories, all these archives, all this documentation that do not give birth to a single idea, all these plans, programmes and decisions that do not lead to a single event ... " Intellectuals, break off' (1993, xxi).

Now, it seems to me that it is the acceptance by Cohen of Baudrillard's *symmetry*, of juxtaposing nihilistic capital as all absorbing sponge and nihilism as a fantastically creative springboard, of an opposition between reactive and active nihilism (and as we shall see in the next section, the *juxtaposition* of event against representation, of language which ties and language which undoes, between 'normal' history and the abnormal temporalizings of Lyotard and Deleuze, and between the continued presence and the disappearance of history ...), that all of this schizoid tension confirms what I have already hinted at, namely, that Cohen is essentially a *binary* thinker. For I cannot detect in Cohen much evidence of any kind of *sublation*, any trace of dialectics, of syntheses. Just oppositions leading to possible openings: 'I no longer project academic writing as a transcendence (resolution) at all; its products are not part of any dialectic whatsoever, regardless of the fate of any specific academic text' (1986, 5). Cohen therefore has always thought, I think, in twos not threes; it is not obvious – and I don't think Cohen wants it to be obvious – where we might 'end up': 'How can we make a sense of "destiny"', he writes, 'that is less narrative and more a question of selections created from different levels of existence? How to make goals less interesting than new processes of engagement with the world ... [how can we make sure *not* to shrink] the future to our [existing] political and cultural sizes' (2006, 9.17). Well, yes indeed, and so I would not want it to be seen as a *complaint* against Cohen that he thinks in twos, in oppositions without end, since it is precisely Cohen's oppositional (take no prisoners) approach, his refusal to essay comfortable outcomes, that casts into such sharp relief so much of contemporary 'historical culture'. Accordingly, in the short expositions that follow I want to indicate why I think that Cohen's oppositional thinking is so very productive and (as we shall see in conclusion) so indexical – even 'inevitable'.

On four oppositions

At the risk of arbitrary compartmentalization it might be useful, expositionally, to place just four of Cohen's oppositions into separate sections: (1) on passive versus active nihilism; (2) on reactive versus active language; (3) on narrative versus the event; and (4) on the continuation versus the disappearance of history – Cohen going with the *latter* term in each of these couplets.

On passive versus active nihilism

Cohen distinguishes passive from active nihilism, approving of the latter. Thus, active nihilism might be seen (as in, say, Nietzsche and Deleuze) as creative and inventive such that the power of transformation, based on will, is the primary definition of activity. Here active forces are seen as the exclusive sources of action and energy. Consequently, as the names suggest, passive or reactive forces are not in themselves an originary force so much as 'the form that active force (which alone acts) takes on when it is interiorized or reflected back against itself' (Hallward 2006, 64).[4] Passive/reactive nihilists are thus on this reckoning the vast bulk of humanity who, recognizing (intuitively, perhaps) the meaninglessness and absurdity of life, shy away from confronting this 'catastrophe' by variously disavowing it as they recode meaninglessness into various forms of domesticating reassurances, including historiographical ones: 'the uses and abuses of history refers [to the way history is] brought to various cultural functions, such as making hierarchies (of time, telos), ideals, judgements of taste, political filiation and more' (Cohen 1998, 3). Passive nihilism (misrecognized as normality) thus permeates historical cultures as it negates scepticism and the reduction of value to taste (will). Passive nihilism can thus be thought of as the affect of a near-overdose of order-words; here passive nihilism 'pertains to the suppression of linguistic unreliability rendered in certainties … passive nihilism means we go on and on trying to extract some "surplus" [value] of language and power instead of radically transforming the way we do such work' (ibid., 4). And contemporary academic history is, for Cohen, *par excellence* of the latter type, *re*-thinking, *re*-figuring, *re*-articulating, *re*-considering, *re*-vising, *re*-viewing, *re*-casting ('all the *res*') historical *re*-presentations so that it/they can be *re*-affirmed as *re*-usable, applying 'brake-shoes' to any endless proliferation of readings, of meanings, *re*-turning even sometime aspiring radical texts to safe common-usage in contemporary history cultures. Here Cohen analyses how, in their various ways, texts by, say, Appleby, Jacob and Hunt, Sobchak and Ginzburg (in a brilliant chapter on Ginzburg in *Passive Nihilism*; Cohen 1998, 127–62),[5] Butler and Friedlander and, I'm afraid, Jenkins, all make history safe for ease of consumption: passive nihilists in action.

Thus, by way of example, my own *On 'What is History?' From Carr and Elton to Rorty and White* (Jenkins 1995), by its replacement of the former duo by the latter, makes history *re*-usable by suggesting the abandonment of modernist 'history as such' in favour of making the postmodern histories being advocated 'clean and upfront'. Here the antidote to old modernist fake objectivism is a 'rhetoric that returns to the autobiographic as a better mode of such "dialogue" and "conversation" in which the expression of the "subjective position of the author" is made the minimum condition for even imagining the "objective" and the critical'. Stunningly, writes Cohen, autobiography 'is not "read" in Jenkins' model as a mode of writing, as syntaxes and meaning that might be discrepant with the author, but is maintained as a mode of writing purified of difficulties' (1998, 18). Here 'clean autobiography' – high levels of reflexivity – allows *history* to continue *re*-vitalized, *re*-cycling it back into academia now safely 'brought up to date' where it ends, emasculated, another recommended text on this or that reading list, all energy spent. If only Cohen wasn't so right; this is causing me to worry as to whether I've learnt my lesson!

And so, obviously, Cohen himself does not want to be so *re*-cuperated (it being for this reason that he deliberately writes 'hard books' – no easy assimilation here – and why, ironically, he may see his uncompromising position compromised by this very paper): Cohen's writings stand four-square against passive nihilism. Instead of being *re*-turned into the safe-harbour of 'historical debate', instead of the *re*-turn of his scepticism and relativism into the arms of scholarly caution and liberal pluralism, Cohen's own texts are, he hopes, too *excessive* to fall prey to emasculating *re*-codings. Cohen writes excessively for 'excessive readers' beyond *re*-inscription, not least by his preference for strangifying, difficult, *active* language.

On reactive versus active language

We know, or at least we claim that we know even as we forget, that history is *coded*; that it is language and value-based and, as such, cannot have a 'natural' basis. Consequently, historiography always returns us *not* to the past *per se*, to 'how it essentially was' and 'is', but to training, discipline, convention and norms, cultural operations before they are historical or 'natural' in their formation and outcomes (Cohen 1998, 128). Language as discourse is thus imbricated in power relations (struggles) and therefore acts as a key to the examination of both conserving and deconstructing works, to already well-embedded articulations and future other-ings. And such language, whether conserving or deconstructing/promising, always operates (as representation, as simulacrum) at one remove from being able to definitively know or access phenomena 'plain'. For 'bare' phenomena are always – precisely by being metamorphosed into 'reality' by language – both simultaneously 'revealed' and kept hidden by it. Paul de Man succinctly expresses this anti-representational limit brilliantly:

> … it is not *a priori* certain that language functions according to principles which are those, or which are like those, of the phenomenal world. It is therefore not *a priori* certain that (language) is a reliable source about anything but [itself].
>
> (Cohen 1998, 66)

For both de Man and Cohen it is language which forces the chaotic world – and even our solar system and cosmos – into order: 'look, the sun and the moon *obey* our syntax'. Wherever the chaos and contingency of phenomena are smoothed out, folded up, signed, sealed and neatly tucked up into 'reality', we are in the presence of *reactive* and *violent* language. Thus, language is reactive when 'it employs a syntax that excludes uncomfortable and potentially uncontrollable sense ... to react is to limit the number of concepts in contention' (Cohen 1993, xxii); and it is violent for the simple reason that the claim (by de Man) that language as such cannot definitively coincide with what it is not (which opens out to the much larger suggestion, which Cohen picks up, that it is conceivable that not only is the 'uncontrollable' constituted by language, but also that language is itself 'saturated by uncontrollability'), then, whenever instabilities are closed down, whenever appeals for 'clarity' and 'control' are met, we are in the presence of 'operations that force language to submit to ideology' (1998, 85). Consequently, to allow for the uncontrollability of meaning 'is to allow for the upending of all ideological readings because this allowance plunges one right back into having to choose – what to reveal and impose in any act of language' (88). And it is this uncontrollability which Cohen likes, since it is precisely the textual discrepancies between syntax and semantics which, through the employment of such notions as undecidability, the uncontrollable, the discrepant, etc., open up 'instances of a *war* within representation', a *war* between closure and excess, between reactive and active, excessive readers.

It is on behalf of the excess and excessive readers, and thus against reactive/affirmative uses of language – those carriers of *passive* nihilism – that Cohen gets to work. Cohen has a whole panoply of oppositional concepts all of which help us to read our worded world *disobediently*, surpassing (perhaps) all that has previously been said. For Cohen's *excessive* readers read in ways unthinkable to those writings made for those passive (Nietzschean) 'last readers', new readers who 'scramble' a text's 'marching orders', its instruments for reception, dissembling, disorientating and therefore dispossessing received, dominant codings, producing *discrepancies* that disrupt smooth talk(ers) so opening language up for new *initiatives*.

The 'influences' Cohen draws on to argue all of this (not least Nietzsche and Wittgenstein, de Man, Lyotard and Deleuze) permeate his texts. Thus, for example, Lyotard's notion of *dispossession* is used in several ways. First, it dispossesses 'happenings' of received understandings, emptying out alleged significance. Second, it 'burns up forms': 'the concept acknowledges that things occur that make it impossible for language to represent; this surplus of the signified does not allow for the basic historicist reduction, namely, a representing document' (Cohen 1993, 72). Third, it leaves *events* isolated; unlike the ever-readiness of historiography to familiarize the strange, dispossession opens into what 'remains to be determined; something that hasn't been determined before' (73). Here we are not dealing with an absence, a nothingness or a lack to which meanings can be *re*-stored – for there never was a meaning to lose. Rather there is a *displacement* that opens up spaces for innovation. And finally, in terms of language, dispossession is enacted as a *differend*, a condition of incommensurability, as a thinking that has pulled back from any consensus: 'As the *differend*, dispossession will be like the "unstable state and instant of language wherein something which must be able to be put into phrases cannot yet be"':

> Silence, vague feelings, pausing, postponements, refusal to judge even the most 'obvious' of errors and faults, keeping one's subjectivity out of the way for the 'reception' of regimes of possible signs, and constant delay in affixing names situate 'phrasing' within a virtual bind of (1) the 'impossibility of indifference' and (2) the 'absence of a universal genre of discourse to regulate events. One is always making phrases that are incomplete ...
>
> (74)

Similarly, de Man's notion of *discrepancy* (namely, the impossibility of making any actual expression *necessarily* coincide with what has to be expressed), allows for something *other* to be said: 'the impossible, the uncontrollable, the discrepant, the sublime, all figure as a *war* within representation'. Consequently, to not just allow for discrepancies (and *differends*) but to deliberately produce them so that cracks appear in even the tightest 'epistemic fixture' becomes important: thinking in excess. Always.

Cohen is thus led, by way of summary here, to the point where language allows for the proliferation of semiosis since signs/texts are always caught up within *perplexity*: 'signs are too few for the naming of reality, meanings are too numerous for the precise and unequivocal expression of [one's] "own" ideas ... Meaning outstrips signs' (1998, 90). Yet of this unavoidable condition historians want to know little; to hear nothing of their own terror. History wants 'to maintain a hegemony of recoding, "the sign function that reduced ambivalence and the symbolic"' (90).

Now, this emptying out of all intrinsic meanings and values, this raising of everything that happens ('it happens') to multifaceted, multilevelled readings, endlessly, moves us onto the always tense relationship between Events/events and narrative, a relationship Cohen says he regards as '*the* contested terms of historiography today, and perhaps of political culture in general' (2006, 9).

On narrative versus the event

'Of the many thousands of articles and books concerning the historiographic topics of event and narrative – on their distinctions and modes of connexion – there is a pragmatic acceptance that narrative constitutes the sense of events, a pragmatism that is confident about narrative' (Cohen 2006, 9). Arthur Danto's statement (in his *Analytic Philosophy of History*), says Cohen, covers the event 'with a general description and brings it together with like instances [to suggest] just how commonplace it is for us to think of events as already stories, already "nested" in a medium that events seems naturally and socially to belong to. Narrative is that "written land" (Rancièrre) where, as historical representation, "a true body of words [is] substituted for erratic speech"' (9). And despite over 50 years of powerful critiques of narrative and its affects, opines Cohen, this remains the general position today. Yet this (ontologically mistaken) depiction of narratives as being essentially of 'a natural kind' obviously covers a multitude of sins, the most important of which is that, not being of a natural kind at all (in a culture 'no such thing'), then this leaves histories as always being 'histories for someone' – and especially those someones who benefit from the existing arrangements of capitalist social formations. Accordingly, for Cohen, historical narratives have a far from natural double function; namely, 'that they narrate each past, or segment thereof, putting our knowledge of consequences, often little more than present rationalizations, into a story the past did not know belonged to it', reading 'what never was written', so to use it to 'legitimise strong, contentious, present interests' (254), these two functions allowing me to restate Cohen's central thesis: that narrative historicizations aim to prevent the appearance of new claimants on the future. For historical writing/narration has now become

> virtually a war over claimants in every zone ... claimants over names and processes, claimants to 'firstness', claimants to intensity – to *historicize* ... means to lend time as a power to an existing claim. It is this sense of historical knowledge as deeply selective that marks *to historicize* as a transpolitical manoeuvre carried out in the very act of narrating.
>
> (11)

Such narratives are ubiquitous but, as noted already, always at the cost of keeping the past alive 'otherwise'. In effect, then, in the processes of transforming past *events* into 'historical events' (a process of production since no events ever come to us already 'historical'), the stuffing is knocked out of them. Purged of awkward resistances, bottling-up contingent events so that order is preserved, historical narratives quite literally '*sentence* events to death', disallowing the past to go with any one (else). And Cohen's writing, from beginning to end, resists such sentencing and such imprisonments in the name of a future that will indeed ring with the voices of new claimants and thus, in the process, deprivilege the past: making the future come *first* makes the past and present, before and during, *irrelevant*. For Cohen only the future matters, a future as an event 'to come' and which can come not least by wrenching events *per se* from their settled, narrative-assured locations, and reactivating them excessively, eternally, cutting once again the umbilical cord that sustains the future by way of substances derived from the past. Cohen is thus looking (with Lyotard and Deleuze) to leave the past 'behind'; he suggests that we turn our energies to making events happen again and in the future (returning 'eternally') in ways unforeclosed: 'The mode of the event is the problematic ... sensitive crisis points, turning points, boiling points, knots ... a *tangled tale*' (255).

This reference to Lyotard and Deleuze introduces us again to two of Cohen's favourite theorists and, as usual, they serve him well. In his writings he has used them for all kinds of insights but perhaps never more so than when polemicizing against historical narratives in the name of the disruptive power of the *event*.

Cohen's ways of privileging the event within historical narratives – returning them to ruin – litters so many of his texts that, once again, only the slenderest of accounts can be given here. But the general gist of Cohen's arguments *après* Lyotard and Deleuze might be illustrated by recounting parts of his 'Philosophical Prelude' to *History Out of Joint* (2006) wherein both are used – plus further comments drawn from elsewhere.

Lyotard's most sustained elaboration of narrative and event, Cohen tells us, occurs in his essay on Kant and the French Revolution, 'The Sign of History', wherein he argues that 'Westerners' attunement to historical experience is based on a linguistic and social *inflection*, the name *common being*' (2006, 11), which delivers a pseudocognitive rule of telos or finality or fulfilment. But given that all one has in 'making up' the journey to such an ending are (contingent) traces of the past considered as signs – and because such signs are endlessly polysemic – then such signs, irreducible to just one ending, cannot guarantee (and therefore historical *research* as the search for such a guarantee by embedding signs in nonsaturable contexts cannot guarantee) any definitive objective sense, no real 'common being', but can only present yet just another reading. Thus whereas common being (dominant discourse) would like every representation to turn signs into a genetic or telic pattern, events/signs resist this by their equivocal status.

So, instead of historians being able to make what happened ('it happened') necessary (though not fully determined given capital's – and capitalists' historians – embrace of pluralism and intellectual *laissez faire* – up to a point), so rendering up the past into safe hands, equivocal events can instead act as 'energetic signs' (as 'tensors') whereby events become *agitated* such that narrative forms become actually or potentially incommensurable – 'out-of-joint'. Here smooth absorption flounders, here Cohen's argument that an event transmits an excess of meaning surplus to requirements means that narrative holdings become inadequate vehicles for representation. Consequently (Cohen's) Lyotard argues for the re-emergence of the idea of the sublime; the reassertion of the *external* unfigurability of events such that it is not clear when narration can *ever* become *the* adequate mode of representation. For signs 'indicate that things have happened that require phrases that have not been said, and may not be sayable' in ways we're unaccustomed to; highly strung historians can suffer nervous breakdowns here.

Deleuze compounds Lyotard's arguments, not least in his *Difference and Repetition* (1968), wherein the usual notion of repetition (as the same) is rearticulated as 'repetition as *difference*' and thus as critique, 'connecting it to "reflections, echoes, doubles and souls," to reciprocity and self-implication, as well as to "theft and gift"; that is, repetition as a new kind of *production*, displacing concepts such as beginning, finished, over, telic origins and finalities, a mode of active thought where "at any point in time the returns so far as truth is concerned are not all in"' (Cohen 2006, 14). Here the conjunction of past event and repetition – in a new 'place' – is 'closer to transgression' and not 'a single past that returns in the future': how can 'any rational person not laugh hard at the idea that capital entered the world isomorphic with a benevolent "historical" narrative'? (1993, 91). Repetition, then, is the return of the demand that a previously unknown past be recognized and given power to disturb all that which hadn't yet spoken its name. Deleuze offers events as 'disturbance of narrative containment, conflict between event and narration' (Cohen 2006, 14), a way of negating 'command discourses', slipping events past dominant power politics.

A Deleuzean historiography is therefore against narrative politics of any kind; it resists belonging to any law, to any nature, to any pre-given. Events belong to only one thing: *the future.* Events can become nonlaws and repetitions – considered as event and concepts – tests for the holding power of representations. Deleuze will affirm that consciousness can be made a theatre, one that does not represent but *performs* repetitions, bypassing opposition and mediation – in short, *working* pastness for passage to the future (Cohen 2006, 16). Deleuze asks us to leave events 'hanging' in semantic free-fall, to confront 'asymmetry in the cause'; that is, that we think of events as 'Part of the power of beginning and beginning again … forces of thought which are not the forces of recognition, today or tomorrow … an unrecognised and unrecognisable *terra incognita*'. What dangers can such historiography elicit? (254) Here the negative does not return

> … the identical does not return. The Same and the Similar, the Analogous and the Opposed, do not return. Only affirmation returns – in other words, the Different, the Dissimilar … neither the default nor the equal, only the excessive returns.
>
> (255)

Well, such thoughts as these are not, concludes Cohen, much in discussion in university-based history writing or exchanges in seminar rooms (or anywhere else very much, come to that), and they're not to be expected in the corridors of power where history is built to last by yoking historicizations of temporality to dominant claimants. 'Not to drag their generation to the grave' was the injunction of Nietzsche's 'unhistorical and super-historical, self-experimental quasi-subject' manifested in Lyotard's (and Deleuze's) writings, this to 'the point where … as experimentation with subjectivity … one might invent "allusions to the conceivable which cannot be presented". Of this, contemporary historiography knows almost nothing' (2006, 202).

On the continuation versus the disappearance of history

The theme of 'the end of history' is not, in Cohen's eyes, a version of *post-histoire* (too nostalgic, too historical etc.), but the version of a death – like the death of Nietzsche's God – occasioned by our neglect; out of our having better and more urgent things to talk about. Again this theme pervades so much of Cohen's works that I need to repeat that I can only scratch the surface of one of his richest/'deepest' seams. And for that 'impression' I turn to what I think of as one of Cohen's very best papers; namely, Chapter 4 ('The Disappearance of History') of *Academia and the Luster of Capital* (1993), the following summary of which brings me towards the end of this introductory reading of Cohen.

In a nutshell, then, Cohen's argument – which I put initially into tabular form – goes as follows. *First*, as he traces certain conceptual reasons for the disappearance of history from contemporary social formations, the suggestion arises that *none* of the actual day-to-day problems one confronts are themselves 'really' historical in the very concrete sense in which, say, financial or health problems are concrete (Cohen 1993, 81). Besides, what exactly is *added* to the phrase, 'people living in conditions of poverty in the 1930s', when rephrased as, 'people living in *historical* conditions of poverty in the 1930s'? *Second*, if you cannot give both in general and in particular a material sense to the words 'history' and 'historical consciousness', if there is no compelling sense – no compelling need – 'to the constancy of any "name of history"', then is there any need for any analysis to defer to a so-called 'historical' one? *Third*, despite this lack of conceptual definitiveness, as a discursive practice, as a way of ordering people around, a way of framing events to control them, historical consciousness both prohibits and allows all manner of practices but, strangely, it never seems to legitimate thinking anti- or ahistorically – odd for a profession valorizing disinterest (objectivity). *Fourth*, compounding its lack of definitiveness and thus drawing attention to the arbitrariness of hegemonic usages (closures), is something few historians want to admit; namely, the impossibility of 'historicity': 'to fully "historicize" (contextualize) complicated phenomena of the present-future is intellectually futile, since the more one embeds the "real" in narrated context(s) the more that something will – if it releases any active energies – show itself to be unamenable to our narrative designations' (84). Of course, there are forces (structures, agencies, agents, etc.) 'out there', but these remain uncapturable – think of writing a total or comprehensive or true or objective or authentic 'history of yesterday': what could that possibly be, possibly not be? *Fifth*, when one speaks of having a 'historical sense' one really means 'being able to "recreate" some event or another. [But] this … "recreating the real" by means of narratives … is disappearing both as normal practice and as an increase in revisionism' (84). *Sixth*, historical reason as typically construed is the occasion for laughter:

> If capital ceaselessly redynamizes social relations, where all the historical clocks are transformed into hourglasses on their side, then how could the

> obvious absurdity of there never appearing in person this 'historical reason' linger on? Capital, if it thinks, must think of every raising of the name 'history' in all its forms as the epiphany of the triumph of the spirit world, the past that is waiting for us to 'close it'. This idiotic projection into the past of its being turned towards us is just another figure which suppresses what historical writing despises: those 'strange flows which circulate' (Deleuze) and not in ways that return to ... [familiar] conjugations.
>
> (83)

What is strange here is the idea of a past that is turned towards us rather than seeing its 'flows' as just 'flows', irrecuperable into any particular/necessary *unity*, cut adrift from any 'specific heading'. Here the disappearance of history is that slipping out of control, that lack of correspondence between a time-consciousness and a directionality ostensibly possessing one's objective or subjective identity with capitalist-driven times/timings. History quietly drifts away here. It's reductive equations, whose 'typical form is that of a past recognized by present names, which in turn equals the construction of a future that resembles the present', is now faced by a surfeit of names that, uncontrollable by 'history' as they cannot be 'plugged into existing "uni-forms" and identities', break free, recognizing that the narrated past as something objective – with its linear perspectives, appropriate emplotments, resolutions of conflicts, absence of subjective markers – is simply a sleight of hand whereby the attempt is made to try and ensure a falsely objective future as the necessary one. Well, no such thing.

Against all of which failings Cohen suggests as the antidote linguistic scepticism and political intervention whereby the past and the present do not add to the burden of the future, whereby a new aim can be articulated: *to try not to injure the future*. And, starting with that section of his chapter entitled 'Leaving is Not Psychological', Cohen sketches out, in some of his most positive writing, the clear benefits of leaving the (historicized) past behind.

Let me retabulate as I briefly list just some of these benefits. Thus, *first*, the disappearance of history means that historical consciousness has now been replaced by all sorts of new modes which suggest radical deterritorializations that stress the achronicity of dominant social forms: 'this avoids projecting a symmetrical reversal represented in the normalization of "decline" which seems to be the reflex when the social does not "move forward"' (Cohen 1993, 111). *Second*, instead of a direct confrontation with the powers that be, 'one might imagine the "disappearance of history" as a freeing of one's mind from a burdening weight now acknowledged as unnecessary', and, since historians cannot help with this delinearization, then this might be thought by its difference from order words:

> In the order-world life must answer the word of death, not by fleeing but by making flight act and create. There are pass words beneath order

> words. Words that pass, words that are the components of passage, whereas order-words mark stoppages or organized, stratified compositions · (112)

Pass words are words, and timings, that know nothing of origin or result, beginning and outcome, but await invention. This is an ahistoricity that problematizes the future, a welcoming of events that come from other than the past, creating events 'outside of what is recognized'.

Third, the disappearance of history means that the narrative texts that we customarily deploy are put out of reach 'by treating events as an *excessive being* that provokes one to "respond to a case without criteria" ... Strangify: never historicize' (Cohen 1993, 114). What matters is to effectively amplify the energy, not to succumb to the evasions and stupidities of one's epoch, regardless of what this 'looks like'. And never think in terms of *post-histoire*, which implies an 'after' and hence a recoding. Instead think of how to 'jam the codes', all the terms of 'transportation' that normally carry us safely 'from' and 'to'. Here it is a question of there being new (Deleuzean) 'planes of immanence' which don't offer resistance as much as imply

> ... reverse causalities or 'advanced' determinisms, decoded innate functions related to *acts of discernment* or electron rather than to linked reactions; and *molecular combinations* that proceed by noncovalent bonding rather than by linear relations – in short, a new '*pace*'. (115)

A new *pace*. Exactly. Here the question is whether untimeliness can be taken to new highs and lows; to

> accelerate it or slow it down to the point where it does *something* other than promote linear causalities which are always 'behind and ahead' of necessity forms. In other words, the category of the 'untimely' raises the question of the dislocation from the concerns of going players. (116)

This is, adds Cohen, 'language on the spot' where the only timeliness is that of a generalized *bricolage*. Here, no one series commands the others, the unhistorical is 'plugged in'; chances abound, 'swept on by time without forming a whole or presupposing one ... academic historiography remains Platonic to the extent that it is 'unable to think itself in difference'. 'Platonism' is what one thinks 'when one *knows* in advance what things "look like", the emergent forced to fit with and conform to the already-existing weight of already known sign-systems, the reactive force of *ratio cognoscendi*' ... yet there 'is so much that it is unable to say' (120–21). To say the unsayable, to think the unthinkable, is what Cohen wants to say and think. The aim is a Nietzschean one, a surpassing of what has previously been said, a newness that is not *re*-subjectifying, which knows nothing of all those *res*.

This is a disappearance of 'history as we have known it' that is relaxed and, in a Baudrillardian way, simply *indifferent*. It is *not* the end in the sense of a *re*-volution, or an eschatological break, but precisely the coming to an end of all which has previously made sense – without fuss, without nostalgia, without 'before' and 'after' having any chance of re-establishing an older, social order:

> What I have called a 'disappearance of history' concerns the possibility that reality – as modernity – itself makes 'history' an increasingly archaic connection; nonetheless, as language, this relation belongs to a semantic control code, whose purpose is the historicization of experiences, their verbal reduction to the games and rules of the existing players. I have not minimized how difficult it is to engage in a critique with this formation, but it is disappearing. As it does, so appear possible transformations without 'history'.
>
> (Cohen 1993, 122)

Conclusions

I have three conclusions to draw. *First*, I want to say something to those who already like Cohen, *second*, to those who may need more persuading as to why they should do so and, *third*, to those who would dismiss him pretty much out of hand. And I want to spend most time talking about this last group. For I want to argue that, ironically, far from Cohen being out-of-joint with 'our' times and therefore irrelevant to them, he is in fact indexical with them and that, that being the case, taking Cohen seriously because of his indexicality may make opponents hold less firmly to their anti-Cohen (and their anti-postmodern) position since, not to do so, would make *them* out-of-joint, would make *them* anachronistic/irrelevant. In effect, I want to argue that Cohen is *unavoidable* today. Now, this argument may seem confused and/or just plain wrong, but I hope to make it look right (attractive) in the few paragraphs remaining.

In this paper Cohen is presented as being centrally concerned with academic history and the way in which he embeds this in the wider historical culture read as an ideological component of capitalist reproductive processes/practices. Here it is understood that Cohen offers *nothing* to make existing historians get *smarter* at what they already do by adding some or other theoretical insight, methodological advice or heightened reflexivity. Rather, assuming academic history/historians have (in the main) been and are imbricated in academia *not* to perform the role of radical critique (the thesis of *Academia and the Luster of Capital* 1993), such affirmative/passive history and historians are left to pretty much wither on the vine. As I say, this is the Cohen of this paper, a reading I hope I have made look attractive to those who are already admirers, anything (everything) I have omitted and/or missed being able to be compensated for by their own readings.

To those who may be newer to Cohen or who may need more convincing as to why they ought to take him seriously, I am concerned that the Cohen I have presented may be 'too thin'. By which I mean that, by concentrating only on what Cohen has to say about history and history culture without embedding it within his analyses of the wider culture he himself embeds it in, I have sold him short. Thus, in this paper I haven't touched upon Cohen's detailed analyses of, say, (neo)psychoanalysis, scientific discourse, multiculturalism, 'theory and Los Angeles', Taiwan, Barthian semiotics, aesthetics and art-criticism widely construed, and that whole plethora of critical socio-economic-cultural-ideological analyses which find expression in 'Consumption in an Age of Information' (Cohen and Rutsky 2005), nor the areas I have expected the other contributors to this *Issue* to consider: Derrida, Deleuze and that whole raft of theorizations on academia and the function of history therein. In other words, that whole range of concerns that makes reading Cohen's texts – along with their notes and references – a veritable gold mine for further thought and which I have barely attended to. Behind the 'thin Cohen' presented here there is a very much 'fatter Cohen' who repays close attention massively.[6]

And there is one more thing which possibly unconvinced readers may baulk at but shouldn't; namely, that it is easy to think that Cohen's analyses are just too black and white; that he is swept away by his own good versus evil rhetoric, by his own schizoid framings (by his failure to find, as Lyotard failed to find, an uncompromised *avant-garde* yet his optimism that things can get better), and that his gestures towards future alterities are empty ones. And the Cohen I have presented here – the binary/oppositional theorist – is a Cohen who could all too easily be read as an expression of a previous moment, a sort of throw-back to the 1960s' liberationary rhetoric of a hippyish counterculture, 'let a thousand flowers bloom' type; a futuristic dreamer whose grip on the actual possibilities of current life is slight. What Cohen wants is just not going to happen: best ignore him. And I would urge readers not to dismiss Cohen for any of these reasons, nor succumb to feeling shy about being (though I know it's frowned upon) *enthusiastic*. In other words, I would urge that readers keep their nerve at this point and not dismiss Cohen because he has no blueprint/template for the future he might wish to see realized. For not only is this lack of a detailed futurity perfectly understandable – as I hope to show below – but his *enthusiasm* is precisely what makes him unattractive not least to a discourse – mainstream academic history – that is so serious, so grave. Conversely, what I like about Cohen is his radical, uncompromising dreams of otherness, his infectious celebration of untapped creativity which, in these utilitarian dog-days of business as usual fed by the imperatives of economic efficiency, keeps the spirit of resistance and hope alive. In other words, what I like about Cohen – almost irrespective of whether his analyses are correct or not – is the tone of his work and the *image* of Cohen as exuberant resistance fighter against a contemporary capitalism that cannot, surely, be the best of all possible worlds. But, as it happens, I don't think

Cohen's analyses are wrong nor his (unavoidable) vagueness about the future an impediment to his acceptance, these remarks taking me to my final comments with regard to the *indexicality* of Cohen with 'our' times.

The argument goes like this. 'We' live today in a bourgeois capitalist social formation where the economy has no time or place for *intrinsic value* but only for market value and thus for *exchange value*. And exchange value is, by definition, relative value: the value of X has a value relative to Y depending on supply and demand pressures that are contingently related to the machinations of market forces, etc., etc. Consequently, here in the West – and globally wherever the market cash-nexus is the determinant of value – then exchange/relative value (and thus relativism) runs too. Accordingly, it is inconceivable to think that in social formations so absolutely saturated with relative values that cultural expressions of value – for example the values/value of history – should escape relativism. And they don't. As a result, the days of metanarrative histories (histories where everyday happenings were collected together to form an (imagined) immanent *unity*, a meaning-full whole, thence to be yoked to some or other teleology, a trajectory taking us from the past to the present to an assured future whose contingencies were caught up in 'historical necessities'), well, those days have long gone. And the fragmentation of such (alleged) unities has impacted upon *academic petite*-narratives too which, by no means escaping the desire for unity (for truth, objectivity, the synthetic account, epistemic surety, etc.), have lacked the power to resist their own fragmentation, splintering and breaking apart all those vain attempts to form homogeneous discourses. Here we witness (to put it into Baudrillardian terminology) the *revenge* of the aleatory and the *ludic*, the revenge of the contingent and the relativistic as the (temporary) phenomenon which attempted to bind *everything* together (namely, the attempt by that famous 'experiment of modernity' to achieve 'human rights communities' in bourgeois and proletarian forms – attempts wherein both *meta* and *petite* narratives were integral parts), fell short of its realization amongst the death camps, the gulags and the nation-state sponsored genocides of that most bloody century on record – the twentieth – it being the shortfall of this trajectory, the aftermath of that experiment and the unravelling of the ties that were to bind the particular to the universal, that we are living *through* today. This is our 'post' modern condition, our condition of utter contingency, relativism and anti-foundational/anti-essentialist nihilism. This just is where we are; this is the condition Cohen engages with.

In which case, 'post' modernity and postmodernism (the condition of postmodernity raised to the level of theoretical consciousness), with all its undecidables and its ubiquitous *aporias*, is precisely *indexical* to market capitalism in its 'current phase'. Fredric Jameson's famous verdict is right: postmodernism is the cultural logic of (contemporary) capitalism; postmodernism (shadowing capitalism's flexibilities and its multiple modes/styles of production, circulation, consumption, etc.) just is what the doctor ordered: a capitalism that has to survive by managing high levels of contingency as best it can;

market/exchange value without any unitary end. And until capitalism changes, exchange/relative value is here to stay.

Now, to all those historians who don't seem to get this (because if they did then they surely couldn't write and phrase their anti-postmodern and anti-relativist polemics in the way they do – anti-relativism being what their positions ultimately come down to), historians whose number include the Spiegels, the Bentleys, the Applebys, the Friedlanders, the Ginzburgs, the McCullaghs, the Gormans, the Cannadines, the Roths, the Megills, i.e. pretty much the bulk of the history profession, then postmodernism and relativism merely constitute a temporary *blip*, a blip that might have slightly discomforted some historians and perhaps have made them more reflexive, but which a sensible dose of neo-realism or neo-empiricism or neo-epistemology – or some kind of direct, real, concrete and thus authentic/true experience (sublime or not, it scarce matters) will overcome and see off. Well, I don't think so. For the saturation of capitalist social formations by exchange/relative values *means* saturation, and there is currently no alternative. Relativism just is the air we breathe and there is no other air. And there doesn't need to be. We can live with it, use it.

I think this is exactly what Cohen does. For Cohen *reflects* (if I can use this inadequate concept here) both the exigencies of current capitalist market forces *and* the impossibility of seeing how to *precisely* get out(side) of them. Cohen's texts, as premised on exchange value, relativism, contingency and nihilism, are thus used by him to *both* undercut any residual totalizing tendencies in epistemic and ethical/political closures on the basis of using relativist freedoms offered by the market to (theoretically) free up all those who, within capitalism, need such freedoms (empowering emancipations), *and* to articulate the further hope that such freedoms will escape capitalism's grip as the currently *axiomatic* basis for all thought, so as to usher in substantive freedoms which capitalism cannot itself dream/realize for fear of its very existence.

Accordingly, it is now clear why Cohen is the very last person to conceive this future 'to come' through any kind of definitive scenario which will *arrest* the meanings of words and things. Which is why he can only gesture towards multiple possibilities and creative acts without foreclosure: massive creativity but without prescription ... to make up rules in the absence of rules. It is Cohen's task not just to affirm a different future but to make that future more difficult to control, to hold steady. Breaking the hold of history as it attempts to weld together past, present and future does that. And in this I think he takes his lead from Lyotard and Deleuze and Baudrillard *et al.*, and their arguments against totalizing closure, which such theorists never stopped articulating given their obsessive and wholly justifiable fear of any type of totalitarianism coming back – returning 'differently' of course – but returning nevertheless.

And I like Cohen, just as I like Lyotard *et al.*, for exactly these reasons. We are all – if I might use the royal 'we' – both the products of capitalism (and therefore indexical with it), whilst not being fully governed or determined by it, since freedom conceived otherwise (not least by postmodernists) is not the *property* of capital but is something which, unfulfillable within capital, goes beyond capital's own more formal gestures to seek new worlds. To this way of thinking Cohen, like postmodernity/postmodernism as actuality and potential, is absolutely *not* some mere *blip*; neither, being indexical, can go away, but neither think that capitalism is the alpha and omega of social living. And so for all those who think that history (returning *much more narrowly* now to history/history culture) in its late twentieth- and early twenty-first-century manifestations has somehow withstood relativism and has shrugged off the undecidables and *aporias* of postmodernism, I would just want to say that, whilst such historians as Spiegel *et al.* may well think that they have finished with postmodernism (and Cohen), I'm afraid that postmodernism (and Cohen) have not yet finished with them.

Notes

1 The argument in this paragraph does, of course, apply to all historians/theorists, including Cohen, who has by no means escaped such 'mixed origins'. But at least Cohen recognizes this and is therefore happy to explicitly position himself and then argue for that position as best he can, always falling short of definitiveness. Cohen should not therefore be seen as offering knock-down logical arguments but rather as trying to make his proposals (analyses) as plausible as possible in the hope that they might resonate with others. Who can do more? For this mode of 'argumentation' see the Introduction to Rorty (1989). See also, on argumentation, Bennington's brilliant paper (2001).

2 Ermarth (2004) writes in ways which link up with aspects of Cohen's arguments at this point: 'The purpose of modern historical method … is to permit discovery of the abstract, emergent forms and causalities operating invisibly in sequences of particulars: sequences that otherwise might look random or chaotic if recorded, say, by a giant world-historical camera. Traditional historical writing selects to produce; that is its purpose … Whether the process of empirical rationalization is historical or scientific it treats particulars as evidence or "clues", in other words, as minor material manifestations of larger, more abstract principles and laws. The particulars are discarded once they have yielded their generalizations' (77–8). The problems inherent in this (those of *inference* and *historiality*) are much underestimated by historians.

3 For the kind of politics that are based on the axioms of hegemony and agonistics see, for example, Ernesto Laclau *Emancipations* (1996) and *On Populist Reason* (2005). I'm not certain about Cohen, but I find the position of Laclau close to my own.

4 Hallward's text provides, I think, one of the very best introductions to Deleuze's thought.

5 The chapter on Ginzburg in *Passive Nihilism* is one of Cohen's finest.

6 As will already be clear from my references/notes, I have (primarily) based my reading of Cohen on his books. I have read many – but not all – of his papers. My decision to restrict myself to books was made for two reasons. First, it is Cohen's books that I suspect (new) readers will almost certainly go to initially and I see my introduction as an introduction to aspects of those texts and, second, Cohen's 'position' is found in most detail in his books, and it was this that I was most interested in. I urge readers to go to Cohen for themselves with the hope that I haven't misled, not least because, given the density of Cohen's text, they remain, as I said in the general introduction, 'almost summary proof'. *Apropos* of which (and relating back to note 1) in an email exchange with Martin Davies, to whom I had mentioned the density, the 'summary proofness' and the epigrammatic nature of so much of Cohen's writings, Martin responded as follows: 'Thinking about your comments on Cohen,

it occurred to me that one reason why he is so difficult to summarize is because his readings {writings} are a *performance* rather than an argument. An argument can be summarized and its force still retained, but if the performance is reduced to essentials, these may seem inadequate in relation to the performance. Every so often Cohen produces something pithy and quotable ... but it still isn't like reading Cohen himself.' I think this is spot on.

References

Badiou, A. 2007. *The century*. Cambridge: Polity Press.

Bennington, G. 2001. *For the sake of argument (up to a point)*. In *Arguing with Derrida*, ed. S. Glendinning. Oxford: Blackwell.

Cohen, S. 1986. *Historical culture: On the reading of an academic discipline*. Berkeley: University of California Press.

—— 1993. *Academia and the luster of capital*. Minneapolis: University of Minnesota Press.

—— 1998. *Passive nihilism: Cultural historiography and the rhetorics of scholarship*. New York: St. Martin's Press.

—— 2006. *History out of joint: Essays on the use and abuse of history*. Baltimore: Johns Hopkins University Press.

Cohen, S., and S. Lotringer, eds. 2001. *French theory in America*. New York: Routledge.

Cohen, S., and R. Rutsky, eds. 2005. *Consumption in an age of information*. London: Berg.

Ermarth, E. 2004. *Ethics and method. History and Theory* 43, no. 4: 61–83.

Hallward, P. 2006. *Deleuze and the philosophy of creation*. London: Verso.

Jenkins, K. 1995. *On 'What is History?' From Carr and Elton to Rorty and White*. London: Routledge.

—— 2009, forthcoming. *At the limits of history*. London: Routledge.

Laclau, E. 1996. *Emancipations*. London: Verso.

—— 2005. *On populist reason*. London: Verso.

Rorty, R. 1989. *Contingency, irony, and solidarity*. Cambridge: Cambridge University Press.

17 Cohen *contra* Ankersmit

This, the last paper, was written as a review essay for *Rethinking History* journal.

Here I put together Cohen's *History Out of Joint* (Baltimore: Johns Hopkins University Press, 2006) and Frank Ankersmit's *Sublime Historical Experience* (Stanford University Press, 2005) because, although very different books indeed, I thought I could fruitfully juxtapose them around a theme – central to Ankersmit, more marginal in Cohen – of the sublime. Because (as I explained in the *notes* to the paper) I was beginning to put together the 'Cohen Issue' for *Rethinking History* journal (see pp. 271–294), I dealt at greater length with Ankersmit on this occasion.

Along with Hayden White, Frank Ankersmit had been a major influence on me; I owe him a lot. But I found his *Sublime Historical Experience* a disappointment. I cannot really see – and this not for want of trying – what Ankersmit is trying to do with the idea of sublimity he has for any understanding of historical consciousness, and my review reflects this. This is not to say Ankersmit – like Cohen, like White – is not 'right' about so many things historical; it is only to say that, for me, this latest stage of his historical thinking doesn't really convince.

No one can accuse Sande Cohen and Frank Ankersmit of writing easy books. Indeed, it may well be that the difficulty of their texts has had the effect of lessening their impact on students of history in general (construed here as all of those who produce, or intend to produce, historical works), rather than increasing it; certainly few professional/academic historians or their progeny have the taste or constitution for theorization at this level. But there are doubtless other reasons too, the most important probably being the fact that their specific theorizations make uncomfortable reading for those who populate the more traditional highways and byways of contemporary 'history culture', threatening it with ruin. Taken seriously, Cohen's and Ankersmit's texts raise critical perspectives on both the ideological functions of our history culture and the inevitable shortfall of those empirical/epistemological strivings that overwhelmingly characterize the work(s) of those who live within it. No surprise, then, that they should be relatively ignored or, if and when they are actually 'known', be somewhat disavowed.

But as someone who is also critical of 'traditional' history producers and their continued allegiance to a reductive empirical/epistemological mind-set despite the intellectual/methodological bankruptcy of such a position being, by now, abundantly clear, and who reads all historical productions (including his own) as wall-to-wall theorizations governed by ideological positionings, then Cohen and Ankersmit are vital. With regard to Ankersmit, I have long been influenced by his notions of, for example, narrative logic and narrative substance, by his relatively early and relatively unequivocal championing of postmodern approaches to 'history', by his valorization of the aesthetic nature of history texts and to his work on intertextuality, representation, metaphor and so on. Apart from Hayden White, few others have made me stop and think, take stock of and take in, the problematicizing implications of such 'critiques' of 'normal history'. With Cohen it has been different. Over the years I have read his major texts (*Historical Culture* 1986; *Academia and the Luster of Capital* 1993; *Passive Nihilism* 1998), as well as some of his articles and chapters. But I'm ashamed to say that I have *used* Cohen much less than Ankersmit as a guide to what to best think about contemporary mainstream history/historians and the 'affirmative nature' of the(ir) discourse. Indeed, before reading the book under review – *History Out of Joint* – I had recognized but not fully appreciated just how brilliant Cohen actually is, whereas Ankersmit's excellence had long been registered. And I want to explain, relative to these last remarks, how reading Cohen and Ankersmit together, back-to-back as it were, has made me much regret my sometime neglect of Cohen whilst seeing, for the first time in Ankersmit, a kind of unwelcome pessimism as well as some unconvincing arguments in support of it.

Let me begin to explain this last remark a little before proceeding. For reasons that suit my position, I find Cohen's *History Out of Joint* a blast of fresh air in a discursive practice that is all too often intellectually stuffy and theoretically backward; Cohen is vital, alive, alert, perspicuous. Admittedly, his text is somewhat uneven, and Cohen's style is not only challenging but made more difficult by some odd sentence constructions. But this is nothing. For Cohen's text has made me turn to his other works such that, in my now more attentive mode, I realize just how good Cohen is for all those who would like to think otherwise, 'outside the box'. And in this review essay I want to try to give just a flavour of Cohen in the hope that readers will be moved to read him themselves: he deserves to be – but he is not – on every reading list of every university history course that has the ambition of critically examining 'history today' and its less and more desirable practices and cultural/ideological affects.[1]

On the other hand – and with even a sense of betrayal given my long-term reliance on Ankersmit for so many insights – his *Sublime Historical Experience* is disappointing. Why? Well, it's not because Ankersmit breaks relatively new ground – albeit in a book ten years in the making – and that this is unwelcomingly disorientating. No; newness is always to be welcomed if not always accepted. Moreover, Ankersmit is at pains to stress that although readers may think some of his arguments are 'off the wall', they might also believe them to be a recantation of his previous positions. And this is *not* the case: '[T]his is a book about sublime historical experience', he writes,

> *and not about anything else* (such as historical explanation, causality, narrative, or representation) ... [it] does not question the conviction that there is, or rather, has been a past existing independently of what we may say or write about it, that we can make statements about it that are either true or false, that we can explain the past by mentioning causes or in terms of texts representing the past, that all these things can be rationally discussed and, finally that there is no occasion for historical scepticism. ... '
>
> (Ankersmit 2005, 14)

and these are indeed all old Ankersmitean themes. Which is fine; it leaves the Ankersmit I like intact. And it's also fine that Ankersmit's 'new' object of enquiry – sublime historical experience (henceforth SHE) – is attended to with all the scholarly rigour that is his trademark. Ankersmit's remarkable erudition and its insightful use is, as usual, formidable – even intimidating. No, my objection to Ankersmit's treatment of the sublime is to do with the melancholic and pessimistic cast of mind (let me call it that for now) he seems to bring to it and bathe it in. Moreover, although he knows very well that this is just his personal spin on the sublime (discussed most openly in Chapter 7), there is a strong enough pressure through the constant use of the universalizing 'we' to suggest that this is 'surely' the way we are 'all' struck by the experience of the sublime (as loss, trauma, disorientation – both personal and collective, etc.), such that the arguably fantastic, imaginative potential for joyful inventiveness and politically radical and emancipatory work (so obvious in other 'theorists') just slips out of the picture – or rather, never really gets into it. Of course, I'm aware other readers may not have, or will not have, picked up on those pessimistic motifs that cast what the sublime could be into dark relief. And I'm also aware that the way I have read Ankersmit here may seem to suggest that, once set on a course, I seem hell-bent on creating a *mood* not actually present in his text. But my conviction, my 'feeling', my 'experience', of reading Ankersmit is that what I think is there is there and that I can *propose* it as a way of understanding Ankersmit's text. And why am I so struck by Ankersmit's *negative* sublime? Because of *intertextuality* – another old Ankersmitean stomping-ground. For compared to Ankersmit, Cohen's 'historical' use of the sublime is just so upbeat, is such a dynamic and optimistic force. To be sure, the notion of SHE that patterns Ankersmits text is not so overtly articulated in Cohen, but his sometimes working of it and its implicit presence throughout energizes Cohen's writing. And so although this *review essay* (a genre that gives the reviewer something of a licence to be discursive), sometimes does what reviews generally do – review the books – I want to focus here primarily on the different treatments of the sublime in Cohen and Ankersmit in the hope that my championing (on this occasion) of the former over the latter on this matter is productive. I start with Cohen.

We all have our intellectual heroes and Cohen's just happens to be Jean-François Lyotard. It's an excellent choice. Of course there are other influences operating in *History Out of Joint*. Nietzsche, Deleuze, Guattari and Derrida are regularly invoked and chaptered; Baudrillard permeates, Kant is critically engaged, a host of 'proper' historians have walk-on parts, a range of aesthetic and other theorizations are called upon. But it is Lyotard who on this occasion – as on others – is the nearest to Cohen's heart. Thus, 'Chapter Seven', Cohen writes in his Introduction,

> is a synthesis of Jean-François Lyotard's theory of historiographic representation … This is the only chapter that veers towards intellectual 'homage' as I think that of all the so-called postmodern philosophers, Lyotard has the most acute things to say about historiography as what it most manifestly is, a modulation 'in the family of narrative cultures', never separate from 'savage, primitive, underdeveloped, backward, alienated, composed of opinions, customs, authority, prejudice, ignorance, ideology'.
> (Cohen 2006, 8)

For both Cohen and Lyotard, then, history has mixed/impure origins (of power, resentment, affirmation, denial, self-seeking, etc.) which no amount of archival work or 'the facts' or 'realism' or 'objectivity' can negate or nullify: history is a dirty discourse, affected by suasive desires, always for someone or something even when it's allegedly just for itself – 'as if'. And for Cohen and Lyotard most history is for the wrong things (affirming on-going culture in all its maldistribution of power, etc.) and the wrong people (for those who benefit accordingly and unjustly). Accordingly, Cohen's book is pretty much about substantiating his verdict that history in our culture is indeed guilty of acting *affirmatively* – as support for dominant/consolidating interests – whilst going on to essay possible escape routes *beyond* history. As he says on the last page of his Introduction:

> Part One [consisting of chapters on Nietzsche, Taiwan, Art Criticism, figuring the historian of today, historical anecdotes] is mostly critical of the tactics and strategies of normal historical representation; Part Two [on Derrida, Lyotard, Deleuze, Guattari] argues that we can conceive history so that its critical uses are transgressive, or a welcoming of events, which might involve activating public disputes that cannot be 'returned' to narration. Part One is concerned with how various senses of the public are given history in ways that are actually abusive, culturally and intellectually speaking. Part Two locates theory of history within changed conditions of capital, and stresses new uses of thought and criticism that are, perhaps, ahistorical.
> (Cohen 2006, 17)

And it is Lyotard who best serves both of these parts. So what does Cohen's engagement with Lyotard look like and how is the sublime treated radically and optimistically? Well, let me move towards Cohen's sublime and its historiographical consequences by working in from the general to the particular, and let me begin where Cohen does by focusing on what he considers to be *the vitally contested* terms of both historiography and politico/historical culture today: *narrative* and *event*.

About the many hundreds of works concerning the historiographical uses of the notions of narrative and event, one can say that most historians are confident about the capacity of narrative to *control* events: Embedding events in familiar(izing) narrative 'contexts' (short, medium and long term; often all three) is what historians do. Here narration *absorbs* events (especially potentially disruptive ones); historical narration is that orderly 'written land' where a 'true' body of words (description, explanation, significance …) is substituted for 'erratic speech' and erratic events. An event, to become a 'proper' historical event, cannot be left unexplained or inexplicable, only the explicable is 'historical' (which helps to 'explain' why the Holocaust – seen as an unimaginable/unrepresentational 'event' – seems to remain beyond our understanding, giving the slip to [historians'] sense and reason). Events, then, to become 'historical events', have to be integrated into received understandings via approved methods just to be recognized as historical. Such historical narration thus purges events of their differential, excessive, awkward elements – which makes them available for interminable rereadings – smoothing the rough edges and shaping them to the best fit, made to measure, bespoke style. Here a controlling 'synthesis' is the aim, 'coming to terms with the past' its most 'often heard phrase' (201). Here continuity, linearity and coherence, fabricated and preserved as a bulwark against the unruly and the chaotic, is its ideological locale/function. In fact such 'historical coherence' – with its talismanic notions of continuity and change, similarity and difference; with its meaning-laden beginnings, middles and ends, its structures, patterns and watersheds, its directional switching points which ensures that the 'right' past rolls right up to us spot on cue, bang on time – is *never* a *found* coherence but always a coherence issuing *entirely* (and I mean *entirely*) from the applied form(s) of the narrative genre itself; well, all this is misrecognized by most historians. Coherent narratives thus work to control the serendipitous, the aleatory, the ludic and the 'other' against charges of radical contingency, against the charge of the Lyotardian notion of *unpresentability*. By which idea – the unpresentable – Lyotard doesn't mean that things not capable of being definitively presented now will one day (and in principle) be presented. No. The unpresentable is not merely another version of what is missing from representation, but is rather those 'eventful experiences' ('just about everything') unable to *ever* be fully historicized. Moreover, this unpresentable is not ontologizable, is not 'any-thing', but is rather that intuited *excess*, that necessary outside that makes the 'contextualized' inside always less than saturable and thus always temporary and fragile, haunting all attempted closures with their impossibility and thus ruin. Unpresentability is comparable here to Deleuze and Guattari's idea of 'non-thought', which is not a negation or a 'no', but refers to things (events) that have not yet been successfully placed in representations and which cannot ever be so placed, thus requiring endless thought experiments without determinate origins or ends: here intentionality, meaning and teleology become and remain 'troubled' as endless differences and loosed events signal the *aporetic* nature of decisional undecidability. Here events wait in limbo for that settling decision that can never actually arrive: there is 'no last instance', no 'last judgement', no hope – thank goodness – of any 'final solution'. Here, thinks Cohen, once sure-footed, empirically confident, epistemologically driven (modernist) history wobbles over; here the old tried-and-tested glue that seemingly stuck together subject and object, fact and value, becomes 'tacky'; here the 'before now', the past ('too reified a term'), slides free of any real or certain meaning; the 'before now' remains both sublime and sublimely indifferent to meaning-full closures, knows nothing and cares less about our desires for completion and fulfilment.

And for Cohen (and Lyotard) this is the *very best of things*; both, one way or another, embrace unpresentability, celebrate the incommensurability of phrase-regimes, construe the possibility of activating the *differend* as indexical of freedom, valorize endless multiplicity and thus that general *excess* that defies fixity: rest assured, no historical representation will ever get things right; a 'true representation' is oxymoronic. And so Cohen and Lyotard joyfully accept the sublime indifference of the world and world's past, that skip free of every simulacrum ('mistaken for reality'), and every anthropomorphic conceit. This is a 'sublime' that opens everything up and keeps them open, that permits everything; a post-modern stance which, in its relishment of being able to make up new rules in the absence of rules *after* and not before 'the event', invites ceaseless invention. Here what passes for the sublime (experienced in ways that are always disorientatingly *out of joint* with attempted/extant 'historical closures', always beyond the controlling embrace of the beautiful), holds no feelings of terror, no feelings of loss or lack, knows nothing of trauma or angst or pessimism. No, 'the past' has gone, the trick now is forget it, to 'get out of it', to 'get over it'. A Nietzschean optimism takes over here; the creative person must learn to forget, to practice standing naked on an unsupported single point without fear or giddiness, not to deny the past but to 'will to forget it' and thus, slipping out from under the burden of history, create on the 'basis' of sublime nothingness ('creating something out of nothing is the story of our lives') that which is currently desired. As Hayden White once put all of this so unerringly right:

> The dissolution of the notion of an historical semantics is, at the same time, the dissolution of the dream of a method by which history in general can be endowed with any sense at all. The historian is liberated from having to say anything *about* the past; the past is only an occasion for [the] invention of ingenious 'melodies'. Historical representation becomes once more all story, no plot, no explanation, no ideological implication at all – that is to say, 'myth' in its original meaning as Nietzsche understood it, 'fabulation'.
>
> (Hayden White 1973, 372)

Exactly; except for the fact that this way of reading things is very precisely *ideological*. For nothing as advocatory as this can escape ideological intent (least of all Nietzsche's own politics which just do constitute 'Nietzsche'), and certainly this kind of sublime does political work for Cohen: for him the injunction to 'always historicize' always reads 'always ideologize'. For Cohen sees history as always governed by ideological desires which, along a dominant–marginal spectrum, overwhelmingly benefits the dominant interests of 'capital', it being the resultant inequalities and injustices which Cohen wishes to 'deconstruct ('to put it mildly'). And Cohen considers that one way of doing this is to undercut the way 'history now' is predominantly used to *affirm* 'capital' as if there was 'no alternative' to it (by construing history per se as the way to understand the world we live in: by arguing that understanding 'today' means situating it in a narrative of 'arrival'; by using our 'cultural memories' to confirm that our current reality is not only real but rational/reasonable; by establishing its reality/realism by backward glances which affirm that the way things are the way things have to be). And for Cohen these 'narrations' actually displace our attention from the present and the future (where we live now and tomorrow) by insisting that 'today' can only be 'understood' by never actually examining it. Such a 'dissemination of models of history', writes Cohen,

> promotes cultural subjects who are encouraged to think about non-narrative relations – capitalism, justice, and contradictions – in a narrative manner. Narrating screens the mind from the non-narrative forces of power in the present as 'historical' narration reduces present semantic and pragmatic thought (connotation) to forms of story, repetition, and model, all of which service cultural redundancy ... what actually occurs by means of 'historical thought' is the destruction of a fully semanticized present ... I [thus] argue that critical thinking is not possible when connected to academic historical thinking.
>
> (Cohen 1986, 1–2)

Now, this position, taken from *Historical Culture* (Cohen 1986), still informs *History Out of Joint* twenty years later as Cohen tries to answer the questions animating the latter text: who should have the power to decide the culturally important? What are we doing when we make ourselves subjects to one particular history and not another? How does Nietzschean anti-production bureaucratize and install misinterpretation as cultural truths? How does the culturally lasting get made endurable and affect public life? Who can believe the truth of any 'periodization' that would put us into coherent narrative orders (commands) when we know that history is always 'out of joint'? And, thanks to Nietzsche, must we not conceive of language not just as a vehicle for transparent messages and correspondence, but as a *mixed* system – reference on one side, madness on the other – the actual and the virtual contaminated, the same language enabling us to be both a teller of truth and a teller of lies?

And – and this is Cohen's big question – isn't the excessive *sublime* something which must be controlled, beautified, ontologized and thus territorialized and boxed into quietude and negativity so that its use as a radical potential power for newness is neutered?

Both Cohen and Lyotard, then, want to welcome events 'without *to historicize*, infinitive mode' operating:

> 'Not to drag their generation to the grave' was the injunction of Nietzsche's unhistorical and superhistorical, self-experimental quasi-subject, manifested in Lyotard's writings, among other phrases, as experimentation without subjectivity, this to the point where one might 'invent allusions to the conceivable which cannot be presented'. Of this, contemporary historiography knows almost nothing.
>
> (Cohen 2006, 202)

Enter Ankersmit.

Ankersmit's text is complex. Composed of a Preface, Introduction, eight lengthy chapters and an Epilogue where the devil is in the detail – and there is an awful lot of detail – it's almost summary-proof. Just when you think you've got it a new argument loosens your grip: 'challenging' is not an adequate word for this supple and subtle text as it ranges, seemingly effortlessly, across complicated analyses of Rorty and Huizinga, Gadamer and Burkhardt, Rousseau and Hölderlin and a host of well- and lesser-known philosophers, artists, novelists, poets and theorists. Of course the *leitmotif* of 'the sublime' holds things together, but it is only in the very last chapter – 317 pages in – that Sublime Historical Experience (SHE) is extensively addressed.

This being the case my treatment of Ankersmit's text is – like Cohen's – highly selective and lacking in those fine distinctions Ankersmit's pages are littered with. But, to get a reasonable, initial overview of Ankersmit's concerns and intentions (if not the *mood* – to which I'll return), one could do worse than summarize his Preface and Introduction. Baldly put, their 'arguments' might be presented as follows.

Since the Second World War, two 'topics' have been central to historical thinking: that of truth and that of the narrative representation of 'the past'. In the 1950s and 1960s the first topic predominated, focusing on the epistemic status of historical explanation (covering laws, etc.). But, in the 1970s and 1980s, with the widespread recognition that 'truth' in history was expressed not at the level of the statement/sentence but the (whole) text – and with the impact of Hayden White's *Metahistory* (1973) slowly increasing as it was swept along by the more general currents of the 'linguistic turn' – then the centre of gravity shifted toward narrative representation and 'textuality' until the whole world, and world's past, became 'texts'. And Ankersmit explains that, although he has never renounced his 'commitment' to both of these 'topics' – he is an adherent of empirical/epistemological accounts of the historical for 'whatever takes place in the historical text on the level of the statement while being ... an adherent of a theory of historical representation for the text as a whole' (xiv) – nevertheless, the thrust of his work has clearly been on narrativist representation and textuality.

But, Ankersmit goes on, such emphasis on the text has now gone too far. For one aspect of how we relate to the past has escaped the intellectual matrix of both historical truth *and* representation, namely, the question of the origins and status of historical consciousness: '*What makes us aware of the past at all*, what should happen, or must have happened to a nation or a collectivity to become fascinated by the problem of its past? This is the approach that will be adopted in the present study' (Ankersmit 2005, xv). And this, says Ankersmit – somewhat disingenuously – is a supremely impractical question that has no bearing whatsoever on what historians do and why they do it; SHE is 'useless' from the point of view of the 'practising historian', it simply increases historical consciousness.

Now I say disingenuous because it becomes very clear merely from reading Ankersmit's *Introduction* that to get this kind of historical consciousness into our heads quite a lot of mental spring-cleaning (which arguably *will* affect our practices as we begin to see the whole point of going to the past differently) will have to occur if we are to make space for the sublime in general and SHE in particular. So what will have to be reconsidered? And the answer is essentially to do with scaling-down the imperializing 'thrust of language'. For while Ankersmit acknowledges all that has been done for history by the 'linguistic turn' (White is again indexical here), nevertheless, a high price has been paid; namely, that as a result of textuality a historical theory has been developed for which '*il n'y a pas de hors-texte*' has eliminated all our other categories (linguistic or otherwise) for making sense of the actuality of the world and of the past (10). Consequently, Ankersmit claims that his book is an attempt to

> do away with all the (quasi) transcendentalist conceptions we may find not only in tropology but also in hermeneutics, deconstructivism, (post) structuralism, or semiotics. It can therefore be seen as an uncompromising attack on all that came to be known over the last twenty to thirty years by the name of 'theory' ... [This] will be rejected here in the name of the notion of *experience*.
>
> (10)

As a consequence of which rejection, this will involve:

> the 'Romanticism' of an approach to the past involving all the historian's personality and not just (or even merely primarily) the formalism of his or her cognitive faculties. More specifically this book is a rehabilitation of the romanticist's world of moods and feelings as constitutive of how we

> relate to the past. How we *feel* about the past is no less important than what we *know* about it.
>
> (10)

Accordingly, the experience of 'feeling' the past before language 'gets at it' is crucial here. Ankersmit again.

> Historical experience involves, in the first place, a Gestalt-switch from a timeless present into a world consisting of things past and present. This gives us the discovery of the past as a reality that has somehow 'broken off' from a timeless present. This is 'the moment of loss'. But at the same time historical experience aims at a recovery of the past by transcending again the barriers between past and present. And this could be characterised as 'the moment of desire or of love'. All [sic] of historical writing is to be situated in the space enclosed by these complementary movements of the discovery (loss) and the recovery of the past (love) that constitute together the realm of historical experience ... *The sublimity of historical experience originates from this paradoxical union of the feelings of loss and love, that is, of the combination of pain and pleasure in how we relate to the past.*
>
> (9)

From which position the chapters that follow – on Rorty, Gadamer, Huizinga, Burkhardt *et al.* – are all, in their different ways, about Ankersmit getting rid of 'linguistic transcendentalism' since no compromise is possible between language and experience: '[W]here you have language experience is not' – and vice versa. For we have language very precisely so that we do not have to face 'the fears and terrors that are typically produced by experience'; language is 'the shield protecting us from the terrors of a direct contact [sic] with the world as conveyed by experience'; language presents us with images of the world (*simulacra*) but, as such, it can offer 'only a shadow of the terrors inhabiting the world itself and the fears it may provoke' (11). Ankersmit thus wants us to abandon our linguistic safety-blankets and upholstered existences so that we can not only experience the past direct at the level of our singular, existential 'selves', but also to draw attention to SHE as it pertains to how a past *civilization* might *collectively* relate to *its* own past:

> It is argued that if we wish to grasp the nature of (Western) historical consciousness, we shall have to focus on ... 'experiences of rupture' in which a civilization discards a former identity while defining its new identity precisely in terms of what has been discarded and surrendered. The identification and investigation of these sublime experiences of rupture – think of the Renaissance and of The French Revolution – could be seen as the 'research programme' suggested or implied by this book ... So it will be the difficult but challenging future task of the historical

> theorist to liberate the history of historical experience from the heavy and oppressive weight of (the historian's) language and to unearth experience from the thick sedimentary strata of language covering it. What is the experience of the past underlying the language used by the historian? That is the question asked in this book.
>
> (13–14)

These are arguably the various concerns governing Ankersmit's text, then, and one might ask what could be objectionable about them. And at one level the answer is nothing; in his own intellectually swashbuckling way Ankersmit is off on an adventure to set the historical world to rights, to re-romanticize it. And it even gives the appearance of being even-handed. The sublimity of historical experience – to revisit one of the above quotes – is found in the *union* between loss *and* love, pain *and* pleasure. And yet – and here I want to register my first 'reservation' – while Ankersmit will certainly retain this 'relationship', any attempt at evenness gets short shrift. For we have already seen a few hints as to the darkness and terrors that really constitute the Ankersmitean sublime and SHE, and there are more examples in the very first pages of the book I have referred to so far.

Indeed, the first indication of the negativity of the sublime appears in the Preface where, commenting on Martin Jay's *Songs of Experience*, Ankersmit writes that 'we both know how desperate and lonely one can sometimes feel when having "to cross the swamps of experience" as he once so poignantly put it in a letter to me' (xvii). And in his Introduction, forebodings of what is to come are plentiful. Thus, after inviting us to see his book as a rehabilitation of the 'romanticist's world of moods and feelings', he adds: 'and so I invite the reader of this book to enter the dark and sometimes even sinister world of the profoundest and quasi-existentialist layers of our relationship to the past' (10). And other expressions of those feelings which accompany 'historical ruptures' in addition to '1789' are also seen negatively: '[O]ne might think of how in the US South the trauma of the Civil War can still be felt and of how this may stimulate a feeling of loss and regret in even an occasional visitor to the South (like myself in 1985). Similarly, one might well ask the question of how the past is nowadays experienced in Russia after the two dramatic *caesurus* of 1917 and 1989' (13). And all of this is just the tip of a very large iceberg that one only gets the dimensions of by 'experiencing' the whole of Ankersmit's text – something obviously not possible here. But, to try and give an early indication of the *mood* of Ankersmit's writing – and as I've said *Sublime Historical Experience* is all about moods – it might be possible to rearticulate Ankersmit's Preface and Introduction in a slightly different idiom which might better prepare us for Ankersmit's massively unbalanced account of the sublime and of SHE – I mean, just think of the joy and liberation, the solidarity and the creative freedom attending the idea that mankind was not only made by, but was the *maker* of, 'history' – in 1789, 1917, 1989, the Civil War, etc. So, let me now, briefly, put things other-wise.

Thus, let us say that at the centre of Ankersmit's book, its governing thematic, is something like Nietzsche's dictum that we need lies in order to live, and that these 'lies' can be seen as the various ways in which social formations have constituted 'reality' – and especially the way they have expressed this through language. And I think Ankersmit shares Nietzsche's view that if we stripped away these carapaces of the real ('reality effects') to reveal 'bare life' then, without our usual fictive, fabular shelters, we would be quite literally exposed to the nature of actuality plain before human beings got at it and (contingently) real-ized it. And this glimpse into formlessness, nothingness, into this 'void of being', is portrayed by Ankersmit in the way this yawning void – the sublime – has been 'classically' construed. That is, as engendering fear and dread, angst and terror as 'we' totter on the edge of the abyss(mal) and yet, also and simultaneously, as engendering exhilaration, excitement and creative tension since, rid of all our previous, familiarizing gestures, we feel we might become free again, open to the forces of Deleuzian-like 'creatings'. And in Nietzsche's own case, he welcomes all of this. Nietzsche is anxious that the most 'dreadful of thoughts' (nihilism) is *experienced* by both those who cannot bear it (and who are thus primed to accept any meaning rather than none at all), and those, the *übermensch*, who can both stand it and who can offer, through their creative productions stimulated by it, 'meanings' by which the weak – the herd – can live. Nietzsche thus embraces the unfathomability of the sublime, its empty horizons that 'recur eternally', as the ontological (quasi) foundation for exuberant 'will-to-power' lives:

> In fact, we philosophers and free spirits feel ourselves irradiated as by a new dawn by the report [which has finally reached us] that the old God is dead. Our hearts overflow with gratitude, astonishment, presentiment and expectation. At last the horizon seems open once more. Granting even that it is not yet light, our ships can at last put out to sea in the face of every danger; every hazard is again permitted ... this sea, our sea, again lies before us; perhaps never before did such an open sea exist.
> (167)

And Ankersmit, I think, also wants us to experience *something* of *this* sublime, such that his task is (also) to remove our fabular protections – and especially those epistemological shelters expressed through our linguistic and other representational 'turns' – so that we can indeed face the past, present and future aware of, and so close to, some kind of authenticity; that our experiences of the sublime awakens us to experiences denied us by that soothing tissue of lies (linguistic/textual) which allows us to pass through life as if sleepwalking. At which point Ankersmit's task becomes clear. He will clear away the covers of 'textualizations', engage with Rorty *et al.* and mine the resources of Huizinga, Gadamer, Rousseau, Hölderlin and others so that we might prioritize the 'raw over the cooked', and he will amplify and project existential experiences of the sublime onto collectivities such that they become sometime bearers of SHE.

Now, again, I find little objectionable in this version; it is, after all, not a hundred miles away from Heidegger; it's close to Camus' absurd, Deleuze's creatings, Badiou's Event and, indeed, Cohen and Lyotards' sublime. In fact, it's the bread-and-butter of most existential and most deconstructionist theory associated with post-structuralists, postmodernists and so on – and which Ankersmit dismisses as antagonists rather than embracing as the helpful friends they are. And because of this dismissal – the dismissal of the works of Lyotard and Deleuze *et al.* (Cohen's friends) – friends who have surely worked the sublime and its cognates far more profoundly and adventurously than Burke and Schiller and other Ankersmitean heroes of a gloomy, pessimistic, conservative/reactionary kind have ever done, something happens as Ankersmit goes to the *wrong* sources *if* it's both pain *and* pleasure, loss *and* love that he *really* wants. For, recall, there are two dimensions to the sublime (and SHE). On the one hand there is much fearful wailing and hand-wringing, on the other creative gaiety, new horizons and pregnant possibilities. Aware that because 'nothing' is necessary then everything is permitted, Lyotard (and let Lyotard stand in here for umpteen 'postist' theorists), *embraces* the sublime and plays with it. And Ankersmit, although obviously very aware of that creativity occasioned by absence (it's also writ large in the works of Hayden White which Ankersmit knows so well), Ankersmit plumps *not* for this response to the sublime but its other. Sublime experience (and SHE) is, for Ankersmit, an overwhelmingly mournful, traumatic affair (trauma – we learn later – being the 'psychological equivalent of philosophical SHE'). And hence the overall pessimism of his text, which suggests that, although it is necessary to experience the sublime, and although experiencing it within the context of 'actual history' (as collective SHE) adds a dimension to historical consciousness, these experiences are, overwhelmingly, angst-ridden.

Now, how in a little more detail does Ankersmit cast experience of the sublime/SHE into such shadows? Well, here I can do no more than give a few substantiating examples that will have to stand in for a welter of similar occurrences which I think even the most inattentive reader surely cannot miss. I go to Chapter 8 for the (bulk of) the *how*, Chapter 7 for the (bulk of) the *why*.

In Chapter 8 Ankersmit details four types of 'forgetting' that help him to set-up SHE. The first two are relatively inconsequential (we might forget, say, the name of a once school friend; we might forget a (possibly) formative moment because it didn't register at the time); the third (a forgetting of a possibly 'collective' type where the memory is too painful to be admitted into our 'collective consciousness' – for example the way the Holocaust was 'forgotten' for two decades after 1945), leads on to the fourth, which occupies Ankersmit for the rest of the chapters, SHE, for which the French Revolution of 1789 is the paradigm case. For 1789 figures in Ankersmit's text as the most dramatic of ruptures, as one of 'the most decisive and profound changes that Western man [sic] has undergone in the course of history' (323), since, in that year, mankind entered a whole new world only on the condition of 'forgetting a previous world and of shedding a former "identity"' (323). And this abandonment, this tearing up of a traditional, customary and familiar old world was, argues Ankersmit, always 'extremely painful, and it was always experienced as such', an experience that *remains* as a constant presence:

> The historical transformations occasioning this variant of forgetfulness are always accompanied by feelings of a profound and irreparable loss, of cultural despair, and of hopeless disorientation. In this sense such historical experiences are undoubtedly traumatic too ... a trauma for which no cure is to be found'.
>
> (324)

Here the past accompanies as a lost love might, absent now but 'because of this, always so very much and so very painfully present', a love to which no return is possible however nostalgic or love sick the yearning for that 'lost paradise' that takes on the characteristics of 'myth' (325). Here the trauma is likened to both the permanent loss of a former self *and* the loss of a once 'collective identity', and 'what loss could possibly be greater – for is this not as close to death as one may come?' (325). And this is indeed how the 'conservatives and reactionaries' read 1789 (to investigate such trauma '[o]ur best point of departure will be the reactionary and conservative reaction to the French Revolution' (325)), it being these groupings which stand metonymically for those 'whose loss was the greatest', all this, let us note, at the expense of the revolutionaries/radicals (widely construed) who most benefited from 1789 and who scarce get a mention. And, of course, such conservatives and reactionaries certainly did read 1789 negatively: as a sort of self-inflicted death, a kind of suicide since all that had made sense – since all that just was the *ancien régime* – began to pass away. And the mode of its passing, its violent death pangs and its works of mourning, argues Ankersmit, have contaminated for ever both impending and distant futures, creating the sorts of conditions that are (tautologically) in 'total agreement' with the 'relevant facts' about the sublime. For the sublime experience of SHE is of a wounded world so shattered that 'every normal pattern of experiences lies disrupted; ruined' (346). At which point – and really for the first time in the book – the nature of SHE is defined: SHE is the experience a 'civilization' undergoes when, as in 1789, that collectivity

> has to discard or to dissociate a former self from the self that we are having had the sublime experience in question. Sublime [Historical] Experience, then, is the kind of experience forcing us to abandon the position in which we still coincide with ourselves and to exchange this for a position where we relate to ourselves in the most literal sense of the word, hence, as if we were *two* persons instead of just *one*. This, then, is

> how identity, (traumatic) dissociation, and the epistemological paradoxes of sublime [historical] experiences all hang together.
>
> (347)

Consequently, the fact that this experience cannot be discarded or neutralized but can only be *endured* ('if you're lucky'), means, for Ankersmit, that 'historians rejoicing in, for example, the triumphs of monarchs, soldiers and heroes will never be able to give us that essence' (355). To be sure, intense narrativization, historicizing and 'textualizing' may take place afterwards; new identities may and indeed will be formed. And yet, despite such attempts to absorb 1789 into the weft and weave of a more comfortable and palatable form, its governing trauma can still be *re-experienced* by historians *beneath* all the attempts to 'cover it up'. A historian can, if very fortunate, peer through the odd 'hole' in the ever-accumulating clouds of historiography and experience what lies beneath *direct*, uncluttered by those very histories (texts) that has led one to the edge of the 'void' in the first place. Here, for Ankersmit, historians momentarily lose their footing, here they are as strangers to their previous historical understanding; here they feel despairingly lost: this is *their* own sublime moment of authenticity, of real 'historical consciousness', of feeling 'in your bones' what it was really like to be 'back there'. And who knows, also, that that 'back there' cannot be brought 'back here'; the 'inexplicable gift of what is given to the historian by such a sublime experience is, simultaneously, informed by a no less intense experience of 'losing it'. And, once again, we should not mistake this loss for something which was in our possession, for we never possessed it 'in the way we may possess a house or even a beloved' (177). Because the past always gives back the love the historian bestows on it in unrequited ways. And all of this, Ankersmit insists, is an epistemological and not a metaphysical matter. For although

> this feeling of despair is … intense [and] although it may have been occasionally a work of art, a poem, or by what has provoked a historical experience, all of these are at the same time experienced as a reminder of the unattainability of all of the world and of the past. These objects then *exemplify* this sad feature of our *condition humaine*, and with the unfilled promise of this painting, of this poem, we weep the loss of all the world and of all that the world had promised us when it presents itself in its attire of sublimity.
>
> (178)

For all of these (and other) reasons, then, sublime experience is *never* accompanied by feelings of liberation or redemption (after Benjamin, for example); the present always falls short of a full, permanent, union with the past. This is the pathos of the shortfall of historical knowledge and understanding, the tragedy of historiography. This is why Ankersmit's book is – as he knows himself all too well – so sombre, so mournful, so pessimistic.

And *why* does Ankersmit feel this way? Well, in Chapter 7 – where much against his better judgement as the very private man he is but feeling 'compelled' by the thematic of experience – he explains why he now experiences the past in the way he does. Here, the intermingled 'confessions' and arguments that constitute Chapter 7 are, as usual, richly digressive (there is much here on Francesco Guardi's *capriccio*, the boredom generated by prolonged illnesses which punctuated his 'happy childhood', by flower-patterned bedroom curtains, engraved grotesques, rococo art and other generators of 'moods'), but it is, perhaps, '1789' that deserves pride of place. The arguments here are again complex and cannot be rehearsed, and so I quote at length from a footnote where *enough* of Ankersmit's *soul* is laid bare for our (empathetic) consideration:

> The transition from childhood to early adolescence on the one hand and this nostalgia for the eighteenth century [ancient regime] on the other are, for me, most intimately linked. I must have transferred my feelings about the loss of my happy childhood days to 1789 – and I am well aware of what things made me do this at that time in my life. Undoubtedly this is why I can now still feel the awareness of what we lost in 1789 with an intensity with which one experiences the great losses in one's personal life and why, for me, 1789 is still the historical event *par excellence*. This also moulded my relationship to the past, and this book is, in fact, an attempt to come to terms with the pain I can still feel about 1789. Needless to say, I fully recognise that all this is peculiar to me and that I will not share my attitude toward the past with many others. On the one hand, was *History*, as we presently know it, not born from the rupture of the great revolution from the West's childhood days of the ancient regime? Is *History* – again, as we presently know it – not the offspring of the unhappy marriage of past and present that was celebrated in 1789?
>
> Perhaps one more admittedly quite personal effusion will be allowed to me. Is History not something that we predominantly have on the European continent, which has gone through the experience of the French Revolution and its aftermath but that is much less a presence in the Anglo-Saxon countries, where both in how people behave and in politics the *ancient regime* clearly still persists? We, on the European continent are therefore in a certain sense people of a fundamentally *later* stage in history because of all the unprecedented disasters that we have had to go through here in the two centuries between 1789 and 1989, where later certainly does not mean 'more modern' or 'better'. Quite the contrary – as the brute facts of two world wars, a near third one, and of a Holocaust sufficiently suggest. It is true the French Revolution has given us social democracy … but it also gave us Hitler and communism – and the permanent possibility of their return … The European continent is traumatized by its terrible past and stands with its back to the future – and the pathetic helplessness of the European Union, that is, of the

> institution symbolizing how we try to overcome our dismal past, epitomizes it all.
>
> (442)

Of course, as Ankersmit says in the above, his 'attitudes' are singularly his. But despite these and similar restraining gestures, Ankersmit's analyses are couched such that – childhood not withstanding – his way of experiencing the sublime is 'surely' the way we could – or should – *all* experience it. For certainly there is little attention in his (paradigmatic) treatment of SHE with regard to 1789 about that outburst of freedom and liberty that helped turn French peasants – and later most of us – into citizens. Alain Badiou has somewhere commented that, whilst France both before and after the *Event* of 1789 was 'full of peasants', it was not full of *these* peasants, not these peasants that hung the clergy out to dry, cut off the heads of local aristocrats and declared life, liberty, equality, and the virtues of republicanism – not these peasants. To be sure, Ankersmit is right about one thing. That 'experiment of modernity' that began around 1789 has, in its working out and through, failed (with more than a vengeance) to establish on its own terms those 'human rights communities' it variously promised, an 'experience' giving rise to, I think, that past/post-modern retrospective, that post-mortem dissection of modernity's experiment where elements of what may have caused things to go so wrong 'last time' are analysed for possible future re-use as 'we' fail to give up (as Derrida urged us never to give up) on that great 'fable' of emancipation. And maybe this is the whole point. Postmodernists – *people who have got over modernity* – are people who have not given up ('despite everything') on 'the next time', a possible 'next time' that helps give them a positive spin to the present and the future and places the past where it categorically belongs – *behind us*. In this construal the past isn't something we should nostalgically dwell in or on, but something we should get out of, not least by stressing the positive aspects of sublime experience – viz. freed of necessity, everything is possible. Here Cohen (and Lyotard) and many highly sensitive 'others' are testament to an optimism Ankersmit scarce seems able to imagine.

***

Now, at this point – a point where I could have brought things to a conclusion – I underwent something of an experience of my own. Because when I read back over the draft of what you yourself have just read on Ankersmit before I went on to write that which now follows, I felt unhappy with it. There was something – a lack of focus, perhaps – that disturbed me (although I obviously didn't rewrite the above 'since there it is'). And it took me a while to put my finger on what was worrying me. Then, slowly, I began to get it. For, whilst I had initially thought that I was dissatisfied because I hadn't managed to adequately *connect* the two things that inform Ankersmit's text – sublime experience (as the historian's existential experience of the sublime) and the collective SHE – as I reflected on this I began to realize – too late in the day – that these two elements did not actually (and certainly did not necessarily) connect up anyway: that the historian's experience of the sublime and of SHE are *totally different*, separate things.

In fact, what we have here are two books in one. For although on the surface and from the title – *Sublime Historical Experience* – it looks as if that's what the book is about – namely the collective feeling that a civilisation experiences when it undergoes a rupture so profound that in its semantic free-fall everything collapses irretrievably – in fact the *bulk* of the work is actually on the experiences historians (apparently) feel when 'the past' they thought they knew becomes strange as all that was solid indeed 'melts into air'. And it is *this* phenomenon that the book is primarily about; it is this which constitutes the vast bulk of the first seven chapters of this eight-chaptered text. Because having this feeling – which collapses subject and object, which reduces the epistemological element of histories to an over-determined fragment of a much wider history now resolutely *aesthetic* – is the stick by which Ankersmit can beat up his old previous friends with whom he has so long been in cahoots. As Ankersmit puts it in his own summary of SHE in *History and Theory* (2006) and repeating sentiments we have already cited: 'Taken as a whole, this book is a fierce and uncompromising attack on all that has been known as "theory" in the last three or four decades (for example, structuralism, post-structuralism, deconstruction, semiotics, tropology, all variants of hermeneutics, and so on).'

And so, once I had realized Ankersmit's two-in-one, then my unease about being able to convey the joined-up nature of the book or capture its coherence vanished as I recognized that the book was never coherent in the first place, that it is about two very different phenomena which just cannot be elided.

Then, musing on this, I began to see *why* Ankersmit had probably 'abandoned' the sort of 'theory' he had long pretty-much aligned himself with (whilst insisting that he had not recanted his previous positions). I had once read somewhere that 'George Bernard Shaw was a good man fallen amongst Fabians', and it now occurred to me how Ankersmit might be seen similarly as 'a good man fallen amongst the currently trendy purveyors of *presence*'. And I think that this fall is a huge mistake since, as Hayden White has summarily put it: '[H]istorical memory is a contradiction in terms' (2005, 335).

Ankersmit then – and this is my argument – seems to me to have been badly smitten by developments in memory studies work (work he once correctly characterized as the 'privatization of history' and thus not really history at all) and has thus been bewitched by the crazy notion of accessing 'historically' some or other aspect of the past direct, of being able to get back there without (despite) textual assistance ('For the moment there is only the past itself, revealing to him [sic] its quasi-noumenal nakedness with an unusual directness and immediacy') (125). And, of course, at the level of personal memory (though not, I think, 'collective memory') such a thing does have some credibility, does seem possible to achieve, albeit always 'to an extent'. I mean, my own memory *can* indeed be jogged by, say, the sight of a photograph that captures the moment, long ago and long forgotten, of a young boy – me – sat on a tricycle outside the kitchen door, complete with Fair Isle pullover and laced-up boots. At this moment that occasion can indeed come flooding back to me, seemingly unmediated. Here I don't need to read countless texts on the socio-economic-cultural conditions of rural working-class childhood in England in the early 1950s to 'get it'. *But* I can only remember that past without the help of such texts because *I am the text*. I can 'remember me' because I have everything I need to recall the young boy of 5 or 6 or 7 I once was since he's still inside me; I'm still him – just grown older. But I cannot remember Palmerston's Foreign Policy, or the reign of terror as played out in revolutionary Marseilles, or the collapse of the Anglo-Saxon Kingdom of Mercia non-textually – *and nor can even the most amazing memory-man*. For this we need texts as the indispensable prosphetics to 'memory' which they are. But, note again, that this artificial aid – which *contra* Ankersmit does indeed go 'all the way down' to taint all our experiential/knowledge claims – does *not* extend memory's reach, since about such historical phenomena I have *no* memory. Accordingly, the difference between memory and history is *not* a difference in degree but a difference in kind, a category difference, an ontological difference.

I am perplexed how Ankersmit could apparently *forget* this difference operationally. How could he apparently *forget* that whilst there are bits of as yet unprocessed 'otherness' out there ('just about everything') to get them 'in here' a process of mediation takes place through the very (textual) procedures that has allowed them to be 'experienced' in the first place – and that the very literature on the sublime and presence and immediacy he and we have read cannot but mediate and contaminate his and our (putative) experiences of them. And how can Ankersmit apparently forget that the sublime is not – to recall – a 'thing' to experience *as if* it pre-existed the experience, but is rather the name of an evaluative response to the very experiential 'performance' that constituted 'it' in the first place. And how can Ankersmit apparently forget that any use of the sublime as a resource – as the *empty-mechanism* it is – is never the use of a (non-ontologizable) sublime per se but a mere version giving to him (like Cohen and Lyotard's version gave to them) what he requires from it. Tautologies of all kinds lurk here. And so on and so forth ...

***

Cohen *contra* Ankersmit, then? Well, yes indeed. But this opposition is not, finally, because they don't have common 'enemies' in view. Actually, both know the fabular, fictive, rhetorical, aesthetic nature of history – history as *illusio* – and thus as being beyond both authenticity and truth. Both know history is *more* imagined than found, and locate this literary artefact over against empirical, epistemologically striving, modernist histories. Both know that mainstream 'history culture', the history establishment, is part of affirmative culture. Of course. And both want, albeit differently, to refigure histories such that they are no longer of the kind they predominantly are, or occupy the ideological spaces they currently occupy. And both work the idea of the imagined sublime in terms of the way it could variously affect the particular parts of historical practice they polemicize against. In all these and other ways both Cohen and Ankersmit are radicals: outsiders. Consequently their differences lie in the way they figure the sublime as governed by their particular suasive intentions, their differences lie in *why* they seek to use these *axioms* (for that is all the sublime – and SHE – can ever be) to get what they want. And, in terms of what they want, Ankersmit goes for a rearticulation oriented around nostalgic loss, whereas Cohen – and Cohen's Lyotard – go for the exhilarating potential of making something new out of nothing.

Two books, then, both brilliant in their own ways, both inevitably flawed in their own ways but yet, in terms of their different agendas and their modes of working them through, *reflecting* and *refracting* that *richly splintered* condition of our contemporary out-of-joint history culture that is actually both Cohen's and Ankersmit's object of enquiry. And what is arguably most valuable in all of this is that, in the course of their very different enquiries, they *fragment* that history culture even further. Which is, of course, *excellent*.

Note

1 My treatment of Cohen is, on this occasion, shorter than my treatment of Ankersmit, the reason being that this special issue of *Rethinking History* is devoted to Cohen's work.

References

Ankersmit, F.R. 2006. Books in summary, *History and Theory* 45, no. 1: 147–52.
—— 2005. *Sublime Historical Experience*. Stanford: Stanford University Press.
Cohen, S. 1986. *Historical culture: On the recoding of an academic discipline*. Berkeley: University of California Press.
—— 1993. *Academia and the luster of capital*. Minneapolis: University of Minnesota Press.
—— 1998. *Passive nihilism: Cultural historiography and the rhetorics of scholarship*. New York: St. Martin's Press.
—— 2006. *History out of joint*.Baltimore: Johns Hopkins University Press.
Jay, M. 2004. *Songs of experience*. Berkeley: University of California Press.
White, H. 1973. *Metahistory*. Baltimore: Johns Hopkins University Press.
—— 2005. A reply to Dirk Moses. *History and Theory* 44, no. 3: 333–8.

Afterword

Alun Munslow

In writing this brief Afterword I am happy to admit to being partial. As Keith has noted, I published several of the articles in this collection in the journal I co-edit *Rethinking History: The Journal of Theory and Practice*. Indeed, the journal's title is a straight lift from Keith's first and revolutionary text *Rethinking History* (1991). I also wrote a short preface to the second Classic Edition of that text (2003) and conducted the interview with Keith published in that book.[1] In addition, our collaborations over the years have included the editing of *The Nature of History Reader* (2004) and, with Sue Morgan, *Manifestos for History* (2007).[2] Keith and I have also offered mutual support on a variety of conference and lecture platforms over the years warding off the brickbats and even enjoying the occasional approval of the audiences. Not that Keith ever needed much help from me. His clarity of reasoning, unwillingness to suffer empiricists gladly and pugnacious attitude towards all critics usually saw off the invariably grumpy opposition. More often than not I just sat there and appeared rather meek and mild. Indeed, as a member of one audience once said to me it seemed to be a case of good cop and bad cop.

And this leads me to an important point. Keith's analysis of the state of history thinking – summarised in 1997 in his essay included here from an early issue of the journal *Rethinking History: The Journal of Theory and Practice* – has all too often been met with the disapproval of historians of a particular kind (his description as I recall, but one I now use regularly). In this article he asked why we should bother with history. He has no regrets about his answer and nor should he have. As a self-professed disobedient historian as described in a *Rethinking History* essay published in 2003 and also reprinted here, he has always welcomed the opportunity to confront what I will call conventional empirical–analytical thinking and its vain efforts to deflate his arguments especially when he ran his 'end of history' thesis. But, and most importantly for me, Keith has also been energetic in his efforts to rectify the situation of low esteem in which historical theory and philosophising about history was and is still held by many historians.

It is an index of this situation that so much of Keith's work continues to be met by hostility and outrage. Probably because there have generally been far more of them, I tend to recall the criticisms more than the congratulations. It surprises me that so many conventional historians still seem to think it is 'business as usual' and that history must remain a non-philosophical but sternly empirical–analytical and representational act. Why is it that so many still think this way given Keith's lucid and, at least for me, largely unanswerable position? Well, for some it is probably because the profession generally remains philosophically pre-literate and fearful of anyone who says epistemology is an intellectual choice not a given. But fear of Keith is only in part perpetuated by the professional disciplinisation of school and university history teaching. Although our contemporary accounting and managerial culture demands measurable outcomes which are the direct result of the prevalence of the epistemological choice, there is also the perception of an intellectual menace in the multiple scepticisms that Keith has consistently demonstrated.

For philosophically pre-literate historians concepts like truth, meaning and explanation are understood in ways that Keith has consistently rejected and not least because of the collateral belief that history matters because it 'teaches' us right from wrong if done properly. That historians who believe this still plough their epistemic and inferential furrows has only served to stimulate Keith's deeply critical epistemological, ontological and semantic scepticism. For Keith history cannot teach us how to be better people. As he described it in the essay reprinted here and published in the journal *Rethinking History* in 2007 the affair is over for history and its entailment of ethics. I will return to Keith's argument shortly.

Since the early 1990s publication of *Re-thinking History* (1991) through to this collection with its typically disputatious Jenkinsite introduction, Keith has confronted the stubborn desire among so many practitioners to disregard the nature of any inquiry that takes them beyond their empirical, inferential and representational belief system. And yet, despite this fear of any historical thinking that takes us beyond simple empirical scepticism, his first polemical text remains a best seller.[3] The paradox in this may be because it still shocks and, while the death of postmodernism is now a conventional cliché, the analysis that that text (now a Routledge Classic) contains remains one of the most devastating critiques of both the attitude and professional practice of such historians.

In reading the texts collected here, I recalled Hayden White's famous comment that the discipline of history is defined by what it refuses to think about. Taking up this argument Keith cast himself as an outsider as he argued for a post-epistemological and post-empirical position that insists history is an aesthetic discourse that in effect has demonstrated its own death. As is confirmed in this collection he insists that history as conventionally construed remains ignorant of its aesthetic ontology and that its claim to referentiality remains a *relatively* insignificant feature of the historicised production process we call 'historical knowledge'. What this collection demonstrates to me (and why I was always happy to publish Keith's work in the journal *Rethinking History*) is the ironic edge his work always possesses. For me this means that, to be loyal to the absent past, we just have to let go of conventional notions of history if, by sticking with them, we block out all other epistemic decisions, approaches and expressions. So, instead of 'discovering *the* meaning' of the absent past through its empirical remains and then writing it up as a series of statements of justified belief endowed with the ontological status of a facsimile, Keith re-imagined history, as he says in his own Introduction here, as other than a translation exercise. This has led him to accept the idea that conventional historians are authors who create narratives about the past but who exist in a state of denial as to their epistemic status and functioning. It is a result of this denial and his analysis of what goes into it that pushed Keith to his postist (history (of a particular kind)) argument.

As this book title suggests, understanding the limits to history (and they are substantial) will help us all come to terms with Keith's postist position on history. Only by rejecting history as an epistemic undertaking that (a) always places content before form (aka the past must be *the* transcendental signifier), (b) that meaning has to be defined as the ontological act of discovery, (c) that explanation is the re-presentation of *the* story, and (d) that description equates with representation, can it be unmasked. I believe Keith long ago gave up on the belief that he might persuade historians to think in anti- and post-epistemological ways but he has persisted in placing his arguments before them. He has consistently and doggedly argued that there are alternative legitimate (more legitimate?) ways to think about and practise history as a series of complex epistemic and aesthetic decisions. That this may result in the death of history of a particular kind is not to be regretted. It is in substantial part due to my reading of Keith's work in this way that I have come to believe that without a full understanding of the nature of scepticism, aesthetics, and historical authorship, history cannot be rethought in terms of experiment and expression.[4] That this produces (at least in my mind) an ironic sensibility that feeds back into the formulation of my assumptions and beliefs is Keith's most important legacy to me.

As Keith maintains in his Introduction, history is an unnatural act. It is an invention that can only appear to equate with the past (at least 'good' history is supposed to) for dyed-in-the-wool metaphysical realists. But, unhappily for them, the past is not with us anymore even if they choose to believe it mystically retains a presence today. The inability of historians to bridge the ontological gap between past reality and present history can only work if one invokes a kind of 'magic (metaphysical) realism' whereby personal memory is somehow a template for all historical thinking. But, as Keith has always argued, this idea is so wide of the mark it beggars belief. Of course, as he has again pointed out, rejection of that idea is not that original. Indeed, it (and Keith) has to be located within a strong tradition of epistemic scepticism which can be read in the work of the Pyrrhonists through to Southgate.[5]

The massive intellectual inconsistency of the 'magic (metaphysical) realism' of conventional historians can only be lived with by either ignoring it or by accepting the argument that content (the past) always determines form (as history). This both valorises the notion of 'representation as imitation', and allows claims that honest factual description equates with truthful meaning and explanation. Now, while this might work for figuring out a bus timetable, it certainly does not for securing the truthful meaning of the French Revolution. And, of course, the conventional claim that history is an interpretation that is open to revision as new data is 'discovered' is a rather small fig leaf.

Now, onto this insight (unpleasant for conventionalists) Keith has attached the notions of relativism and subjectivity. There is, perhaps, little that is more intellectually unconvincing than a self-professed objective historian in cold pursuit of the truth. As Keith has pointed out, relativism is not merely unavoidable, but it is valuable precisely because it impairs any historian's commitment to discovering 'the true nature of the past'. Moreover, just because a Holocaust denier peddles empirical/factual lies this does not mean they can be lumped together with epistemic sceptics. Telling lies about Hitler or the Holocaust is not connected to matters of epistemic relativism. Only empiricists who believe in a given and knowable truth could possibly see it in that way. I am apt to argue that if epistemic relativism and scepticism makes life awkward for realists it is not the fault of epistemic relativism or scepticism. Getting *the* data straight is not the same as getting *the* story straight.

The intellectual backwoodsism that was prevalent in the late 1980s and early 1990s especially among the British historical profession resulted directly from the little impact that multiple sceptical (aka postmodern) ideas had made at that time. In the 2003 'classic' edition of his book Keith said the book's success had surprised him given that the discipline of history was 'rabidly anti-theoretical' but it was 'a niche market ... which *needed* to be opened up'.[6] His aim was overtly disobedient and disruptive inasmuch as he believed students ought 'to know something about the product they are making ... And they still do.'[7] Delivered in a no-nonsense style his argument was that history students should have the right to understand and, if they choose to, escape from the archivally industrious yet perpetually stultified empirical–analytical vision of what history could only ever possibly be.

Keith began his key work by making what now seems such an obvious point (that even a few British professional historians do admit it) that the past and history are different things. History is a discourse – a different category – to that 'which it discourses about'.[8] But, more than this, the past and history 'float free of each other' as, he says, there are many ways to read a discourse.[9] This was a distinction that he pursued exhaustively in a variety of texts that, over subsequent years, became more complex as he analysed a whole variety of the misconceptions professional historians had (and most still have) about what they do. Among the more important of these misconceptions was the failure to understand that the history they write is, plainly, just another text and one that is not privileged in terms of truthful knowing simply because of its referential pretensions. It is thus because we, as human beings let alone as historians, cannot escape our narrative-making universe in order to somehow check how our texts correspond to 'reality'. We can't escape the gravity well of our narrative making. We can refer to past reality – but we can't escape back to it by visiting the archive or 'feeling its presence'.

Although, as I have noted, a number of philosophers of history have long examined the matter of the epistemological status of history as a truth-acquiring undertaking, it was Keith who brought matters to a head for the conventional practitioner historian and, more importantly, for their students. In arguing that history was principally a philosophical activity rather than a simple empirical and analytical practice, he made the devastating point that history as well as epistemology more broadly was intellectually brittle. He did this by reiterating and developing the arguments of Meiland and other sceptical philosophers that knowing the truth about something that no longer exists is impossible.[10] Although historians can 'evidence' that something happened by reference to the sources this act cannot in and of itself sort out the elementary predicament of knowing what it truthfully means. History – analogically – is thus quite unlike a court of law. This analogy while appealing to the epistemologist is just plain wrong. Only the briefest understanding of the process of underdetermination should squash such a practical-realist misconception. Once it is acknowledged that the references can be the seat of more than one interpretation then the relativism at the heart of epistemology has surfaced. As Keith pointed out with his usual dogged determination this situation of uncertainty can only do more good than harm. As he has long and regularly pointed out: 'truthful interpretation' is an oxymoron even if such an insight remains lost on all epistemologically inspired historians.

The epistemological vulnerability of history results, for Keith, from (a) the situation whereby evidence is selected rather than being self-selected, (b) that because representation always fails history cannot be a facsimile of the thing-in-itself, (c) that historians are authors who create historical narratives, and (d) they cannot escape their own powers of creation (ontological and semantic). All this is a broadside against objectivity and their favourite oxymoron. The repugnance engendered in conventionalists has resulted in the claim that Keith is arguing that historians cannot 'tell the truth about history'. And of course they were right – but not for the empirical and analytical reasons they offered. In a sense all Keith is saying is that it is unfeasible to tell the truth about a representation. In an echo of Ankersmit, depictions have no truth value even if they have referentiality. Only by denying this can historians open up a world where claims can be made that historians can 'tell the truth about the French Revolution' or worse that they can learn their ethics from history.

As Keith has also long argued history of a particular kind is especially dangerous when it makes the claim to educate us about the present. What constantly surprises him is the extremely hazardous notion that we can learn anything ethical from history. That contemporary and exploitative Western capitalist culture widely deploys this idea does not mean it has any epistemic validity. So, if we reverse content and form and recognise the fictive nature of history writing then this ought to force us to acknowledge that all we are comparing are histories – representations – and not history and the past. But all we have are narrative representations we have authored. We have histories of things that do not exist (the absent past). So, trying to learn ethics (and better management of political choices in the present) from the past via the ontologically different category of history seems rather odd. Ironically, then, claiming that we can learn our ethics from the past is actually to say that we can learn from *a particular history*. Given the ontological status of a magic (metaphysical) realist history all we can do is weigh up competing *narrative representations*. That so many historians seem unwilling to come to terms with this idea does not mean they must be right. And this is, of course, the central point concerning epistemic scepticism. Although the belief in empirical scepticism will do much good if it reveals empiricists who choose to lie about data, it does much harm when it makes us ignore bigger epistemic issues.

Until his book *Why History?* (1999) Keith was sworn postmodernist. This, I think, is because he believed (as did I) that deconstruction offered the prospect of liberating history from its magical (although the preferred term was practical) realist belief.[11] He had hoped postmodern histories might offer an escape from a history possessed by the evil genie of 'knowability'. But, with *Why History?*, his exasperation really emerged. He then started to argue that if conventionalists would not evolve then, in effect, they should go the way of the dinosaurs in what would be a catastrophic and global epistemic explosion of multiple scepticisms. In the new post-epistemological world Keith argued we ought to simply 'forget' history. Henceforth we could live with the imaginaries provided by theorists like Foucault, Derrida, Lyotard, Baudrillard, Rorty, Ermarth, and more recently Cohen. Without the concept of foundations we could do away with the very concept of history. Then, in *Refiguring History* (2003), Keith argued for a new way of thinking about the past drawing on Said and Badiou (and others) as intellectuals who could dispense with history offering alternatives that must at best refract and refigure 'the before now'. The truly disobedient intellectual had arrived. Now Keith had a duty to be doggedly discontented.

Our collaboration on *The Nature of History Reader* (2004) was a practical effort to illustrate the variety of epistemic positions that conventional (or as I have called them reconstructionist and constructionist), unconventional and experimental (deconstructionist) and 'postist' historians occupy. But, embedded in this book, was the largely Jenkinsite argument (for which I held his coat) that conventional history is intellectually moribund – a corpse that only when viewed in a certain epistemic light still seems to twitch. This theme was echoed in his 2008 articles in the journal *Rethinking History* when he defended the contribution of Hayden White and Sande Cohen to a radical rethinking of how we come to terms with the past.

As Keith suggests, history is out of joint and he sees in the work of Ankersmit and Cohen that both have fragmented our history culture and that this is not just a good thing, it is excellent. Although I have taken a path different to Keith in that I want to see many different understandings of history in the future rather than just forgetting it, I am indebted to his willingness to go where no historian has dared go before. And this is truly an excellent thing. I do not wish to summarise what I have said as a conclusion. In this Afterword I have merely selected a few ideas I have personally associated with Keith – the duty of the historian to be disobedient, his 'end of history' argument, a programme of epistemic scepticism, the perpetual failure of representation and the unbridgeable gulf between 'the past' and 'history'. But I have omitted others. I leave it to you to reach your own conclusion about Keith and his work. But, whatever conclusion you do reach, please read more of his work than you may already have.

Notes

1 Keith Jenkins, *Re-thinking History* (Classic Edition), London and New York: Routledge, 2003)
2 Keith Jenkins and Alun Munslow (eds) *The Nature of History Reader*, London and New York: Routledge, 2004; Keith Jenkins, Sue Morgan and Alun Munslow (eds) *Manifestos for History*, London and New York: Routledge, 2007.
3 Jenkins, *Re-thinking History*, op. cit.
4 See Alun Munslow, *Narrative and History*, Houndmills and New York: Palgrave Macmillan, 2007.
5 See variously and recently Michael Oakeshott, *Experience and Its Modes*, Cambridge: Cambridge University Press, 1933; Benedetto Croce, *History: Its Theory and Practice*, New York: Russell and Russell, 1960; Jack W. Meiland, *Scepticism and Historical Knowledge*, New York: Random House, 1965; Peter Unger, *Ignorance: A Case for Scepticism*, Oxford: Oxford University Press, 1975; Leon J. Goldstein, *Historical Knowledge*, Austin: University of Texas Press, 1976; Barry Stroud, *The Significance of Philosophical Scepticism*, Oxford: Clarendon Press, 1984; J. Annas and J. Barnes, *The Modes of Scepticism*, Cambridge: Cambridge University Press, 2003; Beverley Southgate, *Postmodernism in History: Fear or Freedom?*, London and New York: Routledge,2003; and, most recently, Stephen D. Hales, *Relativism and the Foundations of Philosophy*, Cambridge, MA: The Massachusetts Institute of Technology Press, 2006.
6 Jenkins, *Re-thinking History*, op cit., p. xvii.
7 Ibid.
8 Ibid., p. 7.
9 Ibid.
10 Jack W. Meiland, *Scepticism and Historical Knowledge*, New York: Random House, 1965. See also Michael Oakeshott, *Experience and Its Modes*, Cambridge: Cambridge University Press, 1933; Benedetto Croce, *History: Its Theory and Practice*, New York: Russell and Russell, 1960; and Leon J. Goldstein, *Historical Knowledge*, Austin: University of Texas Press, 1976.
11 Alun Munslow, *Deconstructing History*, London and New York: Routledge, 2006 [1997].

Name Index

Manifestos for History

Edited by Sue Morgan, Keith Jenkins and Alun Munslow

Written by some of the world's leading historians and theorists of history, *Manifestos for History* draws together a series of Manifestos that address the question of what kinds of histories we ought to be considering and making in and for the twenty-first century. With a foreword by Simon Schama and an afterword by Hayden White, these Manifestos – critical, innovative, reflexive, inspirational – are absolutely essential reading, not just for those embarking on the study of history, but for all those who would think seriously about `the nature of history' in its present and possible future forms. This collection establishes a benchmark for all future considerations upon the discourse of history.

ISBN13: 978-0-415-37776-8 (hbk)
ISBN13: 978-0-415-37777-5 (pbk)
ISBN13: 978-0-203-96234-3 (ebk)

For Product Safety Concerns and Information please contact our EU representative GPSR@taylorandfrancis.com
Taylor & Francis Verlag GmbH, Kaufingerstraße 24, 80331 München, Germany

www.ingramcontent.com/pod-product-compliance
Lightning Source LLC
Chambersburg PA
CBHW071755110726
47908CB00006B/1813

* 9 7 8 0 4 1 5 4 7 2 3 6 4 *